GREATER INDIA SOCEITY PUBLICATION NO. 2.

HINDU LAW AND CUSTOM

GREATER INDIA SOCIETY PUBLICATION NO. 2.

HINDU LAW AND CUSTOM

BY

JULIUS JOLLY

Professor of Sanskrit, Wuerzburg University,
Tagore Law Lecturer, Calcutta University (1883).

Authorised Translation

By

BATAKRISHNA GHOSH

Research Scholar, National Council of Education, Bengal.

GYAN

Published by

GYAN

Gyan Publishing House
5, Ansari Road
Daryaganj, New Delhi-110002
Phone: 011-47034999, 9811692060
E-mail: books@gyanbooks.com

Distribution Network
gyanbooks.com
India, USA, Canada, UK, Australia, France

ISBN : 978-81-212-2562-5 (HB)
First Published, 1928

2nd Impression 2021

Printed at: Gyan Press, Delhi.

Hindu Law and Custom
Author: Julius Jolly

GREATER INDIA SOCIETY PUBLICATION No. 2.

HINDU LAW AND CUSTOM

BY

JULIUS JOLLY

Professor of Sanskrit, Wuerzburg University,

Tagore Law Lecturer, Calcutta University (1883).

Authorised Translation

BY

BATAKRISHNA GHOSH

Research Scholar, National Council of Education, Bengal.

GREATER INDIA SOCIETY

91, Upper Circular Road,

CALCUTTA

1928

INTRODUCTORY NOTE

Dr. Jolly's valuable researches into the history of ancient Hindu law and custom do not stand in need of an introduction at this time of day. His *Recht und Sitte* has long occupied the rank of a classic in this field.

In placing the first authorised English edition of this well known book before the public, the Greater India Society wishes, first of all, to place on record its grateful appreciation of the sympathy and encouragement of members and well-wishers of the Society, but for which it could not have undertaken this task so soon after the publication of *Champa*, the first volume in its series, Ancient Hindu Colonies in the Far East, by Dr. R. C. Majumdar.

To Dr. Jolly the Society is under a deep debt of gratitude not only for his authorisation and the trouble he has taken to obtain, on its behalf, the consent of his German publishers, but also for personally going through considerable parts of the manuscript, suggesting corrections and improvements and for writing a new preface for this translation. This and the valuable notes and references which have been added by the author and the translator with a view to bring it in line with the latest researches, make this translation a new edition rather than a mere translation of the original book.

The translator, Mr. Batakrishna Ghosh, a young Indologist of great promise and an enthuriastic member of the Society has spared no pains to make his work as accurate as possible. He has also made certain modifications in the text at the suggestion or with the consent of the author.

The Society also feels that it cannot let the book go out to the public without a word of acknowledgment as to what it owes to the promptitude and the courtesy of the managers of the Prabasi Press who have given it every facility in their power and have gone to the length of supplying, at a sacrifice to themselves, special types with diacritical marks indispensable for a technical work of this kind. The credit for the timely publication and the typographical merits of the book is entirely theirs.

As for the Society, it will deem its efforts fully rewarded if the book encourages research into the vast domain of ancient Indian culture and proves to be helpful to those readers who could not use the work in the original.

CALCUTTA
September 1, 1928.

KALIDAS NAG
Secretary, Greater India Society

FOREWORD

The subjoined work is a translation of my German work on "Recht und Sitte" which was published in 1896 as the first part of the Encyclopaedia of Indo-Aryan Research of the late lamented Dr. G. Bühler whose researches have done so much towards clearing up the legal history of India and whose untimely death owing to a boat accident was universally felt as such a heavy loss to science. During the more than thirty years which have elapsed since the publication of "Recht und Sitte" the study of Sanskrit law has been progressing with rapid strides and it is a matter of regret that my advanced age and ill-health should have prevented me from thoroughly bringing my work up to date, before it was translated into English. It is hoped, however, that the learned notes added by the translator will to some extent supply this deficiency.

Generally speaking, the most important recent discovery in the field of Ancient Hindu Law is that of the Arthaśāstra which though a text-book of Polity is replete with useful information on Law and Judicature as well. Many of its legal rules, it is true, agree literally with the law of the Smṛtis, but others differ widely from it or treat of subjects not found in the Smṛtis. What is more, the general tendency of the Arthaśāstra is directed towards Artha or gain as the name of the book implies, whereas the Dharmaśāstra lays down rules of Dharma, i. e. of dutiful and pious conduct, and ordains superiority of Dharma whenever it comes into conflict with Artha. This explains the fact that the law of evidence in the Dharmaśāstra includes the administration of ordeals as belonging to the religious side of law, whilst the Arthaśāstra omits ordeals but introduces judicial torture of various kinds instead. The antiquity of judicial torture in India is proved by its occurrence in the Daśakumāracarita and in the Mṛcchakaṭikā. Another characteristic feature of the law of evidence of the Arthaśāstra consists of the extensive employment of spies for finding out corruptible judges, perjured witnesses, forgers, wizards, poisoners, thieves and others. The Dharmaśāstra on the other hand tries to establish truth by addressing long admonitions to witnesses in a case and admits perjury to be expiated by a penance in cases where the life of a person is at stake. Religious law in general is passed over in the Arthaśāstra which confines its attention to worldly subjects. The punishments inflicted are chiefly fines and a special chapter is devoted to a number of rules regarding the conversion of diverse corporeal punishments into fines. It should not be overlooked that judicial fines were an important source of income for kings and judges. In the Family Law the strict religious standpoint of the Smṛtis, which does not allow the remarriage of widows, is not shared by the Arthaśāstra in which divorce is not forbidden. In all such questions the rules of this recently discovered book may be supposed to agree more closely with actual practice than the rules of the Dharmaśāstra. For a detailed analysis and examination of the Arthaśāstra I may be allowed to refer to my introduction to the Lahore edition (1923) of that work.

Important additions to our knowledge of Dharmaśāstra literature has been supplied by the publication in India of such valuable texts as the Bālakriḍā of Viśvarūpa, the earliest gloss on Yājñavalkya, Aparārka's commentary of the same work and Bālambhaṭṭa's (not Lakṣmīdevi's) commentary of the Mitākṣarā. The merits of Viśvarūpa and of some other early commentators have been well brought out by P. V. Kane in the recent paper on the predecessors of Vijñāneśvara. The same scholar has examined the Vedic basis of Hindu Law and is engaged on a history of Dharmaśāstra. The labours of Dr. Jha are chiefly directed towards the elucidation of the Code of Manu and its commentaries, Medhātithi's especially. The merit of having edited the Vyavahāramātṛkā of Jīmūtavāhana, the renowned author of the Dāyabhāga, belongs to Sir Ashutosh Mukherji. The Tagore Law lectures, Sacred Books of the Hindus, Madras Law Journal, Ānandāśrama texts and other periodical publications abound in valuable information regarding Sanskrit Law. Several new collections of

Smṛtis have been printed. The Smṛticandrikā and other old Nibandhas have been edited in the original Sanskrit or in translations. The collections of Smṛti fragments from quotations has been continued by Herberich for Vṛddha-Manu, by Scriba for Pitāmaha, by Kane for Śaṁkha-Likhita and by Bandyopadhyaya for Kātyāyana. Manuals such as Ghose's Principles of Hindu Law go deep into historical questions. Prof. G. Mazzarella of Catania in Italy has written a vast Italian work, six volumes of which have hitherto been published, on Indian Law (1906 foll.). In Germany quite recently Prof. Meyer has proposed a new chronology for the principal Smṛtis and Dr. Losch has tried to trace the Yājñavalkyasmṛti to its original form in the Purāṇas.

The translator has spared no pains to make his translation as accurate as possible. He has also corrected a number of misprints and mistakes in the German text.

Würzburg, July, 1928. J. JOLLY.

CONTENTS

ABBREVIATIONS

Adhy.—Adhyāya.
Āp.—Āpastamba.
Apar.—Aparārka.
App.—Appendix.
AR—Asiatic Researches.
Arch. Surv. W. I.—Archaeological Survey of Western India.
Aśv.—Āśvalāyana.
AV—Atharvaveda.
Baudh.—Baudhāyana.
BG—Bombay Gazetteer.
Bijdr.—Bijdragen voor de taal-, land- en volkenkunde van Nederlandsch Indië.
Bṛh.—Bṛhaspati.
C., Cat.—Catalogue.
C. C.—Catalogus Catalogrorum.
C. H. I.—Cambridge History of India.
CII—Corpus Inscriptionum Indicarum.
C. P.—Central Provinces.
Dāyabh.—Dāyabhāga.
Dhs. or Dhs. (Calc.)—Dharmaśāstrasaṁgraha, Calcutta 1876.
Dhs. (Bomb.)—Dharmaśāstrasaṁgraha, Bombay 1883.
Dig.—Colebrooke's Digest.
EI—Epigraphia Indica.
Ess.—Essays.
Gaut. Gautama.
Gaz.—Gazetteer.
Gobh.—Gobhila.
Gṛ.—Gṛhya.
Hār.—Hārīta.
Hem.—Hemādri.
Hir.—Hiraṇyakeśin.
IA—Indian Antiquary.
IG—Hunter, The Imperial Gazetteer of India (2nd. ed., Lond. 1885-87, 14 vol.).
I. O.—India Office.
I. St.—Indische Studien.
I. Str.—Indische Streifen.
JAOS—Journal of the American Oriental Society.
JBeAS—Journal of the Asiatic Society of Bengal.
JBORS—Journal of the Behar Orissa Research Society.
Kāmas.—Kāmasūtra.
Kāty.—Kātyāyana.
Kauś.—Kauśika.
Kauṭ.—Kauṭilya.
Kum.—Kumārila.
Lassen IA. LIA—Lassen, Indische Alterthumskunde.
M.—Manu.
Mādh.—Mādhavīya.
Mah.—Mahābhārata.
Mān.—Mānava.
May.—Vyavahāramayūkha.
Medh.—Medhātithi.
Mit.—Mitākṣarā.
Mṛcch.—Mṛcchakaṭikā.
MS—Maitrāyaṇī Saṁhitā.
Nār.—Nārada.
Not.—Notices.
N. W. P.—North-Western Provinces.
N. W. P. G.—North-Western Provinces Gazetteer.
Pañc.—Pañcatantra.
Par.—Parāśara.
Pār.—Pāraskara.
Pitām.—Pitāmaha.
Quot.—Quotations.
Raghun.—Raghunandana.
Rājatar.—Rājataraṅgiṇī.
Rām.—Rāmāyaṇa.
Ratn.—Vivādaratnākara.
Rechtsschriften.—Über das Wesen der altindischen Rechtsschriften und ihr Verhältnis zu einander und zu Kauṭilya.
RV—Ṛgveda.
Sāmav.—Sāmaveda.
Śāṅkh.—Śāṅkhāyana.
SBE—Sacred Books of the East.
SII—South Indian Inscriptions, ed. by Hultzsch.
Śl.—Śloka.
Smṛtic.—Smṛticandrikā.
Sū.—Sūtra.

Tag. Lect.—Tagore Law Lectures, 1883, by J. Jolly.
TS—Taittirīya Saṁhitā.
Vai., Vaikh.—Vaikhānasa.
Vas.—Vasiṣṭha.
Vi.—Viṣṇu.
Vikr.—Vikramāṅkadevacarita, ed. Bühler.
Vīram.—Vīramitrodaya.
Vivādacint.—Vivādacintāmaṇi.
VS—Vājasaneyi Saṁhitā.
WIL.—Weber, Indische Litteraturgeschichte.
WZKM—Wiener Zeitschrift für die Kunde des Morgenlandes.
Y.—Yājñavalkya.
ZAL—Zimmer. Altindisches Leben.
ZDMG—Zeitschrift der Deutschen Morgenländischen Gesellschaft.
ZVR—Zeitschrift für Vergleichende Rechtswissenschaft.

I. THE SOURCES

§ 1. *The sources of law in general.* In India as in other oriental countries the law (*vyavahāra*) is an integral part of religion and ethics (*dharma*) and the law-books (*dharmaśāstras*) therefore offer us overwhelming data about religious purification and penance, prayer and sacrifice, pohibitions about food and drink, punishment in hell and rebirth, philosophy, eschatology, creation, funeral ceremonies and sacrifices to the dead, the study of the Veda and asceticism, the manner of living and customs of Brahmans and Kings and other things which we do not generally expect in a law-book. Many Dharmaśāstras give nothing at all about law proper and only a few later compilations such as the Nāradasmṛti may be called purely juridical works. According to the law-books the Vedas should be regarded as the first and foremost source of the *dharma* which are therefore frequently quoted, specially in the Dharmasūtras which generally follow the Vedas very closely and may, on the whole, be regarded as the oldest source of law. The Vedas in a narrow sense contain many data about sacrifices, penances, prayers and other features of the *dharma*, which are important for the history of customs, but they contain only occasional notices about legal affairs. What the Dharmasūtras quote from the Vedas on this subject, is based partly upon mere juridical construction of utterances originally absolutely irrelevant ; for example, Āp. 2, 14, 11 quotes a Vedic passage—the purport of it is that Manu divided his property among his sons—to demonstrate that unequal division of property is forbidden. Actual references to legal institutions such as e. g. compensation for murder (§ 44), are of course of great value for the earliest history

Oriental conception of law.

Vedas, the primary source of law.

of law. In the Dharmasūtras on the contrary, so far as they have come down to the present time, are always found particular sections about the law of inheritance, law of government, legal procedure and other features of law proper as it was taught and traditionally handed down in the oldest schools of the Brahmans. Even in those cases where the Dharmasūtras are called by the general designation Dharmaśāstra in Mss. they can be easily recognised by their style which they have in common with other Sūtra-works such as, for example, the grammatical and the philosophical Sūtras. Their connection with the Vedas is most evident where they are still handed down as part of a greater collection of Sūtras belonging to one or another Śākhā of the Veda, such as, e. g., the Āpastambīya Dharmasūtra.

Dharma-sūtras.

Metrical works of the second stage.

The second stage of the legal literature is represented by the very numerous metrical works which have come down to the present time under the name of Dharmaśāstra or Smṛti. They differ from the Dharmasūtras composed partly or wholly in prose, first in form, inasmuch as they are throughout written in verse, mostly in simple *ślokas*, then however also in their character, of which in § 5. Yet these works, to which the Mānava-dharmaśāstra, the most esteemed and illustrious of all Indian law-books, belongs, appear partly to have originated out of older Dharmasūtras and are, therefore, at all events, connected with the Vedic literature, indirectly at least. The name Smṛti which is given to the Dharmasūtras and Dharmaśāstras and also to many other works, properly signifies "memory", in the sense that the memories of the holy Ṛṣis of antiquity are recorded in them in contradistinction to Śruti, "revelation", i. e. the Vedas, which is given the greater authority in points of dispute. The Mah. too may be reckoned among the Smṛtis without hesitation; it is treated on the same footing as a Dharmaśāstra and is quoted as authority, not only in the mediaeval and modern law-books, but it was regarded as the great Smṛti, based on the Veda and proclaimed by Vyāsa, even by the famous Kumārila of the eighth century A. C. The epic literature includes also the Purāṇas which are mentioned as a source of law already in Gaut. 11, 19 and which are actually frequently quoted in the later law-books (§ 10).

Commentaries and Compendiums.

The latest stage of Indian legal literature is formed by the commentaries and systematic works which have been developed from the Smṛtis from the early mediaeval age. As the products of a new age and inspired by mighty princes and ministers, these extensive compilations gradually drove the Smṛtis so completely out of vogue that at the time of the establishment of British rule in Eastern India, the Mitākṣarā, a law compendium of the eleventh century, was the standard work in the greater part of India. For the historical study of Indian Law, for which the clearing of the beginnings must be of particular importance, this group of works, whose number is legion, is important and indispensable, specially as they are helpful to understand the Smṛtis.

The customary law.

Besides the traditions contained in their holy books, in the Vedas and the Smṛtis, the Brahmanical authors of the Smṛtis themselves recognise as the third source of law the ways of living and the teachings of pious men *Sadācāra*, *Śiṣṭāgama*, etc. In connection with law proper particular customs and manners of particular countries, castes and families are often emphasised as standard, of course only so far as they are not opposed to the sacred law.[1] The important position given in this

1. Kātyāyana is most emphatic on this point. He says that the customary law shall be recorded in books and as much care should be paid to it as to the Veda:—यस्य देशस्य यो धर्म्मः प्रवृत्तः सर्व्वकालिकः। श्रुतिस्मृत्यविरोधेन देशदृष्टः स उच्यते ॥ देशस्यानुमतेनैव व्यवस्था या निरूपिता। लिखिता तु

respect to the customary law is certainly thoroughly in conformity with facts and renders it a duty to those who deal with the history of law to search after the traces and survivals of the Indian customary law. This task is all the more important, because the inclination to theorise and the class interest have strongly influenced the Brahmans in their juridical literary activity, so that their rules of law cannot be accepted without criticism. Of course the sources of Indian customary law are scanty. Only for the present day a rich and trustworthy material is at our disposal in the laborious collections of English scholars. For earlier times, besides the reports of Greek, Chinese, Arabic and other foreign observers, occasional data in the epigraphical, historical and poetical literature are particularly valuable.

Apastamba Dharma-sūtra.

§ 2. *The proper Dharmasūtras.* The term Dharmasūtra in its proper sense applies only to those works which still form part of a greater collection of Sūtra works. The best preserved and earliest investigated and printed of these Dharmasūtras is that of Āpastamba (Āpastambha). The Āpastambīs or Āpastambs are a sect of Brahmans still represented in Southern India.[1] According to the census report of 1891, there were, e.g. in Bombay (Presidency Division), 267 "Apastambs"; in Berar too "Apatambs" are found among the Brahmans.[2] Already the Mahārṇava says that their home was in Southern India, to the south of the Godāvarī and that they were in this country already at an early period is further evidenced by a Pallava inscription of the fifth or sixth century A. D.[3] The Veda followed by

---

सद्यः धार्या मुद्रिता राजमुद्रया ॥ शास्त्रवद्यत्नतो रक्ष्या तां निरीक्ष्य विनिर्णयेत् । See quotation in Devaṇṇabhaṭṭa's Smṛticandrikā, vol. III. Part I, p. 58. *Translator.*

1. Bühler SBE 2, XXXff.

2. Cf. BG. 18, 1, 111 (Puna); 21, 89 f. (Belgaum); census of India, 1891. 8, 183 (Bombay); 6, CXVI (Berar).

3. Bühler l. c. Fleet I. A. 5, 135.

the Āpastambīyas is the Black Yajurveda, and in fact they represent one of the five sub-divisions of the Khāṇḍikīya school which on its part is a branch of the Taittirīya school.[1] Their canonical work, however, at the present day is, and perhaps has been since when they became a particular school, the great Kalpasūtra in 30 closely connected chapters, of which our Dharmasūtra (ed. Bühler) forms the 28. and the 29. chapters. Its contents chiefly deal with the study of the Veda and other duties of the Brahman students, purifications, forbidden foods, penances, duties of Snātakas and Gṛhasthas and similar other subjects of the sacred law. Of secular law, only the law of marriage and inheritance and criminal law are briefly dealt with, but in a singular manner. Linguistically this work is full of archaic and anomalous forms and phraseology which can be explained only on the hypothesis that it was finished before the canon of Sanskrit language established by Pāṇini attained to ruling power. This fact combined with a few other criteria has induced Bühler to assign the date of composition of this Dharmasūtra to the fourth or the fifth century B.C.[2] The reference to Śvetaketu, who appears as a Vedic teacher even in the Śatapathabrāhmaṇa and the Chāndogyopaniṣad, in Āpastamba (1, 5, 4 ff.) as of a modern *avara*, is of particular importance in this respect.[3] On the other hand, this author cannot be one of the earliest Vedic leaders of schools, for according to the tradition, which is corroborated by the result obtained by comparing the preserved works,

Date of Āpastamba.

---

1. Simon, Beitr. zur Kenntnis d. ved. Schulen 18 f.

2. Hopkins (C. H. I. p.249) says that Āp. is probably not older than the second century B.C. The archaisms in the language, in his opinion, may be due to the fact that the Andhras retained linguistic peculiarities long after Pāṇini fixed the northern usage. *Tr.*

3. I have tried to prove that Āp. is the oldest Dharmasūtra. See Ind. Hist. Quart. 1927, pp. 607-611. *Tr.*

Baudhāyana and other authorities anticipated him as founders of new schools.[1]

Home of Āpastamba.

As regards the home of Āpastamba (no matter what real name lies hidden behind this patronymic), he distinguishes himself as an inhabitant of the South by referring (2, 17, 17) to a custom prevailing among the peoples of the North (*udīcya*) with disapprobation. Perhaps he was a native of the Andhra land i.e. the country between the Godāvarī and the Kṛṣṇā, because he quotes the Taittirīyāraṇyaka in that version which is prevalent among the Andhra Brahmans, and also according to the notice in the Mahārṇava, already referred to, the Āpastamba-school had its seat in the Andhra land. The southern home of this school likewise indicates a comparatively late origin for it, for the South is generally not at all mentioned in the Vedic Saṁhitās and the Andhras in the Aitareyabrāhmaṇa still appear to be barbarians.[2]

The Dharmasūtra of Hiraṇyakeśin.

The Dharmasūtra of Hiraṇyakeśin is closely connected with that of Āpastamba, and its unimportant differences from it, consisting chiefly of variations in readings, have been collected by Bühler in an appendix to his second edition of the Āp. Of the collection of Sūtras of the Hiraṇyakeśin school, consisting of 36 chapters, the Dharmasūtra represents the 26. and the 27. chapters.[3] The tradition says that Āpastamba preceded Hiraṇyakeśin,[4] who dissented from the older Āpastamba school and founded a new school settled between the Sahya mountains (in the Konkan and further south) and the Southern Sea, which, however, even now appears to admit its dependence on the Āpastamba-school.[5] The fact that a Hairaṇyakeśabrāh-

1. Bühler l. c. XV-XXX.
2. Ibid. XXXIII-XXXVII.
3. West and Bühler (3rd. ed.) 34.
4. WIL (2nd. ed.) 110.
5. Bühler l. c. XXIV, XXXI; L. v. Schröder, MS. 1, XXVII. Also according to BG 13, 1, 73f. there are still in Thana pretty numerous Brahman sects which bear the designation "Apastamba Hiranyakeshi".

man is mentioned in a Pallava inscription of the fifth or the sixth century A. D., affords a lower limit for the date of the separation of this school from the Āpastambīyas which, however, took place probably much earlier.[1] For the authenticity of by far the greater part of the Āpastambīyadharmasūtra, we find a much wished for confirmation in the exactly corresponding text of Hiraṇyakeśin's Dharmasūtra.

Baudhāyana Dharmasūtra.

Baudhāyana (Bodhāyana) is the alleged author of the oldest Dharmasūtra to the Yajurveda and it has been preserved as part of a Sūtra collection.[2] Its high antiquity at once follows from the tradition recorded in two interpolated passages in Baudh. (ed. Hultzsch) itself, that the Baudhāyana-school is older than the Āpastamba-school and that on the whole it is the oldest of the Sūtra-schools connected with the text of the Taittirīya.[3] However, also a comparison between the contents of the two works which are related to each other and not seldom agree with each other verbatim, shows that Āp. is the younger author, for he expresses stricter and therefore probably later views than Baudh. about adopted sons, levirate, Paiśāca marriage, about the preference given to the eldest son in inheritance and other points. The same is the case with their corresponding Gṛhyasūtras, and the style too of Baudh. is more archaic and awkward than that of Āp.

Contents of Baudh

The subjects dealt with by Baudh. are multifarious; thus he discusses the difference of customs in various lands, the duties of the Brahmacārin and the Snātaka, contamination and purification, sacrifice, mixed castes, duties of the king and the executive duty of the penal judge, hearing of the witnesses, the marriage law, penances, law of inheri-

1. Bühler l. c. XXXIII. XXIV.

2. Bühler l. c, XVIII-XXII; SBE. 14, XXXV-XXXIX.

3. According to Meyer, Rechtsschriften (*passim*), Baudh. is the oldest Dharmasūtra. *Tr.*

tance, position of women, bathing, the five great sacrifices and the four stages of life (*āśrama*), regulations about food, sacrifice offered to the dead, rules for ascetics, householders, hermits, minor sacrifices, penances and propitious ceremonies. Nevertheless the fourth Praśna of this work which is almost wholly composed in Ślokas, is probably a modern interpolation, and even the third Praśna is not above all suspicions,[1] although many doubtful things in it, such as the Adhy. 6 about *prasṛtiyāvaka*, now receives some support from the analogous passages in the newly discovered Hārita. The original position of the Dharmasūtra within the whole Kalpasūtra of the Baudhāyana school may be fixed pretty accurately from the mutual references inspite of the wretched manuscript materials ; the arrangement of the work seems to have been similar to that of the Āpastambiyas.[2]

In the Mss. it is generally called the Baudhāyana-dharmaśāstra, for which reason Hultzsch has chosen :this title for his edition ;[3] yet the designation Dharmasūtra too occurs [4] in the Haug Ms. 163, and also the designation Baudhāyanasūtra is found in quotations out of the Baudh. As regards the continuation of the Baudhāyana school,[5] Bühler knows modern Baudhāyanīyas only from hearsay ; neither does this term occur in the census reports for the year 1891. On the other hand a Brahman

Baudh, a southerner.

studying the Sūtras of Bodhāyana is mentioned in an inscription of Vijayanagara of 1354-5 A. D., and under the title Pravacanasūtra which is certified also in the literature, this work is mentioned in an inscription of the ninth century likewise belonging to the South. The family of the

---

1. SBE 14, XXXIII-XXXV.
2. Ibid. XXX, cf. Caland, Altind. Ahnencult 18f.
3. In H.'s new ed. it is called Dharmasūtra. *Tr.*
4. Cf. ZDMG 31, 130 f.
5. Bühler, SBE 14. XXIX,XLII.

famous Sāyaṇa too belonged to the Baudhāyana school.[1] As the Mss. of this Dharmasūtra come mostly from the South and the contents of the same exhibit a close acquaintance with the South and the literature thereof, it may well be taken for granted that this school like that of Āp. was originated in the South.[2]

§ 3. *The revised Dharmasūtras.* Those Dharmasūtras may be called revised Dharmasūtras which are not actually handed down in the manuscripts as part of a collection of Vedic Sūtras but in form and contents are like the proper Dharmasūtras and are quoted in the law-books of the mediaeval age or even earlier. The best preserved of these works, so far as it is yet known, is the Dharmasūtra of Gautama (ed. Stenzler) wholly written in prose. The Gautamas are mentioned in literature as a sub-division of the school of Rāṇāyaṇīyas belonging to the Sāmaveda, and from Kumārila we learn about Gautama's Dharmasūtra that it is fundamentally a work belonging only to the Chandogas, i. e. the followers of the Sāmaveda.[3] The Rāṇāyaṇiyas had their principal seat in Mahārāṣṭra and Telinga-sāmavedīs are still said to exist in eastern Hyderabad who are considered as Rāṇāyaṇīyas and are divided into 7 gotras one of which is called Gautama.[4] Of course the occurrence of the name of the Gautama school here may be accidental, as is the case with the Gautam-Brahmans in Bombay and other places[5] for Gautama is a well-known gotra name. That our Gautamīya Dharmaśāstra belongs to the Sāmaveda, is confirmed

Gautama Dharmasūtra.

1. Burnell, Tanjore Catalogue, 20b ; Clemm, Saḍvimśabrāhmaṇa, 16.
2. Bühler l. c. XLIff.
3. Simon, Ved. Schulen 28-31 ; Kum., Tantravārttika 179 ; Bühler SBE 14, XI ; 25, 613.
4. Simon l.c. 27 ; J. Wilson, Indian caste 2, 54.
5. Census of India 1891, 8, 184.

by an examination of its sources, for the whole of the 26. Adhy. is taken word for word from a Brāhmaṇa of the Sāmaveda, the Sāmavidhāna ; the five Vyāhṛtis(1, 51) are wholly derived from this Veda and the expiatory prayers (19, 12) are partly taken from it.[1]

The contents of Gaut.

The contents which often appear to be very archaic, deal with the sources of law, duties of the Brahman students, ascetics and fathers of families, the laws of marriage, rules of salutation, the position of the Brahmans, the sacrifices and other obligations of a Snātaka, the modes of life of the four Varṇas, the duties of the king, law and justice, impurity and the removal thereof, sacrifice offered to the dead, the study of the Veda, the position of women, Prāyaścitta and the law of inheritance All these things are dealt with as in proper Dharmasūtras, only metrical passages are altogether wanting. The repetition of the last word in every Adhy. is an archaism, but on the other hand the language contains few obsolete forms and also the system of mixed castes including the *Yavanas* (4, 21) gives the impression of a modern origin.

The Quotations from Gaut.

The quotations from Gaut. are of primary importance for the determination of the age of this work, of which the one in Baudh. 1, 2, 7 and the reference to a view of the son of Utathya i. e. of Gaut. in M. 3, 16, may be traced in substance, if not literally, in Gaut. 11, 20 and 4, 26.[2] About the quotation in Vas. see below. The Bṛh. 25, 38 too quotes our Gaut. (28, 18). Of older law teachers Gaut. mentions only M. (21, 7), by which however, is meant not the well-known law-book of M. but an older work (cf. § 4) if it does not refer merely to the mythical first parent M. who is often quoted as an authority. Another important

1. Bühler SBE 2, XLVII f.
2. l.c. XLIX ff., cf. West and Bühler (3rd. Ed.) 34, 39.

fact is that Baudh. appears to have borrowed the last Adhy. of his third Praśna from Gaut.[1] With the conclusion reached by Bühler (in his translation), that the Gaut. is the oldest of the preserved (printed) Dharmasūtras, agrees, by the way, also the view of its editor Stenzler, who in his manuscript remains (ZDMG 47, 621) held Gaut. to be the oldest author on Dharma on the ground of a notice derived from earlier times. Gaut. should probably be placed centuries before Āp. and perhaps even before Baudh.[2]

Vasiṣtha Dharma-sūtra.

The Dharmaśāstra of Vasiṣṭha[3] unfortunately has been preserved only in wretched uncommentaried and often incomplete manuscripts. Führer was able to use four complete Mss. for his edition, but other Mss. contain, instead of 30 Adhy. only 6 or 10, or 21¼ such as the Calcutta edition, or 28½ or 29½ Adhy.[4] Internal evidences too indicate that Adhy. 25-30 are mostly appendages to a work—the torso—probably of an earlier date, although isolated passages from Adhy. 28 are quoted already in the Mit. Even in the earlier portions some Sūtras are hopelessly corrupt.[5] Nevertheless we should never fail to understand that this work consisting of a mixture of prose and verses and in many comparable passages still showing the archaic Triṣṭubh instead of the later Anuṣṭubh of M. and other authors, is directly to be reckoned among the proper Dharmasūtras, and in a quotation it is even called "Vasiṣṭhasūtra".[6] The passage 5, 6 f. which of course is derived from the TS is quite Vedic.

---

1. Bühler l.c. LI.
2. Meyer (Rechtsschriften, *passim*) says that Gaut. is the last of the Dharamasūtras. He even suggests (p. 119) that Gautama used the commentaries on M. though elsewhere (p. 324) he says that Gaut. must be older than Bṛh. *Tr.*
3. Cf. Bühler SBE 14, IX-XXVIII and Indian Studies 5, 6 (1895).
4. Cf. Führer, Vās. 5; Jolly ZDMG. 31, 130; Eggeling, Cat. No. 1253 ff.
5. Bühler l.c. and ZDMG 31, 704 ff.; Böhtlingk ZDMG 31, 480 ff
6. Vivādacint. 152.

Contents of Vas.

The subject matter of Vas. likewise resembles that of the Dharmasūtras and includes *inter alia* the sources and the jurisdiction of law, the duties and the origin of the four castes, specially the Brahmans, the law of hospitality, impurity and the removal thereof, laws about women, the daily duties, the four Āśramas, the law of marriage, the obligations of the hermit and the ascetic, the position of the fathers of families and Snātakas, the study of the Veda, the rules of salutation, restrictions about food, excommunication out of the caste, legal procedure, the law of inheritance, the mixed castes, duties of a king, public and private penances and charitable gifts and institutions. Moreover, the rules of Vas. are in many cases of a particularly primitive character ; thus in 1, 28 ff. he enumerates like Āp. only six forms of marriage instead of the orthodox eight, but designates the purchase of women as the "form of human marriage" (mānuṣa-vivāha).

Relation with Ṛg-veda.

According to Govindasvāmin and even according to Kumārila (8. century) the Dharmaśāstra of Vas. was studied only by the followers of the Ṛgveda, but was however, recognised on all hands[1]. That these notices do not relate to the other Smṛtis ascribed to Vas. may be proved by the ancient quotations from the Vas. which can be traced only in this work. In this Smṛti Vas. has been specially quoted or referred to three times as authority, and in some way or other the whole reminds one of the Vasiṣṭha known to us from the Ṛgveda which also corroborates its connection with the Ṛgveda. As Vas. evinces a leaning towards the works of northern India in his quotations of Vedic Saṁhitās and Sūtras, this part of India is probably his birth place or the land of origin of his school. This could hardly have been concluded from the designation holy land he gives to the modern

1. Kum. l.c. ; Bühler SBE 14, XI ; SBE 25, 613.

North-Western Provinces, because this theory of holy land was a common property in the Brahmanical tradition and is found also elsewhere, e. g. in Baudh. and M.

References to other teachers of law in Vas.

As regards Vas.'s relation with other teachers of law, quotations from Yama, Prajāpati, Hārita, Gautama and Manu are found in Vas. The quotations from the three first mentioned authors are not present in the Smṛtis ascribed to them. The quotation from Gaut. in 4, 36, seems to refer to Gaut. 14, 44. Particularly interesting are the numerous quotations from M. (cf. §5), which so far as they are not references merely to the mythical M. are manifestly derived from a work which was in substance related to our M. but was yet composed like the Dharmasūtras in a mixture of prose and verses, partly Triṣṭubh. On the other hand our M. 8, 140 contains a quotation from Vas. which actually occurs in our Vas. 2, 51. Accordingly our Vas. is older than M. but later than Gaut., yet one should always ascribe a high antiquity to a Vedic school which was connected with the Ṛgveda and apparently belonged to Northern India, and so our work may be placed several centuries before Christ.

The Viṣṇusmṛti.

The Vaiṣṇava Dharmaśāstra or the Viṣṇusmṛti,[1] a very extensive work in 100 Adhy., is presented as a revelation from the god Viṣṇu in the introductory portion and the final chapter. Also in several other passages of this work he (Viṣṇu) holds conversation with the goddess of the earth. Yet we have here manifestly the remodelling of the work by a member of the Viṣṇuite sect of the Bhāgavatas. The main stock of our book which is also quoted under the name Viṣṇusūtra, thoroughly resembles the Dharmasūtras in form and substance and in the metrical passages it agrees in many cases word for word with

1. Cf. my translation SBE 7 and edition in the Bibl. Ind.

these works and with M. and other metrical Smṛtis as well. Still more important are the special relations of our Vi. with the Kāṭhakagṛhyasūtra and other works of the Kāṭhaka school, out of the Veda,--the Kāṭhaka,--of which school many of the Mantras cited by Vi., are taken while passages common with the Gṛhyasūtra of this school, which are often very extensive, are seen particularly in connection with the Śrāddha ritual, Vaiśvadeva sacrifice and the Vṛṣotsarga. As these rites are performed within every Vedic school only according to its special ritual, Vi. may directly be regarded as the Kāṭhaka Dharmasūtra which was alienated from its special school and became a generally recognised law book by the same process as is demonstrated by historical evidences in the cases of Gaut. and Vas. Even at the time of Govindarāja (12. century) a Sūtra work of the Kaṭha school about Dharma seems to have been in existence, for the Smṛtimañjarī quotes a rule in prose of a Kaṭhasūtrakṛt about the atonement for the murder of a Brahman, which, however, cannot be found in Vi[1].

It may be called the Kāṭhaka Dharmasūtra.

The canonical works of the Kaṭha school whose original home was in the Punjab and Kashmir may be reckoned among the oldest remains of Indian literature. Of course our work in its present form, even excepting the Viṣṇuite interpolations, contains a series of passages of modern character, such as the mention of the seven days of the week including the designation of the Thursday as *jaiva* (78, 1-7), the passages about widow-burning (25, 14 and 20, 39), about books *pustakas* (18, 44 and 23, 56), about places of pilgrimage in all parts of India (85, 1-52), about Trimūrti (30, 7), the vague definition of the limits of the Aryan land 84, 4 (Āryāvarta), etc. Even though most of the passages of this sort may be readily rejected as later interpolations yet the age of the redaction of our work as

Uncertainty of age. Cannot be older than the third century A. D. in its present form.

1, Bühler. SBE, 25, XXI.

it is now existing, still remains doubtful to some extent.[1] The juridical sections seem to belong to its oldest part specially the duties of the king in Adhy. 3 and the penal law in Adhy. 5 and also the law of inheritance along with the doctrine of mixed castes in 15-18, while the laws of debt and legal proceedings in 6-14 appear to be less ancient. The Adhy. 19- 96 deal with sacrifices to the manes, impurity, laws about women, the sacraments, the study of the Veda, sins and the penances for them including the doctrine of hell and the transmigration of the soul, the duties of the Gṛhastha and the Snātaka, the Śrāddha, charitable gifts and the duties of the Vānaprasthas and the ascetics. The language shows few archaisms but is also almost completely free from corrupt readings, because the text was probably commented upon carefully already at an early period. There are no references to older teachers of law and also Vi. in his turn is not quoted by other Smṛtis. In subject matter, next to its relations with M. those with Y. are most remarkable. The Viṣṇuite revision of our work can by no means be assigned to a period earlier than the third century A. D. if the Greek designation of the Thursday is ascribed to the reviser

The Dharmaśāstra of Hārīta.

The newly discovered and still unpublished Dharmaśāstra of Hārīta consists of 30 Adhy. like Vas. but is, however, more extensive than any of the above mentioned works excepting Vi. Before the appearance of the Ms. of this work which until now is the only one available, discovered by V. S. Islampurkar in Nasik,[2] a Dharma-

---

1. Meyer (Rechtsschriften, pp. 195-252) has tried to prove that Vi. is later than Yājñavalkya but considerably older than Gaut. (p. 253). In a word he is an "elender Skribent." Neither does Meyer believe that Vi. had undergone a rehandling at the hand of a Vaiṣṇava, but he does not give any reason for it. The legal chapters in Vi. taken to be old by Jolly, are of a late date according to Meyer. *Tr.*

2. I owe to Bühler the chance of being able to use this Ms., who had it brought from India and placed it at my disposal along with his copy of a part of the same.

sūtra of Hārīta was known only from quotations and from them I in 1889 compiled the Vyavahārādhyāya of H. and W. Caland in 1893 gave a synopsis of H.'s. treatment of the Śrāddha ritual in his "Ahnencult". These passages, so far as they appear to be ancient in language and substance may be traced almost fully in the Ms.,[1] but on the other hand the metrical quotations among them about legal procedure and law of debt, whose modern character I had pointed out, are not found in it. Apparently these quotations are derived from a later work, as several metrical works of modern times ascribed to H. are still in existence (§8). Other ancient quotations mostly in prose, on the other hand, about Śrāddha, impurity, penances, rules about food and bathing and other parts of the sacred law, are found in the Ms. although our work seems to have undergone much damage since the time of Hemādri (13. century) who gives an enormous mass of such quotations. In the fourteenth century the Dharmasūtra of H. is frequently quoted in the famous commentary of Mādhava on the Parāśarasmṛti, and the editor of this work, V. S. Islampurkar, who has been already mentioned, has traced most of these quotations in this Ms. Of other ancient Smṛtis the Sūtra-work of Uśanas (§4) in Adhy. 4 contains a reference to the view of H. about the issues of a union with a Śūdrā which remarkably agrees with a passage in H. 21 (Caland).[2] It must be admitted at all events that U. refers to the special case where a son is born of such a union.

Quotations from H.

As thus the existence of H. in the mediaeval age and earlier is proved as satisfactorily as in the case of the works hitherto dealt with, the H. also agrees with them in form and substance as far as possible. The

H.'s points of agreement with other Smṛtis.

1. Yet Meyer (Rechtsschriften, p. 225) says that H. is certainly a late "Machwerk" (bungling work). *Tr.*

2. Correspondence by letter.

prose, which on the whole is predominant, alternates with Anuṣṭubhs and Triṣṭubhs ; the verses are often introduced with the typical *athāpyudāharanti* of the Dharmasūtras ; quotations from the Veda are pretty frequent. The contents deal with the sources of law, Brahmacārins, Upakurvāṇaka as well as Naiṣṭhika, Snātakas and Gṛhasthas, Vānaprasthas and Yatis, restrictions about food, Pratigraha, Ṛtvij, Śrāddha, including Paṅktidūṣakas and Paṅktipāvanas, duties of the Snātaka, Ācāra in general, the five Pākayajñas, study of the Veda and Brahmacarya, Yama and Niyama, impurity and the removal thereof, penances for various infringements, procedure with the witnesses, judicial affairs and the temporal law, laws about women, principal sins, fooding of the Brahmans, particular penances, expiatory prayers etc. In one of the quotations from H. which however, I cannot trace in the Ms., there appears to be a reference to the Śrāddhakalpa in the Śrautasūtra of H. (Caland)[1].

Contents of H.

The particular Vedic school too out of which this work has arisen, can be determined. On the ground of a passage mentioning Maitrāyaṇi quoted in a commentary, Bühler first gave out the suggestion that the H. is Maitrāyaṇīya[2]. Caland has adduced two other quotations from H. to corroborate this suggestion (loc. cit.) in which likewise Maitrāyaṇi is mentioned and he has pointed out cases of remarkable agreements between other quotations and the Maitrāyaṇīyapariśiṣṭa and the Mānavaśrāddhakalpa. The Ms. contains not only the quotation of Bühler and almost all the quotations forwarded by Caland, but it shows other connections with the Maitrāyaṇīya school, for it even introduces the *bhagavān maitrāyaṇiḥ* and quotes Mantras from the Maitrāyaṇīya Saṁhitā, such as the well-known Mantra *śatadāyo vīro* in Maitrāyaṇīya Saṁhitā 1, 7, 5.

H. belongs to the Maitrāyaṇīya school.

---

1. Correspondence by letter.
2. SBE 14, XX.

The comparatively numerous quotations from H. in Āp. and Baudh.[1] also indicate that he was a Sūtrakāra of the Black Yajurveda ; however, none of these passages is found in the Ms. The Ms. is derived from Nasik and this city is at the same time the find-spot of two Mss. of the Maitrāyaṇiya Saṁhitā. The Maitrāyaṇīyas otherwise lived farther in the north, probably in the neighbourhood of the Kaṭhas who are closely related to them and like them are reckoned among the oldest Vedic schools[2]. The word *kaphella* used in a quotation, which is a Kashmirian word according to the commentary (Hemādri 3, 1, 559), seems to indicate a Kashmirian home for H.

H. is perhaps the oldest Smṛti in existence

Our H. is perhaps the oldest Smṛti in existence. H. does not refer to older works on law, and when he quotes Prajāpati, M. (manur abravīt is the probable reading for munir abravīt in about 19 cases) and Ācāryāḥ and if it often agrees almost word for word with all the other Smṛtis, such analogies do not indicate borrowing, but are derived from the common tradition of the Vedic schools. Unfortunately, the Ms. is throughout so full of mistakes that an edition of the important work on the basis of the same is inconceivable. We should hope, therefore, that other Mss. may be discovered and particularly the ancient commentary referred to by Hemādri 3, 1, 559[3].

Vaikhānasasūtra.

Much more correct than the H.-Ms. is Bühler's Ms. of the Vaikhānasasūtra in the Vienna University Library, consisting of a "Gṛhya" in 7 Praśnas and a "Gṛhyadharma" in 4 Praśnas. The latter chiefly deals with the four Āśramas in which 4 kinds of Brahmacārins and Gṛhasthas respectively and 2 kinds of Vānaprasthas along with numerous sub-divisions, have been distinguished (Pr. 1), and it also deals with the special religious

1. l.c. Index s. v. Hārita.
2. L. von Schröder, MS. 1, XIX ff.
3. Aufrecht C. C. 766.

duties of the Vānaprastha, Snāna, Bhojana, Snātakadharma, the ways of life of the Vānaprastha and the Bhikṣu, mixed castes etc. (2,3) and the *pravaras* (4). The law proper is not touched in this work which of course is a Gṛhyadharma and not a Dharmasūtra; the duties of the forest hermits who, as is well-known, are called Vaikhānasa after Vikhanas appearing in this work as an authority (*ityāha vikhanāḥ*), are more exhaustively dealt with in this work. The term Vaikhānasa occurs already in Gaut. 3 2, and Baudh. 2, 11, 14 and M. 6, 21 refer to the *vaikhānasa-śāstram* or *matam* when describing the duties of the forest hermit, by which, accordtng to the commentators, is meant a Sūtra-work of Vikhanas about the duties of the Vānaprastha [1]. Has this work been preserved in our Ms.? The Śrāmaṇakāgni or the establishment of the fire *śrāmaṇakīyena vidhānena*, the exact time for retiring into the forest (putraṁ pautraṁ ca dṛṣṭvā), distinction between the Sapatnīka, who is accompanied by his wife, and the Apatnīka who goes alone into the forest (1, 6-8; 2, 1 ff.) and many other rules characteristic of our work are actually seen in the Smṛtis, while other things, such as the Phenapa, Audumbara, Kuṭīcaka and other kinds of hermits, may be, on the other hand, traced only in the Purāṇas or in the Mah. in the present state of our knowledge. The numerous passages connected with the cult of Nārāyaṇa appear to be very recent which like a red band stretches over the whole length of this Sūtra-work. Further, the expression *budhavāra* too occurs in it (Bühler) [2]. The allusion to widow-burning too in Vai. gṛ. 7, 2 should be considered as a sign of its late origin: *sahamaraṇe...dampatī dāhayati*, if *sahamaraṇa* here is not to be explained in any other way (§20). The Vaikhānasa school is clearly

Vaikh.-referred to in earlier works.

Detailed rules about forest hermits.

1. Bühler SBE 25, XXVII-XXIX.
2. Correspondence by letter.

considered one of the youngest schools of the Black Yajurveda according to Mahādeva (WIL 110). The connection of this work with this Veda is proved by the quotations of Mantras from it and the reference to the Yajuḥsaṁhitā. Many Mantras, however, a point emphasised to me by Dr. Caland [1], appear to be quite post-Vedic and in the case of Yajus texts, mere Pratīkas would have been sufficient. If this work forms the counterpart of the still unpublished Vaikhānasa-śrautasūtra[2], it may be reckoned among the class of proper Dharmasūtras. As the prospect of a treatment of the whole Vaikhānasa-sūtra has been announced from a certain quarter, I shall not go deeper into this matter.

Vaikh. belongs to the Black Yajurveda.

§ 4. *The secondary and fragmentary Dharmasūtras.* The composition of Sūtra-works on Dharma may be traced even in the hoary antiquity, for they have been mentioned even in Patañjali's Mahābhāṣya and even in Yāska's Nirukta a series of legal maxims in Sūtra style have been quoted[3]. But on the other hand the extinction of many Vedic Sūtracaraṇas and the rise of numerous metrical works on Dharma could not at any time drive the Sūtra style wholly out of vogue, so that a Sūtra-work on Dharma can be assigned to the oldest period of Indian law, only when there are other criteria, specially those furnished by ancient quotations. Thus the small Budhasmṛti[4] which contains a concise treatment in prose of the Saṁskāras, sacrifices, Varṇa, Āśrama and Rājadharma, is by no means authenticated by quotations. Budha is not mentioned in the lists of authors of lawbooks in Y., Par., Paiṭhīnasi, Śaṅkhalikhita and in the

The spurious Budhasmṛti.

1. Correspondence by letter.
2. Cf. Aufrecht l. c. 610.
3. Cf. West and Bühler (3rd. ed.) 37 f.
4. Eggeling, Cat. No. 1323 ; Dhs. (Bomb.) 854-56 and the Madr. ed. ; Burnell, Tanjore Cat. 125 ; Weber, Verzeichnis No. 1753.

Padmapurāṇa and even in the law-books of the middle ages he is very rarely mentioned. A metrical text which Hemādri 2, 1, 150 quotes from Budha is not found in his Smṛti as it has been published. Accordingly it is probably a modern compilation. More important is the yet unpublished Uśanas[1], composed in a mixture of prose and verses, among which even Tṛṣṭubh is found, which in 7 Adhy. deals with contamination and purification, castes, penances, Śrāddhas, selling of prohibited articles and punishments. The greater part of the Śrāddhakalpa and long passages from the Śaucakalpa in this yet unpublished work are quoted by Hemādri, and a few passages also in the Mādhavīya[2]. On the other hand this Uśanas does not contain any one of the 21 texts, mostly in verse, which are ascribed to him in the Mit. Likewise also the texts regarding law proper are wanting in it which Vīramitrodaya, Mayūkha and other juridical works quote from this author, as well as the quotations concerning all parts of Dharma in other Dharmanibandhas. Our U. on its side seems to quote a verse from Manu[3]; and it also refers to M. frequently as an authority[4] which of course, however, does not mean much, and quotes Vasiṣṭha, Hārīta, Śaunaka, and Gautama in a passage about the issues of a marriage between a Brahman and a Śūdrā[5]

The important Smṛti of Uśanas.

Uśanas quotes M. Vas., H., Śaunaka and Gaut.

1. West and Bühler (3rd. ed.) 36; Mandlik 291 f.; Eggeling 1316; ZDMG 31, 129 and Tag. Lect. 53.

2. I owe this reference to Dr. W. Caland of Breda who in the most liberal manner also placed at my disposal his collations of 4 Mss. of this work.

3. Cf. Bühler SBE 25, XXXV. The reading *manur āha* is found also in the Haug. Ms. and two Mss. used by Mandlik. Dr. Caland is of opinion that the prose passage following these words, is not the quotation but the fragment of a verse reminiscent of M. 5, 62, preceding them, is the real quotation and regarding the *sumantur āha* he draws attention to an analogous quotation from *Sumantu* in Hemādri.

4. Cf. Bühler l. c. LXII.

5. l. c. XXVII; ZDMG l. c.

which exactly agrees in a remarkable manner with M. 3, 16. Three of these quotations, though not exactly in the same form, appear in our Vas. 1, 24 ff., Hār. 21 (cf. above, §3) and Gaut. 4 26. Accordingly our U. would be later than M., Vas., Hār., and Gaut., but older than Hemādri (13. century) and at all events it is but incomplete as we have it, for many of the old quotations are not found in it and some of the most important features of Dharma are not dealt with in it at all. The Mss. are truly very bad and contain large lacunae particularly in Adhy. 1 and 2. The ancient Ṛṣi Uśanas is considered the author of another Smṛti [1] as well, which contains some prose passages. This work, however, which has been published, many times already, is clearly not the U. of the quotations as none of them are found in it. It consists of 618 Ślokas and 2 Sūtras in prose in the 9. Adhy. which deal with the daily duties—Śrāddha, impurity, penance and often agrees verbatim with M.

The Smṛti of Kāsyspa.

The small Smṛti of Kāśyapa [2] or Upakāśyapa deals at first in prose but afterwards is Ślokas, with the duties of the Gṛhastha, Ācāra and Prāyaścitta. Yet this work may at best be but a sketch of the original Dharmasūtra of Kāśyapa who is well-known as a Ṛṣi and a teacher of law, for he is frequently referred to as author of Ślokas and prose texts on the law of inheritance, pious gifts and other parts of the law, which are not found in this work. Atri, famous as a Ṛṣi and even quoted by M. 3, 16 as a teacher of law, is considered to be the author of various Smṛtis and one of them which is still unpublished,[3] consisting of 9 Adhy., shows a mixture of prose and verse, e.g., Adhy. 1-3, 6 and 9 contain altogether 61 Ślokas while Adhy. 4 wholly and Adhy. 7 and 8 for the most part,

Various Smṛtis of Atri.

1. Dhs. (Calc.) 1, 501-554.
2. Dhs. (Bomb.) 856 ff., cf. Eggeling 1317 ; Burnell 124.
3. Eggeling No. 1305 f.; Burnell 124 ; ZDMG 31, 128.

are written in prose. Its contents exclusively deal with penance and expiation in this world and the next for various sins and transgressions and is mostly identical with the published Laghu-Atri, which however, contains a short prose section only in the fourth Adhy. and with the Vṛddha Atri [1] which has also been published and is closely related to the latter; only in the last named work I was able to trace a quotation occurring in the Dharmanibandhas :(Mādh. 1, 432). Śātātapa (or Vṛddha-Ś., Bṛhacchātātapa) is referred to by Y. and Parāśara as a teacher of law and is often quoted by Hemādri, Vijñāneśvara and other mediaeval writers as the author of rules mostly in verse about penances, contamination, charitable gifts, alms, Śrāddha and other features of the sacred law. At least one of these quotations, in prose, concerning the penance for murdering a Brahman (Mit. on Y. 3, 243) occurs at the beginning of the Ms. described by Eggeling Cat. 3 No. 1362, which in 12 Adhy. deals with Vaiśvadeva and Śrāddha sacrifices, rules of diet, impurity and other religious questions in a mixture of prose and verses. Related with this Ś. is the Dharmaśāstra of the same author[2] (Ibid. No. 1361)—at first in prose but later on containing 139 verses. The Smṛti of Vṛddha-Ś. on the other hand is quite a different work consisting only of 63 verses and 2 prose passages, in which Mandlik (326) has found a quotation from this author in the Nirṇayasindhu.

The Smṛtis of Śātātapa and Vṛddha Śātātapa.

The unpublished Bṛhaspati[3] in prose in the manuscript collection of the R. As. Soc. in London, has nothing to do with the renowned teacher of the same name of whom so many metrical texts on law proper are quoted, but rather seems to be a religious work of a new sect. From certain

The Spurious Smṛti of Bṛhaspati.

1. Dhs. (calc.) 1, 1-12 ; 47-59

2. Mandlik, who found in it a reference to the *trimūrti* clearly describes (326f) the same work.

3. Tag. Lect. 52.

The interesting Smṛti of Śaṅkha.

aspects the most interesting of all these works is the Smṛti of Śaṅkha (Bṛhat or Vṛddha-Ś.)[1] in 18 Adhy., two of which 11 and 12, are written partly in prose and the rest, however, are throughout written in verse. The multifarious contents of this work deal with Varṇa and Āśramadharma, baths, ablutions, prayers, the holiness of the Gāyatrī, offering of water to the manes, Śrāddha, purification and penances. I find nearly 30 Ślokas quoted from Adhy. 4, 8, 9, 11, 16 and 17 alone in Mit, (on Y. 3, 30, 260, 264, 290, 293, 309), Mādh. (1, 236, 238, 250, 274, 284) and in Jīmūtavāhana's Dāyabhāga (p. 212), so that the authenticity of this Smṛti is sufficiently warranted for. Of course many other quotations, particularly the prose ones, are not found in it; yet the verse about *parivitti* (17, 43) seems to agree with a prose rule on this subject quoted in Mit. on Y. 3, 265. Thus this work represents, as Bühler has aptly remarked, a stage of transition from the Dharmasūtras to the metrical Smṛtis.

The Sūtra-work of the Mānava School.

Of the fragments of Dharmasūtras which are known only from solitary quotations, those on the whole may be regarded as the oldest which are referred to in other Dharmasūtras. Particular interest attaches to the ancient quotations from a Sūtra-work of Manu or the Mānavas[2], on account of their relation with the law-book of the same name. Thus a remarkable quotation from a Mānavam about the slaughter of animals is found in Vas. 4, 5-8. The passage, partly in prose and partly in verse, is exactly in the style af ancient Dharmasūtras and may have been derived from a Mānavaṁ Dharmasūtram,[3] supposedly the source of the Mānavam

1. Dhs. (calc.) 2, 343-374; Eggeling No. 1357 f.; Burnell 127; Mandlik 314 f.; West and Bühler (3rd. ed.) 40 f.

2. Bühler SBE 25, XXXI-XXXVIII.

3 I have tried to prove (Ind. Hist. Quart. 1927 pp. 808 ff.) that a Sūtra work of the Mānava School was never in existence. *Tr.*

Dharmaśāstram, for the metrical portion of this quotation occurs in M. 5, 41, 48, only with this difference that in M. 5, 48 meat-eating is forbidden without exception in conformity with the later principle of ahiṁsā. The other quotations from M. in Vas. including the stereotyped *manurabravīt*, are in verse, and 6 of them are found in our M. word for word or with slight modifications, but 3 (Vas. 12, 16 ; 19, 37 ; 23, 43) cannot be traced in M. Leaving out Vas., the above mentioned passage (M. 5, 41) occurs also in the Śāṅkhā.-gṛhya 2,16, 1. Even Gaut. 21,7, refers to a prose M. as an authority for the maxim that the first three principal sins are inexpiable and our M. (11, 90-92, 104 f., 147) too teaches practically the same thing, for the penances prescribed there are equivalent to suicide. About the rather doubtful quotation from M. in the Dharmasūtra of Uśanas see above and p. 21, note 3. The two passages about the teachings of the Mānavāḥ in the Nītisāra of Kāmandakī 2, 3 and 7, 24 f. (=M. 7. 155-157) appear to be ancient, and the Mānavāḥ in it appear to be a Vedic school, though not yet generally recognised. More such references are found also in the latest of Smṛtis, e.g. in a quotation from Kātyāyana in Ratn. 332, where a view of the Mānavāḥ about the punishment for theft is quoted which approximately corresponds to our M. 9, 270.

Quotations from the Mānava-dharma-sūtra.

See §3 for the ancient quotations from Hārīta. The metrical quotations from Yama in Vas. 11, 20 ; 14, 30 ; 18, 13-16 ; 19, 48 need not have been derived from a Dharmasūtra of the mythical "King of Dharma." Of the Sūtra texts quoted in the mediaeval and modern Dharmanibandhas, I shall first mention a prose text, of course a solitary one, of Vṛddha or Bṛhan-Manu, about the penance for a Brahman who has stolen gold [1]. The "Old" or "Great" M. is moreover

Quotations from H. and Yama.

Vṛddha-Manu.

1. Herberich, Zitate aus *Vṛddhamanu* (Würzb. 1893) No. 82.

considered to be the author of Ślokas whose recent origin is betrayed by the reference to the signs Aja and Kanyā of the Zodiac, the right of inheritance of the widows, and other points. Compare § 8. Long prose texts mixed with metrical ones, about all the features of the Dharma are ascribed to the two brothers Śaṅkha and Likhita[1] whose names have become proverbial for their righteous-

Saṅkha-Likhika.

ness, and who are already pointed out by Parāśara 1, 24 as the standard authority for the Dvāpara age. According to Kumārila[2] the work of Śaṅkha-Likhita was in his time followed *(parigṛhīta)* mostly by the school of the Vājasaneyins, although, as is the case with all the books of the Vedic schools, it was at the same time considered as binding on everybody in general. Independent of it, Caland has proved that the texts of these two brothers about Śrāddha, collected by him, accurately agree both in the Mantras and in the ceremonies, with the rites of the Vājasaneyins [3].

Paiṭhīnasi and Kātyāyana.

On the other hand, the Dharmasūtra of Paiṭhīnasi, likewise consisting mostly of prose texts and important for the law proper, seems to belong to the Atharvaveda, as Bloomfield has already conjectured[4] and Caland[5] proved the probability of, on the ground of the similarity of the Śrāddhakalpa of this author, collected by him from quotations, with the Atharva ritus. The prose quotation about adoption from a Kātīyalaugākṣisūtra might also have been derived from a Gṛhyasūtra. Similarly a rule in prose about the damage done to merchandises is associated with the name of

1. P. V. Kane has collected the quotations from Śaṅkha-Likhita and in his opinion the date of their Smṛti should be placed between 360 B. C. and the first century A. C. *Tr.*

2. Tantravārttika 179 ; Colebrooke, Ess. 1, 339 (Ed. Cowell).

3. Altind. Ahnencult 100, 136 ff., 252 f., 264.

4. Kauś. XVIII.

5. l. c. 99, 109 f.

Kātyāyana who, as is well-known, was a Sūtrakāra of the White Yajurveda. It is quoted by Medhātithi on M. 8, 215, from a Kātyāyanīyaṁ Sūtram [1]. Kātyāyan Brahmans are still found e.g. in Puna, although it is not clear whether they are connected with the Vedic school of the same name or not. See §9 for the metrical Smṛti of Kātyāyana. A Kātyāyanagṛhya is quoted by Hemādri 3, 1, 1324, which is different from the Pāraskara and contains a cross reference to the Śrautasūtra. Isolated prose rules of Devala, Pracetas, Bhṛgu, Vyāsa and others are also quoted, who are known to us otherwise only as authors of metrical Smṛtis.

§ 5. *The Law-book of Manu.* Comparatively only a few miserable remnants of the almost innumerable Vedic schools, in which the Sūtras known to us from the Caraṇavyūha and other works were once taught, have been preserved to the present day ; and this is the case also with the Dharmasūtras. Of the Brahmans who are still acquainted with their ancient literature—their number on the whole is not large—only a portion, the class of the Vaidikas, adhere to the ancient customs of learning by heart the canonical works of their particular school and to recite them for alms[2]. Also in the social life of the Brahmans the classification based on the differences of the study of the Veda is disappearing before classifications based on other grounds, mostly of a geographical nature. Thus, for example, intermarriage is not allowed between the Kankanasths and Devarukhes in Puna, but inside of these two sects there is connubium[3] between the Rigvedis and the Apastambs or Yajurvedis. Besides the Vaidikas, we find the Śrotriyas and Hotṛs, who are

Lost Sūtra-caraṇas.

Present day state of Brahmanical learning.

1. Bühler IA, 14, 324.
2. Bühler SBE 25, XLVII ff. ; Haug, Brahma und die Brahmanen 47 f. ; Bhandarkar, IA 3, 132 ff.
3. BG. 18, 1, 111, 160.

familiar with the Śrautasūtras and know how to perform sacrifices according to them; the Yājñikas who study the Gṛhyasūtras and perform the Saṁskāras according to them; the Jyotiṣins—astrologers, the Śāstrins or Dharmaśāstrins who are familiar with the law-books and can explain them, and other specialists[1] whose number is still very great at a centre of Sanskrit learning such as the Sanskrit College in Benares.

Specialisation set in at on early date.

This specialisation certainly is not merely of a recent date, but is the natural result of the widening of the sphere of learning which took place at an early date and rendered it impossible, in spite of the long period devoted to the study of the Veda, to master it by committing it to memory[2]. That the study of the sacred law, which specially interests us here, had already become a specialised subject before the time of the Dharmasūtras of Vas. and Baudh. is proved by these works themselves, for they mention also the Dharmapāṭhaka[3] along with those who are acquainted with the four Vedas or the Vedāṅgas, or with Mīmāṁsā, as member of an assembly of authorities *(pariṣad)*, by which term clearly a Brahman is meant who has studied the several Dharmasūtras of the different schools, because the Dharmasūtra of a particular school, as part of the Kalpa, is already included among the Vedāṅgas[4]. A still further specialisation

1. Bühler l. c.; M. Williams, Hinduism 160; Nesfield, Caste System 53 ff.

2. Bühler l. c. L ff.; Tag. Lect. 41 f., 347.

3. Meyer (Rechtsschriften, p. 38) thinks that the Dharmapāṭhaka was an expert in secular law whereas the others were experts in religious law. As Gaut. does not mention the Dharmapāṭhaka, Meyer argues (p. 317) that in the days of Gaut. the legal works had been ruined by the works on Dharma. This theory of Meyer is based on pure imagination and cannot be harmonised with the other theory of Meyer himself that the Nāradasmṛti—exclusively devoted to secular law—is older than Gaut., for Medhātithi, who in his opinion is not far removed from Gaut., often quotes Nārada. *Tr.*

4. Bühler l. c.

may be found in Vi. 83, 6 ff. where among the Paṅkti-pāvanas, those who would sanctify an assembly, one who has studied only a particular Dharmaśāstra is mentioned along with those, who have studied only one Vedāṅga or the Purāṇas, the epics or grammar. Also the fact that the law-books of the different schools, in the opinion of the commentators and to some extent also in the opinion of the authors themselves, were intended to supplement each other, indicates the early advent of specialists and schools of Dharma, clearly to be traced from the Dharmajña, Dharmavid or Dharmapravaktṛ and Pariṣad of the Smṛtis, from the Dharmaśāstrin of Bāṇa's Harṣacarita[1] and from the Dharmanibandhakāras and Ṭīkākāras of the mediaeval age—often very eminent persons, to the court Pandits and Shastris formerly attached to English law-courts and to the popular courts of arbitration *(pañc)* of the present day. That the law-books had received general recognition about 700 A.D., is proved by the statement by Kumārila to the effect that they were indeed evolved and continued within particular Vedic schools, but at his time they were also generally recognised[2].

Further specialisation.

Now, the Smṛtis which at the present day are studied and consulted by the authorities on Dharma in all parts of India, are primarily metrical Smṛtis, above all, the Mānavaṁ Dharmaśāstram and the commentaries and systematic works annexed to it. How early the authority of this work spread over the whole of India is best shown by the numerous commentaries composed in various countries, which go back to the early mediaeval age and refer to even earlier sources. In my edition of the text of M. (London 1887) the variations of the text in these different commentaries were marked as fully as possible,

Importance of metrical Smṛtis at the present day.

1. Calc. Ed. 204.
2. Tantravārttika 179; Colebroke, Ess. 1, 339.

Text of M. was the same even 1000 years ago.

but they are unimportant comparatively and it cannot, therefore, be doubted that our M. was essentially the same as it is to-day even 1000 years ago. A still more ancient testimony for the existence of a work at least very closely resembling this Smṛti is Bṛh.[1] whose fragments, which should be assigned to about the sixth or the seventh century A.D., exhibit an intimate acquaintance with M. Thus Bṛh. 10, 13 speaks about the different weights described by "M." with clear reference to M. 8, 132-137. The famous passage M. 9, 57-68, where Niyoga is at first prescribed and then forbidden, is already turned to account by Bṛh.; regarding the permissibility of gambling he points out (26, 1) the disagreement which exists in this respect between M. 9, 221 ff. and other teachers of law, and when Bṛh. 25, 33 speaks of the 13 sons, who were mentioned "by M.," it is only seemingly in contradiction to the 12 sons in M. 9, 158, 180 ; for according to M. 9, 127 ff. the Putrikāputra may be regarded as the thirteenth son. The superiority of M. over all other teachers of law is emphasised by Bṛh. 27, 3. In 13, 1 he mentions Bhṛgu instead of M. and thereby betrays his acquaintance with those passages of M. where Bhṛgu figures as the real author. Nārada too seems to presuppose our M. although his relation to our M. is not quite so clear as that of Bṛh., and Nār. is to be assigned to about 500 A.D. (§7). The Burmese and Javanese law-books are not less dependent on M. (§13). Kumārila (8. century) is the more important as a witness, because the ancient commentary often cited by him frequently refers to our M.[2] The inscriptions too corroborate this, at least in so far as they mention M. at the head of the teachers of law and this is done even in a Valabhi inscription of the sixth century A. D.[3]

M. drawn upon by Bṛh. and Nār.

The evidence of Kum. and of the inscriptions.

1. SBE 33, Introd. ; cf. §9.
2. Cf. Bühler l. c. 613.
3. l. c. XCIII ff.

The relation between our M. and the Mah., which of course is of a very complicated nature, is remarkable[1]. Thus in Mah. 12, 56, 23 ff. two Ślokas are mentioned which M. had sung *sveṣu dharmeṣu.* One of these Ślokas agrees with M. 9, 321 and the expression *dharmāḥ* is often used to indicate a Dharmaśāstra. In Mah. 13, 46, 30 ff. there is a still clearer reference to a Śāstra composed by Manu—the more so because the rule cited here is the same as M. 9, 87 in substance and even agrees with it word for word to some extent. In the story of Śakuntalā in Mah. 1, 73, 8 ff., Manu at least, if not his manual, is mentioned as the authority for the list and description of the eight forms of marriage—a passage which agrees in its main features with M. 3, 20-26. Of course, in other comparable passages it appears that the Mah. represents an older state of things than our M., so that the law proper in it is expounded in an altogether disorderly fashion and without any trace of the 18 titles of law. Besides, M. contains a whole series of references (particularly 7, 41 ; 8, 110 ; 9, 23, 66, 129, 227, 314, 315 ; 10, 108), which betray an accurate knowledge of the saga of the Mah. ; but it is true that most of these references occur in those parts of our M. which seem to be of later origin. Particularly remarkable are the numerous parallel passages in these two works which in the Mah. are not mentioned as quotations from Manu. According to Bühler's researches there are more than 260 such verses, i.e. about 1/10 of the whole of the M., in the 3., 12., and the 16. Parvans of theMah. alone. As sometimes the one and sometimes the other of these two works contains the better reading, this agreement cannot be the result of borrowing but goes back to a common source and this common source is to be sought in Indian "Spruchweisheit."

M. and the Mah.

Mah. represents an older state of things.

1. l. c. LXXIII ff. ; cf. Hopkins JAOS 11, 257 ff. ; Holtzmann D. Mah. in O. u. W. (Kiel 1895) 114 ff.

'Spruchweisheit' in the Smṛtis.

The fondness for adages and parables which is still common in India found a particularly rich field of activity in the sphere of Dharma. M. reads like a didactic poem and even rises not seldom to poetical altitudes. Even the Dharmasūtras are full of verses which are again seen in M. for the most part, word for word; Vas. thus has 39 Ślokas and Vi. more than 160 Ślokas in common with M. Thus, if it is certain that a large mass of memorial verses were existing at an early date, it was in all probability just for the Dharmaśāstrins, who knew these verses by heart, to draw up whole works in metre and to versify the existing Dharmasūtras, be they of their own or of other Vedic schools.

Transition from Sūtra to Sloka.

The theory that the transition from the Sūtra form to the Śloka form was connected and coeval with the transition of the sacred law from the Vedic Caraṇas to special schools of Dharma, must, in the nature of things, remain a hypothesis, which, however, gains a great amount of probability for reasons of various kinds. Thus from the close relationship between the M. and the Mah. it becomes understandable that the epic Śloka was selected for both, be it that the epic already existed at an earlier time in its present form or was brought into this form at the same time as M. Like the epic, M. too is meant for the great mass of the people or at least for the educated, acquainted with Sanskrit. And as the epic was transformed from a simple description of battles and war-scenes into a didactic poem—a Smṛti,[1] there developed out of the Dharmasūtras, the handbooks of the schools of the Brahmans, the metrical presentation of the Dharma which should be equally binding on everybody. Also the time of origin of our M. and the Mah. in their present form is approximately the same. As M. in its essential parts and

1. Cf. Bühler and Kirste, Contrib. to the Hist. of the Mah (Wien 1892).

in view of its relations to Bṛh. and Nār. can hardly be assigned to a period later than the 2.-3. century A. D., so the Mah. too according to the researches of Bühler, must have existed in approximately its present form at least about 300-500 A. D. [1]

Date of M.

As the Mah. at the time of its revision was considerably extended in view of the advanced Brahmanism, so the Dharmasūtras too received a great deal of accretions. The narrow, exclusively religious standpoint of the Vedic schools permitted many important questions to be dealt with only by a hint, specially as the Sūtra-works were committed to memory and thus had to be as concise as possible and, as has already been pointed out, were from the first destined to supplement each other. On the other hand a work which was intended to be studied and recited by every member of the three higher castes (M. 2, 16 ; 12, 126), would have to go much more into details and include a much wider circle of subjects [2]. Thus an exhaustive treatment of law proper, which in the Dharmasūtras was treated rather in a step-motherly fashion, was necessary in such a work. In fact the juridical section i. e. the 8. and the first part of the 9. Adhy. covers more than one fourth of the whole of this extensive work (713 of 2684 verses) while in the Dharmasūtras they occupy comparatively much less space. Particular laws and maxims are illustrated by instances from the Mah. as has already been mentioned above.

Effect of this remodelling.

Exhaustive treatment of law in the Dharmaśāstras

Even the sphere of the duties of the king (7, 1-226 ; 9, 294-325) was considerably extended and supplemented compared with the Dharmasūtras, e. g. Vi. Adhy. 3. It contains, *inter alia*, the daily routine of the king (M. 7, 145 f., 151 ff., 216, 221 ff.) seen also in the Mah. 15, 5, 10 ff. and in Daṇḍin's

Later additions to the text of M.

1. l. c. 21-27.
2. Bühler SBE 25, LXVI-LXXIII.

Daśakumāracarita 8 (p. 156 ed. Godabole), and particularly the exaggerated glorification and deification of royalty (M. 7, 1-15 ; 9, 294-311 etc., cf. Mah. 1, 82, 18, etc.) which is quite consistent in a work intended for the Kṣatriyas and their advisors while in the Vedic literature and the Dharmasūtras royalty is as a rule extolled only in connection with Brahmanism. The philosophical portions of the 1. and the 12. Adhy. are based, as Garbe [1] has proved, on a later Purāṇic form of the Sāṁkhya philosophy. Also in the other chapters there is much which was probably added to the original work only at the time of its versification—such as the philosophico-medical excursus 2, 89-100, the classification of the *pitaraḥ* 3, 193-201, discussion about the means of subsistance of the Brahman 4, 1-24, the introductory remarks before the laws of diet 5, 1-4, the remarkably detailed account of the mixed castes 10, 1-74, and the uselessly repeated laws about the duties of the castes 10, 101-131 etc.[2]

Better arrangement in M.

As in its contents, so also in the arrangement of the subject matter the M. exhibits a remarkable advance on the Dharmasūtras. The old Vedic designations for divisions and sub-divisions, Praśna, Paṭala and Khaṇḍa (Khaṇḍikā) have indeed been retained practically only in the proper Dharmasūtras while in other works the division in Adhy. is followed as in M. Of the 12 Adhy. in which the M. is divided the first six deal with the creation of the world and the duties of the four Āśramas including the Śrāddha, Vaiśvadeva and other sacrifices ; the other six deal with the duties of the king, particularly the administration of justice and the right to punish, the occupations of the four castes and the mixed castes, the penances, and the transmigration of the soul.

---

1. Die Sāṁkhya Philosophie (Leipzig 1894) 44-47.
2. Bühler l. c. LXVI.

The law proper according to M. is divided under 18 titles : 1. Recovery of debt, 2. deposits, 3. sale without ownership, 4. concerns among partners, 5. resumption of gifts, 6. non-payment of wages, 7. non-performance of agreements, 8. recission of sale and purchase, 9. disputes between the owner of cattle and his servants, 10. disputes regarding boundaries, 11. assault, 12. defamation, 13. theft, 14. violence, 15. adultery, 16. duties of man and wife, 17. law of inheritance, 18. gambling and betting. Mill[1] and others have sharply criticised this classification of Indian law, but it is worthy of notice not only as a first attempt, but this classification seems to have been taken directly from actual life and fully corresponds to the necessities of the life of those days. Thus the law of debt, closely interwoven with the rules of court procedure occupies the first place on account of its great usefulness ; then follow the question of deposits, particularly important on account of the general insecurity of ownership in those days, the laws of donations and gifts with which the Brahmans are most closely concerned from their class interest, laws of partnership and trade, disputes about boundaries and other topics of the sphere of civil law. The next five topics are connected with criminal law. The particularly detailed sections about the duties of man and wife and the law of inheritance conjointly form the domestic laws. The few verses about gambling and betting represent a short supplement[2].

The 18 titles of law in M.

The classification is based on actual life.

Coming back from these later elements in our M. to the original parts of this work as they can be traced out by a comparison of the same with the Dharmasūtras, we are confronted with the further question whether a particular work of this kind may be said to have been the

1. Hist. of India 1, 195.
2. Cf. ZVR 1, 246 ff.

M. and Mānavācārya.

source of our M. or not. Here the well-known hypothesis comes up, which makes the mythical first parent Manu, who in our M. (1, 1-4, 118 f. etc.) is named as the author of the work, identical with the Mānvācārya or Manvācārya, the traditional author of the Mānava Gṛhyasūtra[1] and according to which the Mānava Dharmaśāstra as the law-book of the Mānavas, was originated out of the lost Mānava Dharmasūtra, the supposed Dharmasūtra of the Vedic school of the Mānava-Maitrāyaṇīyas. These hypotheses which were first raised at a time when this school was known only by its name, have received little support from the discovery of several of its chief works. Neither the Gṛhyasūtra along with the Pariśiṣṭa nor the Saṁhitā and the Śrautasūtra of the Maitrāyaṇīyas agree accurately with M.

Parallelisms between M. and the Mānavaśrāddhakalpa.

The Mānava-śrāddhakalpa[2] however, discovered by Bühler and turned to account for this question by him, offers very numerous points of agreement with M. These interesting parallels however, refer only to a certain number of particular verses, while the ritual is quite different, and these verses might have been taken from M. because the Śrāddhakalpa on the whole seems to be a modern work in its present form and many other verses seem to have been taken from the Karmapradīpa and the Caturviṁśatipurāṇa[3].

The comparison with Gṛhyasūtra and the Śrautasūtra of the Mānavas.

As regards the Gṛhyasūtra, it has indeed a rule about begging from relative women common with M. 2, 50, but this law is found also in other Gṛhyasūtras (Pār. 2, 5, 5 ; cf. Āśv. 1, 22, 7) nor is it without further parallels in the Smṛtis (Āp. 1, 3, 26, etc.), so that it may be regarded as a common property of the Sūtra literature. About the time of the Saṁskāras, the

1. Bühler SBE 25, LXIII.
2. l. c. XL-XLIV.
3. Caland, Altind. Ahnencult 78 ff.

forms of marriage, of which the Mānavagṛhya knows two—the Brāhma and the Śaulkadharma, and other decisive points the two works hold wholly divergent views[1]. Regarding the important ritual of Śrāddha the same is the case with M. 3, 214 ff. and the corresponding treatment of the same subject in the Śrautasūtra of the Mānava school[2]. Accordingly, there is no chance of an agreement between our M. and the Sūtras of this school as there exists between Vi. and the Gṛhyasūtra of the Kāṭhaka school or between Y. and the chief works of the Vājasaneyins. However, the existence of a work, supposedly the source of our M., is indicated by the scanty fragments of such a work in ancient quotations discussed in §4. The author of the Dharmasūtra of this school need by no means have been the same person as the author of the Gṛhyasūtra ; thus the Dharmasūtra of the Hairaṇyakeśas which they have taken from the Āpastambīyas, differs considerably from their Gṛhyasūtra in language and subject matter[3]. Indirect relations between M. and the Mānava school may still further be traced through Vi. and the Kāṭhaka school[4]. All these arguments, however, yield only a certain degree of probability to the supposed relationship between M. and the Vedic Mānavas, so that it is perhaps most advisable to reserve the final decision on this question till the discovery of decisive manuscript materials.

Uncertainty about M.'s relation with the Mānava school.

The author of our M. at all events already knew various older law-books as he speaks of the Dharmaśāstras in general as well as mentions several teachers of

1. D. Dharmasūtra d. Viṣṇu und d. Kāṭhakagṛhyas. (1879) 76 ff. ; cf. P. v. Bradke ZDMG 36, 438 ; Bühler l. c. XXXIX.
2. Caland l. c. 198 ff.
3. Bühler l. c. XL.
4. SBE 7, XXV ff. ; P. v. Bradke l. c. 438 ff.

law by name [1]. The Vaikhānasa school for example which he refers to when dealing with the duties of the Vānaprastha, has left us a Dharmasūtra, which though a very late work in its present form, yet in that particular section about Vānaprasthas shows remarkable points of agreement with M. (§ 3). It should not, therefore, be doubted that the author had made use of works of various schools when he intended to write a didactic poem on Dharma binding on all castes and to set it off with the name of Manu, who had so long been glorified as the first parent of mankind and was considered to be descended from Brahman, the universal soul, or was identified with it, and was said to be the founder of the social order in this world, and was renowned as the inventor of sacrificial usages and as the religious law-giver,[2] long before the Sūtra-school of the Mānavas came into existence which very probably was also named after him. The name of our law-book is not in this respect without analogy with the names of authors of other metrical Smṛtis such as Atri, Uśanas, Dakṣa, Nār., Prajāpati, Bṛh. etc., which likewise have also been taken from the world of heroes and gods.

The author of M. made use of previous works.

That the alleged work of M. received so general a recognition even so early, may be explained on consideration of the fame of the mythical M. of whom even in the three Saṁhitās of the Black Yajurveda it has been said that all that M. has said is medicine[3]. The fact that this Mantra and the passage to the effect that M. divided his property among his sons, which is often quoted in connection with the law of inheritance, belong to the Black Yajurveda, as well

The cause of the unusual popularity of M.

---

1. M. 2, 10 ; 3, 16, 232 ; 6, 21 ; 8, 140 ; 12, 111 ; cf. Bühler l. c. XXV-XXX.
2. Bühler l. c. LVI-LXV.
3. Tag. Lect. 43 ; Bühler l. c. XVI.

as the occurrence of a few Mantras specially peculiar to this Veda[1] in M. and its relations with Vi. may be explained on the hypothesis that the sources of law made use of by him belonged, though not to the Mānava school, yet exclusively or principally to the sphere of the Black Yajurveda. But this too is uncertain.

M. and the Black Yajurveda

Bhṛgu's name like that of Manu is mythical, who according to M. 1,60,119 ; 5, 1-4, 122, etc. is the proclaimer of this work which was revealed to him by his father M. and who is therefore frequently represented as discoursing when passing into a new section, although he is not often mentioned by name. It is, however, doubtful whether it will be right to completely differentiate this Bhṛgu, after whom our work is called the Mānavadharmaśāstra in the recension of Bhṛgu (bhṛguprokta, bhṛguproktā saṁhitā), from our M.,[2] particularly because already in Nār. and in the Skandapurāṇa (§ 7) a combination of the names of these two authors is found. However, in the quotations, in the oldest of them, our work is expressly ascribed to M. and Bhṛgu appears as the author of a separate Smṛti.

Bhṛgu as the proclaimer of M.

The heterogenous character of the sources of our M. renders it impossible to utilise the few geographical data occurring in it in order to definitely determine its land of origin[3]. It is, therefore, hardly advisable to insist upon the interesting definitions of the lands, Brahmāvarta, Brahmarṣideśa, Madhyadeśa and Āryāvarta (M. 2, 19, ff.), although they seem to belong to the ancient part of the work, specially because Baudhāyana 1, 2, 9 ff. whose school certainly belongs to Southern India, also locates the lands of the Aryans to the region of the holy rivers in Northern India[4].

The land of M.'s origin is uncertain.

1. Cf. Caland l. c. 206.
2. Cf. Johäntgen, Das Gesetzbuch des Manu 15, 97 ff. ; P. v Bradke l. c. 433 ff.
3. Cf. M. Willioms, Indian Wisdom (3rd. ed.)213 etc.
4. Cf. Bühler l. c. XLV.

M. the first metrical Smṛti.

§ 6. *Yājñavalkya.* While the Dharmasūtras in general represent an older stage of development than our M. this Smṛti is the foremost among the metrical works. In the passage of Kumārila, often referred to, mention is made of Gaut., Vas. and other Sūtra-works, and he also frequently cites our M. whom he considers to be the highest authority in the sphere of Dharma. The great Mīmāṁsaka seems to have known no other metrical Smṛti than M. and an examination of the contents of these works shows that they are less archaic than M. and ex-

Y. posterior only to M

pressly or tacitly, assume him to be their predecessor. First of all Yājñavalkya comes into consideration, about whom Stenzler[1], the editor and translator of Yājñavalkya, is of opinion that in antiquity he is posterior to M. but precedes all other authors and therefore represents the next phase after M. In fact the advance on M. is unmistakable, it is evident even from the more concise form of its contents which enabled Y. to discuss almost all the topics handled by M. in 1009 Śl. instead of M.'s 2684; they are roughly divided into three sections, approximately of equal length, on custom, law and penance. The section on law does not expressly refer to M.'s classification of the law under 18 heads; the commentators however divide it in a similar manner but add to the above 18 two more: conditions of service and miscellany (cf. §7). The order is indeed slightly different in Y. for, the law of inheritance, disputes about boundaries and the transgressions of the shepherd here occupy the 3., 4. and the 5. places,

The advanced views of Y.

gambling and betting the 12. place, etc. In the of law inheritance the widow's claim to property and that of the daughter in the absence of male issue are fully recognised (2, 135), while M. still like the Dharmasūtras, takes a very

1. Pref. VIII ff,

unfavourable view of women's claim to property. In the law of debt Y. (2, 37-67) deals with mortgages and the foreclosure of the same, various kinds of securities and with the liability for debts, much more exhaustively than M. Generally Y. lays particular stress upon private law, specially upon the law of trade—the criminal law being of less importance to him. Y.'s treatment of the hearing of witnesses and, on the whole, that of the judicial procedure are on a decidedly advanced footing. While in M. the evidence is essentially based on deposition and along with it only the water and fire-ordeals are mentioned, Y. 2, 22 mentions the written document as the chief testimony and (2, 84-94) gives elaborate rules of drawing up and testing documents. He describes at length (2, 95-113) five different kinds of ordeals which should be resorted to in default of other means of evidence. He (2, 24-29) also lays down systematic principles about the law of possession and usucaption barely alluded to in M.; the same about appeal (2, 30). The penances likewise are more diverse in character in Y. 3, 316-328 than in M. In connection with social customs I mention only his polemic against the marriage of a Brahman with a Śūdra woman (1, 56). According to the Mit. this polemic is directed against M. 3, 13 and it is quite credible. The fact that M. here is not expressly mentioned by Y. testifies to the high esteem which he must have been already enjoying at the time of Y.

Y. mentions written documents and 5 ordeals.

Y., on the whole, is later than the Dharmasūtras and M., though, e. g., the documentary evidence is already referred to in Vas. 16, 10, 14 f. The analogies between Y. and Vi. are remarkable, even in such cases where both differ from M.,[1] for example, regarding copperplate grants, deeds of debt and all documents in general,

Y. and Vi.

1. Cf. SBE 7, XX ff.; Vi. 3, 82; 6, 24-26; 9-14; 17, 1 f., 13; 19, 7 f.; 96, 54-95; 97, 1, 9.

regarding the five chief divine judgments and their applications, regarding inheritance, distinction between inherited and self-earned property, recognition of the right of representation, funeral ceremonies, and moreover, regarding the composition of the human body and Yoga—topics dealt with also in the medical works[1]. At the same time it is, however, remarkable that in the passage Y. 2, 240 f. which is otherwise closely comparable with Vi. 5, 122 f. the word *nānaka*, a designation for minted coin, is found,[2] which is rightly interpreted as a proof of the comparatively later origin of our Y.[3] It can well be inferred from this that in other cases too Vi. has retained the older version and Y. has drawn upon Vi. or rather upon the Sūtra-work lying at the root of this work. Yājñavalkya is unmistakably related to another work belonging to the Black Yajurveda, namely, the Mānavagṛhyasūtra, with which it has in common a passage about the symptoms and cure of one possessed by Vināyaka (Gaṇeśa) (1, 270-292) which has wrongly been considered as a proof of the later origin of this work [4]. The language, the metre, the concise form, the reduction of the four Vināyakas to one Gaṇeśa, all this proves that here too Y. represents the later tradition[5]. A Vināyakaśānti is besides described in another Sūtra-work of the Black Yajurveda—in Baudh[6].

Y. later than Vi.

Decisive data, however, connect Y. with the White Yajurveda. Even Stenzler, ZDMG 7, 517 ff. pointed out the similarily between Y. 3, 1 ff. and the Gṛhyasūtra of Pāraskara 3, 10[7] belonging to

Y. belongs to the White Yajurveda.

1. Cf. Transact. of the 9th, Congr. of Orient. (Lond. 1893)., 456 ff.
2. There is some confusion in the German text here. *Tr.*
3. Stenzler l. c. XI; cf. WIL (2nd. ed.) 222, 299.
4. Stenzler l. c. IX.
5. P. v. Bradke ZDMG 26, 426-433.
6. Raj. Mitra, Not. No. 1325.
7. Cf. Oldenburg SBE 29, 355-359,

the White Yajurveda and also the relation in which Y.'s name stands to the Vājasaneyi-Saṁhitā. Y. who is also called Vājasaneya, is considered to be the author of this Saṁhitā and figures as the chief authority in the Śatapathabrāhmaṇa belonging to it, particularly in the Bṛhadāraṇyaka; the Yajus-mantras were revealed to him by the Sun-god. Similarly Y. 3, 110 refers to himself as the author of the Āraṇyaka which he had received from the Sun. In conformity with this, in Y. the Mantras which are recited at the Śrāddha are taken mostly from the Vājasaneyisaṁh. and the whole exposition of the Śrāddha 1, 219-271 exhibits a large number of points of agreement with the Śrāddhakalpasūtra of Kātyāyana edited by Caland.[1] Accordingly, it is probable that the Smṛti of Y. is based on a Sūtra-work of the White Yajurveda but at the same time other Sūtra-works and our M. were utilised by the author of this work. The laconic style of Y. should perhaps be regarded as a lingering relic of the original Sūtras.[2]

Y. based on a Sūtra-work of the Wh. Yajurveda.

While by means of the sources made use of by Y. the upper limit of the age of his Smṛti may be fixed, his acquaintance with Greek astrology, according to Jacobi[3], authorises us to hold that he should be assigned to the

1. Caland, Altind. Ahnencult 127-130. 245-252: cf. West and Bühler (3rd. ed.) 47.

2. Meyer (Rechtsschriften, pp. 120-194) says that the whole text of Y. is nothing but a metrical version of what his predecessors in the field had said on Indian laws and customs and that most of all he has copied Kauṭilya. As Y. has broken up and never quoted in full the verses of previous works in his attempt to condense the text as much as possible, Meyer argues that any work which has any verse in common with Y. must be later than Y. These theories of Meyer are however directly opposed to the conclusions reached by Losch. See foot-note 1. p. 44. *Tr.*

3. ZDMG 30, 306 f.

Losch however says that this is no longer quite certain for the Babylonian heptagram might have been directly derived from Babylon and not through the Greeks and this is rendered all the more probable by the recent discoveries in the Indus valley. *Tr.*

third century A.D. at the earliest. In 1, 295 he enumerates the 7 planets in the astronomical order, and in 1, 80 too *(sustha indau)* he gives an astrological reference though without using any Greek term. The word *nāṇaka* already referred to, is not without importance for chronological purposes ; at all events, it is not one of the most ancient coin-names. For the *terminus ad quem*, besides the oldest commentaries (§ 11) and the Garuḍa and Agnipurāṇas with their numerous borrowings[1] from Y. (§ 10), the other metrical Smṛtis are important, whose posteriority will be proved below. Y. therefore falls approximately in the fourth century A. D. The statement in Y. 1, 2 as well as the Vedic references indicate that his home is to be sought in Mithilā (Videha), and the Vājasaneyins also generally belong to the North.

Date of Y.

§ 7. *Nārada.* The Nāradasmṛti[2] attracted great attention already a hundred years ago on account of the

---

1. The first and the third chapters of Y. are found in the Garuḍapurāṇa and the second chapter is found in the Agnipurāṇa. Hans Losch has made a detailed study of these extracts in his little work "Die Yājñavalkyasmṛti verglichen mit den Parallelen des Agni und Garuḍapurāṇa" and has arrived at the following conclusions:—

a. The Rājadharma section at the end of the first chapter is an interpolation.

b. The Agnipurāṇa version of the Vyavahārādhyāya is older than the corresponding chapter of Y. and though it is strongly influenced by the Arthaśāstra literature it is still essentially an independent work. But on the whole the second chapter is a later addition to the text of Y.

c. Verses 60-206 of the third chapter of Y. are interpolated and the Purāṇa version of this chapter is older than the text contained in the Smṛti. *Tr.*

2. Cf. SBE 31 ; Tag. Lect. 54 ff. ; The Institutes Nárada by J. Jolly (Lond. 1876 and Calc. 1885) ; West and Bühler (3rd. ed.) 48-50 ; Bühler SBE 25, XVII, XCV ff. ; Bendall, Journey in Nepal (Lond. 1886), 56 ff.; Conrady, 15 Blätter einer nepales. Palmblatt-Hs. des Nārada (Leipzig, 1891.) ; Ridding, A Ms. of the Nārada Smṛti JRAS 1893, 41-47.

passage in the author's introduction which describes the various recensions of M. and represents Nār. as a fragment of an older and more extensive recension of this work than our M. composed by Bhṛgu. According to this passage referred to by Sir William Jones in the foreword to his Manu and after him frequently by others, the first parent M. is said to have composed a comprehensive work on law, philosophy etc. in 24 sections and 100,000 Ślokas. The Devarṣi Nār., who received it from M., seeing the feeble intellectual power of man, made a sketch of it in 12,000 Ślokas and Bhṛgu's son Sumati further abridged it into 4,000 Ślokas. Only this sketch is now accessible to humanity, but the Nār.-Smṛti preserves the 9. chapter of the sketch prepared by Nār. from M., dealing with law proper. This datum is often taken into account for the history of our M. and conjointly with the quotations from a Vṛddha or Bṛhanmanu, it is regarded as a proof of the fact that only a later revision of the original work of M. has been preserved. Our M. should be regarded as still later, if the version of this introduction to Nār. found in the greater and perhaps the more ancient recension of his work is taken to be true; for this version throws in Mārkaṇḍeya between Nār. and Sumati as another redactor who is said to have made a sketch in 8,000 Ślokas.

Various recensions of M. mentioned in Nār.

A comparison of the contents alone shows that Nār. is not older but decidedly later than M. and that the traditional relation between these two authors must therefore be reversed. It is possible that the tradition according to which Nār., the intermediary between gods and men, received a law-book from the first parent M. is as old as that which connects Bhṛgu with M. in the same manner. The analogous statements however in the Purāṇas and in the Mah. about four successive revisions of the original work of M. mention

The Purāṇic tradition about the successive revisions of M.

Bhṛgu, Nār., Bṛh. and Aṅgiras or Śaṁkara, Indra, Bṛhaspati and Kāvya, as the four redactors. The order here is therefore different, for Bhṛgu, Sumati's father, here comes before Nār.

Advanced views of Nār.

Nār.'s posteriority to M. is evident, for instance, from the 132 sub-divisions of the 18 titles of law, 15 kinds of slavery, 21 ways of earning livelihood, 11 kinds of witnesses, 5 kinds of divine judgment, 3 kinds of principal crime (Sāhasa) and further ramifications[1] which have far fewer categories in M. or on the whole are present only in embryo. Even the fact that Nārada makes law proper the subject of a separate work is a sign of great advancement. In purport too he differs from M. not seldom, but these differences in most cases may be explained if it is held that in Nār.'s days a great advance was made in legal constitution; for example, Nār. declares gambling, which is entirely forbidden by M., to be permissible so long as it takes place publicly under state control (17,1-8); he curtails the right of primogeniture in the law of inheritance (13, 4 f.) and on the other hand, grants the mother and the unmarried sisters equal shares with the sons at the partition of the property after the death of the father (13, 12 f.); in the law of debt he considerably extends the liability to the wife for the debts of her husband (1,17-25); in law-suits he gives great prominence to proceedings in writing and documentary evidence.

Nār. indebted to M.

The impression that our M. is the basic work upon which Nār. has made improvements is further strengthened by the fact that he fully agrees with M. in the arrangement of the subject matter because even the "miscellany," *prakīrṇaka*, not found in M. among the titles of law, and the appendix on theft, have their parallel passages in the section 9, 229-325 of

1. See f.-n., p. 47.

M. which seems to be a supplement to the 18 titles of law The initial verse of the original work of Manu cited in the introduction agrees almost literally with M. 1, 4 which, in fact, is the real beginning of the work and its table of contents likewise approximately agrees with that of our M. ; Nār. frequently refers to M. and in a Ms. Nār. is even directly called *mānave dharmaśāstre nāradaproktā saṁhitā*, just as M. is called the *bhṛguproktā saṁhitā*.

Nār quotes the initial verse of M.

Nār. is posterior not only to M. but also to Y. Indeed, he often agrees, specially in judicial proceedings, particularly with Y., but surpasses him in details and exactitude and a great advance in casuistry as well as in subject matter may be easily recognised. Thus besides the 5 ordeals described in Y. he knows two or four more [1] ; the classifications referred to above are wanting in Y. almost as completely as in M. ; a large number of technical details are found in I, 2, 1 ff. and in Quot. 2, 1-22, 3, 1-12 about the composition of complaints and answers, which are not yet mentioned by Y. ; the theory of legal majority and capacity for business (1, 26 ff.) is peculiar to Nār. alone ; his treatment of witnesses, e. g., the list of inadmissible witnesses in 1, 157-197, is much fuller than that in Y. ; the theory that in some cases witnesses are not necessary (1, 172 ff.) is yet unknown to Y. ; in secular law the doctrines of gifts (4, 1 ff.), of reward, slavery and salary (5, 1 ff. and 6, 18 ff), of dikes and fallow lands (11, 17-26), of impotency and its cure (12, 8-19), of irregular wives (12, 49-53), of divorce (12, 89-97), of defamation (15, 1-14), of gambling and betting (17, 1-8), of confiscation (18, 10 f.), of detection of crimes (Appendix 7 ff. and Quot. 7, 23-29) etc., are developments yet unknown to Y. How far he surpasses Y. in details will appear from the fact that his work contains 1200

Nār. also posterior to Y.

The detailed laws of Nār.

1. Cf. Conrady l. c., who shows that the ordeals further mentioned in the Nepalese Ms. are interpolated from Kāty.

Ślokas including the passages in the Napalese Mss. and the quotations against the 307 Ślokas in the second Adhy. of Y. On the other hand, a still greater development in law than is evident in Nār. is clearly perceptible in the works of the various authors known to us only from quotations—Bṛh., Kāty. and Vyāsa (§ 9).

Nār. mentions the Dīnāra,

Along with these relative criteria for the determination of the age of our Nār. by comparing it with other Smṛtis, another decisive fact should be taken into consideration for definitely fixing the *terminus a quo*—the reference to *dīnāra*-denarius, once as a gold coin and another time as gold ornament (App. 60 ; I, 2, 3a). As the Denar might have reached India only through the Greeks and as the pronunciation of eta as iota begins generally speaking in the days of the empire about the second century A.D. (dinaria for denaria in an inscription of 161-169 A.D.)[1] so the Dīnāras struck in India in imitation of the Denars could hardly have come into existence before the second century A. D., although coins of the weight of a Denar were issued by the Indoskythian Kings.[2] For the *terminus ad quem* it is of importance that Asahāya, one of the earliest juridical commentators who may be dated approximately in the eighth century, has written a commentary on our Smṛti. Accordingly Nār. can be dated approximately at about 500 A. D.[3] In

1. Cf. G. Meyer, Griech. Gramm. (2nd. ed,) §73 ; Brugmann, Griech Gramm. (2nd. ed.) §8.

Winternitz points out that this confusion in pronunciation began from a considerably earlier period (see f.-n., 2). *Tr.*

2. The Indian word Dīnāra appears first in Gupta inscriptions from 400 A.C. onwards. See Winternitz, Hist. III, 496. Jolly.

3. Meyer is convinced that Nār. should be placed several centuries before Christ and certainly before Gaut., M., Y. and Vi. (Rechtsschriften, *passim*). In his opinion the passages in which Nār. mentions the Dīnāra are interpolations (p. 103 ff.). The advanced views of Nārada prove nothing because Nār. is a practical

the seventh century a Nāradīya-dharmaśāstra is mentioned by the poet Bāṇa [1].

As regards his native country, it is perhaps to be sought in Nepal, for according to App. 57 ff. he appears to belong neither to the South, nor to the East, nor to the North-West *(pañcanadyāḥ pradeśe)*, and the oldest and the best, and at the same time a very good Ms. of his work has been derived from Nepal, where an ancient commentary too was composed on Nār. in Newari.

Nār. hails from Nepal

§ 8. *The later metrical Smṛtis.* After it was once customary to present the main doctrines of religion and morality in metrical compendiums—the metrical Smṛtis, new works of this type arose more and more out of the schools of Dharma and were fathered upon various saints and gods while the actual authors persistently adhered to discreet anonymity. Those names were used by preference which had already acquired an established reputation in the field of Dharma and thus it comes to pass that absolutely different works are frequently ascribed to the same author. Thus there are more than one Aṅgiras, Atri, Āpastamba, Uśanas, Kātyāyana, Gautama, Parāśara, Bṛhaspati, Yama, Likhita, Vasiṣṭha, Viṣṇu, Vyāsa,

Rise of the later Metrical Smṛtis.

Different works ascribed to the same author.

politician whereas M., Y. etc. are dilettantes. Regarding the 15 kinds of slavery Meyer says that as Buddhaghoṣa mentions only four kinds of slaves, nothing can be decided from this fact (p. 88 f.). The 21 kinds of livelihood cannot be of any significance because Indians were interested in magic from very early times and by this classification Nār. has tried to ascertain what is magically pure and what is not (p. 93). Many other things in Nār. which appear to be of late origin, are interpolations according to Meyer.

Most of the arguments forwarded by Meyer are very far-fetched and Buddhaghoṣa's testimony cannot be of any value in this connection because Buddhaghoṣa very probably records the actual state of affairs whereas in the Smṛtis we have mostly to do with mere theories. *Tr.*

1. Bühler SBE 25, CVII.

Śatātapa, Hārita, etc., even excepting the works known only from quotations. [1] In many cases the epithets Laghu, Madhyama, Bṛhat, Vṛddha, Pūrva, Uttara, Śloka, etc. are subjoined to these names, to characterise these works according to their bulk and age, and to distinguish them from other Smṛtis of the same author. It can hardly be conceded to the Indian commentators that, for example, Vṛddha Manu or "the ancient Manu" represents a work of the age anterior to the M. we are acquainted with. These distinctive appellatives, which in part seem to be derived from the authors themselves, but which mostly however, appear to emanate from the commentators alone, apparently qualify rather the works than the authors and thus, for instance, terms like Bṛhat, which is often changed into Vṛddha "the ancient", Laghu "the small", Madhyama "the middling," Śloka "the metrical," are used to designate the works of the same author. Historical value cannot be given to the epithet Vṛddha as has been frequently done; rather, where it occurs it is to be regarded as a sign of the late origin of the work concerned, for if there was only one work of the author, it would not have been necessary to attach to it any such distinctive epithet.

Various epithets attached to these works.

These epithets are misleading.

Even without taking into account the occurrence of the epithets referred to above, in the case of by far the greater number of these metrical Smṛtis, so far as they have been printed, there are weighty reasons to consider them to be modern compilations of secondary importance. First of all, these works, for the most part, do not contain the numerous texts about all features of Dharma, particularly about law proper, which are ascribed to their alleged authors in the commentaries and systematic works on law of the mediaeval age.

Other signs of late origin.

1. Cf. Stenzler I. St. 1, 232—246 ; West and Bühler (3rd. ed.), 25-52 ; Tag. Lect. 50-67 ; Weber I. St. 3, 508-513 and Verz. 325-341 ; Mandlik, 275-330 ; Eggling, Cat. No. 1289-1372 ; Burnell, Tanj. Cat. 124-127 ; Jolly, ZDMG 31, 127-130 ; V. S. Islampurkar's Parāśara, Prefatory notes.

None of these works deals with law proper (*vyavahāra*). For example, the metrical Smṛtis of Āp., Gaut., Vi., Śaṅkhalikhita, and Hārita of the works which are still extant can at the best be but partially identical with the works of these authors known to us from mediaeval quotations, because the greater part of these quotations are in prose. The contents too of these Smṛtis often impress us to be quite modern. Thus in Parāśara, for whose Smṛti the commentary of Mādhava belonging to the fourteenth century and the occurrence of most of the ancient quotations in our text[1] secure a comparatively high antiquity, it is found in the author's introduction (1, 24) that he regards himself to be a modern author, the standard author for the Kali age alone, and particularly assigns the works of M., Gaut. and Śaṅkhalikhita to the three previous ages respectively. As his rules are concerned with the present age of sins it is quite understandable that Parāśara makes allowance for the growing tendency to permit agriculture to the Brahmans and he reduces the 12 sons of the ancient Smṛtis to 4 of whom 2 are adoptive sons (2, 2, 6, 13 ; 4, 22). It is also remarkable that Parāśara 4, 30 f. recommends widow-burning, which is referred to in Dharmasūtras only facultatively and does not occur at all in M., Y. and Nār.

Parāśara considers himself to be a modern author.

The Bṛhat-P. "the great P." by Suvrata is of a still later date—an extensive work about five times the bulk of P., with which however, it has a certain similarity in the arrangement of the contents, specially in the first section, so that it should be considered an enlarged version of P. Other signs of modern origin are the passages—certainly interpolated—with the addresses Nṛpa, Rājan, reminiscent

The Bṛhat-Parāśara.

1. Thus according to the collections in Stenzler's literary remains (cf. ZDMG 47, 615-621) 70 Śl. of P. are cited in the Mit. of which 61 are found in the printed text of the former.

of the Purāṇas, while at the same time the whole work is being recited before an assembly of sages, the reference to the laws of M., Gaut., Vi., Y., Hārīta and many others belonging to a preceding age, the extravagant glorification of the cow in Adhy. 3, the Viṣṇuite tendency, the occurrence of artificial metres such as Indravajrā, Upendravajrā, Vasantatilaka, etc.

The Smṛti of Dakṣa.

The text of the small Smṛti of Dakṣa is very well warranted for. Of the 200 Ślokas it consists of,[1] I have found 53 cited by Hamādri, and Kullūka, and in the Ratnākara, Vīram., Mādhavīya and in the Mit. Of course, there is also a number of quotations which are not found in our Dakṣa, but in substance they are in conformity with the other texts and might have been left out of a work which is not protected by a commentary from corruptions through the carelessness of the scribe. On the other hand, Satī is recommended by this author too (4, 18). Saṁvarta[2] has 227 Ślokas, 16 of which I find cited in the Mit., and by Hemādri. On the other hand, the texts about jurisdiction and secular law ascribed to this author in numerous works on law are not found in it. Another suspicious point is that he (35, 61) mentions and recommends only the *brāhma vivāha* of the various forms of marriage.

The Smṛti Saṁvarta.

Kātyāyana's Karmapradīpa.

Regarding the Karmapradīpa of Kātyāyana or Gobhila (also called Chandogapariśiṣṭa, see Eggling's Cat. pp. 595, 524) which has been much talked of[3] and in part has been even edited in Germany, I wish to say only this that this work documents its connection which the Sāmaveda

1. Dhs. (Calc.) 2, 383-402. The Haug Ms., and the I. O. 1320 have only 197 Śl.

2. Dhs. 1, 584-603. The Haug Ms. and I.O. 1366 contain 210 Śl., I.O. 1367 has 73½ Śl.

3. Cf. Bloomfield ZDMG 35, 534 ff.; Knauer, Gobh. 2, 10-14; Schrader, Der Karmapradīpa, Introd.; Caland, Altind. Ahnencult 110-121.

by four times referring to the doctrines of Gautama whose relation with this Veda has been discussed in § 3[1]. Moreover, although a certain amount of antiquity is warranted to it by the commentary of Āśārka and by the quotations—for example, in the Mādh. and by Hemādri who quotes it as "Kāty.", Śloka-Kāty. (as in Hem. 3, 1, 1549=Kāty. 1, 18 ; 2, 1) or as Karmapradīpa—it can yet be reckoned only among the latest spurs of this species of literature because it quotes the Gṛhyasaṁgraha and Vasiṣṭha's Śrāddhakalpa [2]. It has nothing to do with the Smṛti of Kātyāyana (§9) which is very important for law proper.

Vyāsa, Bṛh. and Atri.

Similarly the little work now figuring under the name of Vyāsa can at the best be fragments of the Smṛti of Vyāsa which is likewise particularly important for jurisprudence, although several of the quotations about other features of the Dharma are found in it[3]. Satī is again recommended in Vyāsa 2, 53.[4] A similar incongruity exists between the c. 700 verses on law proper alone which are ascribed to Bṛhaspati and the 66 verses on Dāna of which his printed Smṛti consists. Yet some of these verses are ascribed to Bṛh. by Hemādri[5] and some other verses agree with the usual promissory and imprecatory formulas in

1. 13, 13 ; 17, 21 ; 20, 4 ; 24, 13.
2. Caland l. c. 113-116.
3. Dhs. 2, 310-342. Thus Laghu-Vy. 1, 2 f.=Mādh. 258 (Bomb. ed.) ; 1, 4-6=ibid. 259 ; 2, 71 f.=ibid. 415. Vy. 3, 64=416 ; 4, 29 f.=186 ; 4, 51=395. Further Vy. 4, 15, 18, 31. 33, 35=Hemādri 1, 5, 7, 25, 33.
4. Cf. the elaborate rules about Satī and its exaggerated glorification by Vyāsa as quoted by Mitra Miśra on Yājñ. I. 86. Vijñāneśvara in his commentary on the same verse of Y. quotes a few verses of Vyāsa on Satī which are evidently taken from the Mah. What is most peculiar, two of the verses ascribed to Vyāsa by Mitra Miśra are attributed to Śaṅkha and Aṅgirasa by Vijñāneśvara. *Tr.*
5. Dhs. 1, 644-651. 7, 8, 17=Hem. 122, 505, 507.

the landgrant inscriptions [1]. The metrical Atri which in 238 verses deals with Ācāra and Prāyaścitta, does not contain any of the none too numerous texts about Dāna, Prāyaścitta, Śrāddha, adoption and other features of Dharma, which are dscribed to A. [2]

Various other spurious metrical Smṛtis.

Other works of this class are the metrical Śātātapa, which deals with sins, penances and Karmavipāka in 6 Adhyāyas and appears to be merely a fragment of an extensive work on Karmavipāka of this oft-quoted author[3]; Likhita[4], whose little Smṛti with its motley contents appears to be a mere sketch and contains none of the quotations though of course they are very rare; Aṅgiras, whose booklet dealing with penances is characterised as modern by the prohibition of indigo-coloured clothes for widows in verse 21, in conformity with the present custom [5]; Uśanas, who in 51 Ślokas gives us a system of mixed castes including men of the most diverse professions such as coppersmiths, potters, barbers jewellers, scribes, physicians, etc.[6]; Yama, whose 98 verses deal only with various penances and do not agree with the numerous quotations from Yama with the exception of verse 22, which is cited in the Mādh. 131[7]; the metrical Āpastamba whose 237 Ślokas are devoted to penances alone[8]; the small Smṛti of Viṣṇu[9] devoted to the cult of Viṣṇu having as little in common with the Dharmasūtra discussed in §3 as the little Hārīta, equally decided in its Viṣṇuite tendency, with the Dharmasūtra of

1. 26-33 and 46 and also a few similar verses in the other recensions of Bṛh. in Eggeling 1324-1329.
2. Dhs. 1, 13-36. Eggeling 1307 has 369 Śl.
3. Dhs. 2, 435-455. Cf. Raj. M. Not. No. 526; Eggeling 1364.
4. Dhs. 2, 375-382.
5. Dhs. 1, 554-559. cf. Mandlik 293.
6. Dhs. 1, 497-501.
7. Dhs. 1, 560-567.
8. Dhs. 1. 568-583.
9. Dhs. 1, 60-69.

the same author discussed in §3 [1]; the extensive Vṛddha-Hārīta in 2587 Ślokas [2], which is full of Viṣṇuite references and mentions *inter alia* the *pañcasaṁskāra* of the Vaiṣṇavas in Adhy. 2 and refers to the different incarnations of Viṣṇu in Adhy. 3.

Vṛddha-Gautama, a part of the Mah.

The Vṛddha-Gautama too falls in this class and it has nothing to do with the Vṛddha Gautama of the quotations but in spite of that it may similarly be recognised to be a Viṣṇuite work even from its very title "Vaiṣṇavadharmaśāstra." V. S. Islampurkar has detected it to be a part of the Mah. and though it cannot be found in the printed editions of the Mah., yet it occurs in an ancient Ms. of the Āśvamedhika Parvan discovered by him and under this title it is often quoted in the Mādh.[3] The metrical Śaṅkhalikhita (Madras ed.) and Pulastya (Bombay ed.) belong to this class and the same is the case with the numerous still unpublished works of this species as with the published ones, so far as I can judge them by a critical examination or by the available extracts and descriptions. The Viṣṇuite tendency is particularly in evidence.

The works following the Sūtras.

A special group, however, worthy of notice, is formed by those works which follow the ancient Sūtras in title and contents. Thus there are the newly published Gautamasmṛti in 14 Adhy. which clearly follows the Dharmasūtra and the Pitṛmedhasūtra of Gaut. discussed in §3, the metrical Āpastambasmṛti, which is still divided into Paṭalas and closely follows the Āpastamba-sūtra in the Mantras and in the ritual at the Śrāddha[4], and we have also other works of this kind.

---

1. Dhs. 1, 177-193.
2. Dhs. 1, 194-209.
3. Dhs. 2, 497-638, cf. Islampurkar l.c. Pref. Notes 6-9.
4. Caland, Altind. Ahnencult 111 f., 48 ff. ; Bijdragen 6, 1. Cf. also West and Bühler (3rd. ed.) 51 f.

Importance of these fragments.

§ 9. *The fragments of metrical Smṛtis.* A far more reliable material is handed down to us in the fragments of metrical Smṛtis in the numerous quotations of mediaeval jurists than in the works discussed in §8. Of course these quotations are not quite sufficient to enable us to exactly distinguish between the texts characteristic of every individual author. There are e.g. texts which are ascribed both to Bṛh. and Kāty., or are cited without any statement about the source. There is as little certainty about retaining or dropping the epithets such as Vṛddha, Laghu, etc. discussed in § 8. The later jurists appear to cite these Smṛtis mostly only indirectly after the quotations in older works, so that it is probable that they possessed complete Mss. of these works no more than we do at the present day. Yet discoveries like that of Hārīta (§ 3) embolden us to hope that yet a Ms. of this or that lost work may come to light somewhere.

Brh. dependent on M.

For law proper the fragments of Bṛhaspati and Kātyāyana are most important. Bṛh.,[1] a Ms. of whose juridical Smṛti must have existed till recent times in the opinion of a Śāstrin (Bühler), closely follows M. whom he declares to be the standard author and comments upon his work and enlarges it (§ 5). Even where he does not expressly mention M. he always adheres to his teachings. Thus he has taken the 18 titles of law from M., divides them, however, into two parts relating to property and injury (2,1-11) respectively, i.e. into civil and criminal law. In the law of debt he explains the peculiar expressions (11, 55-58) by means of which various ways of realising a debt have been described in M. 8,49. Where he differs from M., as is the case in the law of indivisible property (25,79), he takes care not to mention the honoured teacher by name.

1. SBE 31. Introd.

Even compared with Nār., Bṛh. appears to belong to a stage of still further development. Thus in Nārada the actual heirship of the widow is not yet mentioned, while Bṛh. (25,46 ff.) circumstantially develops the theory that the wife is half the body of her husband and therefore she should inherit his property if he dies without male issue. Also the theory of the personal property of the woman (*strīdhana*) is much more elaborate in his work, inasmuch as he extends it even to the immovables. Further, Bṛh. emphasises that his institutes have reference only to the present age of sins and he is therefore no longer inclined to recognise Niyoga and the secondary sons (24, 12 ff.; 25, 39 ff.) fully sanctioned by Nār. (12, 80 ff.; 13, 45 ff.). On the other hand he sanctions Satī (24, 11). In the law of debt Bṛh. distinguishes between four kinds of sureties (11, 40) instead of the three of Nār. (1, 118). In chapter 8 he deals with documents in minute details. He extends the law of partnership even to the joint undertakings of farmers, craftsmen, architects, musicians and robbers (14, 20-32). He keeps closer to M. than to Nār., yet he agrees with the latter in many definitions. He too mentions the Dīnāra (10, 15) like Nār. Accordingly it appears that the account of the Skandapurāṇa, referred to in § 7, about the successive redactions of M. by Bhṛgu, Nār. and Bṛh., in spite of its mythical character, approximately agrees with the actual state of affairs; yet however, there is no great distance of time between Nār. and Bṛh. Bṛh. should be assigned to about the sixth or the seventh century A.D. because already from the ninth century onwards he is quoted by the commentators as an inspired Seer. For the quotations from Bṛh., in Dhammasats which lead us to a similar result, see § 13. The passage (27, 21) about the Pārasīkas indicating an intimate intercourse with the Persians

Bṛh. represents a stage of further development than Nār.

The detailed laws of Bṛh.

Date of Bṛh.

is also worthy of notice. The Bṛh. quotations about other features of Dharma, some of which may be traced in the small Bṛh. (§ 6), are comparatively far fewer in number than those about Vyavahāra; perhaps like Nār. the latter formed a separate work on law proper. From the reference to the Vājasaneyaka-mantra, VS 20, 20, in a text of Bṛh. about Snāna[1], it cannot be concluded that Bṛh. was a Vājasaneyin, for the same Mantra is cited elsewhere too, e.g., in Vi. 64, 21.

Various works of Kāty.

Kāty. is closely connected with Bṛh. as a juridical author. As a teacher of the White Yajurveda he is considered to be the author of several works including the Srautasūtra and the Śrāddhakalpa to this Veda, and quotations are found also from a Kātyāyanagṛhya [2], which is different from the Kātīyagṛhya of Pār. See § 8 for his Karmapradīpa. It is possible that the latter is a fragment of the original Smṛti of Kāty., for it contains many of tho texts quoted in the Dharmanibandhas; yet the juridical texts of Kāty., which are not found in it are so numerous that they might have formed a work by themselves. Very probably these texts are connected with the Dharmasūtra of Kāty., discussed in § 4.

Close relation between Bṛh. and Kāty.

The similarity of Kāty.'s juridical texts with those of Bṛh. is perceptible everywhere in their phraseology and in the arrangement of the subject matter as well as from their contents. It is therefore quite understandable that these two authors, as already referred to, are not seldom confused with one another; many texts also may belong to both. Thur according to Bṛh. as well as Kāty., the legal verdict may be based on one of the four grounds of judgment: Dharma, Vyavahāra, Caritra and Rājājñā, and also in the

1. Hemādri 3, 1, 902
2. l. c. 1324.

definitions of those terms the two authors agree with each other approximately, although the subsections mentioned by Bṛh. cannot be found in Kāty. (Bṛh. 2, 18-27 ; Kāty.[1] 2, 30-34)[2]. Bṛh. is more elaborate also in his explanation of the various grounds for the inadmissibility of a complaint (3, 9-12), while on the other hand, Kāty. (4, 1-23)[3] describes in detail the four methods of answering a complaint and divides them into various subsections. In the law of debt, according to Bṛh. 11, 13 when gold is lent, the capital along with the interest may increase to double the original amount; Kāty. 10, 10[4] extends this law also to jewels, pearls and other precious things. He expands Bṛhaspati's laws about suretyship by adding, for instance, a long list of inadmissible sureties (10, 28-30)[5] and elaborates his laws about the liability for debts and the realisation thereof by a mass of detailed rules about fathers and sons incapable of doing business, women capable of inheriting, slavery for debt, imprisonment for debt etc., (10, 41-90).[6] In the law of partnership, like Bṛh. he too discusses the division of the common profit in the case of a confederacy of robbers, dealers, farmers or craftsmen (13, 3-6).[7] In the law of inheritance he recognises the heirship of the widow in the absence of male descendants, but only with certain reservations (25,46-66).[8] Like Bṛh and Nār. he too knows the Dīnāra. Generally speaking he agrees in many cases with

Kāty. further develops the laws of Bṛh.

Kāty. knows the Dīnāra.

1. These quotations are to be referred to the English translation prepared by me which is now ready for the press. (This translation has never been published and so these references cannot be verified. For the references to Kāty. however I have indicated the corresponding texts in Bandyopādhyāya's Kātyāyanamatasaṁgraha. *Tr.*)

2. Bandyopādhyāya, Kātyāyanamatasaṁgraha, 371-375. *Tr.*

3. Bandyopādhyāya, 108 ff. *Tr.*

4. Bandyopādhyāya, 447. *Tr.*

5. Bandyopādhyāya, 463 ff. *Tr.*

6. Bandyopādhyāya, 389—439. *Tr.*

7. Bandyopādhyāya, 505—508. *Tr.*

8. Bandyopādhyāya, 708 ff. *Tr.*

Nār. and M. and in particular gives definitions of technical terms occurring in the works of these and other authors, such as Prāḍvivāka, Vyavahāra, Anvādhi, Vetana, Utkoca, Sāmanta, Vṛddha, Śauryadhana, Bhāryādhana, Vidyādhana, Strīdhana,. etc.

Authorities quoted by Katy.

Of authorities he most frequently quotes Bhṛgu, i. e., of course, M. in the recension of Bhṛgu (as in 10, 55, 87; 15, 4; 16, 5; 24, 11, 28, 38, 40, 45)[1] and Bṛh. (e. g. 4, 39, 40; 15, 25; 24 ,27, 31, 37).[2] He mentions the Mānavāḥ and Gautamāḥ (21,9)[3] as authorities for a rule about theft which, I confess, cannot to traced in our M. and Gaut. To sum up, however, Kāty. is rather posterior to than contemporary with Bṛh. with whom he has another point of similarity in the number of his juridical texts which amounts to over 700.[4] At all events he is certainly later than M. Y. and Nār.

The Vyāsa-smṛti from quotations.

Vyāsa, of whom over 200 juridical texts have been quoted, deals particularly in details with judicial procedure and agrees in many cases with Nār., Bṛh. and Kāty. Thus he gives the etymology of the word Prāḍvivāka, mentions even the accountant and the scribe among the assessors of the law-court, speaks of registering the plaint on the floor, discusses in details the composition and examination of royal grants and other documents, mentions the four modes of answer and eight kinds of judgment and deals with occupation and usucaption in the same manner as Bṛh. and Kāty. (1, 5, 8 f., 21-26, 34-72)[5]. In the law of debt he refers to 7 kinds of suretyship, i. e. 2 more

1. Bandyopādhyāya, 404, 423, 525, 532, 548, 562, 740, 751, etc.; also Manu, e. g., ibid. 416. *Tr.*

2. Bandyopādhāya, 531, 557, 739, 750, 753. *Tr.*

3. Bandyopādhyāya, 634. *Tr.*

4. In Bandyopādhyāya's collection the number of Kātyāyana's Slokas amounts nearly to 900 including the appendices. *Tr.*

5. See f.-n. 1, p. 59.

than Kāty., 3 more than Bṛh. and 4 more than Nār. (2,12). A striking sign of the modern origin of the Vyāsasmṛti is the glorification of Satī, which Vyāsa recommends and facilitates in every way (12, 3—10).

Pitāmaha from quotations.

Pitāmaha, of whom about 200 juridical texts have been preserved, seems to have been considered a special authority on ordeals and describes all the 9 kinds of same, in which connection he particularly dwells upon the names of the gods appealed to. Even Bṛh. 10, 27[1] quotes him as authority for a rule about the ordeal with a hot gold-piece. This quotation may refer to Pitām. 2, 147[2], but however, it may also be a memorial verse ascribed to Pitām. so that his Smṛti need not necessarily be older than that of Bṛh. His descriptions of the ordeals seem rather to be more detailed than the descriptions of other authors and his 50 *chalāni* and 22 *padāni nṛpajñeyāni*, i. e. offences which should be investigated and punished by the king even if there is no impeachment (1, 7-23), are also indicative of a particularly modern character.

Hārita from quotations.

Hārita[3] appears in the quotations as the author of over 50 juridical Ślokas which are found neither in his Dharmasūtra (§3) nor in the metrical works ascribed to him (§8), and evidently they deal with the law of a very modern period. Thus he describes the course of judicial proceedings and the composition of plaints and answers with the same scholastic subtlety as Kāty. and others (1, 16-29, 31, 38 ff.) and distinguishes between five kinds of sureties in the law of debt (2, 11).

Anonymous quotations.

Still many more names occur in the juridical quotations, to which we should also add the numerous

1. The same passage is found also in the Napalese Ms. of Nār. (Conrady, Fünfzehn Blätter 12, 15).

2. See f.-n. 1, p. 59.

3. Jolly, Der Vyavahārādhyāya of H.'s Dharmaśāstra (Münch. 1889).

texts which are quoted without any more accurate designation than "Smṛti". In most cases these quotations are not numerous enough so that the individuality of the authors concerned may stand out in bold relief, yet in general there is no reason to assign them to an older period than that of Bṛh. and Kāty. Thus the Smṛtisaṁgraha, whose very name betrays it to be a modern compilation, declares the unequal partition of property favourable to the older sons, the levirate and the animal sacrifice to be inadmissible in the present age and gives views about the nature and the origin of ownership which remind us even of the commentaries. Prajāpati gives great prominence to widows' right of inheritance. Halāyudha, Dhāreśvara (Bhoja), Jīmūtavāhana—famous commentators of the mediaeval age are at the same time quoted as authors of Ślokas exactly of the same style as of the metrical Smṛtis.

Many other names in the sphere of custom and religion.

In the wide sphere of customs and religion partly the same names and partly a series of other names are met with in the quotations. Thus even the Mit.[1] quotes as authors of metrical fragments on Ācāra and Prāyaścitta, Angiras, Atri, Āśvalāyana, Upamanyu, Uśanas, Ṛṣyaśṛnga, Kaśyapa, Kaṇva, Kātyāyana Kārṣṇājini, Kumāra, Kṛṣṇa-Dvaipāyana, Kratu, Gārgya, Gautama, Caturviṁśatimata, Chāgaleya, Jamadagni, Jātukarṇya, Jābāli, Jaimini, Devala, Dhaumya, Pāraskara, Pitāmaha, Pulastya, Paiṭhīnasi, Pracetas, Marīci, Yama, Vṛddhayājñavalkya, Likhita, Laugākṣi, Vasiṣṭha, Vaiśaṁpāyana, Vyāghrapāda, Vyāsa, Śāṇḍilya, Śunaḥpucha, Śaunaka, Saṭtriṁśanmata, Sumantu, etc. A similar but more copious list may be gathered from Aparārka[2]. Still

1. According to the collections in Stenzler's literary remains; cf. ZDMG 47, 616.

2. Cf. Kirste, Analyse der Citate in A.'s Commentar (Wien 1893).

more numerous and multifarious are the quotations, particularly about Śrāddha, in Hemādri and in the Smṛticandrikā, not to speak of later works.

§10. *The epic literature.* The two great epics, particularly the Mah., are often quoted as sources of law, exactly in the same manner as the Smṛtis, and in the quotations from the Mah. either the whole work or a particular Parvan or the Gītā (Bhagavadgītā) is mentioned. The close relation between the Mah. and the Smṛtis is illustrated even by the fact referred to in §8, that the extensive printed Smṛti of Vṛddha-Gautama originally formed a part of the Mah. and is often cited in the Dharmanibandhas as such. Also the Smṛtis of Viṣṇu, Bṛhaspati, Yama, etc., discussed in §8, may be considered to be remodellings or shorter episodes of the Mah. or allied works on account of their form and the addresses like *dvijaśreṣtha* and various references to the heroes of the Mah. That the Mah., whose importance for the history of law will shine forth frequently in course of this treatise, must have possessed its present character of a colossal Smṛti already about 300-500 A. D.[1] has been proved by Bühler[2]. Thus the verses regarding gifts have been quoted from the Mah., even from the fifth century onwards and in an inscription of the sixth century 100,000 Ślokas are ascribed to the Mah., so that, accordingly, already at that time, it had attained approximately its present bulk. At the time of Kumārila, i. e. in the eighth century, the Mah. was already essentially a a didactic poem in which the old sagas figured only as connecting links. According to the united evidence of Bāṇa in the Kādambarī and an inscription from Kamboja, it used to be recited like the Rāmāyaṇa in the temples of

Mahābhārata, a colossal Smṛti.

History of the Mah.

1. "V". Chr. in the German text is a typographical mistake. *Tr.*
2. Bühler and Kirste, Contrib. to the history of the Mah., Sitzungsber. Wien 1892, 4-27.

India and Further India already about 600 A.D. for the edification of the faithful. Rāmāyaṇa has the character of a didactic poem even from the very beginning. Jacobi assigns the date of its composition to the period from the sixth to the eighth century B. C.[1]

Rāmāyaṇa.

The influence of the Purāṇas,

The Purāṇas have influenced the development of Ācāra even more strongly than the Itihāsas. The popularity enjoyed by these extensive collections of legends was certainly attained by them already in the days of the earliest Dharmanibandhas. Thus Hemādri supports his exposition of the Vratas, which forms a great part of his colossal work, almost only on the Purāṇas which are generally his chief source. Even in the Dharmasūtras the Purāṇas are frequently quoted as sources of law and Āp. 1, 24, 6 refers specially to the Bhaviṣyatpurāṇa. Neither is it advisable to sever the existing Purāṇas completely from those of antiquity and to consider them to be worthless modern compilations. The existing Purāṇas[2] are connected with the Vedas and the Smṛtis in many ways. Thus Caland[3] in his exposition of the Śrāddha found a close connection between the Mārkaṇḍeyapurāṇa and the unpublished metrical Gaut. of the Burnell collection, between the Viṣṇudharmottara and Vi., the Caturviṁśatipurāṇa and the Mānavaśrāddhakalpa, the Kūrmapurāṇa and the Smṛti of Uśanas, and between the Brahmapurāṇa and the rites of the Kaṭhas or Kapiṣṭhala-kaṭhas. The Śrāddhakalpa of Y. has passed over to the Agni and the Garuḍapurāṇas; the former contains moreover the whole of the second book of Y. and the latter

Authenticity of the Purāṇas.

1. Das Rāmāyaṇa (Bonn 1893), 100-111. Ludwig arrived at a different result ; Über das Rāmāyaṇa (Prag 1894). Cf. also Grierson IA 23, 52 ff. ; Barth, Bulletin 288 ff. (1894) ; Jacobi ZDMG 48, 407 ff.

2. Cf. Bühler SBE 2, XXVIII f.

3. Altind. Ahnencult 68, 79, 112.

contains almost the whole of the first and the third books of Y.[1] The Bhavişyapurāņa has borrowed long passages from the first three Adhy. of our M.[2] The so-called Smṛti of Laghu—Hārīta is identical with a part of the Nṛsiṁhapurāņa and seems to have been taken from it and purposely stamped as a Smṛti[3]

For the consideration of the age and authenticity of the existing Purāņas, this also is of great importance that a large portion of the quotations from them in the Dharmanibandhas may be traced in our Purāņas. Thus V. S. Islampurkar has traced in the existing editions and Mss. of Kūrma, Nṛsiṁha, Mārkaņḍeya, Liṅga, Vişņu, Śaiva and Skandapurāņas most of the quotations from them occurring in the first part of the Mādhavīya edited by him and at least some of the quotations from the Matsyapurāņa. The same with the Purāņa quotations of Hemādri. Still more important is the fact that Alberuni about 1000 A. D. was acquainted with a work essentially identical with the Kashmirian Vişņudharmottara, and he also knew that Brahmagupta had used the work already in 628 A. D.[4] These religious works are of course less important for law proper excepting certain features of the family law and therefore will be mentioned but rarely in the following treatise. The Smṛtis themselves do not recognise the Purāņic sources of law to be equally authoritative, rather in the case of a conflict between the teachings of the Smṛti and the Purāņas, the former decides the issue[5] ; but the authors of the Dharmanibandhas have little observed this maxim.

Many of the quotations still found in the Purāņas.

Alberuni knew the Vişņudharmottara.

1. Cf. Mandlik LVII f.
2. Bühler SBE 25, CX f.
3. V. S. Islampurkar, Mādh. 1, 9.
4. Bühler, IA 19, 408, cf. SBE l. c.
5. Thus according to Vyāsa 1, 4 ; Saṁgraha in the Prayogapārijāta. Cf. West and Bühler (3rd. ed.) 11 ; Mandlik XXVIII.

The Mīmāṁsakas are the earliest commentators.

§ 11. *The commentaries.* The activity of the commentators in the field of Dharma had begun clearly already at a very early period. The works of the Mīmāṁsā school[1] may in a certain sense be considered as explanatory works on the Smṛtis ; the aim of this school was to explore the Dharma and to investigate the essence of Smṛti and its relation to Śruti theoretically and practically, and the Mīmāṁsā school was, as referred to above, well acquainted with the M. and the most important Dharmasūtras

Medhātithi and his date.

The Mīmāṁsā school has therefore certainly strongly influenced the opinions of the commentators, so that even the colossal Manubhāṣya of Medhātithi, opening the way up for the long line of commentaries on M.[2], quotes Kumārila ; Medhātithi therefore could not have lived before the end of the eighth century but on the other hand he must be dated before the time of Bhojarāja (eleventh century) and Vijñāneśvara (11.—12. cent.) ; he thus belongs to the 9. or the 10. century A.D. at the latest.[3] Very probably his native country is to be sought in Kashmir, although already in early times he is quoted in South Indian works. The Manuṭīkā of Govindarāja, is very useful for the interpretation of the text as it contains a full paraphrase of the text and is marked by a conciseness of expression and philological accuracy, but it is considerably later, and in consideration of its posteriority to Bhojarāja and anteriority to Śrīdhara,

The Manuṭīkā of Govindarāja.

---

1. Cf. Colebrooke, Ess. ed. Cowell. 1, 319-349 ; Thibaut, Arthasaṁgraha (Ben. 1882), II-XV.

2. Cf. Bühler SBE 25. CXVIII-CXXXVI ; Tag. Lect. 4-12 My Manuṭīkāsaṁgraha in the Bibl. Ind. contains extracts from 6 unpublished commentaries and Mandlik's Mānavadharmaśāstra (Bomb. 1886) contains the complete text of 7 commentaries.

3. Medhātithi's significant statement (on M. II, 22) that "Mlecchas even invading Āryāvarta again and again, can never be permanently settled there" may be turned to account to determine his date. *Tr.*

Dharaṇidhara, Nārāyaṇasarvajña, Jīmūtavāhana, Śūlapāṇi and Kullūka, it should be placed in the 12. century.

The Manvarthavivṛti of Nārāyaṇasarvajña however, which is remarkable for originality but goes into details only in the case of difficult passages in the text, can hardly be dated later than the 14. century, for this Nārāyaṇa is mentioned already in a work of Rāyamukuṭa composed in 1431 ; moreover, a Ms. of this commentary was copied in the year 1497. The famous commentary of Kullūkabhaṭṭa, already published several times and probably composed in Benares in the 15. century, has recently been proved to be a piece of plagiarism based on the older work Govindarāja. Rāghavānanda's Manvarthacandrikā mentions the four above-mentioned commentaries, but depends mostly on that of Kullūka ; the author who is otherwise known as a philosophical writer can therefore be assigned to the 16. century at the earliest, but cannot have lived later than c. 1650, for the oldest Mss. of his work belong to this period.

Commentaries on M. by Nārāyaṇa, Kullūka and Rāghavānanda.

There is no certainty about the commentary of Nandana or Nandanācārya ; probably it belongs to a later date ; he appears to have made use of the above mentioned works, specially that of Nārāyaṇa, although he does not mention them, and by the readings he has favoured he betrays his South Indian origin. The still unpublished glosses of an unknown author, found in a Kashmirian Ms. of our M. are at least 200 years old, but are unimportant. The Manubhāvārthacandrikā of Rāmacandra is quite a recent commentary in the opinion of Mandlik, the editor of this work ; moreover, only selected passages are explained in it, apparently following Kullūka in particular, whom, along with the Mitākṣarā, the author mentions in his introduction as his

Commentaries on M. by Nandana and Rāmacandra.

chief source. Moreover commentaries on M. by Kṛṣṇanātha, Rucidatta and Maṇirāmadīkṣita, a contemporary of Shah Jahan (1628-58), are mentioned in manuscript-catalogues[1]. The commentaries of Asahāya., Viṣṇusvāmin, Bhāruci, Viśvarūpa, Bhojarāja, Dharaṇīdhara, Śrīdharasvāmin, Mādhavācārya, etc., are as yet known only from quotations[2]. Of these the first two are older than Medhātithi, the three following older than Mitākṣarā—the reign of Bhoja of course falls in the period between 1021 and c. 1050—Dharaṇīdhara is older than Kullūka who often quotes him but according to the quotation on M. 2, 85, does not reckon him among the "Ancients" like Medhātithi ; for Mādhavācārya see § 12.

Lost commentaries on M.

Next to M., Y. seems to have been most commented upon, and most important is the frequently published commentary of the mendicant *(parivrājaka)* Vijñāneśvara —the famous Mitākṣarā [3], which became a standard work already at an early date in the Dekhan and also in Benares and a great part of Northern India ; even in the English period, it has exercised a great influence on modern judicature through Colebrooke's translation of that portion of it which deals with the law of inheritance. Vijñāneśvara is called a Southern author in the Madanaratna. He himself controverts the opinions of the authors of the North and glorifies the King Vikramāditya of Kalyāṇa, who is undoubtedly identical with the ruler of Kalyāṇa in Haiderabad known from inscriptions of 1076-1127 A.D. and from the Vikramāṅkadevacarita edited by Bühler. The period of

Mitākṣarā on Yājñ.

Date of the Mit.

1. Aufrecht l. c. 451; Stein, Jammu Catalogue (1894) XXXVII.

2. Cf. Bühler l. c. CXX; Tag. Lect. 5; Mandlik l. c. 1, 4; Kielhorn EI 3, 48.

3. West and Bühler (3rd. ed.) 12-17 ; Bhandarkar, Hist. 61-67: Colebrooke l. c. 479.

activity of our author therefore falls in the last quarter of the eleventh century and the first quarter of the twelfth century, and the fame of his work should be attributed more to the power and esteem of the mighty Cālukya princes than to any intrinsic merit of the Mit., which indeed is not a mere commentary, but contains a system of Dharma furnished with numerous quotations.

Commentaries on the Mitākṣarā.

The Mit. in its turn was commented upon by various authors and moreover, on the whole, many of the later legal works now agreeing with it, now opposing it, attached themselves to the Mitākṣarā. I know the commentaries of Madhusūdanagosvāmin (19. cent.), Mukundalāla, Rādhāmohanaśarman and Halāyudhabhaṭṭa on Mit. only from manuscript catalogues. The commentary of Viśveśvara—the Subodhini, which goes into details only in particular passages was composed at the court of the dynasty of Madanapāla ruling in Kāṣṭhā (Kāṭha) to the north of Delhi in Northern India probably about 1350-1360, because the Madanavinoda, the last of the five known works of this author, was written in 1375 and Subodhini was his earliest work[1]. The very elaborate commentary of Lakṣmīdevī Pāyaguṇḍe, called Lakṣmīvyākhyāna,[2] was written about 1750, certainly not after 1782[3]. As proof of the verbosity of this learned female Sanskritist of the 18. century it may be mentioned that in this work the section on Dāyabhāga alone covers 239 pages of a copy belonging to me, as against the 32 printed pages on Dāyabhāga in the Bombay edition of the Mit. (1882). Only fragmentary

The extensive commentary of Lakṣmīdevī.

1. Aufrecht l. c. 454 f.
2. Its Vyavahāra section has been published under the name "Bālambhaṭṭī." *Tr.*
3. Cf. ZDMG 46, 270; Tag. Lect. 15.

Mss. are known of Nandapaṇḍita's commentary on the Mit. (17. cent.)[1]

Aparārka on Yājñ.

Of further commentaries on Y. notably the learned and comprehensive works of Aparārka and Mitramiśra[2] and the short commentary of Śūlapāṇi have been preserved ; all of them are still unpublished. Aparārka[3], a king of Konkan belonging to the dynasty of Śilāhāras, ruled in the 12. century ; yet we have got to choose between two kings of this name of whom one is attested to have lived about 1140-1160 and the other from 1184 to 1187. The commentary of Aparārka or Aparāditya is particularly rich in Smṛti-quotations[4] and was assiduously made use of by later authors. His relation with the Mit. is not clear because though of course he often alludes to it, yet however he does not mention it by name and not seldom differs from the Mit. in views and readings[5].

Mitramiśra on Yājñ.

Mitramiśra's Vīramitrodaya, not to be confounded with the manual of Dharma of the same name (§ 12), is an elaborate and valuable work as tested by Peterson and the date of its composition falls in the 17. century[6].

Śūlapāṇi's Dīpakalikā.

Śūlapāṇi's Dīpakalikā which explains only selected passages is modern in the opinion of Colebrooke[7] ; according to R. Mitra[8] on the other hand, Śūlapāṇi is a contemporary of Lakṣmaṇasena of Bengal (beginning of the 12. century[9]). Śūlapāṇi is quoted by Raghunandana

---

1. Cf. ZDMG 46, 271,
2. Mitramiśra's commentary is being published in the Chowkhamba Sanskrit Series along with the Mit. *Tr.*
3. Cf. Indraji, BG 13, 2, 426 ff. ; Bühler in Denkschr. d. Wiener Ak. 42, 5, 1 (1893).
4. Cf. Kirste in Bühler l. c.
5. West and Bühler (3rd. ed.) 18 ; Tag. Lect. 13 f.
6. Peterson, II. Report 49-53 : Eggeling l. c. 1288: ZDMG 46. 271.
7. l. c. 487.
8. Not. 3. No. 1147,
9. See f.-n. 1, p. 75 *Tr*

(about 1600) and himself quotes no later authors than Bhavadeva, Bhoja (11. cent.) and Lakṣmīdhara (12. cent. ?)[1] ; yet very probably he is later than Jīmūtavāhana (§ 12), for the latter is mentioned at the head of Bengali jurists. Śūlapāṇi lived in Bengal, for he is called Sāhuḍiyāṇa or Sāhuḍīpāla, which Colebrooke identified with Sāhuria in Bengal, and he is called an Easterner by Kamalākara. I know the commentaries of Kulamaṇiśukla, Mathurānātha and Raghunāthabhaṭṭa[2] only from manuscript catalogues and those of Bhāruci[3], Devabodha (both older than the Mit.), Viśvarūpa (the teacher of Vijñāneśvara), Dharmeśvara (older than Śūlapāṇi), etc. only from quotations.

Śūlapāṇi hails from Bengal.

Other Commentaries.

On Āp. and Gaut., we possess valuable commentaries by Haradatta, also called Haradattācārya, and Haradattamiśra, a South Indian author, who is very probably identical with the Haradattamiśra or Haradattacārya quoted by Sāyaṇa-Mādhava[4] in the Dhātuvṛtti and in the Sarvadarśanasaṁgraha[5] and therefore is to be dated about 1300 at the latest. Bühler has published extracts from this commentary on Āp. in his edition of Āp. and has translated many passages of the two commentaries in the foot-notes in SBE 2.

Comm. on Āp. and Gaut.

Mādhava, who has been just mentioned, with his title Vidyāraṇya "the wilderness of learning", famous as a fertile author like his younger brother Sāyaṇa, is the author of the extensive commentary on Parāśara, the Parāśarasmṛtivyākhyā, often quoted by later authors and contains a full encyclopaedia of Dharma, parti-

Mādhava's Commentary on Parāśara.

1. Aufrecht l. c. 660.
2. l. c. 474.
3. Cf. ZDMG 47, 616.
4. Cf. Bühler Āp. (2nd. ed.) VIII.
5. Gough 104.

cularly also of Vyavahāra[1]. In the introduction to this work the author calls himself the Guru and Minister of King Bukka, who is without doubt Bukka I, the famous ruler of Vijayanagara (Hampi on the Tuṅgabhadrā in Bellary) in Southern India ; documents regarding this king, according to Hultzsch, cover the period Śaka 1276-93, so that his reign falls in the third quarter of the fourteenth century. An edition of the first two sections in Telugu has appeared from Madras ; two new editions of the whole work are about to appear in the Bibl. Ind. in Calcutta and in the Bombay Sanskrit Series,—the latter is the best. Burnell in 1868 published a translation of the chapter on the law of inheritance.

Nandapaṇḍita on Parāśara.

The well-known author Nandapaṇḍita wrote a considerably shorter commentary on Parāśara which is still unpublished and scarcely touches law proper ; it was written at all events before 1622 the date of composition of his Vaijayantī, in which this commentary is quoted[2]

Nandapaṇḍita's Vaijayantī on Viṣṇu.

The Vaijayantī just mentioned is a very elaborate commentary on Vi. containing numerous quotations and excurses, which, according to the Mss., was composed by Nandapaṇḍita in the year 1622 at Benares. This learned Dharmādhikārin whose descendants are still living in Benares (§ 12), has left behind him a considerable number of extensive works on law and also in the sphere of philosophy and even poetry. I have myself published extracts from his Vaijayantī in my edition of Vi. in the Bibl. Ind. and in my translation of Vi.

Asahāya on Nār.

Nār. was first commented upon by Asahāya whose high antiquity has been adverted to above ; yet we do

1. Cf. Burnell, Vaṃśabr. XVI ; Klemm, Saḍviṁśabr. 15 ff. ; R. Sarvadhikari, Principles 362-366 ; Hultzsch EI 3, 36 ; SII 1, 161.

2. Tag. Lect. 16; Eggeling l. c. 1301.

not possess his Nāradabhāṣya in its original form; it was revised by a certain Kalyāṇabhaṭṭa, because the text "was spoilt by bad scribes". My edition and my translation of Nār. contain long extracts from it. There is another commentary written in Newari in a Nepalese Ms. of this Smṛti.

Baudh. has been commented upon by Govindasvāmin in his Bodhāyanadharmavivaraṇa, and English extracts from this work are to be found in the notes in Bühler's translation of Baudh. But Bühler does not place this commentary very high in antiquity and in the opinion of Burnell too it is modern. Govindasvāmin on Baudh.

The Karmapradīpa of Kāty. is commented upon by Āśārka or Āśāditya. According to Eggeling I. O. No. 1470, the Vidhānapārijāta written in 1625, and according to Aufrecht Bodl. No. 654, Kamalākara, who wrote at the beginning of the 17. century, quote an Āśārka. Anantadeva of a slightly later age mentions an Āśāditya (Hall. Ind. 190). Schrader's Karmapradīpa contains extracts from Āśārka. Āśārka on Karmapradīpa.

Almost all the works mentioned hitherto contain more or less numerous references to older commentaries on the Smṛtis commented upon by themselves. Moreover, commentaries on other Smṛtis, e. g., Hārita, Vyāsa, Caturviṁśatimata, are mentioned in the manuscript catalogues or are quoted in mediaeval and modern law-books. For some of the commentaries on later works see § 12. The commentaries have as yet by no means ceased to be composed, as, e. g., the valuable commentary on Vas. was composed by Kṛṣṇapaṇḍita only in the seventies of this (nineteenth) century. Other commentaries.

§ 12. *The Dharmanibandhas.* Of the multitude of almost innumerable systematic works on Dharma,—the Dharmanibandhas, only a few of the most import- Nibandhas are innumerable.

ant ones may be noticed here, with special reference to the works which are exactly datable and deal with law proper. The most ancient of the existing works appear to be of the 11. or the 12. century, although quotations from considerably older works are not wanting.

Lakṣmīdhara's Smṛtikalpataru.

Lakṣmīdhara [1], the first minister *(sāṁdhivigrahika)* of a king Govindacandra is the author of Kṛtya or Smṛtikalpataru or Smṛtikalpadruma which in 12 Kāṇḍas deals with Śrāddha, Dāna, Pratiṣṭhā, Śuddhi, Tīrtha and other features of the sacred law as well as with the duties of kings *(rājadharma)* and procedure *(vyavahāra)*. Perhaps the patron of Lakṣmīdhara is identical with the powerful Govindacandra of Kānyakubja, and documents about this king cover the period from 1105 to 1143. At all events Lakṣmīdhara is quoted already by Hemādri and in the Smṛtyarthasāra (see below) and in his turn quotes Medhātithi (9. cent., see § 11) among the commentators, so that he can very probably be assigned to the first half of the 12. century, if not earlier. He s quoted also in various other works from every part of India besides the two above-mentioned ones,—such as the Madanapārijāta, Madanaratna, Vivādacintāmaṇi and Vivādaratnākara, Sarasvatīvilāsa, Vīramitrodaya, and by Kamalākara, Raghunandana, etc.

Halāyudha of Bengal.

To approximately the same epoch as that of Lakṣmīdhara, belongs Halāyudha,[2] the author of the recently published Brāhmaṇasarvasva about the daily duties of the Brahmans, etc., which is assiduously quoted specially by Bengali authors. Halāyudha was the chief justice *(dharmādhikārin, dharmādhyakṣa)* of the famous king Lakṣmaṇasena of Bengal who ascended

---

1. ZDMG 46, 273; cf. EI 2; 358 ff.
2. Eggeling 1640; IA 19, 1 ff.

the throne in 1119.[1] The father of this king was Ballālasena, and the same name happens to be the designation of the author of the Dānasāgara about religious gifts, which according to the introduction in the I. O. Ms. 1704 was composed by Ballālasena, the son of Vijayasena and the grandson of Hemantasena with the help of Aniruddha in the year 1169 (Śaka 1091)[2]. There is no doubt about the correct reading of this date also expressed in words by Aufrecht and Eggeling but from inner reasons it is more probable that it should be read Śaka 1019=1097 A. D. with R. Mitra according to another source. Ballālasena's Dānasāgara.

Of ancient South Indian works there are the Abhilaṣitārthacintāmaṇi or Mānasollāsa of the Cālukya king Bhūlokamalla-Someśvaradeva (1127-38), an encyclopaedia for princes about architecture, politics, amusements, etc.[3] and the important Smṛticandrikā of Devaṇṇabhaṭṭa[4], which is divided into 5 great Kāṇḍas or Adhyāyas on Saṁskāra, Āhnika, Prāyaścitta, Śrāddha and Vyavahāra with numerous sub-sections *(prakaraṇas)*. The section on Dāyabhāga or the law of inheritance in this work has been published and translated. As the Smṛticandrikā quotes Aparārka (§11) and is quoted by Hemādri (see below), it must be dated at about 1200. This work enjoys a high esteem not only in Southern India but is frequently quoted also in North Indian works such as, e. g., the Vīramitrodaya. In a passage of the Smṛtican- The Mānasollāsa. The Smṛticandrikā of Devaṇṇabhaṭṭa

1. Many scholars are inclined to assign the date of Lakṣmaṇasena to a considerably later period, cf., e. g., V. A. Smith, Early History of India (3rd. ed.) p. 403. For other views on this point see, ibid. pp. 415—422 ; R. D. Banerji, Bāngālār Itihās, part 1 (2nd. ed.). *Tr.*

2. Cf. Aufrecht, C. C. 792 ; Pischel, Die Hofdichter des Lakṣmaṇasena 7 ; R. Mitra, Not. No. 279.

3. Burnell, Tanjore Cat. 141 ; R. Mitra No. 1215, 2203 ; Bühler, Vikramāṅkadevacarita 41 note; Aufrecht, C. C. 26.

4. Eggeling 1373 ff. ; ZDMG 46, 271 f.

Śrīdhara's Smṛtyarthasāra.

drikā quoted by Hemādri (Śr. 1360) which, however, I cannot find in the corresponding part of the text of the Smṛtic., a view of the "author of the Smṛtyarthasāra" has been criticised. If the oft-quoted work of this name by Śrīdhara[1] is meant herewith, as is most probable, the latter must have been written before 1200, but however it is certainly not older than 1150 because Śrīdhara refers to the Kalpavṛkṣa (Kalpadruma of Lakṣmīdhara, see above) and to Govindarāja-matam. Govindarāja already mentioned as a commentator in §11 should here again be mentioned as the author of the Smṛtimañjarī[2], which is quoted by himself in his commentary on M. and by other ancient authors.

Govindarāja's Smṛtimañjarī.

Hemādri's Caturvargacintāmaṇi.

The imposing Caturvargacintāmaṇi of Hemādri[3] belongs to the latter half of the 13. century, more accurately, to the period between 1260 and 1309, whose already far advanced publication in the Bibl. Ind. will, it is hoped, be shortly concluded. Of the five Khaṇḍas, the first or Vratakhaṇḍa, the second or Dānakhaṇḍa and a greater part of the fifth or Pariśeṣakhaṇḍa have hitherto appeared, while the third the and fourth Khaṇḍas i.e. the Tīrtha and the Mokṣakhaṇḍas, are still unpublished. Law proper has not been dealt with in this voluminous work, excepting in some occasional remarks in the section on Śrāddha (524 ff.), but it is a real mine of interesting quotations from the Smṛtis and Purāṇas. Hem. was the minister *(mantrin)* and secretary or keeper of archives *(śrīkaraṇādhipa)* to two powerful rulers of the Yādava dynasty in Devagiri (Dowlatabad in Haiderabad)—Mahādeva (1260-71) and Rāmacandra (1271-1309). Bhan-

1. Bhandarkar, Rep. for 1883 f., 46 ; Eggeling 1543 ff. ; ZDMG 46, 279 ; Colebrooke, Ess. 1, 472 f. Jacobi's collection contains an old Ms. of the Smṛtyarthas. of *sam* 1476.

2. Eggeling 1550 ; Bühler, SBE 25, CXXVII ; ZDMG l. c.

3. Bhandarkar, Hist. 88-90, 109-117 ; Eggeling 1376 ff. ; ZDMG l. c. 272.

darkar[1] assigns to about 1230 a Dānavākyāvalī about religious institutions and gifts, which was composed by Vidyāpati at the request of Dhīramati, the wife of the king Narasiṁhadeva of Mithilā. An old Ms. of this work was copied already in 1483 and moreover the name of king Narasiṁhadeva occurs in the traditional family trees of the ancient dynasty of Mithilā, in which the well-known Harasiṁhadeva, whose reign falls in the beginning of the 14. century, is mentioned as his great-grandson.

Dānavākyāvalī of Vidyāpati.

The 14. century is the blooming period of the school of Mithilā, highly important for the development of jurisprudence proper ; it might have been connected with the tradition existing in this country from the time of Y. (§6). Caṇḍeśvara is the author of the Smṛtiratnākara[2],—an extensive digest divided into 7 parts on Kṛtya, Dāna, Vyavahāra, Śuddhi, Pūjā, Vivāda and Gṛhastha, and of the shorter and purely religious work Kṛtyacintāmaṇi. According to the introductions to his works, Caṇḍeśvara was the son of a minister and was himself a minister *(mantrin)* of the king Harasiṁhadeva (see above), conquered Nepal for his master (according to other sources, in the year 1324) and on the banks of the river Vāgvatī (rising in Nepal) he gave away in charity his own weight of gold. As this meritorious act is dated in the year 1314, the composition of our work took place a little later. Hitherto only the Vivādaratnākara has been published in the Bibl. Ind.—an elaborate exposition of the 18 titles of law containing a great wealth of quotations.[3]

Caṇḍeśvara's Smṛtiratnākara.

1. Bhandarkar, Rep. l. c. 52.

2. Eggeling, 1387 ff., 1621 ; ZDMG 46, 273 f. ; WZKM 4, 72 ; R. Sarvadhikari, Principles 319 ff. ; R. Mitra No. 1842.

3. Jayaswal has published (1924) the Rājanītiratnākara of this author. *Tr.*

Misarumiśra's Vivādacandra.

The Vivādacandra[1] is a similar work which received its name from Candrasiṁha the grandson of the king of Mithilā just mentioned and of Lakhimādevī (Lakṣmīdevī), the spouse of this king, and this work emanates from Misarumiśra who was appointed by Lakṣmīdavī to compose it. The Ratnākara is mentioned in this work and it may be about 50 years later and was therefore probably written towards the end of the 14. century. Vācaspatimiśra[2], a particularly fertile author, often cited specially in works of the Bengal school, lived at the court of king Harināräyaṇa of Mithilā; he was a great-grandson of king Harasiṁhadeva and a nephew (son ?) of Candrasiṁha and thus must be assigned to about 1400 or even in the 15. century. His chief work consists of various Cintāmaṇis on Śrāddha, Tīrtha, Nīti, Prāyaścitta, etc. The Vivādacintāmaṇi which was published in Calcutta in 1837 and translated into English by P. C. Tagore in 1863, deals with law proper, as also the still unpublished Vyavahāracintāmaṇi dealing with judicial proceedings.

Vācaspatimiśra.

The Cintāmaṇis of Vācaspatimiśra.

Somewhat earlier, namely at about 1360-70, the Madanapārijāta was composed by Viśveśvara[3] in the North-West under the auspices of Madanapāla (cf. §11). This work published in the Bibl. Ind. in nine Stabakas, deals with the sacred law and of forensic law it deals only with the law of inheritance (St. 8). The author mentions Hemādri and Aparārka, the Kalpadruma and the Smṛtyarthasāra, the Mitākṣarā and the Smṛticandrikā as his sources. According to Aufrecht he copies largely from Mādhava's commentary on Parāśara though, however, he does not mention it anywhere. Quotations from the Pārijāta are often found

Viśveśvara's Madanapārijāta and other works.

1. Aufrecht, Bodl. No. 718 ; Bhandarkar, l. c. 48 ; Colebrooke, Ess. 1. 471.

2. Eggeling, 1398 ff. ; ZDMG 46, 273 ff. ; R. Sarvadhikari l. c. 398 ff.

3. Aufrecht, Bodl. No. 651 ff. ; Eggeling, 1394 f. ; Bühler, SBE 25, LXXV ; Bhandarkar l. c. 47.

in other works, but as this title is very common they need not be taken to refer to this work. After the Pārijāta our author wrote also the Mahārṇava or Karmavipāka and the Smṛtikaumudī, on the rights and duties of the Śūdras, in which the Smṛtimañjarī (see above) is quoted, and lastly his medical work Madanavinoda dated in the year 1375.

Mādhava too, who composed the published Kālanirṇaya and many other unpublished works on Dharma besides the commentary mentioned in § 11, should be mentioned here for that reason. The Kālādarśa is mentioned as source in the Kālanirṇaya and other works ; but this work, also frequently cited otherwise, need not necessarily be taken to mean the Kālādarśa of Ādityabhaṭṭa preserved in the Mss.[1]

Mādhava.

Ādityabhaṭṭa.

The Dharmaratna of Jīmūtavāhana[2] seems to belong to the 15. century. The famous treatise on the law of inheritance popularly called the Dāyabhāga, the chief work of the Bengal school in this sphere, translated by Colebrooke, forms a part of this work. This work contains references only to ancient authors like Govindarāja, Jitendriya, Bhoja, Viśvarūpa, etc., but according to the commentators, the teachings of the above mentioned authorities of the Mithilā school, including Vācaspatimiśra, are criticised in it, so that—assuming this postulation to be correct—it could not have been written before the fifteenth century, but at the same time neither later, for an old Ms. of the Dharmaratna dates from the end of that century and this author is quoted already by Raghunandana. Jīmūtavāhana has been frequently commented upon,—an edition of his

Jīmūtavāhana's Dharmaratna.

Commentaries on the Dāyabhāga.

1. Eggeling 1655 ; Aufrecht, C. C. 98.

2. Eggeling 1499, 1511 ; R. Mitra, Not. 5, Plate II ; ZDMG 46, 278 and 47, 617 ; R. Sarvadhikari l. c. 400-403 ; Colebrooke's Dāyabhāga 2, 27 ; 4, 3, 23 ; 11, 1, 14 ; 11, 4, 3 and Ess. 1, 482 ; Aufrecht, Bodl. No 714.

Dāyabhāga with 7 commentaries appeared in Calcutta in 1863-66. Yet however Ācāryacūḍāmaṇi, the oldest of these commentators, known also as a writer on the same subject, must be assigned to the 15. century, for he is already quoted by Raghunandana, and the same of Śūlapāṇi (see § 11), whose Smṛtiviveka seems to have comprehended all the features of Dharma.

Nṛsiṁha's Prayogapārijāta.

The Prayogapārijāta of Nṛsiṁha, an extensive digest of the sacred law must date from the beginning of the 15. century, for it actually contains a reference to Mādhava's commentary on Parāśara (§ 11), but an old Ms. of this work was

Rāmacandrācārya.

copied already in the year 1437-38[1]. The Kālanirṇayadīpikā of Rāmacandrācārya is based on the above-mentioned work of Mādhava on Kāla ; it is a South Indian work

The Madanaratna.

of 1450, commented upon by a son of the author[2]. The Madanaratnapradīpa, in short Madanaratna[3], is an encyclopaedia of law in 7 books, called Uddyotas. The Vyavahārodvekkoddyota in my hands contains a very elaborate treatment of law proper distinguished by valuable quotations from the Smṛtis. The Mādhavīya is the youngest of the later works and authors cited therein, such as the Mitākṣarā, Kalpataru, Halāyudha, Asahāya, Smṛticandrikā, and in fact, Mādhava is mentioned frequently and with special respect, so that this work, according to a well-known rule, must be at least 100 years later and should thus be assigned to the latter half

Quotations from the Madanaratna.

of the 15. century. Quotations from the Madanaratna are found cited by authors of the first half of the 17. century such as Kamalākara, Anantabhaṭṭa, Nīlakaṇṭha, Mit-

1. Tagore Lect. 21 ; Eggeling 1396 ; R. Mitra, Bikaner, No. 942 ; Aufrecht, C. C. 355 f. ; ZDMG 46, 275 f.

2. Bhandarkar l. c. 50, 58-60 ; Eggeling 1659.

3. According to a Ms. lent me by Bühler,—a copy of No. 2437 of the Mss. of the Raghunātha temple in Jammu. Cf. Eggeling 1681.

ramiśra, and even by Padmanābha belonging to the latter half of the 16. century (see below). It is worthy of notice that our author mentions no works of the Mithilā school later than the Ratnākara. As he glorifies Delhi and polemises against the authors of the South and East, it proves that he belonged to the North-West; yet, as the family-tree is quite different, he cannot be identical with Madanapāla also belonging to that part of the country (see above).

The Nṛsiṁhaprasāda of Dalapati[1], is a similar work divided into 12 Sāras; he speaks of himself as the prime-minister or Viceroy *Sāmrājyadhuraṁdharamahīpati* of Nizam Shah, i.e., very probably, of the founder of the dynasty of Ahmednagar which bore the same name (1489-1508). This learned compendium, in which law proper too has been dealt with, proves that in Devagiri, Indian Law was studied even after the installation of Islam and that the example of Hemādri (see above) did not fail to induce emulation. The above dating of the work finds support from a Ms. of same copied in 1511-12 at Benares. A Ms. of the Smṛtisāra of Harinātha was copied already in the year 1472-73. I have in my possession a transcript of the section on law proper—the Vivādaparicceheda—of this work, it extends over 67 pages. This work, therefore, falls in the 15. century at the latest. Only ancient authors like Śrīkara and Bālarūpa and ancient works like the Kalpataru, are quoted by Harinātha; on the other hand, much importance should not be attached to the references to a Smṛtisāra found in old quotations[2] for this title is very common.

Dalapati's Nṛsiṁhaprasāda.

Harinātha's Smṛtisāra.

1. Tag. Lect. 18 f.; Eggeling 1467; Benares Cat. 150,
2. ZDMG 46, 278, cf. Festgruss an B. 46.

Raghunandana and his works.

Raghunandana, the learned son of Bengal, deserves to be mentioned at the head of the authors of the 16. century. His chief work, the Smṛtitattva[1], has already been published many times. Of the 28 Tattvas into which this great digest is divided, the law proper is dealt with in the Divya, Dāya and Vyavahāratattvas on ordeals, inheritance and judicial proceedings respectively ; the last two have also been separately published and the Dāyatattva has even been translated. Several Tattvas had been commented upon at quite an early period. As Raghunandana in his Jyotiṣatattva speaks of the year 1498 he must have lived about that time, as is apparent also from his contemporaniety with the famous reformer Caitanya (1486-1527). King Pratāparudrasena of Orissa (1503-1524), who was a contemporary of Caitanya and was converted to his religion by him, composed the Sarasvatīvilāsa, an extensive work on law, perhaps before his conversion about the year 1515 ; the Vyavahārakāṇḍa of this work dealing with the law of inheritance, has been edited and translated by Foulkes (Lond. 1881). This work, which has received great esteem in South India, specially in the native country of the author, does not follow the Bengal school but the Mit. and the Smṛtic.[2]

The Sarasvatīvilāsa of Pratāparudrasena.

Ṭoḍaramalla's Ṭoḍarānanda.

The Ṭoḍarānanda[3] of Ṭoḍaramalla, the famous finance-minister of Emperor Akbar (1556-1605), can boast of an author hardly less blue blooded. The part of this work dealing with judicial proceedings and forensic law is called the Vyavahārasaukhya; an old Ms. of this section was copied in the year 1581, and also a Ms. of the Vratasaukhya, copied in the year 1582-83, is still in existence. The Vyavahāramayūkha and the Śūdra-

1. Colebrooke, Ess. 1, 489 ; Eggeling 1405-1438.

2. Foulkes l. c. Pref. and § 557

3. Tag. Lect. 19 f. ; Aufrecht, C. C. 214 ; R. Mitra, Bikaner No. 1030

kamalākara (see below) contain quotations from the Ṭoḍarānanda.

Two families distinguished for learning, still living in Benares, may be traced back upto the 16. century[1]. Rāmeśvara (with whom the epithet Bhaṭṭa, common to whole family, begins) was a son of Govinda who came from South India and settled down in Benares about the beginning of the 16. century. His son Nārāyaṇa wrote various works on religious law and philosophy, some of which are still in existence with the dates 1535-36, 1556-57 and 1568-69. His Prayogaratna, published in Bombay in the year 1861 is still regarded in Western India as an authoritative work in matters of household usages. Śaṁkara, the son of Nārāyaṇa is particularly known as the author of the Dharmadvaitanirṇaya which should thus be dated somewhere towords the end of the 16. century; it is a disquisition on the problems of law; the portion of this work dealing with adoption has been edited and translated by Mandlik[1]. Rāmakṛṣṇa, another son of Nārāyaṇa, was also active as an author in the field of of Dharmaśāstra[2].

The works of Nārāyaṇabhaṭṭa and his sons.

The second family likewise comes from the South, but was however settled in Benares for six generations when its famous member Nandapaṇḍita was born whose Vaijayantī, written in 1622, has already been discussed in §11. A poetical work of this author bears the date 1598-99. His Dattakamīmāṁsā on adoption, already published many times and translated by Sutherland is the best known of all his works. To the 16. century belong also Acala's Nirṇayadīpaka[3] written in

Nandapaṇḍita and his works.

Other writers of the sixteenth century.

1. Cf. Mandlik, LXXII (where family trees are given), 54-56.
2. Aufrecht. C. C. 509.
3. Eggeling, 1580 ff.

1518 on religious usages, the Jaṭamallavilāsa[1], written in the North-West before 1600, perhaps even in the 15. century, the Nirṇayāmṛta, written at the instance of a prince of the well-known family of the Cahamānas of Ekacakrā on the Jumna, which however not being the only work of this name is hard to fix[2]. Also the Samayāloka of Padmanābha[3] and other works belong to this century.

The activity of the family of Rāmeśvara.

The 17. century which we enter upon herewith, presents to us first of all the representatives of the family of Rāmeśvara of Benares. Nīlakaṇṭha,[4] a son of Śaṁkara, already referred to, wrote his chief work Bhagavantabhāskara divided into 12 beams (Mayūkhas), published in Bombay and Benares, in honour and at the request of the Rajput prince Bhagavantadeva of the family of the Seṅgaras of Bhareha (Bhareh) at the confluence of the Jumna and the Chambal in the N. W. Provinces, which still belongs to this Rajput family. The portion dealing with law and law-court which is called the Vyavahāramayūkha, already separately published several times and translated by Borradaile and recently by Mandlik,[5] appears to follow the Madanaratna in particular; in the theory of adoption the author follows the views of his venerable father (*tātacaraṇāḥ* p. 40 ed. Mandlik) laid down in the Dvaitanirṇaya (see above). The Dvaitanirṇayasiddhāntasaṁgraha[6] written by Bhānu, a son of Nīlakaṇṭha, is a sketch of the latter work. A brother of this author who was a namesake of his grandfather Bhaṭṭaśaṁkara, wrote in 1671 among other works on Dharma the Kuṇḍoddyota-

Nīlakaṇṭha.

Bhānu and Bhaṭṭaśaṁkara.

1. l. c. 1593.
2. Bhandarkar l. c. 49 f.; Aufrecht 298.
3. Eggeling 1680; Peterson I, 101.
4. West and Bühler (3rd. ed.) 20 f.; Mandlik LXXIV ff.; Eggeling 1444 ff.; Atkinson, NWPG 4, 1, 417.
5. New translation by P. V. Kane. Jolly.
6. Eggeling 1575.

Divākara and Vaidyanātha.

darśana[1]. Divākara, a son of a daughter of Nīlakaṇṭha wrote *inter alia* the big Dharmaśāstrasudhānidhi in 1683 and an Ācārārka in 1686; his son Vaidyanātha wrote tables of contents to two of his books[2].

The works of Kamalākara and Dinakara.

A son of the above mentioned Rāmakṛṣṇa named Kamalākara, who was also a cousin of Nīlakaṇṭha, was enormously productive[3]. His comprehensive work Nirṇayasindhu, written in 1611-12 and published several times, is considered even to this day to be the highest authority on questions of religious ceremonies in the Mahratta country. His Śūdradharmatattva, in short Śūdrakamalākara, which likewise has been published, forms a part of his great Dharmatattva. His Vivādatāṇḍava is a valuable treatise on law proper following the Mit. and polemising against the Bengal school. His brother Dinakara[4] wrote along with other works the Karmavipākasāra of which work we have a Ms. copied in the years 1639, and the Dinakaroddyota divided into a series of Uddyotas like the Madanaratna. A Ms. of the Vyavahāroddyota of this work is with me. This elaborate treatise on law proper chiefly based on the Mit. contains the statement found also in other parts of the work that it was completed by the son of the author Viśveśvara or Gāgā, who was a contemporary of Aurungzebe.

Other members of the family.

Lakṣmaṇa, a younger brother of Kamalākara, wrote a sketch of daily duties—the Ācārasāra.[5] Anantabhaṭṭa[6], a son of Kamalākara, wrote among other works a Rāmakalpadruma, at all events before 1674-75, the date of a Ms. of

1. Ibid 1684.
2. Ibid. 1616, 1708 ff.
3. Ibid. 1502, 1584 ff.; 1630, 1650 ; West and Bühler (3rd. ed.) 23.
4. Eggeling 1504 f., 1766 f. ; Aufrecht, C. C. 252 f.
5. Eggeling 1612.
6. Burnell, Tanj. Cat. 133 ; Aufrecht, C. C. 13.

this work. Divākara[1] is connected with this learned family through his mother; he was the son of a daughter of Nīlakaṇṭha and wrote the Dānacandrikā published in Benares. The same is the case with Rāmacandra[2] with the family name *Tatsat*, who wrote the Kṛtyaratnāvalī in 1648; his mother was a great-grand-daughter of Rāmeśvara of Benares.

The works of Mitramiśra.

Mitramiśra, already mentioned in §11, descends from another family but was likewise a native of Northern India; the portion of his Vīramitrodaya[3] dealing with Vyavahāra has been published several times and the section of this portion dealing with the law of inheritance has been edited and translated by G. Sarkar. In the law of inheritance Mitramiśra closely follows the Mit., on which he has even written a commentary and combats the theories of Jīmūtavāhana and other jurists of Bengal. His patron, the Bundela Vīrasiṁha, after whom the Vīramitrodaya has been named, murdered the famous Abul Fazl in 1602 and lived till the reign of Shah Jehan (1628-58). It is important for the purpose of fixing the date of Mitramiśra that a work dedicated to the younger son of Vīrasiṁha was written in 1635.

Various other works of the seventeenth century.

Other works of the 17. century are the two digests Smṛtimuktāphala of Vaidyanātha (c. 1600) based on the Smṛticandrikā and divided like it into Kāṇḍas on Vyavahāra, Śrāddha, etc.,[4] and the Vyavahāranirṇaya of Varadarāja, a Tamil of the end of the 16. or the beginning of the 17. century, of which the chapter on the law

---

1. Eggeling 1709.
2. Bhandarkar l. c. 50; Eggeling 1623, 1670.
3. West and Bühler (3rd. ed.) 21-23, Eggeling 1288, 1224; ZDMG 46, 269-271.
4. Burnell l. c. 134; Aufrecht 747.

of inheritance has been translated by Burnell[1]. Both of these works were written in South India and have been described by Burnell. We have also the little work Gotrapravaranirṇaya of c. 1620, a register of Gotras, by Raghunātha[2]; the religious calendar Kālatattvavivecana also written in 1620 by Raghunātha, the grandfather of Rāmacandra, referred to above[3]; the Vidhānapārijāta, an elaborate work of the year 1625 by Ananta[4], dealing also with law proper; the Rāmaprakāśa[5], a comprehensive digest of religious usages, composed under the auspices of Kṛpārāma, a contemporary of Jehangir (Jāhāṁgīra, 1605-1628) and Shah Jehan (Sāhajāhāṁ, 1628-58); Raghunāthasūri's hand-book of religious usages—Prayogatattva[6] written in 1655; the Tithinirṇaya, Kālanirṇaya and other religious works of Bhaṭṭojidīkṣita specially known as the author of the Siddhāntakaumudī, who should be assigned to the first half of this century and who was known as a teacher about 1620[7]; Raghunātha's Smārtavyavasthārṇva of 1661 also dealing with the law of inheritance[8]; the partly published Smṛtikaustubha (also dealing with law proper) of Anantadeva, whose patron Bāz Bahādur Candra is identical with a king of Kumaon assignable to 1644-64[9]; the sacrificial calendar Parvanirṇaya of the year 1685 by Gaṇapati Rāvala[10], etc.

Various works of the seventeenth century.

---

1. Burnell l. c. 143 and "The law of partition" (Mangalore 1872), XVf.
2. Eggeling 1781.
3. Eggeling 1667 f.; Bhandarkar l. c. 50.
4. Eggeling 1468; Aufrecht 13.
5. Eggeling 1600 f., 1664 ff.
6. Eggeling 1578.
7. Aufrecht 395; Bhandarkar 51 f.; Burnell 129 f., 139; Weber, Verz. No. 1176; Eggeling 1677; Aufrecht ZDMG 45, 306.
8. Eggeling 1491.
9. ZDMG 46, 277 f.
10. Eggeling 1674.

Various works of the eighteenth century.

The most prominent works of the eighteenth century are Ratnākara's Jayasiṁhakalpadruma[1] of 1713, so named in honour of King Jayasiṁha of Mathurā; the South Indian work Vyavahāramālā[2] on judicial proceedings and forensic law, which is only partly written in Sanskrit and is very much in use in Malabar; the Vratarāja or Vrataprakāśa by Viśvanātha on fasts and other Vratas[3], composed at Benares in 1736; the sketch of the law of inheritance—the Dāyakramasaṁgraha by Śrīkṛṣṇa Tarkālaṁkāra of the beginning of the 18. century[4], which has been published in Calcutta and translated by Wynch; the juridical work Vivādārṇavabhañjana, the result of the collaboration of 12 Pandits from different parts of India *(nānādeśanivāsin)*, which, on account of the reference to Śrīkṛṣṇa Tarkālaṁkāra, can at the earliest be dated in the middle of the last (eighteenth) century, etc.[5].

Digests compiled under British rule.

The last named work reminds us of the category of digests originated under English influence, specially works like the Vivādārṇavasetu[6] written at the order of Warren Hastings and published in Bombay,—an elaborate treatise on law and judicial proceedings, which was written in 1773-75 by a commission 11 Pandits from every part of Bengal and was translated into English by Halhed in 1775. The sources, mentioned in the introduction, all belong to the Bengal school with a few exceptions. Similar works are the Vivādasārārṇava composed for Sir W. Jones in 1789 and the two works Dharmaśāstra-

---

1. Aufrecht, Bodl. No. 665 ff.; Eggeling 1595.
2. Eggeling 1509; Burnell, Dāyavibhāga XIII.
3. Aufrecht, Bodl. 663 f.; Eggeling 1692 f.
4. Cf. Colebrooke, Ess. 1, 482 f.
5. Peterson II, 53, 118; Bhandarkar l. c. 48 f.; Tag. Lect. 22; Aufrecht, C. C. 580.
6. Eggeling 1506; Colebrooke l. c. 464 f.; Code of Gentoo Laws (Lond. 1781), Pref. LXXIV, XC f.

saṁgraha and Siddhāntapīyūṣa written towards the end of the century at the order of Colebrooke. Most remarkable however is the Vivādabhaṅgārṇava[1] written by Jagannātha of Calcutta at the instance of Sir W. Jones, which (with the exception of the part dealing with criminal law) was translated into English by Colebrooke at the order of Sir John Shore. This translation, completed in 1796 by Colebrooke in 3 volumes, along the translation of M. by Jones, was the starting point of the study of Indian law in Europe. The Indian original too possesses lasting value as, so far as it goes, it is the most elaborate exposition of Indian jurisprudence based on a profound study of the literature on this subject.

The 19. century too has produced many important works. As a specimen of same and at the same time of the activity in French India in this sphere, I mention here Sicé's French translation of a Tamil sketch of the Smṛticandrikā[2] composed in the thirties by a Tamil,—Professor of Tamil in Madras. An interesting category is made up of the numerous Vyavasthās "legal judgments" of the court Pandits or Shāstrīs consulted at the Anglo-Indian law-courts, a few specimens of which I have in my possession.

Activity in the nineteenth century.

§13. *Buddhist law-books.* The Buddhist law-books, in so far as they record the legal usages of non-Aryan peoples, do not come within the sphere of this encyclopaedia. Yet among Buddhist peoples outside India,—particularly in Burma—in consequence of the installation of of Indian law among them—remarkable traces of Indian legal views and expressions are found which are interesting as reflex of same and supplements thereto.

Indian law outside India.

1. Aufrecht, C. C. 580 ; Eggeling 1531 ff.

2. Sicé, Vyavaharasarasangraha ou Abrégé substantiel du droit (Pondichéry 1857).

Work of European scholars in the field of Burmese law

After Sangermano, who lived as missionary at Ava and Rangoon from 1783 to 1807, for the first time presented in his description of the Burmese Kingdom, which was published only after his death, an "extract out of the Burmese law-book called Damasat",[1] Dr. Richardson in 1847 (second edition, Rangoon 1874) edited the "Damathat or the laws of Menoo" in Burmese and English and in 1850 R. Rost wrote about the Manusāra composed in Pāli and about its relation with M.[2] These studies eventually became of great importance when by the act of 1875 the Buddhist law was officially prescribed for the Buddhists in Burma. Colonel H. Browne, Commissioner of Pegu had extracts from four Dhammasats edited by Moung Tetto in 1875-77 and instituted searches in Ceylon for the sources thereof which he thought, would be there, but the searches were fruitless. A. Führer in 1881 copied six palmleaf manuscripts of the Manusāra and in 1882 published in the J B *BR* A S in two articles a summary of the contents of this work consisting of 1134 Śl. along with parallel passages from M. and later Indian law-books. These works about the Burmese law however received the most lasting impulse when J. Jardine was appointed Judicial Commissioner of Burma and not only discussed a series of legal questions of this country important for the practice of law in his eight "Notes on Buddist Law" in 1882 f. and edited the writings about the sources which had been handed over to him in Rangoon by Dr. Forchhammer, who had died before, but induced this excellent Pāli scholar to write a greater work about the history of Burmese law distinguished for thoroughness and deep knowledge by announcing a "Jardine Prize."[3]

1. A description of the Burmese Empire by the Rev. Father Sangermano. Rome 1833; second edition by Jardine, Rangoon 1885.
2. Ind. Stud. 1, 315-320.
3. The Jardine Prize. An Essay on the sources and development

Forchhammer has proved that the Burmese law-books which mostly bear the title Manudhammasaṭṭham, i. e. Manudharmaśāstram, have come to the Burmese through the Talaings who are superior to them in culture. The Dhammavilāsa, perhaps the oldest law-book of the Talaings, was composed in 1174 A. D., but now it is not preserved in its original form. The second oldest Dhammasaṭṭham ascribed to King Wagaru of Martaban (1281-1306) was edited and translated into English by Forchhammer following a Ms. dated in the year 1707, which contains the Pāli text besides an interlinear Burmese version. This important work betrays its Indian origin on every side,—by the mythical introduction about the first parent M., who of course is here transformed into a nobleman of King Mahāsammata, who mounted to heaven and saw the law written in characters of the size of a grown-up cow on the boundary wall of the universe including the 18 titles of law, the 12 sons, the periods of waiting for women regulated according to the cause of the absence of their husbands—for those whose husbands are travelling or have disappeared, reversion of the uninherited property to the king, the partition of the property among sons of different ranks born of the rightful marriage, the seven kinds of slaves, various kinds of inadmissible witnesses, the slight and serious bodily injury, reduplication of the punishment for this offence if two men assault a single person, etc[1].

Law-books of the Talaings.

Indian origin of Wagaru's Dhammasaṭṭham.

But these analogies are not restricted to M. or any other particular law-book; they extend over Smṛtis of the most various characters,—from the Dharmasūtras to the latest metrical Smṛtis, such as Bṛh., Kāty. and Vyāsa. Only a few rules of the law-book of Wagaru are not derived from some Indian source. Only in the 17. century the

Even the latest Smṛtis are drawn upon by the Burmese law-books.

of Burmese Law, with Text and Translation of King Wagaru's Manu Dhammasattham. Rangoon 1885.

1. Wagaru l. c. §§ 2, 83 f., 46, 79, 81, 115, 184, 149, 153.

Indigenous element asserts itself only at a later period.

native element exercised a strong influence on the legal literature; the verdicts given in law-suits by Buddhist priests composed in view of Buddhist morals—the Pyattons, were incorporated into the Dhammasats and at the same time the religious practices of the Brahmanical colonies and the laws of the order of the Buddhist monasteries in Burma were taken into consideration as well as the canonical literature of the Buddhists. Thus in the third period of the Burmese law, there arose at the instance of the powerful King Alompra, the Manu Kyay composed by his war-minister in Burmese in 1756—the extensive law-book translated by Richardson.[1]

The erroneous views of Forchhammer.

The results of the careful and laborious researches of Forchhammer who has enumerated more than 50 Dhammasats and Pyattons and described them as far as necessary, may so far be accepted without the slightest modification. The conclusions however drawn by him from the lack of any element in the oldest Burmese law-books which is connected with the Vedic and the Neo-Brahmanical cultures, are more disputable[2]. The assumptions that animal sacrifice and other Brahmanical elements were added to Indian law-books at a comparatively modern period, and that the Burmese Dhammasats have risen out of an older recension of same, are refuted by the Dharmasūtras which prove the animal sacrifice and the entire Brahmanism to be the oldest element of the Smṛtis. Yet Forchhammer does not seem to have stuck to this opinion in his last and the most mature work, for in it he only combats the assumption that the oldest Burmese law-books are direct translations of Brahmanical works and derives them from a Buddhistic Manu or Mānava school which flourished in India in the 7.-9. centuries and from there reached the Tala-

1. Forchhammer, Essay 96-104.
2. Jardine's Notes on Buddhist Law 4, 27 ff.; cf. Tag. Lect. 290 -98.

ings in Burma in the 10. or the 11. century[1]. Only the later Indian Smṛtis like Nār. are purely juridical works like the Dhammasats and it is quite possible that a law-book of this sort was shaped in a Buddhist form already at an early period by the Buddhists of Southern India and was then transferred to the Talaings on the opposite coast whose oldest epigraphical alphabet is identical with the South Indian Vengi alphabet of the fourth century A.D.[2]

The influence of Indian law spread much farther beyond Burma towards the east and the south. Thus in Siam there is found the tradition of a law-book of M.[3], and the extracts which Low published in the first volume of the Journal of the Indian Archipelago (1847) from a Siamese law-book of 1614 A.D., contain much that is Indian, though Low has spoken about the "Hindu Origin" of this work with some reservation of doubt. Thus the Pāli formulas and usages at the conclusion of a marriage ceremony, the rule that the interest in case of a debt should never exceed the amount of the capital, that the King inherits a property for which there is no legal heir, that the boys should be brought up in Buddhist monasteries, the long list of inadmissible witnesses, etc. are clearly of Indian origin. Indian law in Siam.

It is well-known that the island of Java once received along with Indian culture also Indian law and that from that time onwards up to this day it is maintained as the prevailing system of law in the neighbouring island of Bali.[4] The laws of ancient Java and Bali, about which already in 1849 Friederich gave interesting informations[5], Indian law in Java and Bali.

1. Easay 62 f.
2. l. c. 27.
3. Führer l. c.
4. See Tyra de Kleen, Mudrās auf Bali, for numerous customs and superstitions clearly reminiscent of the Indian source. *Tr.*
5. Journ. of the Ind. Arch. 3, 243.

may best be judged from the ancient Javanese law-book edited, translated and compared with Indian sources by Jonker [1]. Here too we meet with the tradition of Prabu Manu the originator of the system of law [2], and of a Mānavadharmaśāstra [3], and here too there are in fact parallel passages not only to M. but also to Y., Nār., Bṛh. and other later authors [4]. Agreement with Indian sources is to some extent less accurate than in the case of Burmese law-books, so that in the doctrine of the 12 sons here we find besides the Indian element also a powerful and independently developed native element. "It is clear" says Kern "that in Java the redaction was made by experts in law, in Burma it was done by the monks" [5]. That the reception of Indian law in Java must have been accomplished already in the 10. century A. D., is proved by a copper-plate discovered there bearing the date Śakavarṣātīta 849 which contains a verdict of the court *(jayapattra)* composed quite in agreement with the rules laid down by later Indian jurists such as Bṛh. [6]

The Jayapattra discovered in Java.

It is remarkable that in Ceylon, which has borrowed so much from India, traces of Indian law are far scantier than in the distant Java. Not a single Pāli law-book exists in Ceylon, although in that part of the Mahāvaṁsa which has not been edited by Turnour, a King has been praised because he gives judgments according to M. [7] The Nīti-Nigaṇḍhuva, a collection of native customary laws composed about 1818 under British auspices by a commission of distinguished Sinhalese gentlemen of

No trace of Indian law in Ceylon.

1. Een oud-javaansch wetboek. Leiden 1885.
2. Friederich l. c.
3. Jonker l. c. 11 ff.
4. l. c. 19. 175, 231.
5. Kern, Bijdr. 4. V., 10, 4 (S.-A. p. 4.)
6. J. Brandes, Een Jayapattra of Acte van eene Rechterlijke Uitspraak, Veltevreden 1887.
7. Rh. Davids in "Academy" of 14. March 1885.

Kandy, which was translated into English by Lemesurier[1], contains only very little of Indian element, such as the doctrine of the four castes of "Brahmins, Kxetriyas, Waisyas and Goiwanse" and the classification of the slaves into four classes of which the *antojāto, dhanakkito,* and *saaman dāsaviopagato* are reminiscent of the *gṛhe jāta, krīta,* and *tavāham ityupagata* of Indian law (Nār. 5, 26 f.)[2]. I must here refrain from a closer examination of this interesting work but I mention only this that it dicusses in details the group marriage of several brothers who enjoy the family property and a wife in common[3]. The customary laws of the Thesalaweme, a collection of the legal usages of the Tamil inhabitants of Jaffna in Ceylon, prepared at the instance of the Dutch Government in 1707 is exclusively Dravidian in character[4].

§ 14. *The customary law and European treatment of Indian law.* The Smṛtis were written by Brahmans for Brahmans and they bring out the caste privileges claimed by them in the rudest manner. The Kṣatriyas too appear beside the Brahmans as a privileged class, but the bulk of the population, particularly the mass of the Śūdras, stand so low, that it is considered hardly worth the trouble to examine their customs and legal usages. Leaving the details about classes and castes to be dealt with in State-antiquities[5] I content myself here only with this (cf. §1) that the authors of the Smṛtis themselves fully recognised the necessity of the existence

The Smṛtis are written by Brahmans for Brahmans.

---

1. Colombo 1880. I owe Mr. E. Kuhn the chance of being able to use this rare work.
2. Nīti-Nigh. 5,7.
3. l. c. 82-89.
4. Mayne § 42.
5. A part of the Encyclopaedia of which the present work is the first part. This part however has never been published. *Tr.*

of other laws and regulations. It is a significant remark, that the science of law (*vyavahāraśāstra*) like grammar (*vyākaraṇavat*) is based on usage (*ācāra*)[1].

Causes of self-contradictions in the Smṛtis.

The authors of the Smṛtis and the commentators too always strive to accommodate themselves with the spirit of the time, inasmuch as they declare obsolete rules to be no longer admissible in the present age of sins (*kalivarjya*), or, as the Smṛtic. says about several forms of ordeals, "obsolete at the present day" (*adyotsanna*). This does not prevent them however from laying down older customs immediately after those of a later period, for by that time they come to be regarded as belonging to the revelation (*śruti*). In this way a part of the contradictions of which the Smṛtis are full, may be explained away. A second source of these discrepancies lies in the differences of local usages and views of different schools which likewise had to be taken into consideration.

It is impossible to distinguish between theory and practice in the Smṛtis.

If even from the incompleteness and inconsistent character of the laws of the Smṛtis the necessity of testing and supplementing them by means of other sources is felt, this desideratum becomes all the more palpable, when we consider that the Smṛtis themselves offer us few data by which to distinguish between the pious wishes and theoretical disquisitions from the actual state of things. However, the Brahmanical jurists in many cases succeeded in procuring general observation for their maxims[2] as, for example, the wording of the ancient donative documents (*śāsana*) shows, which agrees even in the minutest details with the rules of the later Smṛtis. Even at the present day it is quite a common practice among the aspiring castes to observe among themselves

1. May. (ed. Mandlik) 56.
2. Cf. ZDMG 44, 342-362.

child marriage, prohibition of widow-remarriage and other characteristic institutions of the Brahmans, to earn for themselves greater esteem in public opinion. It should, however, never be forgotten that the Smṛtis are purely private works and cannot be placed on the same footing with the law-books of other countries.

English works on Indian customary law.

Indian customary law has received due consideration only in the English epoch. The official census reports (of 1891) [1] contain the most up-to-date and the best materials, of which, of course, only the chapters on age and sex, civil condition, marriage and castes, tribes and races come into consideration for legal affairs and social condition. The value of this monumental work is enhanced by numerous statistical tables and charts[2]. Risley's "Tribes and Castes of Bengal" Vols. 1, and 2 appeared simultaneously along with his "Ethnographic Glossary" (Calc. 1891 f.)—an alphabetical list of Bengali castes containing also descriptions of their customs and usages. The older works about castes should be discussed in State-antiquities.[3] The Gazetteers contain a full geographico-statistical description of India which however, in part, are of an older date. In what follows particularly the Bombay Gazetteer Vols. 1-24 have been used, whose exhaustive descriptions of caste usages, especially of the Brahmans, afford excellent materials for the history of laws and customs. The well-known Imperial Gazetteer of India by Hunter in 14 volumes (second edition Lond. 1885-87) is an alphabetical sketch

The Gazetteers.

1. We have of course now other census reports *Tr.*

2. The India Office agreed to my request for a few important official publications indispensable for the present work by sending me the 26 volumes of the census report for the year 1891 as well as all the available volumes of the Gazetteers of India and the 2 volumes of the Ethnographic Glossary of Risley,—a liberality for which cannot be thankful enough.

3. See f.-n. 5 p. 95. *Tr.*

of all the Gazetteers [1], and the sixth volume of the same work contains an historico-political outline. The two following works which have been much used in this treatise are based on official enquiry about the castes—Tupper's "Punjab Customary Law" (3 volumes Calc. 1881) and Steele's "The Law and Custom of Hindoo Castes within the Dekhun Provinces" (second edition, London, 1868). They contain a full treatment of the customary law in the Punjab and in Bombay. The land tenure system is discussed in Baden-Powell's "Manual of the Land Revenue systems and Land Tenures" (Calc. 1882). Grierson in his well-known work "Bihar Peasant Life" (Calc. 1885) has described the life of the farmers in Bihar; it also possesses considerable importance for antiquarian researches on account of the rich linguistic materials which show many points of agreement with the phraseology of the Smṛtis.

The works of Tupper and Steele.

Besides these and other official publications there is an extraordinary abundance of private works which, of course, are not so valuable. In the following treatise, along with other works the following books have been used: Mallick, Essays on the Hindu family in Bengal (Calc. 1882); Sir A. Lyall, Asiatic Studies (London, 1882); Bose, The Hindoos as they are (Calc. 1881); Phear, The Aryan Village in India and Ceylon (London. 1880); Tod, Annals and Antiquities of Rajasthan (Lond. 1829-32, 2 vols.); M. Williams, Modern India and the Indians (third edition, Lond. 1879); Malcolm, A Memoir of Central India (Lond. 1824, 2 vols.); Dubois, Peoples of India (Lond. 1817). Particularly the older works are, under present circumstances, more valuable, for under British rule the customs have changed more and more; this is the cause of the importance of the sketches

Private works on Indian customary law.

The older works are more important.

1. We have now the third ed. in 26 volumes. *Tr.*

of older travelling accounts of Fryer (1697) and others given by T. Hunter in the fourth volume of his History of India. For the mediaeval age, Alberuni's description of India (about 1030) is the most important work.[1] Among the travelling accounts of the Chinese the well-known work of Hiouen Thsang (7th century) is the best of all.[2] The Greek accounts of India contain little that may be turned into account for the history of legal practices; but they are important for their antiquity.

Customary law from Indian sources.

The value of the data about law and custom found in the ancient indigenous literature excepting the legal sources, is somewhat attenuated by the fact that it was almost exclusively in the hands of Brahmans and therefore does not represent a true picture of the actual state of things. In the first place there are the inscriptions which contain interesting and axactly datable data about institutions and gifts, administration and officials, widow-burning, rate of interest and various documents. The Gṛhyasūtras will be dealt with by Hillebrandt.[3] The Kāmasūtra contains a few notices useful for family law. Of the historical literature the Rājataraṅginī (ed. Stein) comes specially into consideration. The fables, particularly the Jātakas, and the poetical works likewise contain much materials which should of course be used only with caution. The scientific literature too contains many occasional remarks as is proved by Weber's collection of the materials about the history of law from the Mahābhāṣya[4].

As yet there is no monographical treatment of the whole history of law which shall be attempted

1. Sachau, Alberuni's India (2 vols. Lond 1888).
2, According to St. Julien and Beal.
3. See the valuable work of Hillebrandt—"Ritualliteratur" in this encyclopaedia. *Tr.*
4. Ind. St. 13, 466-71.

Treatment of various aspects of Hindu law by different scholars.

here. The ancient Indian law of inheritance and a part of the family law, on account of their extraordinary practical importance, have been very frequently dealt with, specially by English and Indian jurists. The older works of this sort,—those by Sir Th. Strange and his son Th. L. Strange, by Macnaghten, Morly, S. G. Grady and others, possess now only historical value. Of the more up-to-date treatises, particularly West and Bühler's Digest of Hindu Law (3rd.ed. Bombay 1884) and Mayne's Hindu Law and Usage (Lond. 1878) have been used here. The former work discusses in detail the laws prevalent in Bombay, the latter those in the whole of India ; both the works have not only practical purposes but also historical purposes in view and the former contains Bühler's introduction quoted above which laid the foundation to the history of the Smṛtis. H. H. Wilson's "Glossary of Judicial and Revenue Terms" (Lond. 1855) still remains indispensable. Mandlik's "Hindu Law" (Bombay 1880) contains useful gleanings from various sources which are scarcely available in Europe, although there are many mistakes in it. A series of volumes of the Tagore Law Lectures appearing in Calcutta, deals with the law of inheritance or a part thereof,—such as Cowell's "Hindu Law" etc. (1870-72, three volumes), G. D. Banerjee's Marriage and Stridhan" (1879), T. Mitra's "The Hindu Widow" (1881), R. Sarvadhikari's "Law of inheritance" (1882), my own "Outlines of an History of the Hindu Law of Partition, Inheritance, and Adoption" (1885), G. Sarkar's "Hindu Law of Adoption" (1891), etc. I have elsewhere attempted a monographical treatment of the law about women, the law of debt, the system of Indian law, the documents and child marriage[1]. A. Mayr in his work "Das indische Recht"

1. Sitzungsberichte 'der phil.hist. Klasse der bayerischen Akade-

(Vienna 1873) has tried to prove that Sir J. Lubbock's theory about the primitve family and particularly the theory that women were originally the common property of the clan, may be traced also in Indian law. His arguments are based on the materials collected in the first edition of West and Bühler's Digest. Of German jurists Kohler[1] and Leist[2] have recently dealt with the history of Indian law,—the former from the standpoint of the science of comparative jurisprudence with particular reference to modern customary law, which he has constructed systematically on the basis of the Gazetteers; the latter with the purpose of reconstructing the state of things in the Indo-Germanic period. An older work of a Frenchman in India contains parallel passages to the Indian civil law from the pandects and the French coutumes[3]. Special works will be mentioned in proper places; for the works on Buddhist law see §13; Hodgson's works have been used for Nepal.

The works of Kohler and Leist.

---

mie der Wissenschaften 1876, 1877; ZVR 1. 234-260; ZDMG 44, 350-360; 46, 413-426.

1. Altind. Processrecht (Stuttgart 1891); ZVR 3 and 7-11.

2. Gräco-italische Rechtsgeschichte (Jena 1884); Alt-arisches Jus gentium (Jena. 1889); Alt-arisches Jus civile, first part (Jena. 1892) etc

3. E. Gibelin, Études sur le droit civil des Hindous (2 volumes Pondichéry 1846 f.).

THE FAMILY LAW AND THE LAW OF INHERITANCE.

§ 15. *Polyandry and promiscuity.* Can we find traces and relics of sexual promiscuity, matriarchy, polyandry and allied institutions in the ancient literature of India, which, according to modern theories, have everywhere formed the starting point of the development of family law ?[1] As the levirate (*niyoga*) even may be explained away in another way (§ 20), the clearest trace of institutions of this kind lies in polyandry or group-marriage. The best known and oft-quoted example of same—the marriage of Draupadī with the five Pāṇḍava brothers, the heroes of the Mahābhārata, [2] seems to have been reflected in a passage of Āp. (2, 27, 2ff.)—as most of the usages of the epic literature are reflected in the Smṛtis—who declares the practice of marrying a girl to a whole family to be an obsolete custom prohibited in his time. Bṛh. 27,20 speaks even more clearly about it, who says that group-marriage (*kule kanyāpradānam*) is prevalent only "in other lands" i. e., in the South,—there however even at the present day (*samprati*)[3]. Also in the few other cases over and above

Traces of Polyandry in Sanskrit Literature.

1. Cf. A. Mayr. D. ind. Erbrecht 72 ff., 99, 103, 109—114, 152 ff.: Mc Lennan, Studies in Ancient History (Lond. 1876) and Fort. Rev. 1877 ; Mayne, Hindu Law and Usage §§ 57-69; West and Bühler (3rd. ed.) 289, 417 ff. ; Kohler ZVR 3,342-442 ; Bachofen. Antiquar. Briefe 1,171f. ; Leist. Altar. jus gentium 419 ; Delbrück, D. indog. Verwandtschaftsnamen 541-553 etc.

2. Holtzmann, Zur Gesch. u. Krit. d. Mah. 32 f. (further literature given there) ; Hopkins, Ruling caste 354 f.

3. ZDMG 44. 340 ff. ; Tag. Lect. 155. The commentary on Āp. indeed connects the whole passage with Niyoga, but the wording goes against such an interpretation,

the marriage of Draupadī, which may be taken from the Mah. as proof of polyandry (*bahūnām ekapatnitā* or *ekasyā bahubhartṛtā*), it is principally only the matrimonial connection of one woman with a number of brothers. Even the well-known law (M. 9,182 etc.) that the son of one of several brothers may be regarded as the common son of all may refer only to group-marriage if we connect it with polyandrous connections disregarding the intepretation of the commentators.

Polyandry in modern India.

There is an unmistakable similarity between the polyandry of the Sanskrit literature and that of the present day, which, as Sir R. West remarks, is much more common than is generally believed[1]. Thus in Kumāon group-marriage is practised among the Brahmans as well as among the Śūdras and Rajputs,[2] in this particular form that all the brothers marry only one woman like the Pāṇḍavas and the children belong to the eldest living brother[3]. This form of polyandry is in evidence also among the hill tribes of the Punjab but the children are divided among the brothers as in Sedrāj, Lahoul and Spiti. It is said that poverty and the desire of keeping the family property undivided are the causes of this polyandry (as also in the case of the polyandry of the ancient Spartans)[3]. Similar customs are, in general, widely prevalent in the Himalayas.[4] It is alleged that among the Jats of the Punjab the wife of the eldest brother has often to accept the younger brothers as consorts, because they have no means to meet the expences of a marriage [5]. There are similar reports

1. West and Bühler 3rd. ed. 289.
2. Bh. Indrājī IA 8,88.
3. Tupper, Punjab Customary Law 2, 186 ff.; Census of India, 1891, 191, 124 (Punjab).
4. West and Bühler l. c.; IG 121,195; BG 18, 1, 543 ff.
5. IG l. c., cf. Census l. c.

about the people of the opposite extremity of India [1]. The Nairs of northern Kanara have gradually given up their infamous polyandry only under British rule. Among the Thiyens the legitimate wife of one brother is the wife of all. The women of the Tottiyars and Vellars of Madura have sexual connection with the brothers and other near relations of their husbands. Also among the Todas of the Nilgiris the wife is the common property of all the brothers. Other polyandrous tribes and castes exist principally in Cochin, Travancore and Malabar. About group-marriage in Ceylon see § 13.

Polyandry need not have been confined among Non-Aryans.

In order to explain away the contradiction between these rude usages and the idealistic and lofty views of the Brahmans, polyandry has been declared "Non-Aryan." In fact, it is seen at the present day principally among the "Non-Aryans," particularly among Dravidian and Tibetan tribes. Yet it cannot be proved that the polyandry of the ancient times was confined among the Non-Aryan tribes.[2] Only this much may be said that the Brahmans were always jealously antagonistic to it. The discordant passages in the marriage hymns ṚV 10,85 and AV 14,2 should be strictly left alone as mere mythology.[3]

Hetaerism in ancient India.

Cases of sexual immorality are much more frequent than polyandry, but of course they can hardly be regarded as survivals of the ancient hetaerism. Adulterous connections frequently come into play in Vedic

---

1. Dubois, 3; Buchanan, Mysore 3,16; Mandlik 445 ff.; West and Bühler (3rd. ed.) 284; Nelson, Scientific Study 103 f., Hindu Law 141 ff. Mayne § 58; Madras Census Report (1893) 151f., 214 ff.

2. Meyer (Das Weib im altindischen Epos, p. 82) says that polyandry must have been a purely Non-Aryan practice and the Pāṇḍavas were certainly Non-Aryans. *Tr.*

3. Cf. Delbrück, l. c. 541-545.

rituals. Besides the passages discussed by Delbrück,[1] we should take into consideration also those Mantras which, according to Caland's plausible interpretation, were recited by the illegitimate son *(anyatrakaraṇa)* at the sacrifice to the dead, in order to cut himself off from his natural father and remain the son of his legal father, i. e., the husband of his mother.[2] Prostitution is frequently referred to in the Vedas,[3] and in the Smṛtis it is a legalised institution protected by law.[4] Already the Veśyās or Dāsis clearly form therein a distinct class, the Devadāsī[5] corresponds to the modern temple-servants and Basivis; the Svairiṇī occupied a higher place (Nār. 12,49 ff.). The ideal character of Vasantasenā in the sphere of the dramas and the free treatment of amorous intrigues in the literature of fables and fictions should be remembered in this connection.[6]

Traces of an age of unrestrained debauchery.

An ancient Gāthā quoted in Āp. 2, 13, 7 and Baudh. 2, 3, 34, contains a veiled allusion to a period when little value was placed on the conjugal faith of a woman. The tradition about an age of unrestraint

---

1. l. c. 545 ff., cf. Weber, Ind. St. 10, 83 f.
2. Altind. Ahnencult 193-197.
3. Pischel and Geldner, Vedische Studien 1, XXV.
4. Nār. 6,18 f.
5. The word Devadāsī (Devadaśikyi) has however been used in the Yogimara cave inscription to denote simply a dancer. see Bloch, Archaeological survey of India, 1903-4. *Tr.*
6. There is reason to believe that the *gaṇikās* so frequently mentioned in the Sanskrit literature were not mere common harlots. The Bharātīya Nāṭyaśāstra describes the *gaṇikā* as an accomplished lady with a deep knowledge of many of the sciences (XXIV, 109 ff.) and learned enough to be able to speak Sanskrit on the stage (XVII, 37-38). According to the Lalitavistara XII, 139, Suddhodana wanted his daughter-in-law to be as accomplished as a *gaṇikā*. The *veśyā* was a common harlot, but a *gaṇikā* compares not unfavourably with an Aspasia. Vātsyāyana says—अभिरभ्युच्छ्रिता वेश्या शीलरूपगुणान्विता ॥ लभते गणिकाशब्दं स्थानं च जनसंसदि ॥ Kāmas. (Benares ed.) p. 40. For further details on this point see H. C. Chakladar, Sir Asutosh Mukerjee Silver Jubilee Volumes, pp. 377 f. *Tr.*

and debauchery contained in the Mah., which was put a stop to by Śvetaketu[1], may perhaps be compared with it.[2] Most of the Smṛtis mention the "secretly born" *(gūḍhaja, gūḍhotpanna)* as one of the subsidiary sons, who can inherit the property of the husband of his mother, although he is his illegitimate son by another man. A. Mayr[3] sees in it "a recognition of the right of the other members of the clan upon the married woman" and "one of the most potent proofs of the sometime community of women among the Indian Aryans." According to Bṛh. 2, 30 the women of the east were unchaste *(vyabhicāraratāḥ.)*

Nothing to prove the existence of matriarchy in India.

These and other data, however, do not, of course, authorise us to conclude that there was a period of matriarchy in India, something like the state of things among the pre-Islamic Arabians[4]—the famous statement about the Gāndhāra Brahmans in the Rājatar., of whom it is said that they lived in incest, has now turned out to be an interpolation.[5] The recognition of the *anyatrakaraṇa, gūḍhotpanna* and other illegitimate sons should be attributed to the unusual importance attached to male descendants. Toleration of prostitution has not hindered the growth of a strict law of marriage. The sagas about an earlier period of immorality are utilised directly to represent the lax views about legitimate and illegitimate sons as obsolete. The unfavourable opinion

1. Mah. 1,122, 4 ff.
2. Meyer (Das Weib, p. 92, foot-note 3, last para) says that as even the Indo-Germans had developed a well regulated family life before they dispersed and the Vedic literature knows nothing of promiscuity we should not take these legends to represent the state of affairs in early society. *Tr.*
3. Erbrecht 113.
4. Cf. Robertson Smith, Kinship and Marriage in early Arabia (Camb. 1885).
5. Rājatar. ed. Stein, 1, 308.

about the conjugal faith of women of the eastern countries is perhaps based upon old accounts about Tibetan and Further Indian tribes among whom even now the married life is very lax.

§ 16. *The eight forms of Marriage.* The anomalies in the family law of the Brahmans are explained in their essence quite simply if it is comprehended what a high value was attached to the possession of a male descendant from economic and religious motives and by a crude conception about the position and vocation of the woman it was held, *inter alia*, that the children of the wife belong to the husband who is the owner of the woman even when he is not their father, just as the crops growing in a field belong to the owner of the field even though he has not sowed it (M. 9, 31-56 ; Nār. 12, 55-57 ; Vas. 17, 6-9 ; Āp. 2, 13,6 f. ; Baudh. 2, 3, 33-35 etc.). This view has however been challenged already in the Veda (*śruti*) and in some of the Smṛtis it has certainly been repudiated like the theory of subsidiary sons. A similar contrast between cruder and finer conceptions is met with also in the Indian law of marriage, in which beside the extremely rigid and lofty ideal of marriage we find matches being made by purchase or robbery or by defrauding the woman of her portion.

Anomalies in the family law explained.

Marriage by capture is one of the famous eight forms of marriage the names of which are graduated according to the hierarchical order of the gods and demons whose names are connected with these forms of marriage. Marriage by capture however is generally permitted only to the Kṣatriyas if not altogether forbidden. Its designation Kṣātra Vivāha "the form of marriage appropriate for Kṣatriyas" (Vas. 1,29,34) expresses most clearly its connection with the warlike nobles ; even the unpublished Hār. 24 (as

Rākṣasa and Paiśāca Vivāha.

well as Mah. 13, 47, 10, where: however it is used in another connection) knows of this designation and besides it of course also the usual designation Rākṣasa Vivāha "demon marriage," which like other authors he defines as forcible abduction. The Paiśāca Vivāha is the lowest form and is generally altogether rejected. According to Āśv. 1, 6, 7 however it is not merely an euphemism for rape as according to other interpretations, but consists of secret abduction and is therefore superior to the Rākṣasa Vivāha, abduction effected by means of violence and fighting.

Vātsyāyana's descirption of Rākṣasa and Paiśāca Vivāha.

The Kāmasūtra 230 likewise places the Paiśāca Vivāha above the Rākṣasa Vivāha ; the former is said to take place in this way : the foster sister or the maid (*dhātreyikā*) of the young lady, on understanding with the wooer, makes her drunk and in this state delivers her up to him, or he proceeds in this way without the help of the *dhātreyikā*. On the other hand, the Rākṣasa Vivāha is said to consist of forcible abduction of the young lady by pouncing upon her when she is journeying or is in another village or a garden and to put her guards to flight or to kill them. Whether connections formed in this way could afterwards be legalised by the celebration of the nuptial ceremony, is a controversial point. Otherwise capture of women is considered to be a crime punishable by death (M. 8, 323) at least when the abducted woman is of a caste higher than that of the ravisher (Y. 2,287) ; only she who has not been married off by her father at the proper time may be seduced with impunity (Vi. 24,41 ; M. 9, 93).

In the Mah. forcible abduction of women is ascribed to the most famous heroes such as Duryodhana, Bhīṣma, Arjuna, and it is often called the form of marriage thoroughly becoming in a Kṣatriya[1].

1. Mah. 1,73,11 ; 1,102,16 ; 1,219,22. Cf. Hopkins 356 ff : Holtzmann, Zur Gesch. 23.

Also some of the ceremonies of marriage described in the Gṛhyasūtras seem to have originated out of the marriage by capture. The high antiquity of marriage by capture becomes evident from its wide prevalence among other Indo-Germanic peoples,[1] and it is well-known that it is a universal custom and is particularly connected with exogamy, as is the case also in India (§ 18). At the present day only a few traces of this marriage by capture seem to be left in India,[2] principally among the rude hill tribes; the sham abduction which owes its origin to the marriage by capture is found more frequently as a marriage ritual, e.g., among the Rajput tribes, that is to say, among the descendants of the ancient Kṣatriyas.[3]

Marriage by capture in Mah., Gṛhyasūtras and traces thereof in modern India.

Similarly the choosing of husband (*svayaṁvara*) described in the epics, which is well known specially from the episode of Nala and Damayantī, seems to have been confined among the Kṣatriyas.[4] The father of a marriageable princess arranges that princes of his own standing should present

The Svayaṁvara of the epics.

1. Cf. Dargun, Mutterrecht und Raubehe (Bresl. 1883). 92 ff.: L. v Schröder, Hochzeitsgebräuche 56 ff.; Schrader, Sprachvergleichung und Urgeschichte (2nd. ed.) 553 f.

2. Every Hindu bride has still to put on an iron wristlet immediately after her marriage which she never lays down unless she has the misfortune of becoming a widow. This seems to be reminiscent of the ancient times when marriage by capture was the order of the day and naturally the brides at first had to be kept in chains. *Tr.*

3. Mandlik 445 (Bhils); Risley. the Tribes and Castes of Bengal (Calc. 1891f.) 1,340 (Kamars): 2.142 (Oraons) : Tupper, Punjab Customary Law 2, 90—94 ; BG 3.221 (Bhils), 5,49 (Kṣatris). 6,31 (Bhils). 8, 120 (Rajputs). 11, 60 (Kunbis). 12, 61 (Marvadis), 12,90 (Bhils), 18, 1, 304 (Kunbis), etc. ; Lyall, Asiatic Studies, 219 f. (Rajputs) ; Lyall's Gazetteer for the Hyderabad Assigned Districts 188 (Gonds); Hunter, Orissa 2,82 f. (Kandhs): Kohler, Zeitschr. f. Vergleich. Rechtswissenschaft 7. 227; 8, 103, 144, 266; 9, 325; 10,74—77 ; 11, 167. Many of the ceremonies of marriage considered to be connected with abduction may, in my opinion, be explained otherwise.

4. Mah. 1, 189, 7; 219, 21.

themselves at the Svayaṁvara of his daughter and in the festive assembly the *patiṁvarā* as a sign of her choice puts the garland round the neck of the chosen bridegroom.[1] This custom, seemingly worthy of an age of romance and courtesy to women, which moreover is mentioned already in the ṚV[2], is by no means irreconcilable with the practice of abducting women, as is shown in the case of Duryodhana who being rejected in the choice of husband carries off the princess by force.[3] Arjuna too carries off Subhadrā at the instigation of her own brother Kṛṣṇa who explains to him that although the Svayaṁvara alone is customary with the Kṣatriyas it is also allowed them to take possession of women by force and that it can hardly be expected that his sister would be able to express herself at the Svayaṁvara.[4] The Svayaṁvara has always been a favourite theme eagerly utilised by the poets, cf. Raghuv. 6, Vikramāṅkad. 7-9, etc. The Svayaṁvara sung by Bilhaṇa falls in the 11. century, and that known from the story of Prithvirāj of Delhi falls in the 12. century,[5] and according to Tod, Svayaṁvaras took place occasionally among the Rajputs even to very recent times. The trial of strength or wit at which the bride is given away to the victor, is an interesting and perhaps an older[6] variety of the Svayaṁvara. In this way in the Mah. Arjuna gets Draupadī, in the Rām. Rāma gets Sītā and other instances are found in the Purāṇas and in the marriage of the Buddha.

Svayaṁvara described by poets.

Of course, the festive Svayaṁvara of the epics is not found in the Smṛtis and the choice of husband is allowed to the young lady only if she is not married

Svayaṁvara of the Smṛtis.

1. Cf. Hopkins, 356 f.; Holtzmann 21 f.
2. Pischel, Ved. Stud. 1, 16 ff.
3. Mah. 12, 4.
4. Mah. 12, 219, 21ff.
5. Cf. Bühler Vikramāṅkadevacarita, Introd. 39f.
6. Pischel, l. c. 30.

even after some time has passed after her attainment of puberty; in doing so however she forfeits all claim upon the inherited family jewels while on the other hand, the bridegroom too need not in such cases pay the nuptial fee to the bride's father (M. 9, 90-93); he may even kidnap the bride (see above). The motive in this is that the father loses his authority over the daughter through his delay in giving her away in marriage and from this point of view it is understandable why the Brahmans do not count the Svayaṁvara among the eight forms of marriage. The Kṣatriya Rajputs have not quite accurately observed the Brahmanical custom of child-marriage[1] and so the custom of the choice of husband attended with festivities, which presupposes a grown-up bride,—thus Sāvitrī is *yauvanasthā*, Damayantī is *prāptayauvanā*—could be maintained among them. Of course, even in the Svayaṁvaras of the epics the bride is given away by the parents *(svayaṁvare dattā)* and there are indications that their choice was not a free one; it may be assumed *a priori* that in these high class matrimonial alliances politics exercised a considerable influence. See §17 for the Svayaṁvara in the Kāmasūtra.[2] The liberal Kṣatriyas.

The Gāndharava Vivāha too—the love-marriage without the consent of the parents—seems in the first place to have Gāndharva Vivāha.

1. Cf. Bühler in Festgr.an R. von Roth, 46.

2. Four kinds of Svayaṁvara can be clearly distinguished,—three of the epics and one of the Smṛtis. The Svayaṁvara of Sāvitrī is a unique instance of the absolute freedom of a princess to choose her husband. Alone Sāvitrī travels through various countries in quest of a husband and at last meets Satyavān. But it is hardly probable that a princess of a proud noble family already shackled by fetters of long-standing traditions should be allowed to proceed in this way and Hopkins is very probably right when he says that this was the earliest form of Svayaṁvara (JAOS XIII, 168 ff., 357 ff.). Another form of Svayaṁvara is that the bride is *vīryaśulkā*, i.e. she is to be won by a feat of prowess as in the case of Sītā and

been a privilege of the nobles and therefore can be connected with the Rākṣasa Vivāha (M. 3, 26; Mah. 1, 73, 13), i.e., the bride, on understanding with her lover, is forcibly carried away from the house of her parents. The best known and often (e.g., Kāmas. 227) quoted example of a pure Gāndharva marriage out of the epic is the story of Śakuntalā and Duṣyanta and a secret marriage of this sort without nuptial ceremonies (*nirmantra*) has even been called the most appropriate form of marriage for the Kṣatriyas in Mah. 1, 73, 27. Historical instances of love affairs of Indian princes are found, for example, in the Rājataraṅgiṇī.

Vātsyāyana on Gāndharva Vivāha.

There was a difference of opinion as to whether the usual marriage ceremonies are necessary or are superfluous in case of a Gāndharva Vivāha. Already Devala recommends the performance of these ceremonies and Kāmas 228 f. too advises the lover (*nāyaka*) to perform sacrifices into the fire and to take the bride thrice round the household fire, because the marriage would therewith be as good as concluded, and the parents, in order to avoid public scandal would have to give their consent to it. The Gāndharva marriage is moreover praised (l. c. 233) as being on the whole the best form of marriage and it is otherwise a common designation for love affairs. It is also opined in the Smṛtis (Nār. 12, 44; Baudh. 1, 20, 16 etc.) that this form of marriage is open to all castes alike.

Āsura Vivāha.

As a counterpart to the above-mentioned mainly aristocratic forms of marriage there is the plebeian form Āsura Vivāha, i.e., the purchase of women, which

---

Draupadī. The usual form is well-known but it is hardly possible that the bride could follow her own inclination in such a festive gathering dominated by her father. The Svayaṁvara of the Smṛtis however is a sad contrast to these brilliant marriage parties; here the father of the bride had to hang down his head in shame. R. Schmidt (Indische Erotik, first ed., p. 649.) has excellently brought out this contrast. *Tr.*

is allowed only to the Vaiśyas and the Śūdras (M. 3, 24; Mah. 1, 73, 11 etc.).[1] Of course, general protests against every form of the purchase of women is one of the favourite themes of the Smṛtis. According to M. 9, 98 ff. (cf. Baudh. 1, 21, 2 f. etc.), even for a Śūdra it is prohibited to accept price for his daughter when giving her in marriage as it would be an act of trading in a veiled form which was never heard of in the past. Even the giving away of the bride for a cow and a bull at the Ārṣa Vivāha, allowed to the Brahmans, should be taken merely as a homage to the bride (M. 3, 51-54). Even the recompense of 100 cows for the bride is said to be merely a formality, specially as the bridegroom receives the present back (Āp. 2,13,12). It is possible that the Ārṣa Vivāha had already changed into a mock purchase in which a cow and a bull were given to the bride's father by the bridegroom only for form's sake and which were given back to the bridegroom by the latter as the commentary on Baudh. 1, 20, 4 expressly lays down. Of course, the *gomithunam* of the Smṛtis has a striking similarity with the Zeugos Boón (yoke of oxen), in exchange for which, according to the oft-quoted statement of Strabo, Indians used to buy their wives from their parents. Ārṣa Vivāha.

It is also unmistakable that the price of the bride (*śūlka*) mentioned in the Smṛtis often signifies merely a present from the bridegroom to the bride or from the husband to the wife,—thus, for example, it is mentioned as a part of the Strīdhana (Vi. 17, 18; Y. 2, 144) and Vṛddha M. speaks of the *śūlka* as a present from the husband to the wife. Elsewhere however this term may have only the meaning "price of the bride," for example, when M. 8, 204 says that if a false bride is presented to a bridegroom he should be granted two The *Śulka*.

1. Cf. Hopkins 345 ff., 358 ff.; Holtzmann 23 f.; A. Mayr, 155 ff., 170 f.; West and Bühler 3rd. ed., 273 ff.; Tag. Lect. 76.

brides for the *śulka* he has paid, or when M. 9, 100 says that to give away the daughter "for the price settled upon as *śulka*" is a covert act of selling. On the other hand however M. 9, 97 says that in case the bridegroom dies after the *śulka* has been paid, the brother of the bridegroom shall represent him. The wife is even mentioned as a means of earning money (Vi. 58, 10, Nār. 1, 46). It should also be noticed (see below) that in Vas. and the unpublished Hār. the purchase of women has been called the Mānuṣa Vivāha, "form of marriage appropriate for men".

Purchse of women mentioned in Vedic literature.

The Smṛtis have all the more difficulty in opposing the practice of purchasing women because many Vedic passages may be quoted in favour of this custom. Thus MS 1, 10, 11 and Kāṭh. 36, 5 speak of a woman who has intercourse with other men although her husband has bought her[1] and in ṚV 1, 109,2 the rich presents of the son-in-law seem to be referred to[2]. Of the Gṛhyasūtras Pār. and Śāṅkh. speak quite freely of the above-mentionod present of 100 cows and a cart to boot to the father of the bride and the still unpublished Gṛhyas of the Mānavas and the Kāṭhakas[3] contain the ceremonials for the purchase of women (*śaulkadharma*). Here it appears to be the usual form of marriage in which the father of the bride receives the price of the bride in

Mah. on purchase of women.

gold. Like the Smṛtis the Mah. too condemns the purchase of women on principle but allows it in practice and that not

1. Ind. St. 5, 311.

2. Cf. Bühler's note on Vas. 1, 37; Zimmer, Altind. Leben 310 f[f]

3. Of course, now they have been published in the editions of Knauer and Caland respectively. A new edition of the Mānavagṛhyasūtra along with the commentary has recently appeared in the Gaekwaḍ Oriental Series. *Tr.*

only among Vaiśyas and Śūdras, and often refers to the price of the bride as *śūlka*. Thus Pāṇḍu had to pay a great amount in gold, jewels, ornaments, various stuffs, elephants, horses, carts etc. to the Madra king Śalya for the hand of his sister Mādrī, and this purchase of women is called a Kuladharma—even Paradharma (1, 113, 9 ff.).

Purchase of women in modern India.

The state of things at the present day shows that the opposition of the Brahmans was only partially successful. Thus it prevails in Bengal, chiefly only among the low castes[1]; in the Bombay Presidency however it is very much in vogue even among the higher castes. In Guzerat the sale of girls is said to take place even now secretly, even among such people who publicly denounce it, and in the city of Bombay often an earnest money is paid by depositing valuable objects[2]. Among the Sāmavedis, a respectable and strictly religious sect of Brahmans in Thana, the father of the bride gets from 200 to 1,000 rupees as the price of the bride[3]. Also in the Madras Presidency the payment of price for brides is customary among various castes;[4] the same in the Punjab.[5] In Assam marriages are effected almost only by purchase—it is common even among the Brahmans.[6] Of course in Bengal and elsewhere besides the price of the bride there is also the price for the bridegroom, because the custom of child-marriage has increased the demand for men in the marriage-market. Thus in the Smṛtis the exhortation for early marriage goes hand in hand with the polemic against the purchase of women, cf. § 17.

---

1. Risley l. c. 1, 138 (Birhors), 1, 352 (Juangs), 1, 380 (Kaibarttas), 1,496 (Kocchs), 1, 531 (Kurmis), 2, 96 (Muchis), 2, 102 (Mundas), 2, 229 (Santals), etc.
2. West and Bühler. 3rd. ed.. 275, 277. Cf. Kohler, l. c. 10,77–81.
3. BG 13, 1, 32.
4. Madras Census Report (1893). 274 ff.
5. Tupper, l. c. 2, 116, 194 ff., 220 f. Cf. Kohler l. c. 7, 227 f.
6. Census of India, 1891, Assam Report 113.

Only the first four forms are pure.

The law of marriage recognises as orthodox and appropriate for Brahmans only the first four forms of marriage in the usual list. Only of those marriages pure children are said to be born who should atone for the sins of their forefathers and descendants—in case of the Brāhma Vivāha up to the 10. generation or even to the 21. generation, and the sons born of the three lower forms of marriage would atone for the sins of correspondingly fewer and fewer generations. The women married according to the Brāhma rites are said to go themselves to the heaven of Brahman after their death; if married according to other forms they would go to the heavens of Viṣṇu and other gods respectively. The husband has a claim on the Strīdhana of his wife only if he has married her according to one of the higher four forms of marriage.

Characteristics of these forms.

The characteristics of these forms of marriage are as follows: in the Brāhma Vivāha, the bride is offered out of free will and presented to an honourable man while in the Daiva Vivāha the bridegroom is a sacrificial priest, *ṛtvij*; in the Ārṣa Vivāha the father of the bride receives a pair of kine as already mentioned above, and in the Prājāpatya or Kāya Vivāha the offer of marriage comes from the wooer. These differences are not important and are apparently based on the religious conceptions of greater or lesser merit of an alms- the bride is here regarded as such—according as it is given away freely or is solicited or is presented to a man of more or less respectable position. The sacrificial priest is, as is often the case, inferior in position to a virtuous and learned Brahman; on the other hand his position is raised if he is just at that time engaged in a sacrifice just as the murder of a man engaged in a sacrifice is a still more heinous crime (Vi. 50,7).

Āp. 2, 11, 17ff. and Vas. 1, 30 ff. omit the Prājāpatya

Vivāha and therefore have altogether only six forms of marriage, the Paiśāca Vivāha too,—the last and the worst form, being omitted by them. In the unpublished Hār. the two forms Prājāpatya and Ārṣa are wanting. In their place however Hār. adds the Kṣātra and the Mānuṣa Vivāhas, so that the number at least remains eight. In Mah. 13, 44, 3 ff. only five forms are enumerated—three good ones, namely Brāhma, by which according to the commentary both Ārṣa and Daiva are to be understood, Kṣātra, i. e., according to the commentary, Prājāpatya, which is appropriate for Brahmans and Kṣatriyas, and Gāndharva, and two bad forms, namely Āsura and Paiśāca or Rākṣasa. In Mah. 13 19, 2 only three forms are mentioned as regular which however are here called Ārṣa, Prājāpatya and Āsura. In other passages of course the traditional eight forms of the Smṛtis are given and even the Svayaṁvara is added to them as the ninth,[1] see above.

Vacillating number of the forms of marriage

In the Gṛhyasūtras we find the description of the difference between a Brāhma and a Śaulkadharma which are therein regarded as the two chief forms of marriage, and in Kāmasūtra 190 ff., according to the commentary, the four regular forms have been dealt with comprehensively. Accordingly, it is probable that the Brāhma Vivāha with its double meaning represented originally the form of marriage appropriate for the Brahmans in contrast to the Kṣātra Vivāha, abduction of women, the marriage form of the Kṣatriyas and the Mānuṣa Vivāha, purchase of women, the marriage form of the common people, and only at a later period this form of marriage was connected with the name of god Brahman and the hierarchy of the eight

Speculation as to the original significance of the principal forms of marriage.

1. Cf. Hopkins 356 ff. Inspite of Mah. 1 102, 12 ff., I think there is no similarity between *Prājāpatya Vivāha* and the *Svayṁvara.*

Vivāhas was established on analagy with the hierarchy of gods and demoms.[1] At all events at the present day too there is no difference between the first four marriage forms. The nuptial ceremonies now in practice are generally identified with the Brāhma Vivāha of the Smṛtis.

The nuptial ceremonies.

The Smṛtis do not deal with the actual nuptial ceremonies because these things properly belong to the sphere of the Gṛhyasūtras which deal with the particular usages of the different Vedic schools. Thus in Kāmas. 228 too it is said that the sacrifice into the fire on the occasion of the marriage ceremony should be performed *yathāsmṛti* what is explained in the commentary by *svagṛhyaproktavidhinā.* Yet occasional notices of marriage ceremonies in the Smṛtis as well as in the Rām. and the Mah. and elsewhere, prove that there was a wide consensus of opinion regarding them.[2] Thus the giving away of the bride in the midst of festivities to the bridegroom (Kanyādāna, Sampradāna), the *dextrarum junctio* (Pāṇigrahaṇa), the Vedic Mantras accompanying these ceremonies (Pāṇigrahaṇikamantra), the sacrifice into the fire and the three courses round the nuptial fire, the seven steps together of the young couple (Saptapadī), taking the bride home (Vivāha) after which the whole ceremony has been named, and other usages were universally observed and may be traced to the Vedic age and in some parts even to the hoary past of the Indo-Germanic period and even at the present day they are very widely observed.

§ 17. *Child marriage.* Marriage is a necessity; celibacy is allowed only to the monk (*naiṣṭhika brahmacārin*) and the nun (*parivrājikā*), who however are hardly ever mentioned in the Smṛtis. Therefore, care must be

1. Cf. Tag. Lect. 74 f., Hopkins l. c.

2. Cf. Winternitz, D. altind. Hochzeitsrituell 60, in d. Denkschr. d. Wiener Akademie 1892, 60 ff.

Insistence on child marriage in the Smṛtis.

taken particularly for girls, that they early enter the estate of matrimony, [1] because a marriageable daughter who, without being married, continues to remain in her father's house, becomes a Śūdrā (Vṛṣalī) and her father who did not take care to get her married at the proper time commits a great sin thereby. As the result of this sin he forfeits the nuptial fee for the bride as well as his authority over his family; the daughter, who now has to get herself married independently as Svayaṁvarā, suffers loss of wealth and can even be abducted with impunity (§ 16), and her husband, at least according to the later writers, should be an outcast as a Vṛṣalīpati and avoided in society.

A fovourable marriage can not be contracted too early.

A marriage which is advantageous and in conformity with the laws of caste, cannot be contracted too early; in the pessimistic views of the Smṛtis with regard to the virtue of a woman, only in this way the virginity of the bride may be warranted for; the right of self-determination for the parties concerned was perfectly inconsistent with the ruling ideas about the non-independence of women and also of the sons permitting only the Gāndharva and Rākṣasa marriage recognised as an odious privilege of the Kṣatriyas. In this way the well-known Indian custom of child marriage (*bālavivāha*) becomes quite understandable and it has parallels among various other peoples. But it still remains to be explained how and when the Vivāha which, according to its name and the Vedic marriage hymns, was originally a marriage festivity, came to be transformed into a ceremony of betrothal which was indeed legally fully binding but the bride went to the bridegroom's house—therewith the conjugal

1. Baudh. 4,1,11 ff.; Vas. 17,67—71; Vi. 24,41; M. 9,90 ff.; Parāśara 7,5 ff. Cf. my Rechtliche Stellung der Frauen 8 f.; ZDMG 46,413—426; 47, 143-156, 610-615.

life began—only a few years later when the bride attained puberty.

The Nagnikā recommended in the Gṛhyas.

Already in the Gṛhyasūtras in the enumerations of the qualities which one should have an eye on when choosing a bride, we often come across the requirement that she should be *nagnikā* e. g. Vaikhānasagṛ. 3, 2, 1 (*nagnikāṁ kanyām*), Hiraṇyakeśigṛ. 1, 19, 2 (*sajātāṁ nagnikām* instead of which however there is also the other reading *sajātānagnikāṁ* which conveys just the opposite sense) and further Gobh. 3, 4, 6 (*nagnikā tu śreṣṭhā*) and Mānavagṛ. 1, 7 (*nagnikāṁ śreṣṭhām*) where however, if the last passage is interpreted according to the former, it would appear that the Nagnikā is only recommended as the best. It is all the same whether following some commentators the term *nagnikā* is interpreted literally as a girl still going naked—who wears no clothes, plays with grains of sand, is still a virgin and does not cover her nakedness for shame in the presence of a man or whether following the usual explanation it is taken to be a technical term for a girl not yet marriageable—a girl who is not yet grown up.

The Anagnikā too is recommended sometimes.

On the other hand the Jaiminigṛ. speaks of an Anagnikā (*jāyāṁ vindetā 'nagnikām)*[1] and the same expression is used by Gobhilaputra 2,27 *(prayacchet tv anagnikām)* where the reading however is not certain; the rare term *rātām* too of the Āpastambagṛ. and Yādavaprakāśa's Vaijayantī[2] seems to be doubtful. Anagnikā signifies a marriageable girl. In those Gṛhyasūtras in which there is, so to say, nothing about the age of marriage, e. g., in the Āśv., it may perhaps be assumed with Prof. Bhandarkar[3] that by

1. Bhandarkar ZDMG 47, 154.
2. Winternitz, D. altind. Hochzeitsrituell in d. Denkschr. d. Wien. Ak. 1892, 34-36.
3. l.c. 153.

this reticense the puberty of the girl is presupposed, for cohabiting, going to live with the husband, and other features of the nuptial ceremonies may apply only to grown-up brides. But as these ceremonies are found also in those Gṛhyasūtras which declare themselves absolutely for child marriage or at least fovour it, there is therefore a self-contradiction in these works. It may be assumed that this self-contradiction is to be explained on the consideration that the Smṛtis contain later and older views side by side as in the case of the theory of Niyoga, for the latter being a part of the traditional Dharma could not be left unmentioned. Thus the authors of the Gṛhyasūtras themselves, e. g., Āp., often circumstantially reproduce ancient marriage hymns in a garbled version and that for wrong application [1] merely because they are pieces from an older and sacred age. Moreover the *prattā strī* of Āśv. 4, 4, 23, at whose death her blood-relations are impure for three days, mentioned also in Vi. 22, 34,[2] is to be considered as an early married girl remaining in her father's house till her maturity.

An instance of self contradiction.

In the province of Smṛti literature even the oldest works take the standpoint adverted to above that it is a sin to let mature girls remain unmarried. In conformity with the general views about the function of women and the purpose of marriage, the loss of a *ṛtu*, i. e., the day regarded as appropriate for the raising of progeny, involves the sin of killing an embryo (*bhrūṇahatyā*). This is no doubt the reason why marriageable daughters who are not yet married may after three *ṛtus* herself go out to seek a husband; some authors lay down three years

It is a great sin to remain unmarried after attaining puberty.

1. Cf. Winternitz l.c. 9-13.

2. I beg leave to submit that Vi. in this passage refers to a girl who happens to be in her father's house when giving birth to her child: we have nothing to do here with a *prattā strī* which means the betrothed *(vāgdattā)*, see e. g. *Dāyabhāga* 63. *Tr.*

instead of three *ṛtus.* Utterances such as this that it is better for a girl to remain unmarried till death in her father's house than to be married to an unworthy person (M. 9, 89) are, according to Nīlakaṇṭha and others, not to be taken literally, and, moreover, such utterances are rare. Thus according to Baudh. 4, 1, 11 marriage with even an unworthy suitor is to be preferred to remaining in the parents' house.

Guardians who had to look after the marriage of a girl.

If the father is not alive the relatives who act as the guardians of the girl in the place of her father, have to look after the marriage of the girl and for that reason they are called "Kanyāpradāḥ", "those who give away the girl in marriage". In the lists of these "Kanyāpradāḥ"[1] mostly only the male relations are mentioned,—the brother, the grand-father paternal and maternal, the uncles etc.—while the mother is often placed very low in the list. If there are no relatives at all the king himself should take their place. In the law of inheritance too the brother appears as the next Kanyāprada after the father; he should get his sister married and give her a fourth part of a son's share of the inheritance (Y. 2, 124), i. e., according to the plausible interpretation of some of the commentators, he has to bear the costs of a marriage worthy of his position which, without doubt, were very high already in ancient times as they are to-day. Thus in the Mah. 1, 113, 9 ff. Śalya gives away his sister in marriage.

Conflicting data about the age of marriage.

The rules that the Vivāha should take place before puberty, that the bride—this too is often expressly mentioned in this connection—must be *nagnikā*, are common to all the Smṛtis. Many of them however go further and lay down a fixed age for marriage and the

---

1. M. 9, 4; 5, 151; Y. 1,63; Vi. 24,38 f.; Nār. 12, 20-22; Saṁvarta 67; Par. 7,6.

later the work the earlier is the age.[1] Thus according to M. 9,94, a man of thirty years of age should marry a girl of twelve, and a man of twenty-four years a girl of eight.[2] On the other hand according to the later Bṛh. the age of the bride in those cases should be 10 and 7 respectively. Dakṣa and Saṁvarta recommend the age of 8. Other authors have prescribed the age of 10 or 12 as the upper limit and the age of 7 as the lower limit. There are also texts in which 4-6 and 8 years form the lower and the upper limits. Many occasional remarks prove that such rules did not remain dead letters.[3] Thus in the law of hospitality (M. 3, 114; Y. 1, 105; Vi. 67, 39) the *Kumārī* has been distinguished from the *Suvāsinī* or *Svavāsinī*—now called *Suasin*[4]—by which term a married daughter is meant who still remains in her father's house, i. e., a bride who is not yet mature. If such a girl dies her blood-relations will have to observe a shorter period of mourning, while otherwise for married daughters their blood-relations do not observe mourning at all (Vi. 22, 33 f.). The rare category of "remarried virgin widows" (*akṣatayoni-*

Stray references which prove that child marriage was not a mere theory.

---

1. Cf. ZDMG 46,414.

2. This is merely a pious wish as the commentators too have hinted at. The author of this verse sees nothing beyond the fact that a man must be thirty before he is able to finish the study of the Vedas and that Indian women attain puberty about the age of twelve and forthwith he makes the rule that a man of thirty should marry a girl of twelve. But. naturally enough, this rule has been little observed; we do not find a single instance in Sanskrit literature—in the epics, dramas etc.—where a man is marrying for the first time at thirty. Daśaratha intended to get Rāma married (Rāmāyaṇa. 1, 18, 37) when he was fifteen (Ibid. I, 20, 2). Buddha too was married long before he was thirty. We shall perhaps get a glimple of the true state of things from the verse quoted by Yaśodhara on Kāmas. III, 1,12 which declares that the bride should be younger than the bridegroom by four to eight years : चतुर्थादष्टमं यावत् कनिष्ठा वत्सरे वरात् । कन्यां परिणयेच्छस्तां नेतरातिवयाश्च या ॥

3. ZDMG 46, 418 f.

4. Grierson, Bihar Peasant Life § 1295.

punarbhū, Nār. 12, 46; M. 9, 176; Vas. 17, 20; Vi. 15, 8) may be explained only on the hypothesis that it was considered a marriage if the nuptial ceremonies alone, particularly the act of "grasping hands" (*pāṇigrahaṇa*), took place, even though no consummation followed on account of the tender age of the bride. The expression *kaumārapati* "the bridegroom of youth," whom a *punarbhū* deserts to live with another man (Nār. 12, 47), is significant; here too it is only a bridegroom and not a husband. For that reason in an anonymous Smṛti the husband, i. e., the bridegroom, has been denied the right of having conjugal relations with his bride until she is mature.[1]

Courting, betrothal and consummation.

Negotiations, binding in themselves, used to be carried on before the *vivāha*, and probably even fresh festivals were celebrated at the beginning of the conjugal life. According to Nār. 12, 2 f. the sacrament (*saṁskāra*) of the wedding consists of two parts, wooing or choosing of bride (*varaṇa*), and holding the hand (*pāṇigrahaṇa*) along with the Mantras accompanying these ceremonies, but the courting (*varaṇa*) or the betrothal of the bride (*vāgdāna*) may be regarded as null if any concealed defect (*doṣa*), i. e. deformity or any gross corporeal or spiritual malady, is discovered in the bride or the bridegroom. While courting and betrothal were apparently separated from the wedding only by a short interval, it depended on the attainment of puberty how soon the postponed ceremony of taking the bride to the house of the bridegroom should take place and therewith the conjugal life should begin. At the first *ṛtu*, i. e. on the 5. to the 16. night after the attainment of puberty, or even at a

1. The custom of child-marriage may on the whole be regarded as a later development for no trace of it may be found in the Vedic age. Ghoṣā for instance was married at the age of sixty (Bṛhaddevatā, VII, 41—47)! Old maids too were not unknown (Zimmer, Altind. Leben pp. 305-6). *Tr.*

later *ṛtu*, the ceremony bearing the significant name "impregnation" (*garbhādhāna*) takes place. It is probably even a Vedic custom and it is the first of the 12 or 16 sacraments (*saṁskāras*)of life of the Indians beginning with the germination of life.

The Kāmasūtra too is important for the history of *vivāha*, for it describes in detail the course of an Indian betrothal and marriage from a viewpoint quite different from that of the Smṛtis; however, it often agrees fully with the Gṛhyasūtras. Thus the passage (193 f.) about the girls who should be avoided in choosing a bride is almost literally identical with Āp. Gṛ. 1, 3, 10—13. Now here too a *rākā*, i. e. an already grown-up girl is called unacceptable and, at least according to the commentary, the epithet *phalinī* too has a similar meaning, and moreover according to Kāmasūtra p. 190 the bride must be at least three years younger than the bridegroom.[1] Nevertheless in the following often grown-up brides are talked of; thus on p. 200 a mature bride (*nigāḍhajauvanā*) is mentioned, i. e. one who, as the commentator remarks, has found a husband on account of her other good qualities inspite of this comparatively unimportant defect. If a suitor's courting is rejected, he should try to enter into a love-intrigue (*gāndharvavivāha*) with the girl or to take possession of her through one of the three lower forms of marriage (207—232). Here too apparently the girls are assumed to be grown up as well as in p. 222 where the bridegroom hunting of a *prāptayauvanā* is referred to i.e., one who has remained unmarried because she found no suitor on account of her low origin or her poverty or because she was an orphan formerly. Accordingly, at the time of the

Grown-up brides mentioned in the Kāmasūtra.

1. See f.-n. 2 p. 123 *Tr.*

composition of this ancient work[1] the demands of the Brahmanical customery law were already well-known which however raised too many difficulties in practical life ; the standpoint of the *Kāmasūtra*, which declares the *gāndharva vivāha* to be the best form of marriage (§ 16) is of course quite opposed to the austere views of the Dharmaśāstra

Mah. agrees with the Smṛti.

The Mah.[2] in its didactic portion contains the rule that a man of 30 years of age should marry a girl of 10 who is still *nagnikā* (13,44,15) or that a man of 20 years should marry a girl of 7. As in the Smṛtis here too the *svayaṁvara* is allowed three years after the attainment of puberty and advice has been given not to wait longer in father's house (13,44,14—17). These ordinary *svayaṁvaras* must be distinguished from the festive *svayaṁvaras* which, along with the *gāndharva vivāha*, seems to have been a privilege of the nobles and at the present day too the daughters of the Rajput nobles are married later than the girls of other classes (§16). We must not forget in connection with the ideal maidens of the Mah. as well as of Indian poesy in general[3] that there we have poetical and often conventional portraits which could have corresponded but little to reality. The well-known statement of Greek authors about the attainment of puberty by Indian women at the age of seven as well as the statement

The Greeks on the child-marriage of Indians.

1. Prof. H. C. Chakladar has proved that Vātsyāyana's Kāmasūtra was written about the middle of the third century A.D. (Calcutta University Journal of the Department of Letters, Vol. IV, pp. 85-122). Dr. A. Banerji Sastri is inclined to assign it too the end of the third century (JBORS, Vol. IX, p. 57) and Dr. Jolly to the fourth century (Introd. to Arthaśāstra, Punjab Sanskrit Series, p. 29). MM. Haraprasad Sastri, however, has tried to show in his "Magadhan Literature" that Vātsyāyana belonged to a considerably earlier period. *Tr.*

2. Cf. Hopkins l.c. 339-344 ; Holtzmann 21ff.

3. Cl. Bader, La femme dans l'Inde antique (Paris 1867).

about the six-year-old mothers of India, are wrong in this form, as puberty is generally attained in the twelfth year ; but they may refer only to the observation of the marriage ceremonies of seven-year-old brides. Alberuni (2,154) too was astonished at the early marriages of Hindus.

Child-marriage in modern India.

At the present day child-marriage is the standing custom particularly in all the castes attached to Brahmanism ; it has, however, spread among the Muhammadans too from among them. Thus according to the census of 1891, in the Punjab[1] out of 10,000 girls of below ten years of age, 477 were married among the Hindus and 186 among the Muhammadans. The bride goes to live with her husband (*mukhlava*) a few years after the celebration of the marriage ceremony when she attains puberty. In the North-Western Provinces and Oudh[2], girls are often married shortly after birth ; of every 10,000 girls of 0-4 years of age, 63 are married ; of the same number of girls in 5-9 years of age 999 are married and when of the age of 10-14, almost 9/10 of the whole female population get married. Yet the ceremony of taking the bride to the husband's house—here called *gauna*—takes place mostly 3 to 7 years after the marriage with the attainment of puberty. In north Bengal the average age of marriage of Hindu girls is 11½, in west Bengal 10½, while 6·78 and 11·54 p.c. respectively are less than 10 years of age at the time of marriage.[3] The "second marriage," called *garbhādhāna* or *punarvivāha* by the Brahmans, takes place at the time of the attainment of puberty.[4]

The percentage of child wives is very high in

1. Census of India, 1891, 19, 221, 225.
2. l. c. 16, 246—248.
3. l. c. 3, 185t; Risley l. c. 1, 152
4. Bose, The Hindoos as they are 85.

Percentage of child-wives in various provinces of India.

some districts of the Central Provinces[1] ; thus in Wardha 12 p.c. and in Nagpur 10·1 p.c. of the girls are married when below 10 years in age. In Bombay[2] 1130 of the Hindu females are married at the age of 0-9 and 6064 at the age of 10-14. Here too the second marriage, often called by its earlier designation *garbhādhāna*[3], takes place :at the time of the attainment of puberty i.e., within sixteen days of the marriage and not as laid down in the Smṛtis. The statistics for Madras[4] show very clearly how the child marriage is still very much in vogue among the Brahmans and on the contrary how very seldom it takes place among the Dravidian tribes. Thus there, among the Brahmans, 72·81 p.c. of the female population are married at the age of 10-14 while among other castes it is only 5-10 p.c. Here too the second marriage is called *garbhādhān* among the Brahmans ; here it extends over three days and takes place shortly after the attainment of puberty by the bride.

Child bride-groms.

Among males too marriage at a very tender age is quite common ; thus in the N. W. Provinces, of 10,000 boys 433 are married at the age of 5-9 while at the age of 10-14 only a fraction more than half the population remain unmarried.[5] Yet, for example, in Madras the husbands are on average about 10 years older than the wives which reminds one actually of the rules in M. and Mah. The rule of the Smṛtis, that a mature girl who remains unmarried in her father's house is a cause of shame to the whole family, still rules the modern ideas in a potent form, so that even the lowest castes are more and more running into child marriage.

1. Census 11, 105.
2. l. c. 7, 167, App. A. Tables.
3. BG 18, 1, 140; 23, 137. 140. etc.
4. Census 13. 145. 264.
5. l. c. 16. 246 f.

Defects of a bride.

§ 18. *The hindrances of marriage.* The favourite enumerations of the defects in a bride (*kanyādoṣa*) or of girls who should be avoided when choosing a bride, contain much that is strange and obscure and even the commentaries give us no sufficient help for the clearing up of this long list covering so many as 27 points [1]. The injunctions to avoid a gossiping, hunch-backed, dwarfish, too old, baldheaded, or squint eyed girl and a girl bearing an ominous name etc. as well as recommending a beautiful girl who comes of a respectable family and who has the gait of an elephant and a normal body etc., may naturally be considered as well-meaning advices. For the proper age of marriage see above. It is particularly emphasised not to attach too great importance to wealth. Also according to Kāmas. p. 225 the maidens should prefer a poor but devoted husband to a rich husband who has already been married several times.

Following supernatural hints.

The oracular message about the bride is a superstition but it is an ancient custom; it depends upon the clod of earth which the bride picks up of a number of them placed before her [2]. Moreover the conduct of the bride at the time of courting is to be taken into consideration and it is regarded as an evil omen if she sleeps, weeps, or has gone out when the suitor comes [3].

Examination of the bridegroom.

The bridegroom too, like the bride is examined for his body-marks (*lakṣaṇa*). According to Nār. 12, 8 ff., and Y. 1,55, much care was taken to examine the bridegroom as to whether he was constitutionally impotent or not, which, according to Nār. 12, 16, 97, was also a ground for dissolving a marriage. Yet from M. 9,203 it is clear that such men were mostly married. The astrologers too were consulted on the occasion

1. Cf. Winternitz, Hochzeitsrituell 33 ff.
2. l. c. 37 f.
3. Āp. Gṛ. 3, 10 ; Kāmas. 193.

of these examinations and therefore the Kāmas. (p. 192 f.) lays down that the bridegroom should send his good friends to the parents of the maiden disguised as astrologers (*daivacintaka*) and that they should prophesy to them a brilliant career for the suitor judging by the flight of birds position of planets, etc.

Privilege of seniority as a hindrance to marriage.

The privilege of age is a more important hindrance of marriage, for which reason it is considered sinful in a younger brother to marry before the elder brother and in a younger sister to marry before the elder sister [1]. This rule, in a piece with other privileges of seniority, particularly in the law of inheritance, is to be accounted for by the high expenses of the marriage and of founding a new family, which, according to Indian custom remains with the parents of the husband, and it is found already in the Vedic Saṁhitās and the Śrautasūtras and *in extenso* in almost all the Smṛtis as well as in Mah. Yet however the infringement of this law is only a religious transgression and no crime in the worldly sense and it may therefore be expiated for by a penance in which, *inter alia*, the concluded marriage is dissolved but is afterwards celebrated anew (Vas. 20,7—10). Even now it is customary among the South Indian Brahman sects that the elder brother celebrates a mock marriage with a twig of a tree so that the younger brother may marry without incurring any sin[2]. Modern instances of polyandry too, in which the common wife is considered to be the wife of the eldest brother and her children his children [3], are based on similar views.

Virginity essential in a bride.

The bride must be a virgin. This requirement is mentioned in the laws of marriage in the Gṛhya and Dharmasūtras in general and is self-evident from the custom of

1. Cf. Delbrück, D. indog. Verwandtschaftsnamen 578-86.
2. Nelson, Scientific Study 146 n. 2, cf. Kohler ZVR 3, 372.
3. Tupper, Punjab Customary Law 2, 186.

child-marriage; it is however so much emphasised that it debars even the *remarriage of widows.* It has now been proved [1] that the passages formerly quoted to prove the permissibility of widow marriage in the ṚV and the AV are not what they were thought to be. The "woman who has again become (a wife)" (*punarbhū*), is of course mentioned in AV 9, 5, 27 f. in connection with a sacrifice which such a person performs in order to be united with her second and not the first husband in the next world. It cannot be decided with certainty from these words, either directly or by implication, whether the first husband is still living or not. At all events the latter interpretation is possible and gains in probability from the explanations of the term *punarbhū* in the Smṛtis. Thus the *punarbhū*, who is only one step higher than the wanton woman (*svairiṇī* Nār. 12, 45 ff.), is defined to be a woman who, still a virgin, is married to a second husband or a woman who lived before her marriage with another man though indeed not married to him or who left her first husband because he was impotent, excommunicated from his caste or suffered from a mental disorder, or who has been deserted by her first husband, or who has returned to the husband to whom she was married as a child after living in the meanwhile with others, or one who, in conformity with the custom of levirate, has been given over to a distant relation (*sapiṇḍa*) of her husband on failure of a brother-in-law. M. 9, 175 (cf. 69 f.), Vas. 17, 20, 74 and Baudh. 4, 1, 16 expressly refer to the case where the first husband is dead, but however allow the the remarriage of the widow only if the death of the husband has taken place before the celeberation of the marriage. Moreover the second marriage in the above mentioned Vedic passage appears to be a sin

Punarbhū in AV.

Definition of the Punarbhū in Smṛtis.

1. Hillebrandt ZDMG 40, 708—712; Delbrück l. c. 553-555.

which has to be atoned for by a sacrifice, taking it for granted that the case of the re-married widow has been included in it. In the Smṛtis the remarriage of widows has been considered only in connection with the five cases of necessity (*āpad*) in any one of which a woman may marry another man, namely, if her husband has disappeared or is dead, if he has joined an order of monks or is impotent or is excommunicated out of his caste (Nār. 12, 97; Par. 4, 28),—a passage which is often turned to account by modern defenders of widow marriage in India and which is used even in a Jaina work of 1014 A. D.[1]

Re-marriage permitted under exceptional circumstances.

The case of the disappearance of the husband and the question what the wife will have to do in such cases, have been discussed in detail by other authors. Thus according to Gaut. 18, 15—17 the wife of a man who has disappeared should live in abstinence for six years (and then, after the expiration of this period, she should go to another man); only when he enters a spiritual order should she wait permanently, and when he has gone abroad for Vedic studies she should forbear from having intercourse with other men for twelve years. M. 9, 76 also prescribes a similar period of waiting, which of course has been expounded by a section of the commentators to signify that even after the expiration of this period the wife should live only by manual labour that is permitted to her even if he goes away without caring for her, or that she should pass her life in searching after her husband. According to Vas. 17, 75—80, she should not go to a stranger but preferably to a relation of her husband and he shortens the period of waiting as well as Nār. 12, 98—101 and Devala[2] if the woman has no children and belongs to

Periods of waiting prescribed for the wife.

1. Bhandarkar, Report on 1884-87 (Bombay. 1894) 16.
2. Jagannātha 1, 941 f. of my manuscript—Colebrook Dig. 4,4, CLIII.

a low caste; but on the other hand it should be extended if news is received that the husband is still living.

None of these passages however says anything of a second *marriage*. Thus in the law of debt too we find that a wife or a widow who has lived with another man binds him under certain circumstances to pay the debts of her former husband (Nār. 1, 20—24; Y. 2, 51; Vi. 6, 30; Bṛh. 11, 52) but nothing has been said about their relation being legalised by a fresh marriage. Therefore statements like these hardly affect the general validity of the principle that the Mantras of the marriage are for virgins alone (M. 8, 226). It is also very well known that the daughter is given away in marriage only once [1], and M. 5, 162 expressly remarks that a second husband is never prescribed for a virtuous woman. In the law of inheritance the *paunarbhava*, the son of a *punarbhū* is indeed generally included as one of the twelve sons but he occupies no high place among them and according to M. 9, 160, Baudh. 2, 3, 32, Gaut. 28, 33 and Devala etc. the *paunarbhava* is one of the lower six subsidiary sons and may be regarded only as a relation but not as the heir of his father. However, here too, as in the questions of child marriage, *niyoga* and widow burning (§ 20), the stricter views have arisen only gradually. Thus Kāśypa was the first to extend the category of *punarbhūs* also over such daughters whom their father had promised or intended to give in marriage to some other person or whose mother is a *punarbhū*. The secondary sons (*gauṇaputra*) are for the first time condemned by Bṛh. 25, 41 who were however already passed over in silence by Āp. The general prohibition of marriage with a woman who is already married (*ūḍhāyāḥ punarudvāhaḥ*) is found for the first time in the well-known lists of practices forbidden in the

Second marriage has nowhere been expressly permitted.

Stricter views arose later.

1. Cf. Böhtlingk, Sprüche 6650, 6652.

present age of sins *(kalivarjyāni)* in the Ādipurāṇa and other later works [1].

Widow marriage n modern ndia.

To-day widow marriage—the widow proper or the bride whose husband died at the very beginning of the conjugal life—is indeed allowed by the English law of 1856; but it is so repugnant to the basic principles of the higher castes that e. g. among the Lohars and Mālis of Surat a bachelor is allowed to marry a "widow" duly after his symbolic marriage with a Sami tree or a cotton puppet so that he too may thereby be stamped as a widower; among the Jats of Ajmere he who marries a widow must make good to the family of the deceased husband the cost of his marriage and among many castes in Bombay, the widow may marry only at night or has to come out of her parents' house by the back door, etc. [2] On the whole, there are evidences in the enormous materials in the description of customs contained in the Bombay Gazetteer that among the Brahmans and in almost all the higher castes the widow marriage is absolutely forbidden and takes place only among the lower castes.

Child marriage and prohibition of widow re-marriage.

It is no less dacidedly proved by the data in the census of 1891 that the prohibition of widow marriage goes hand in hand with the spread of of child marriage (§ 17). Thus in N. W. Provinces among 10,000 females 817 are widows among the Hindus and 1054 among the Jainas [3] who are dead against widow marriage. The female population of the age of 20-24 consists of 16.59 and 17.62 p.c. of widows among the Hindus of north and west Bengal respectively. [4] In the district of Wardha in the Central Provinces of 10,000 women of all ages 1610 are widows [5].

1. Vīramitrodaya 2, 1, 11, ed. G. Sarkar.
2. West and Bühler (3rd. ed.) 417 ; Kohler ZVR 10, 94 (according to BG).
3. Census of India 1891, 10, 249.
4. l. c. 3, 186.
5. l. c. 11, 115.

In Madras among the various Brahman castes, although they are all against widow marriage and for child marriage, the number of widows among 10,000 women of the age between 15 and 39 fluctuates between 1994 and 2994. The number of child widows is proportionately large throughout, which, e.g., among tho Kalingis of Madras amounts nearly to 1 per cent of the girls under 9 years of age; this is, as the Report remarks, "apparently a small percentage, but in consideration of the age, it is enormous."[1]

The two parties concerned must be equal in birth.

The necessity of equality in birth is pronounced already in the marriage rules of the Gṛhyasūtras[2] and the Kāmasūtra and it is particularly emphasised in all the Smṛtis as well as in the Mah.[3] Of course in this respect too the gradual progress into harder rules cannot be mistaken. Thus it was an ancient topic of dispute whether the marriage between a man of a higher caste and a Śūdra woman may be allowed or not and, not infrequently, both the views are found one immediately after the other, as, e.g., Baudh. 1, 16, 2, M. 3, 13, Nār. 12, 5, f. and Vi. 24, 1 allow the Brahman to marry women out of the four classes in the order, but on the other hand Baudh. 2, 2, 7 and 4, 1, 5, M. 3, 14 f., Nār. 12, 108, Vi. 26, 4 ff. etc. decisively condemn connections with Śūdra women. Also Āp. 1, 26 7, Vas. 1, 25 f., Y. 1, 56, Pārask. 1, 4, 11 etc. unequivocally declare themselves against the permissibility of such marriages even if they are performed without the usual marriage Mantras, and other ancient authors such as Uśanas, Hārīta, Gautama etc. (cf. M. 3,16, §§ 3, 4 above), fell out only over the question whether in such cases the

1. l. c. 13, 146—149.

2. Cf. Winternitz, l. c. 38. According to Weber, Ind. St. 10, 73-75 there was no fixed norm; the now well-known Gṛhyasūtras were however only partly know to Weber.

3. Cf. Hopkins, Ruling Caste 352.

excommunication of the culprit should take place immediately or later.

Mixed marriages that were permitted.

They were more tolerant towards the marriage of a Kṣatriya woman and a Brahman and generally towards mixed marriages where the female is only one step lower than the male.[1] Thus according to Baudh. 1, 17, 3 ff. (similarly 1, 16, 6 and Gaut. 4, 16), sons of equal status are said to be born of such marriages, and also according to the unpublished Dharmasūtra of Uśanas (§ 4) the son of a Brahman by a Kṣatriya wife will be a Brahman, the son of a Kṣatriya by a Vaiśya wife a Kṣatriya and that of a Vaiśya by a Śūdra wife a Vaiśya. The Mah.[2] too knows of marriages between Brahmans and daughters of Kings.[3]

Mixed marriages that were absolutely condemned.

Marriages between men of lower castes and women of higher castes are universally disapproved and the sons born of those unions are identified with the most hated castes as contrary to the natural order (*pratiloma*). Only the wife of equal position is regarded as the *dharmapatnī* and the mixing of castes is generally a grave sin and the King must take care to prevent it. In later texts the marriage of Aryans (*dvija*) with women of unequal position is mentioned among the usages no longer permissible in this age of sins *(kalivarjya)*.

---

1. It is interesting to note that in the Mālavikāgnimitra (Act I) a brother of the queen is referred to who was inferior to her in caste (वर्णावरो भ्राता) but was not on that account looked down upon for he was appointed Viceroy of the King in the Narmadā region. *Tr.*

2. Cf. Holtzmann, Zur Gesch. u. Krit. 20.

3. That marriage between Brahmans and Kṣatriya women was allowed in very early times is proved by the interesting story of Śyāvāśva in Bṛhaddevatā v, 50-81. Here we find that Śyāvāśva, the grandson of the great seer Atri fell in love with the daughter of king Rathavīti but the king and his consort refused to accept him as their son-in-law as he was not a seer. In fact S. had to be a seer before he could gain the hand of the princess. *Tr.*

Instead of *savarṇā* frequently also the general terms *sajāti, samāna, samānajātīya, sadṛśa* and similar other expressions are used to express the equality of position of the parties concerned in a marriage, and it may probably be assumed that this principle applies to those narrow societies which actually appeared already very early and supplanted the great prehistoric *varṇas*. To-day there is, for example, no connubium between particular Brahman sects ; yet it happens specially among the Kulin Brahmans of Bengal, well-known for their polygamy, that high caste Brahmans take money for their marriage with girls of lower status ; but it is in conformity with the Smṛti rule that misalliances, where the husband is of a caste higher than that of the wife, are not to be absolutely condemned. These questions are to be discussed more minutely in the State antiquities.[1]

The general terms employed to express equality of status apply to the narrow castes alone.

The position and caste should be equal but race and family must be different. As this principle of exogamy is found even in the Gṛhyasūtras there is no reason to doubt its high antiquity[2] although the demands in this respect have been more and more increased. Of the Gṛhyasūtras Gobh. 3, 4, 3-5, Mān. 1,7, Hir. 1,19,2, and Vaikh. 3,2 forbid marriage with a *sagotrā* or *samānapravarā* —Gobh. and Vaikh. forbid moreover marriage with a *sapiṇḍā* of the mother.[3] The expressions *sagotrā* and *samānapravarā* are connected with wider clan organisations (*pravaras*) and of course may be said only of the Brahmans[4]; the *sapiṇḍā* is a proper blood relation.

Gotras must be different.

Of the Dharmasūtras Āp. prohibits the marriage of a daughter with a *sagotra* (of the father) and

1. See f.-n. 5 p. 95 *Tr.*
2. Cf. Weber l.c. 75 ff. and above, f. n. 2 p. 135 and below f. n. 1, p. 138.
3. Cf. Winternitz l. c.
4. Cf. Bülher Āp. 2, 11, 15 ; Gaut. 18, 6 ; M. 3, 5.

Degrees of propinquity hindering marriage.

a blood-relation (*yonisaṁvandha*) of the mother; instead of or besides the *sagotra*, the expressions *samānārṣagotraja*, *samānapravara* etc. are used in other Smṛtis (cf. Mah. 13, 49, 18) and the degrees of affinity hindering matrimonial alliances are defined more accurately to this effect that they consist of relationship traced up to the fifth generation in the mother's side and to the seventh generation in the father's side. The *sapiṇḍas* are reckoned by generations beginning with the common progenitor of the clan. But people did not stick even to these extended rules about the prohibition of marriage. Thus according to Vyāsa 2,2 this prohibition may apply even to a *sagotrā* of the mother, and according to others even to a *mātṛnāmnī* i.e. a girl bearing the same name as the mother of the bridegroom, as well as to the daughter of the spiritual initiator (*guru*) or the spiritual disciple (*śiṣya*). This spiritual relationship is found in the family law as well as in the law of inheritance. Marriages between relations in the prohibited degrees are to be regarded as null according to the commentators, yet the sin incurred by these marriages may in some cases be expiated for by a penance. The local usages too are to be taken into consideration in this connection; thus Baudh. 1, 2, 3 and Bṛh. 27, 19 declare that marriage between cousins is prevalent in the South and such marriages still actually take place in the Deccan among various Brahmanical sects and many other castes in general.[1]

Gradual hardening of these rules.

Affinity still regarded as a hindrance to marriage in India.

The prohibition of marriage within forbidden degrees of propinquity, particularly inside a *gotra*, is mentioned even by Alberuni 2,155 and is now universally observed, at least among the Brahmans, Rajputs and other higher castes. Thus among the

1. Cf. Bühler on Baudh. l. c. Steele, Castes 163. For very ancient testimonies to this local usage of which some are also from the south, see Weber l. c.

various Brahman sects of Madras marriage between persons of the same *gotra* is never allowed.[1] Among the Brahmakṣatris of Puna marriage cannot take place if the *gotras* are the same but if the surnames are same it is no hindrance to marriage[2]; but also in those places of Bombay where the similarity of the surname or *devak*, i.e. the insignia or fetich, is regarded as a hindrance to marriage, it is to be traced back to the same principle, for many *gotras* are denoted by the same surname or the same insignia.[3] In the N. W. Provinces and Oudh marriages within the *gotra* are universally forbidden.[4] The Soti Brahmans of eastern Tirhut keep accurate family registers for their whole sect and produce evidence at the marriage that the bride and the bridegroom are not related to each other in any way that may be a hindrance to their marriage. Those relations among whom marriage is not possible are mentioned in a Behari proverb which declares all the descendants of the uncles and the aunts of the father's side as well as of the mother's side as ineligible to matrimony; yet it is doubtful for how many generations this prohibition continues to be in force[5]. It is a universal rule in Lahore that no man can marry a woman of his *got.* Among the Rajputs of Gurgaon in in the Punjab, marriage even with the relations of the mother or the grandmother of the paternal side is forbidden as well as with any such person who may be proved to be a relation of the paternal side[6]. The exogamy perhaps first came into fashion among the Rajputs

Marriage notallowed between members of the same Gotra.

1. Census of India 1891, 13,264.
2. BG 18, 1, 266.
3. Kohler ZVR 10, 86—90 (according to BG).
4. Kohler ZVR 11, 165 (according to the Gazetteer).
5. Grierson, Bihar peasant Life § 1354; Risley, l. c. 1, XLIX
6. Tupper l. c. 2, 112, 120, 194.

(Kṣatriyas), among whom, in Rajputana, as Sir A. Lyall has beautifully described it[1], it may be studied in its primitive character in connection with the modern mock abduction and the former practice of carrying away women by force and also in connection with the family constitution.

§ 19. *Polygamy, concubinage and divorce.* Although a second husband for the wife "is nowhere prescribed," not even after the death of the first, the husband is to marry anew after the death of his wife without delay (M. 5, 162, 168; Y. 1, 89).[2] But even in the life-time of his wife it is not forbidden for him to get beside her any number of married wives or concubines that he may wish for. Polygamy is in evidence already in the Vedas[3]; thus e.g. in MS 1, 5, 8 the ten wives (*jāyā*) of Manu are mentioned. Yet in such passages of the Vedas and the Śrautasūtras chiefly the princely or noble families alone seem to be referred to, and the dual *dampatī samanasa* "a harmonious couple" and the presence of the one wife (*patnī*) at the sacrifice prove that monogamy was regarded as the usual and natural state of things. The heroes of the Mah.[4] have usually many wives, but there is also a real or chief wife, the Mahiṣī, mentioned even in the Vedas, and in the inscriptions too frequently one single wife is ascribed to the princes Even in the case of the Brahmans of the Mah., although they have several wives, the Brāhmaṇī appears to be the proper and the legitimate wife, the Dharmapatnī.

Polygamy is allowed but monogamy is the general rule.

1. Asiatic studies 219-221; cf. Risley l. c. 1, LIV.

2. Kauṭilya (III, 2) however lays down that a man cannot take a second wife before eight years have passed after his first marriage and even that only if the first wife brings forth no live children or has no male issue or if she is barren. Violation of this rule is even punished by the government. But in the same chapter Kauṭ. says that a man may marry any number of women if he is in a position to make good provisions for all of them. Perhaps only concubines are meant here. *Tr.*

3. Cf. Delbrück, D. indog. Verw. 540 f.; Zimmer AL 324 f.; Kāgi, Der Rigveda 22.

4. Cf. Hopkins 352-354; Holtzmann, Zur Gesch. 22.

Generally a man should at first marry a woman of his own caste and only afterwards proceed to take wives from the lower classes in the order of the Varṇas, so that only the Śūdra is restricted to a single wife of his own caste. Yet the Mah. too sometimes endorses the more austere view that the Śūdra woman can never be taken to wife by the higher classes. The analogous teachings of the Smṛtis on this point have already been discussed in §18. Thus four three and two wives are allowed to Brahmans, Kṣatriyas and Vaiśyas respectively, but excluding the Śūdrā we have only three wives for Brahmans, two for Kṣatriyas, etc. Of these only the wife of one's own caste is the Dharmapatnī and the others are regarded as wives of lower grade or concubines and for this reason their children too are at a disadvantage in the law of inheritance.

Only the wife of one's own caste is the legitimate wife.

The privileges of the eldest i. e. the first married wife is often enlarged upon, for even among several wives of the same caste she, as a rule, holds the premier position. Thus according to Vi. 26, 1—4 he who has several wives (*bhāryā*) of his own caste should perform his religious duties with the eldest; if he has several wives of different castes, the wife of his own caste enjoys this privilege even though she is the youngest; if he has no wife of his own caste, or if the wife of his own caste is absent, the wife of the next highest caste shall occupy her place; but a Śūdra wife shall always be excluded from this privilege. Of course the various wives of a polygamist could not always remain satisfied with this state of things; the historical and poetical literature offer us many an instance of it and even M. 9,83 speaks of the punishment of a "supplanted" wife who leaves the house of her husband in anger. The sad lot of such a wife was proverbial according to Nār. 1, 203. Yet the husband who subordinates her to another wife had to

The eldest wife and her privileges.

The "supplanted" wife.

give her alimony and a present on the occasion of the second marriage (*ādhivedanika*) which according to Y. 2, 148 (in the interpretation of Vijñ. and Apar.) should be equal to the marriage present to the second wife, though of course the Strīdhana which was formerly given to her is deducted from it. Such questions naturally cannot arise if the second wife is no legitimate wife.

Concubines.

At all events concubinage was common and particularly the plural term *striyaḥ* signifies not only the legitimate wives but also the concubines of an individual. Thus according to Nār. 13, 26 the charge of the maintenance of the women (*striyaḥ*) of a deceased person should devolve on his brothers who inherit his property and according to Nār. 52 and Bṛh. 25, 68 the king has to supply necessary maintenance to such women if the property of the deceased, on failure of a proper heir, reverts to him. According to Gaut. 28, 47, at the time of partition, the women connected with one of the coparceners should not be divided. Intercourse with concubines (*dāsī*, *bhujiṣyā*) of another man is regarded as adultery (Nār. 12, 79; Y. 2, 290).

The high position of the legitimate wife.

The commentators too frequently emphasise the difference between a legitimate wife and mere concubines and define the former as a wife who is married according to one of the approved forms of marriage and takes part in the religious duties of her husband and therefore under certain circumstances can also inherit his property. Thus here too the monogamic tendency is clearly perceptible which also characterises the treatment of matrimonial relations in the Smṛtis. As in the law of inheritance the claim only of that widow is recognised who was legally married and is called the surviving part of her husband (Bṛh. 25, 47) so also in the law of marriage man and wife are bound down to mutual fidelity (M. 9, 101), and in the religious law, e. g. at the sacrifices, the husband and the wife are always mentioned as a duality. Āp. 2, 11, 12 expressly lays down that a man should not take any more wives if he has a spouse who takes part in his religious duties and has borne him children.

Divorce odious to the Smṛti writers.

Though among the Dravidian tribes of the south, the Tibetan tribes in the north and the Burmese tribes in the east divorces are very common for which only mutual consent is needed, in Indian law it is considered to be a sin if the married couple separate on account of mutual aversion (Nār. 12, 90). For this reason the Muhammedan Alberuni (2, 154) was struck by the absence divorce in India. The connection established by a public ceremony with great pomp and expense as early in life as possible lays the foundation of a life-long relation and it should not be broken off so lightly. According to the most popular view, as we have already seen, the duty on the part of the wife extended even beyond the grave and the chances of her forming a second marriage are precluded by the general interdiction of widow remarriage even in those cases where such a marriage may be allowed, viz., if the husband is absent for a long time or has disappeared altogether or if he is impotent, or if he has been compelled to secede from citizen life on account of his excommunication out of his caste or if he has joined a spiritual order.[1] Already M. 9, 79 speaks about the conduct of a wife towards an impotent or excommunicated husband and thus presupposes that inspite of this ground for separation she still remains with him. Nār. in 12, 96 grants to the relations of the wife and eventually to the wife herself the right of contracting a fresh marriage if any defect in the husband, previously kept concealed, is discovered ; but even this Nār. in 12, 3 allows

1. Kauṭ. (III, 4) gives elaborate rules about the re-marriage of women, but it is not clear whether re-married women were respected or were treated merely as Punarbhūs. *Tr.*

only an engagement to be broken off in such a case and when dealing with the punishment for concealing the defects in the bride or the bridegroom or for falsely imputing to them any defects of which they are innocent (30-37), he takes only the engagement into consideration and not marriage.[1]

Repudiation of the wife though permitted was extremely difficult,

From the side of the husband of course the repudiation of the wife could be ordained, but the tendency of the legal literature is to render it as difficult as possible. The desertion of a guiltless wife is considered as a crime equal to theft for which a large amount has to be paid as fine (M. 8, 389; Vi. 5, 163; Nār. 12, 95); it also leads to excommunication from the caste and it is said to be the cause of tribulation even in the future life (Vyāsa 2, 47; Dakṣa 4, 16). Āp. 1, 28, 19 prescribes a penance of six months for this crime. Adultery is chiefly mentioned as the crime which justifies abandoning a wife and it is also generally followed by excommunication from the caste. The adulteress in particular cases should even be condemned to a cruel death (Gaut. 23, 14; M. 8, 371; Bṛh. 23, 16 etc.) or should at least undergo severe penances *(prāyaścitta)*; yet according to Vi. 5, 18 the court should interfere only when the husband cannot dispose of his wife single-handed.[2] The

Husband's right of punishing the wife.

means of punishment at his disposal were multifarious. Thus according to M. 9, 84 he could impose upon her a fine if she indulged in spirituous drinks and took part in out-door amusements or according to M. 9, 77 f. he could

1. Kauṭ. (III, 3) at all events permits divorce. "A woman hating her husband cannot dissolve her marriage against his will; nor can a man dissolve his marriage against the will of his wife. But from mutual enmity divorce may be obtained." But the four higher forms of marriage are declared indissoluble. *Tr.*

2. But the remarkable statement of Kauṭilya (III, 2) that "marriage in the basis of all disputes" (विवाहपूर्वो व्यवहार:) proves that marriage was frequently the cause of litigation. *Tr.*

take away her property if she was unamiable and disobedient or even abandon her for three months depriving her of her ornaments and furniture, yet however without withholding her sustenance. According to Nār. 12, 94 a husband should never have intercourse with a wife who is barren or gives birth only to daughters, or if she behaves unbecomingly or if she always disobeys him. In such cases another wife may be taken in the opinion of M. 9, 80 ff., Āp. 2, 11, 13, Vaikh. Gṛ. 6, 2 etc.; yet she should be provided for, and according to M. 9, 83 she should also remain in the house of her husband and according to other authors she should also receive the above mentioned compensation on the occasion of the second marriage of the husband. The husband's conjugal right of punishment such as blows with a cord or a rod is often referred to (M. 8, 299 f.; Śaṅkha 4, 16 etc.)[1]

Even adultery does not always lead to complete expulsion. Thus accordidg to Gaut. 22, 35 and Vas. 21, 8, 15 the adulteress should practise penance for a year and during that period should receive only poor food; according to Y. 1, 70 and Nār. 12, 91 she should get bad food and bad clothes, sleep on earth and must do the menial work of sweeping and cleaning. Par. 10, 15 mentions similar penances for various cases of adultery and speaks of complete expulsion or exile in a foreign land only if the adulterous connection is not without issue or where the wife has cut herself off from the family for good. Similarly Y. 1, 72; Hār. 3, 13 has even expressly opposed the expulsion of the adulteress. On the other hand the expulsion of the wife even for crimes other than adultery has been referred to. Thus according to Nār. 12, 92 f. a wife who is wasteful, brings about abortion or seeks to take the life of her husband should at once be driven out

The Adulteress is punished but not expelled.

Other crimes for which the wife is expelled.

1. See Kauṭ. III, 3. *Tr.*

of the town and a wife who is of a choleric temper, unamiable and eats before her husband should be expelled from the house without delay. According to M. 9, 83 if a wife who has been superseded by another wife leaves her husband's house in anger, she should be confined or expelled from the house in the presence of the family, and in the opinion of Y. 1, 72 every serious crime in general should be punished with repudiation (*tyāga*) though however repudiation for a crime less heinous than adultery belongs to the list of pracices forbidden in this age of sins.

Polygamy and divorce in modern India.

Even at the present day polygamy is as common as it is permissible, and separation proper, at least among the higher castes, is rare. The number of castes in Bombay, among which, according to the trustworthy data in BG "polygamy is permitted and practised" is very large and includes many Brahmanical and aristocratic communities. There are similar data about other provinces too. Nevertheless the percentage of people actually practising polygamy is nowhere very high. Thus in Madras where polygamy is most popular, only 4 per cent of the men have two wives [1] and in the Punjab the number of men wedded to more than one wife does not even amount to than 1 per cent [2]. Sterility of the first wife is usually said to be the cause of polygamy and it is fully in conformity with the principles of the Smṛtis. As it is said in the census report for Madras, separation is allowed even by the modern Brahmanical law of marriage only on account of the adultery of the wife. In the Punjab all the Hindu sects answered in the negative when the question was put before them whether divorce is customary among them; yet sometimes the *tyāg* (=*tyāga* of the Smṛtis) takes place among them, i. e. the husband turns out the wife on account of adultery; but

1. Madras Census Report, 1891, 138.
2. Census of India, 1891, 19, 223.

on the contrary a marriage once consummated is never dissolved even on account of impotence or any other physical defect [1]. Separation is very common among all the Dravidian tribes as the Census Report for Madras shows. In Bombay too among the lower castes separation from the wife frequently takes place, not only because of adultery—in which case she is treated as a slave though she still remains in the house of her husband as laid down in some Smṛtis referred to above—but also on account of impotence, twelve years' absence, disappearance or excommunication of the husband; in these cases the wife may also marry afresh [2]. Probably even in ancient times there were many tribes who cherished such principles, whence the corresponding rules of the several Smṛtis may be explained.

Separation common among the low castes.

§ 20. *Widowhood.* In consequence of child marriage and the prohibition of widow remarriage the percentage of widows in the female population was probably as great in ancient times as it is to-day (§ 18) and therefore the question of the legal position and the duties of the widow assumes great importance.

Widows as numerous in ancient times as they are to-day.

The practice of widow-burning (*satī*), as it is, fits quite well in the frame of the Brahmanical law of marriage as a sharpened form of the severe demands made by the Brahmanical law-givers on the matrimonial fidelity of the widow. Nevertheless this custom is hardly ever mentioned in the whole range of the Vedic literature and the Sūtra-works although the elaborate descriptions of the funeral ceremonies in the Śrauta and Gṛhya Sūtras offer excellent opportunities for their treatment, Only the late Vai.-Gṛ. refers to the Sahamaraṇa in which

Widow-burning hardly ever mentioned in the Vedic and Sūtra literature.

1. Tupper 2, 129, 122,
2. Steele, Castes 168—173, 369.

the husband and the wife are burnt on the same pile of wood (§3). According to the commentators at least the word Sahamaraṇa is a usual designation for widow-burning. Āp., Hār. and Gaut. are indeed quoted as authors of ślokas about *satī*, but these passages are not found in their Dharmasūtras although particularly that of Hār. deals with the duties of women very exhaustively. It is of course mentioned in Vi. 25, 14 and 20, 39 but these two passages were probably interpolated at the time of the later revision. Even the widows of a king, are said to be maintained by his successor according to Vas. 19, 33, although from other sources it is known that widow-burning often took place in royal families. M., Y., Nār. too are reticent about the *satī* in their metrical Smṛtis although they fully discuss the other duties of the widow. Only later authors such as Dakṣa 4,18, Par. 4,30 f., Vyāsa 2,53, the Purāṇas and the fragments of Bṛh. (25,8,11), Aṅgiras, Uśanas, Āp. etc. offer us more or less particular references and descriptions of the Satī. Various Commentaries and digests of law from Mit. (on Y. 1, 86) up to Jagannātha's Vivādabhaṅgārṇava (1,917 ff. of my Ms.=Colebrooke's Dig. 4,2), contain collections of these passages, and on this material Colebrooke's well-known essay "On the duties of a faithful Hindu widow" is based.[1]

The principal Smṛtis are silent about Satī.

Only the latest Smṛtis speak of Satī.

Everywhere however the suicide of the widow appears only to be an optional duty, observation of which brings great merit according to the Mit., beside which however the other alternative of a chaste and retired life (*brahma-*

Satī was merely an option at the best.

1. Cf. F. Hall, The source of Colebrooke's Essay "On the Duties" etc. JRAS 3, 183 ff. (1868). Regarding the well-known passage of the Ṛgveda 10, 18, 7, quoted by Colebrooke as documentary evidence for Satī it can hardly be said that the text has been purposely distorted; at least this distortion must have taken place at a very early date, cf. Ratnākara 442. Originally of course this passage had nothing to do with Satī and the same is also the case with AV 18, 3, 1, cf. Hillebrandt ZDMG 40, 710.

caryapakṣa) has equal merits ; neither can it be explained otherwise how in the same work the right of inheritance of a chaste widow without any son may be recognised. If the widow however decides to follow her husband in death as Satī it is essential that she should be burnt with his body, to the accompaniment of prescribed prayers (*sahamaraṇa*) ; yet if the husband dies and is cremated abroad she may throw herself alone into the fire pressing to her breast a pair of his shoes (*anumaraṇa*). It is regarded as a great sin if the widow repents her decision and as a Citibhraṣṭā leaves the pile.

Sahamaraṇa and Anumaraṇa.

In certain cases, particularly if the widow is pregnant or has a little child she could not be Satī. The Mit. l.c. also quotes a text which opposess the Satī in general of Brahman widows and declares it to be suicide which brings to heaven neither the widow nor her husband. Yet however this text, in a piece with another, should be taken to deal with the Anumaraṇa of Brahman widows alone. Also some commentators, such as Medhātithi on M. 5,157, and Devaṇṇabhaṭṭa are opposed to Satī.

Widow-burning is positively opposed.

The conclusion may be drawn from this that it was never a special Brahmanical institution. Even in the two great epics it occurs only rarely.[1] The Rām. contains a few occasional references to it but none of the widows who figure in the story burn themselves and it has been taken not improperly as a proof of the high antiquity of the Rām. In the Mah. the Satī is somewhat more popular ; thus in 1,74,46 the Anugamana has been declared to be the duty of a true wife, and after the death of Pāṇḍu there is a row among his widows Mādrī and Pṛthā (Kuntī) for the honour of being allowed to be burnt with him in which the former is at last victorious ; yet the Satī is of rare

Widow-burning was not a special Brahmanical institution.

1. Cf. M. Williams, Indian Wisdom, 3rd. ed., 315; Hopkins 172f., 371 ; Holtzmann 28; Jacobi, Rām. 108.

occurrence in view of the enormous bulk of the Mah. and the frequent references to widowed princesses in it.[1]

Satīs in the Rājataraṅgiṇī.

A great contrast to this is the reference to Satīs in historical works and fictions. Thus in the Rājatar. it appears to be a matter of course that at the death of a king one or several widows of the same should burn themselves with him. After the death of king Śaṁkaravarman his chief queen and two other widows as well as four faithful servants of the king mounted his funeral pyre (Ed. Stein 5,225 f.). After the death of Kandarpasiṁha his widow Bimbā enters fire as Satī (7,103). In another case the widowed queen throws herself on the pile of wood from her carriage, and with her three servants and two concubines (*dāsī*) follow the king in death (7,478-481). The 5. Ucchvāsa

Satī in the Harṣacarita.

of the Harṣacarita describes in details how even before the death of the king Prabhākaravardhana his consort Yaśomatī along with other queens prepares to follow him in death as Satī and cannot be swayed from her determination even by the pursuations of her son Harṣa. After the cremation of the royal couple also several faithful friends, servants and ministers of the deceased king accept death by hurling themselves from a high rock. Also in Bāṇa's Kādambarī (169) Mahāśvetā has a pile of wood raised for herself in order to follow her deceased beloved. The Satī is also frequently mentioned in the proper sources of history—the inscriptions. Probably the oldest example known till now of a pillar raised to the memory of the burning of a widow is of the year 509-510 A.D.[2], that is, older than the Satī described in the Harṣacarita by about

1. In the days of Megasthenes however Satī was a common practice. See Mc. Crindle, Megasthenes. *Tr.*

2. CII 3, 92.

a century. The Satī of a queen of Nepal is mentioned in a Nepalese inscription of the year 705[1].

Satī mentioned by Greek writers.

Of the accounts of the classical authors those of Strabon and Diodorus Siculus are most important[2]. The combat between the two widows of the Indian army officer Keteus for the honour of being allowed to burn herself with his body reminds us of the above mentioned row in the Mah. Alberuni (2,155 f.) says that the Indian widow has only the choice between death and self-immolation but prefers the latter alternative on account of the evil treatment they receive; the widows of kings are always burnt even against their will. We have graphic descriptions of later instances of widow-burning till its abolition by Lord Bentinck in the year 1829, e. g. the clear description of the self-immolation of his aunt by I. C. Bose, The Hindoos as they are 273-277. Outside the British dominion this custom continued for some time longer. Thus in 1839 many widows were burnt with the famous Ranjit Singh. In Nepal even in 1877 at the death of the Maharaja Jang Bahadur his widow became Satī. If the entire development of this custom is examined, the later and conditional sanction of the Satī in the Sanskrit literature, the fact that it was chiefly practised only among the princes and the Rajput chiefs—even now in Amber in Rajputana the place where the widows of the princes used to be burnt is pointed out—the sacrifice of the favourite servant along with the favourite wives,—all this seems to show that as among other nations here too the widow-burning was originally practised only by the royal families and was spread only gradually among the mass and was at last received into the official law of the Brahmans.

Satī in modern times.

Widow-burning was practised only among the royal families.

If the widow preferred to live her life was in no way

1. IA 9, 164; cf. 14, 344, 350.
2. Cf. M. Williams l. c. 258.

The life of the widow.

enviable. Even the grass-widow *(proṣitabhartṛkā)* whose husband has gone abroad cannot wear ornaments, cannot show herself at the window, can use no ointment or any other beautifier, cannot loosen her tresses, can enjoy no sweet things, cannot go to anybody else's house or to any festivity, etc. The real widow *(mṛtabhartṛkā)* has to be even more austere. She should eat only once in a day, should not sleep in a bed, should use no scents, daily offer sacrifices to her husband and observe vows and fasts ; she should go on pilgrimage to sacred places and should never pronounce the name of any other man than her husband. If she has grown-up sons she lives under their protection. If not, she comes under the protection of the near or the distant relations of her husband who have absolute authority over her. Only if there is absolutely no male relations of the husband's family should she come back to her father's house and eventually even come under the protection of the king (Nār. 13, 28—31). Of course Nār., who lays down this principle also says (1, 36 f.) that after the death of the father the guardianship of the sons devolves on the mother and Śaṅkha or Śaṅkhalikhita remarks that even after the death of the father the dependence of the children continues so long as the mother is alive ; yet according to the commentaries these rules apply only to that case when the widow is capable of managing the family property ; cf. also § 23 f.

The widow is the guardian of her children.

The widow forfeits her claim to maintenance and the right of inheritance allowed to her in the later texts as soon as she violates her faith to her deceased husband. She is then a "wanton woman" (*svairiṇī*) and even if under the pressure of extreme poverty she surrenders herself to a strangor (Nār. 12,51), she will be excommunicated from the caste if she does not perform one of the prescribed penances and her touch pollutes

The unchaste widow forfeits all her claims

everybody who comes near her (Par. 10,26-35). The son of a Brahman widow (*golaka*, *raṇḍagolaka* in the modern caste lists)[1] belongs to the most hated castes who cannot be invited to a Śrāddha (M. 3, 156, 174).

The life of the modern widow.

Even to this day the harsh treatment of the widow and the widowed bride calls for sympathy. She has to lay down all the ornaments she has worn hitherto, observe complete fast on each *ekādaśī*, that is, twice a month and eat but once a day ; she eats no fish nor any food prepared outside the house, the hair of the head is often smoothly shaved, she has to wear only plain clothes and if rich she has to go on pilgrimage to Benares and other sacred places, etc. Remarriage or entering into a love affair, to say the least, is as much resented as it was before and the reform movement started by Iśvaracandra Vidyāsāgara in favour of widow remarriage has had till now but little success. Yet however the English legislature has given a general sanction to the remarriage of widows and in connection with the law of property it has been taken as a maxim that the property which has once devolved upon a widow cannot again be taken away from her on account of subsequent unchastity.

The levirate and the Kṣetraja son.

Inspite of the stern prohibition of widow marriage the older Smṛtis recommend the levirate in case the widow has no son by her legal husband and therefore receives from the Gurus, particularly from the relations under whose protection she lives, the appointment (*niyoga*) to raise a son through a surviving brother of her deceased husband or, on failure of such a brother, through a near or distant blood-relation of him or eventually through a member of the same *gotra* or at least through a Brāhmaṇa. This son is called Kṣetraja and is regarded as the son of the deceased and after attaining majority he inherits his

1. Steele, Castes 91 ; J. Wilson, Caste 1, 65.

property which is managed till then by his natural father or by his mother (M. 9, 146, 190; Vas. 17, 65). The Kṣetraja may under certain circumstances be heir also to his natural father as "son of two fathers" (Gaut. 18, 13; Y. 2, 127; Vas. 17, 64 etc.; see below).

Various conditions of the levirate.

As the express purpose of this levirate is to assure the safe continuation of the family, in order to prevent thereby the cessation of the sacrifices to the manes and the loss of property, it is quite understandable that the living husband too, who on account of impotence or illness does not any longer hope for progeny, can himself demand levirate. Even the remarriage of the wife of a man who has gone abroad and is considered to have disappeared for ever (as discussed in §18) is taken to be a case of Niyoga by some authors (Gaut. 18, 15—17; Vas. 17, 75—80). On the other hand the view that more than one son may be raised through levirate (Gaut. 18, 8) is condemned by most teachers (M. 9, 61 etc.) and the permission for Niyoga is generally subjected to the fulfilment of a series of strict conditions; for instance, the intercourse between the appointed (*niyukta*) pair shall be discontinued as soon as the woman feels herself to be pregnant or should take place only once, sensuality should have no share in it, legacy-hunting must not be the underlying motive, certain formalities should have to be observed, etc.

Levirate condemned by various law-givers.

These conditions which can hardly be fulfilled at once betray the tendency to render this *niyoga* difficult in every way or to prohibit it altogether as it is quite irreconcilable with the other principles of Brahmanism. It is often openly expressed. Thus Nār., who in 12, 81 lays down very difficult conditions, brands the *niyuktā* with the hated designation *punarbhū* if on failure of a brother-in-law she is given away to a distant relative (12, 48). Hār. 4, 17 allows only the eighteenth (according to the reading of the Ms., the nineteenth) part of the inheritance to a son born of such connections. Āp. 2, 27, 2 ff. declares the levirate no longer admissible on account of the degeneration of the people of the present day and in 2, 13, 6 ff. he points out that the son belongs to the begetter and that the sins which men of antiquity could commit with impunity on account of the greatness of their lustre (*tejoviśeṣeṇa*) are strictly forbidden among the mortal men of to-day; Āp. therefore leaves the secondary sons unmentioned. Already Aupajandhani, an old teacher of the White Yajurveda (Baudh. 2, 3, 33 ff.) had expressed his disapproval of the levirate and the secondary sons. M. 9, 64—70 condemns Niyoga, immediately after recommending it, as a beastly custom (*paśudharma*) which was in vogue only in the reign of King Veṇa and allows it only in the particular case of a betrothed bride whose fiancé died before the marriage. Bṛh. 24, 12 point out this contradiction in M. and explains it by saying that in the present age the sin of Niyoga is no longer permissible.

Niyoga is also reckoned among the usages prohibited in the Kali age and therefore in the Smṛtis it appears to be a custom already falling into disuetude which however was handed down from the Vedic age and therefore had at least to be mentioned. Bṛh. 2, 31 remarks that the Khaśas form matrimonial alliances with the widows of deceased brothers. A kind of Niyoga is mentioned already in the ṚV 10, 40. 2 and this passage was well-known to the commentators.[1] The epic tradition too knows of Niyoga and in the Mah. it is as well theoretically prescribed as it is practically exemplified by the heroes of the poem; yet however in the Niyogas of the epic—

Niyoga declared obsolete.

Niyoga mentioned in ṚV, Mah. and Śrauta-sūtras.

1. Cf. Medh. on M. 9, 66.

of course this form is also known to the Smṛtis—a Brahman and not the brother-in-law receives the appointment, which may also be explained as the result of the modification of the text by the Brahmans from interested motives.[1] Even in the Śrautasūtras a kind of Kṣetraja—the *dvyāmuṣyāyaṇa* or *dvipitṛ*—is often mentioned; he is regarded as the son also of his natural father and the Dvyāmuṣyāyaṇa is mentioned also in the Smṛtis.[2] At the present day, if not Niyoga, at least marriage with the widow of a deceased brother is of common occurrence. Probably it is most popular in the Punjab where so much of what is ancient has been preserved; there it is called *Karewa* and very often causes a man to have two wives at the same time[3].

The theory of sonship, the most striking feature of Hindu family law.

§ 21. *Sonship and adoption.* The twelve kinds of sonship[4], which to some extent are based on the illicit connections of the mother and for the greater part have nothing to do with the blood-relationship of the son with the father, are probably the most striking feature of Indian family-law. The cause of this abnormal importance being attached to male issue is to be sought, according to the Smṛtis, in the offering of sacrifices to the manes which depends upon the male issue; yet however originally an economic motive was perhaps a more important factor in it—to get for the family as many powerful workers as possible. The children belong to

1. Cf. Hopkins 367 f.; Holtzmann 28—30.

2. Caland, Altind. Ahnencult 197.

3. Census of India, 1891, 19, 222 f. There is a kind of *niyoga* in Spiti; there Buddhist monks raise a son and heir for a deceased brother without male issue (Tupper 2, 189 f., cf. Kohler ZVR 7, 209); but it is probably a Tibetan custom.

4. Baudh. 2, 3, 11—35; Gaut. 28, 18 f., 32—34, 39; Vas. 17, 1—39; Vi. 15, 1—30; M. 9,127—147, 158—181; Y. 2, 127—132; Nār. 13, 45—49; Bṛh. 24, 12—14; 25, 33—45; Dev., Yama, Hār., Śaṅkhalikhita, Kālikā and Brahmapurāṇas (according to quotations). Cf. Mayne

the husband—the owner of the wife—even though he is not their father (M. 9, 48—56), and over and above this through adoption he can take into his patria potestas other children out of that of another person. Yet even from the very beginning in the Smṛtis and in the Purāṇas such secondary sons (*putrasthānīya, gauṇaputra*) have been regarded as not equal with the legitimate sons (*aurasa*) and therefore a heirarchy of at least 12 sons has been made among whom each preceding member gets the preference over the succeeding ones in inheritance. The Aurasa is always at the top of the list while the order and nomenclature of the others vary according to particular individual opinions and school traditions. A list of 12 sons differing a good deal from the ordinary list is found in Mah. 1, 120, 32 ff., an enumeration of 5 sons in Mah. 1, 74, 99 and another of 3 sons is found in Buddhistic works.

The hierarchy of 12 sons.

In the Smṛtis generally immediately after the Aurasa we find "the son of the wife" (*kṣetraja*) i. e. the son raised upon her by the husband's brother etc. through Niyoga (§ 20). Five lists mention the "son of the daughter" (*putrikāputra*) in the third place; yet in M. 9, 127—140 he has been placed on an equal footing with the legitimate son and other authors place him at least above the Kṣetraja though Gaut. however recognises him only as the tenth in the order of sons. He is also mentioned in the Mah. 13, 44, 15 and seems to occur already in the ṚV 1, 124, 7 according to the old interpretation which however is extremely doubtful. As on the occasion of Niyoga here too a ceremonius

The Kṣetraja and the Putrikāputra.

§§ 63 ff. (with tables of the 12 sons according to the above mentioned 14 authors); Mayr, D. ind. Erbr. 86—128; Tag. Lect. 144—166; Kohler, ZVR 3, 393 ff.; West and Bühler, 3rd. ed., 872—899; Leist, Altar. Jus gentium 103—111.

endorsement taken place by which, there being no male issue, the daughter is given away to the bridegroom on the condition that his future son should be regarded as the son of his maternal grandfather. According to another opinion such a declaration was unnecessary and the daughter was to be regarded as the heiress if the father only wished it, or in general if she had no brother with evidently better claim to the property according to the general principles of the Indian law of inheritance. For this reason

Yāska refers to the Putrikāputra.

already in the Nirukta 3, 5 the warning is given against marrying a girl who has no brothers, because the son born of such a marriage would belong not to his father but to his maternal grandfather. This right of the grandfather over his grandson could be bought over from him by the bridegroom, but this view is met with only in the commentaries [1]. The heiress daughter may herself be regarded as a son, specially according to Vas. 17, 15 and she occupies a high position in the hierarchy of sons[2].

About the different varieties of the "son of the remarried widow": (*paunarbhava*) see § 15. Out of

The various sons born of mother's adulterous intercourse.

the criminal intercourse of the woman before and after her marriage are born the "son of the virgin" (*kānīna*) corresponding to the Vedic Kumārīputra belonging partly to the maternal grandfather and partly to the later husband of his mother, the Sahoḍha i. e. a son with whom the mother was pregnant even at the time of her marriage, be her pregnancy known or not, and the "secret born son" (*gūḍhaja*, *gūḍhotpanna*), i.e. the son born of wife's adulterous intercourse, but who has seen the light in the house of her husband. The Sahoḍha

1. Cf. Stenzler and Oldenberg on Pār. 1, 8, 18 and Śāṅkh. 1, 14, 16. With Oldenberg I am of opinion that the commentators have wrongly given this interpretation to the Gṛhyasūtras and that *duhitṛmate* simply signifies the father of the bride as Bühler too has translated it in the parallel passage Āp. 2, 13, 12.

2. Cf. Tag. Lect. 147—149.

and the Gūḍhaja are regarded as sons of the husband according to the principle pater est quem nuptial demonstrant (he is the father whom the marriage proves to be so). The Sahoḍha is the lowest of these three sons and is usually given the eighth or a still lower place, probably because marriage with a pregnant woman was considered shameful. The Kānīna often occupies the fourth place and is mostly given preference to the Gūḍhaja who is disgraced with the stain of adultery.

The different kinds of adopted sons.

The adoptive sons are : the "given" son (*datta*, *dattaka*), who is given away by his parents in adoption, the "made" or "artificial" son (*kṛta*, *kṛtrima*), who is adopted when already grown up ; the son who lets himself be adopted of his own free will (*svayaṁdatta*) ; the "expelled" son (*apaviddha*) who is expelled or turned out by his parents without any ground and is adopted as son by another and lastly the "purchased" son (*krīta*) whom his own parents sell to his adoptive parents. In most of the lists the adoptive sons are—certainly because they have blood-relationship with none of the two parents—placed below the sons mentioned above ; so many as four authors assign to the Svayaṁdatta the last place among the twelve sons just :as among the 15 kinds of slaves, those who sell themselves are estimated lowest (Nār. 5, 37). Also the place of the Kṛtrima, Apaviddha or the Krīta is often the last or the last but one.

The son by a Śūdra.

The son by a Śūdra wife or a Sūdra concubine is mostly given the lowest place, as also in the Mah., if he is not altogether ignored, in conformity with the ruling principle of the objectionable character of such connections, cf. § 18.

Already Āp. not only passes over the 12 sons, excepting of course the legitimate son, in silence but also expressly opposes the giving away (for adoption) and selling of a son when he condemns Niyoga (2, 13, 11 ; 2,

The subsidiary sons condemned even from very early times.

27, 2 ff.), which met with opposition already at quite an early period, cf. § 20. The superiority of the son born within the wedlock to all other sons, which is accepted by all the authors generally, led Aupajandhani even so far as to recognise only the Aurasa as the legitimate son and heir (Baudh. 2, 3, 33).

The sons divided into two groups.

In most of the enumerations of the 12 sons (also in the Mah.) they are divided into two groups of six each and only the first six are recognised as heirs and the latter six only as relations but not as heirs to their legal father—a distinction which has been taken over into the Burmese law along with the institution of the 12 sons. The latter group of six sons reminds us of the modern institution of the Dharmaputra, who as the "duty son" or the representative of a son has only to offer sacrifices to the manes and formerly had to set fire to the pyre of a Satī if there was no son and heir to do it [1]. The hard rule that the superior son should always dispossess the inferior son and that the latter has only a subsidiary right of inheritance is of course often avoided but in comparison with the Aurasa the inferior sons get a miserable portion of the legacy, almost next to nothing—only 1/21 part of it, or is only allowed mere subsistence. Bṛh., who in 25, 33-41 admits only the Aurasa and the Putrikā or her son to be legitimate sons and of course recognises faultless adoptive sons and those of a Śūdra wife as sons of middling quality, goes much further and condemns the Kṣetraja and other sons of the wife and in 24, 14 declares all the 13 subsidiary sons to be no longer in vogue. Otherwise all the sons excepting the Aurasa and the Dattaka are usually said to be "forbidden in the present day" (Kalivarjya) and this is also point of view of the later jurists, only besides the Dattaka sometimes all the other adoptive sons and frequently

Only the Aurasa and the Dattaka recognised in the later days.

1. Steele, Castes 185, 226. Cf. West and Bühler, 3rd. ed., 891 f

at least the Kṛtrima, are recognised. It is to be considered a relic of the high position of the Putrikāputra, that where there are no agnate descendants, the son of the daughter is given preference to all other relations in the law of inheritance [1]. At the present day, at least among the higher castes, only adoption is still in evidence; yet Bühler (on Vas. 17, 15) has pointed out an interesting survival of the old custom in Kashmir in which the Putrikā is appointed son and heir and on this occasion her name too takes the masculine form.

Growing importance of the institution of adoption.

The more the other kinds of sonship fell into disuetude through the advance of morality and the increasing prevalence of child marriage, so that they came to be regarded merely as an odious privilege of the Ṛṣis of yore, out of vogue in the present day, the more was the theory of adoption improved and was at last developed into one of the most important institutions of Indian law. The *datio in adoptionem* (giving away in adoption) of a Dattaka is a ceremony in which the parents or the father alone or the mother with the permission of the father give away their son before witnesses to the adoptive parents so that he leaves his own family for ever to enter the family of his adoptive parents. The giving away of the son by his own parents is based on their right of disposition over the son by force of which they can give him away, sell him or turn him out of the house; in this connection the Smṛtis refer to the well-known legend of Śunaḥśepa in the Ait. Br. whom his father Ajīgarta sold to King Hariścandra under pinch of poverty and who was afterwards adopted by Viśvāmitra (Vas. 17, 31ff). According to this legend which was regarded as the Vedic precedent of an adoption [2], the expression *āpadi* in M. 9,

A Vedic precedent.

1. Cf. Mayne § 477.
2. Cf. also Nirukta 3, 4.

168 should be taken to mean the need or poverty of the original parents and not, as some commentators have explained it, the need of the adoptive parents owing to their lack a son. The only son of the original parents should in no way be given away because he is indispensable for the continuation of the family ; on similar grounds sometimes the giving away of the eldest son is forbidden. The rule that the adoption must take place in early childhood before the sacred ceremonies, viz. shearing of hair of the adoptandus (*cūḍā*) and his initiation *(upanayana)*, are performed or when he is not more than five years of age, is based in fact only on a text of the Kālikāpurāṇa the authenticity of which has been questioned by various commentators; yet however it corresponds to the nature of Dattaka-adoption in contradistinction to the adoption of a grown-up boy in the Kṛtrima form (arrogatio). The sacred ceremonies of the boy must take place in the family of the adoptive parents so that he may be fully assimilated to it in conformity with the principle that the adoptandus is the shadow of a real son (*adoptio imitatur naturam*=adoption imitates nature). The adoptive son therefore must be of the same status and caste as those of the adoptive father ; the nearest blood relations should in particular be chosen for this purpose and according to the commentaries first of all the brother's son and eventually a distant agnate relative should be selected, but never the son of the daughter or of the sister. Of the adoptive parents the mother alone has the right of adoption only if the father gives permission and a further precondition for it is that no son of theirs should be living at the time of the adoption.

The only or the eldest son cannot be given away in adoption.

The adoptandus must be of the same caste as that of the adoptive father.

At the time of adoption the relatives should be invited and the king too should be informed. As in the case of every gift, a libation of water (M. 9,168)

The ceremonies of adoption.

and a Dattahoma in particular must be offered. The adoptive father begs for the son and the original father gives him away to him. Then the former dresses his would-be son in two clothes and decorates him with two earrings and a finger ring. There are other ceremonies too. If at a later period the adoptive parents come to have a son born in the wedlock the adopted son gets only a fourth part of that son's share. On the contrary his prospects may brighten up very much if the other sons of his original father die and thus the legacy of the latter reverts to him. Then he is regarded as the "son of two fathers" *(dvyāmuṣyāyaṇa)*—a conception which was originally connected only with Niyoga (§20) but already Kātyāyana expressly extended it also to adoption.

Prospects of the adopted son.

The later jurists have developed a vast law of adoption out of the simple but somewhat vague rules of the Smṛtis [1] and there is a mass of monographs on it—Dattakacandrikā, Dattakadarpaṇa, Dattakadīdhiti, Dattakamīmāṁsā, Dattakakalpalatā, Dattakaumudī, Siddhāntamañjari, Dattārka etc. Dattakacandrikā and Dattakamīmāṁsā of these works have been translated and these translations along with the occasional remarks on adoption in works on the law of inheritance such as the Mit. and the Dāyabhāga are the principal works on which the verdicts given at the English courts and the English text-books on adoption are based. With reference to the latter, particularly to the very exhaustive and instructive treatise of Sir R. West[2], I should like only to remark that many of the hazardous theories which the court practice

Later works on adoption.

1. Cf. Vas. 15, 1—10. Baudh. Par. (SBE 14, 334—336); Bühler JBAS 35 ; Baudh., Gaut. etc. l. c. May. ed. Mandlik 39—46 etc.

2. West and Bühler, 3rd. ed., 859—1237.

Erroneous views in the modern law of adoption.

is now laboriously and gradually trying to strip off, would never have originated if from the beginning also other works had been consulted than those mentioned above. This may be said e. g. of the theory that the ceremonies accompanying a legal adoption mentioned in the Smṛtis are quite indispensable and that it is generally inadmissible to adopt grown-up or nearly grown-up persons or the son of the daughter or of the sister and in general of such a person whose mother the adoptive father could have married and also the theory that any particular stipulation between the parents of both sides is inadmissible in the case of a Dvyāmuṣyāyaṇa adoption, etc[1]. Modern customary law too, about which a few notices will follow, shows that these rules of the Smṛtis are to be taken more as advices than as laws.

Adoption common in modern India.

At the present day adoption is extraordinarily in vogue, specially among the higher castes who are still ruled by the old belief in the necessity of a son for offering sacrifices to the manes, and also among the lower castes who take the higher castes to be their ideal. A father who has no children certainly often postpones the adoption till it is too late, be it that he is afraid of the costs of the ceremonies of adoption and the maintenance of the adoptive son, or that he always hopes for an heir of his own, or that, if rich, he fears to come into close intimacy with the family of the adoptive son or to run the risk of having an ungrateful person in his adopted son who may not be attached to him and may even try to take his life[2]. Thus it comes to pass very often that only after the death of the husband his widow adopts, of course in his name, and it is a disputed point whether a command of the husband given before his death for this act is necessary and whether the widow has eventually to depend upon

Adoption by the widow.

1. Tag. Lect. 159—166.
2. Cf. West and Bühler, 3rd. ed., 901 f.

the permission of the relations; as a rule at least the permission of the relations is necessary particularly in the case of the succession of great landlords and princes[1]. Even most of the commentators have developed out of the Smṛtis the principle, of course in conformity with the spirit of these Smṛtis, that the widow too can adopt, but there is difference of opinion among them as to whether she can do it even without the order of the deceased husband; the Mayūkha[2], for example, represents this view.

Adoption in the customary law of the present day.

In the customary law too the lack of one's own son and heir is regarded as the necessary precondition for adoption and it is also held that the adoptandus should belong to the same caste and even to the same Gotra and moreover nearest agnates are preferred but the adoption of the daughter's son or even the sister's son is not forbidden[3]. As regards the ceremonies of adoption the Śāstrins of Bombay hold that the ceremonies prescribed in the Smṛtis are indispensable, specially the Dattahoma, at least among the Brahmans, while in Madras only the giving away and the adoption of the adoptandus is demanded;[4] in the Punjab even the fact of the adoption of the adoptandus into the family of the adoptive father has sometimes to be proved[5]. That the adoptandus even without any special condition, retains his right of inheritance in his original family a as Dvyāmuṣāyaṇa is often found at least in Bombay, N. W. Provinces and the Punjab[6]. Thus far it is an *adoptio minus plena*

Ceremonies of adoption at the present day.

1. l. c.; Tupper, 2, 154, 178 f., 3, 90 f.; Steele l. c. 176, 187, 391 ff.; 420 ff. Cf. Kohler ZVR 7, 221; 8, 111.

2. See Mayne §99 for the highly important local variations of modern Court practice.

3. Cf. Kohler l. c. 7, 218 ff., 8, 109 ff.

4. West and Bühler, 3rd. ed., 1084.

5. Kohler l. c. 7, 222 (according to Tupper).

6. West and Bühler, 3rd. ed., 898; Tag. Lect. 166; Kohler l. c. 223 (acc. to Tupper).

(partial adoption) as in the case of the Kṛtrima son of the Smṛtis who is of course mentioned only by a section of the ancient authors and is mostly declared as no longer in vogue by the later jurists, but in Mithilā (Tirhut, the home of Y. who in 2, 131 defines the Kṛtrima to be a son adopted by somebody on his own accouut—according to the Mit. an orphan is meant by this term whom the adoptive father induces to let himself be adopted by holding out to him prospects of pecuniary advantage) the Kṛtrima is still officially recognised. There this kind of adoption takes place in this way: the adoptandus has himself adopted into another family as a son entitled to inheritance simply by declaring his wish to do so and at the same time retains his rights in his own family; thus everybody, without distinction of age or family, may be adopted in this formless manner only if he is a member of the same caste[1].

The Kṛtrima son of Mithilā.

There are lingering traces even of the purchased son (Krīta) mentioned in the Smṛtis. Thus adoption by purchase is found in Guzerat; it is the only kind of adoption among several castes of Madras and in the well-known sect of Gosāvīs who cannot marry, children are very often purchased and are regarded as sons in the spiritual sense[2]. In the customary law we may still find traces of the pratice of legitimatising the sons of the wife born without the wedlock, such as the Kānīna, Sahoḍha, Gūḍhaja sons, as for instance in the Punjab[3]. For the law of the illegitimate sons of Śūdra husbands, i. e. the lower castes, see §24.

The "purchased" son of the persent age.

§ 22. *The joint-family.* The basis of the Indian joint-family is that the different members of it should dwell in the same house, take their meals and perform

The external signs of a joint-family.

1. Mayne §§ 81—87.
2. West and Bühler, 3rd. ed., 1143 f.
3. Tupper 2, 185, 203. Cf. Kohler ZVR 7, 209.

the divine service at the same time and enjoy their property in common.[1] The joint preparation of food and eating at the same table are the external signs of homogeniety in the family as well as in the far wider organisations of castes *(jāti)*, and the members of the family are therefore directly called the community of *ekapākena vasatām* i. e. "those who cook in common" (Bṛh. 25, 6). It is quite understandable that the Smṛtis should attach great importance to the "cult of manes, Gods and Brahmans" and therefore recommend the division of property, because in that case the cult which was formerly observed jointly would be separately performed in each household (l. c.; cf. M. 9, 111).

Community of property.

The community of property is absolute and according to Nār. 13, 38 it includes also cattle and rice as well as houses, lands and slaves and even acts of giving and taking, incomes and expenses should have to be done by common consent. Āp. and Baudh. do not even differentiate acquisition from inheritance. Vas. 17, 51 speaks of the self-acquired property of which a double share should belong to the earner. According to Vi. 17, 1 and Y. 2, 114 the father can divide among his sons in any manner he chooses what he has earned himself.

Individual property in the joint-family.

Usually the earnings through learning (among the Brahmans) are specially mentioned as indivisible—that is to say, the remuneration for teaching a pupil, for the recital of Vedic texts, performance of sacrifices etc., and further, the booties of war (among the Kṣatriyas), presents from relatives, the dowry and the property of a wife, lost properties recovered by a particular member of the family etc. are declared to be indivisible ; yet however, every earning, if it is made with the help of the family property, is to be deposited in the common coffer; thus, for example, if a warrior uses a horse or a weapon of the joint-

1. Cf. Tag. Lect. 104—106, 141 f.

family, or if a Brahman student leaves his family in the care of his brother who is not a learned man during his stay with a teacher in some foreign land (Vyāsa; Nār. 13, 10)—whatever is earned in that way becomes the property of the joint-family.

The compass of the joint-family.

The compass of the joint-family was and is frequently very considerable. Not only parents and children, brothers and step-brothers, live on the common property, but it may sometimes include ascendants, descendants and collaterals up to many generations. On account of the custom of child-marriage the paterfamilias may become a grandfather even in the prime of life and often lives even to be a great-grandfather. Originally the circle of Sapiṇḍa-relations, connected with one another through the sacrifices to the manes, extended from the great-grandfather to the great-grandson in the ascending and the descending orders [1]. The great-great-grandson does not belong to it (Baudh. 1, 11, 9), and thus in the opinion of Devala and others the right of inheritance among relations (*kulya*) living together extends to the fourth generation, but by others the limits are still more widened or are, in part, narrowed too.

The family increases during the life-time of the paterfamilias.

The patriarch who was at the head of the family, could not, as a rule, be compelled to divide the property and so until his death the number of the members of the family living with him on the common property would be steadily increasing, particularly as every male descendant brought home a daughter-in-law even in his tender years, the daughters even after marriage remained in the paternal house till they were 13 years of age and over and above the legitimate sons there were adoptive and illegitimate sons of every kind and besides the legitimate wives there were also the concubines.

---

1. l. c. 169 f.

Afterwards the eldest or the fittest son becomes the head of the family.

If the paterfamilias died without previously accomplishing the partition, his place was taken by his eldest son who was either simply regarded as the the heir or was at least considered to be the director of the household and had to look after his brothers and relations as a father (Gaut. 28, 3 ; Āp. 2, 14, 6 ; M. 9, 105—110 ; Nār. 13, 5 ; Mah. 13, 105, 17 etc.). According to another and perhaps later view the eldest son merits this distinction only if he is fit for it and also a younger or even the youngest brother may be the chief of the whole family if he is capable because, the fortune of a family depends on capacity (Baudh. 2, 3, 13 ; Nār. 13, 5). Of course, disputes might easily arise among the brothers over the inheritance and they may go to the length of a partition (§23); yet even after complete partition a re-union of the coparceners may take place who are then called Saṁsṛṣṭins. The inter-relation between the Saṁsṛṣṭins is the same as that between unpartitioned coparceners (Bṛh. 25, 72—77) only there is no right of primogeniture among them. The rule of Bṛh. that such re-union is allowed with the father, brother, or the father's brother, may be interpreted, with a section of the commentators, to mean that these near relatives have been mentioned only as typical examples and that a re-union may include all the members who originally belonged to the family in its entirety, perhaps even such coparceners who did not originally belong to it, cf. § 25.

Partition and reunion of partitioned coparceners.

Absolute authority of the father of the family

The position of individual family-members inside the joint-family was varied according to age, sex and achievements. According to Nār. 1, 32—42, the head of the family rules over his family as a king rules his subjects and a teacher his pupils. His wives and servants are to obey him implicitly and even his sons continue to be dependent on him so long as he is alive even when they have attained majority with the sixteenth year. The father of the family alone can conclude valid legal business and represent the family elsewhere. Whatever a minor or unindependent member of the family does is no better than if it had not taken place at all. Of course, the father's power of acting ceases if there is doubt as to his sanity of mind and according to Hār. 4, 3 the eldest son may take over the management of the property in his place if he is decrepit, (another reading, wasteful), absent or ill. See §19 about the rights of the family-head as the lord of marriage. He can do whatever he likes with his sons—give them away, sell them or turn them out (Vas. 15, 2); yet the selling of children is forbidden already by Āp. 2, 13, 11 and the turning out of a son, excepting when he commits a serious crime, was rendered punishable (Vi. 5, 163; M. 8, 389; Y. 2, 237). The earnings of the sons generally belong to the father—they are in this respect on the same footing with the slaves and the wives (Nār. 5, 14). The supposed exposure of daughters in the Vedic literature is based on an erroneous interpretation of the expression *parāsyanti* as proved by Böhtlingk (ZDMG 44, 494—496).[1] The Smṛtis only say that the father should marry off his daughters as early as possible[2]. He has to support the daughters-in-law even if they are widows (Nār. 13, 28); he can however demand from them in exchange absolute devotion so that a present made to a daughter-in-law in recognition of her devotion was called is called Pādavandanika Strīdhana (Kāty.). In the teachings about venerable personages (Guru) the father mostly stands first; he is the Guru *par excellence* and therefore he is entitled to the

The sons are his slaves.

Prostrate devotion of the daughters-in-law.

1. Yet the exposure of Jīvaka who lived to be the personal physician of Buddha (see Mahāvagga VIII, 1, 4) proves that exposure of children was not unknown in ancient India. Also Kauṭ. XIII, 5 refers to this practice. *Tr.*

2. Cf. § 17.

first place in salutation ; along with the mother he tops the list of those relations who should be saluted not only by greeting but also by touching the feet (Gaut. 6, 1ff.).[1]

The high position of the matron.

As in the regulations about greetings so in other cases too the mother or the matron (*gṛhiṇī*), is frequently placed at the side of the father. In the enumerations of Gurus in the Smṛtis she is to some extent placed even above the father (M. 2, 145 etc.), and the Mah. 13, 105, 15 too gives the highest place to the mother among the Gurus. The real as well as the adoptive mother takes part in the adoption (§ 20). The calumniations in which insulting words are said of the mother is punished more severely than those about the sister or the daughter (Vi. 5, 33 f.). In the law of inheritance, according to M. 9, 217, when male descendants are wanting, the mother or even the paternal grandmother of the testator is to inherit the property and according to M. 9, 190 (otherwise in 9, 146), the widow has to manage the paternal property for the son raised through Niyoga and later if male descendants are lacking she is considered to be the heiress to her husband ; for details about the position of the widow see §§ 20, 23 f.

The position and duties of the mother and the wife.

The privileges of motherhood are certainly as a rule valid only for mothers of sons ; a wife who gives birth only to daughters as well as a barren wife may be replaced (M. 9, 81). Also the general opinion about the inferiority and the evil propensities of the female sex is to be taken into consideration, according to which the woman can never live excepting under guardianship ; in her old age she should remain under the protection of her sons, when a girl she is protected by her father, and when a wife, by her husband (M. 9, 2-18; Y. 1, 85 ; Nār. 13, 31 etc). A gradual independence

1. Cf. Delbrück, D. indog. Verwandtschaftsnamen 556 ff.

of the woman in the field of the partition of property is perceptible in the development of the Strīdhana (§ 25). Hār. 3, 3 gives a graphic description of the duties of a woman. She should concentrate all her thoughts on her household and her husband, carefully prepare the food, eat what remains after her husband and her sons have taken their meals, wash the cooking utensils, besmear the earth with cowdung (it is done even to this day), offer sacrifices to the gods, and before going to sleep respectfully embrace the feet of her husband ; she should serve him, fan him in the hot season, support his head when he is tired, etc. In her home circle the matron rules absolute specially over her daughters and daughters-in-law, the principle of seniority, the ***yathāpūrvam***, is expressly extended also over the female members of the family (Gaut. 6, 3 ff. ; Āp. 1, 14, 9 ; Mah. 13, 105, 19 etc.)

The eldest son is the natural heir.

According to this maxim of the privilege of age the eldest son can, as already referred to, be the chief of the whole family in the case of the death of the father or his permanent disability. As the eldest son or brother holds a high place in the rules about salutation[1] and can marry before his younger brothers (§ 18),[2] cannot be given away in adoption (§ 21), receives an extra share at the time of partition (§ 23) and can alone offer the Śrāddha and other sacrifices of the family[3] etc., he is considered to be the natural family-head after the death of the father. According to M. 9, 213 and Mah. 13, 105, 7 he forfeits his right of primogeniture if he cheats his younger brothers and according to M. 9,214= Mah. l.c. 10 the eldest brother can appropriate to himself nothing of the common family property without compen-

He forfeits his privileges if dishonest.

1. l.c. 560 ff.
2. Cf. l.c. 578 ff.
3. Gaut. 5,7. Cf. Tag. Lect. 109.

sating for it to his brothers. According to Nārāyaṇa this rule is applicable to every member of the family who may manage the property of the joint-family.

Privileges of the manager of the family property.

In this connection let it be mentioned, though it has been already referred to, that a younger brother or a collateral becomes the head of the family if he is particularly fit to be so, but according to Śaṅkhalikhita he can be so only with the consent of the eldest brother. Such a property manager, whoever he may be, is rewarded by his brothers for his labour and receives presents (Nār. 13,35). He may claim however no further privileges and along with the other members of the family he too has to bear the burdens of inheritance such as the maintenance of the widows and the daughters of deceased brothers, marriage of the daughters, initiation of minor brothers, payment of the debts of the father etc. (Nār. 13,26 f., 31 f. etc.). Also the members of the family rendered ineligible to inheritance by illness or corporeal defects etc., are a burden of the inheritance (§ 23), while on the contrary if a brother though able to work does not work for indolence, he may be compelled to separate from the joint-family with a small compensation.[1] The sons had more difficulty with a father who badly managed the family property and therefore it was in the interest of the family principle not to maintain the *patria potestas* in all its rigours but also to afford the sons a direct right of protest and a claim to property. Thus the principle was developed that the father and the sons have equal right of disposition on the property inherited from the grandfather (Vi. 17, 2 ; Y. 2, 121 etc.). According to the later texts even the immovables and the slaves acquired by the father himself cannot be sold without consulting all the sons about it and usually when giving away or selling a family

Burdens of inheritance.

Gradual increase of power of the junior members.

1. M. 9,207 ; Y. 2,116 ; cf. l. c. 97 f.

property the consent of all the members of the family is needed[1].

The menials formed a part of the Indian family as in the case of the family of Roman law and they were without doubt, very numerous as at the present day. Nār. 5, 2—43 distinguishes between labourers *(karmakara)* and slaves *(dāsa)*;[2] the Kauṭumbika who occupies the confidential post of a manager or the major domo belongs to the former category; the slaves are of 15 kinds according as they are bought, born in the house etc. Details about the slavery which as a rule is of a very mild form will be dealt with in the State Antiquities.[3] Besides the relations the Ācārya, Ṛtvij and other spiritual advisors and chief priests are frequent guests in the house who hardly restricted themselves only to one such visit in a year according to the Smṛti-rule[4].

Slaves and servants of the family.

The visitors.

Even now the undivided property of a family is considered to be the normal state of things until the proof is produced that a partition has taken place[5]. The presumption of a joint-family is stronger in proportion as the family-members living together are closely related and therefore among brothers it is more easily acknowledged than among cousins etc.[6], but, as laid down in the Smṛtis, it does not extend to beyond the fourth generation. In Bengal[7] the father of the family exercises a despotic sway over his family; he makes arrangements

The joint-family of Bengal.

1. l.c. 84, 86.

2. *dāsakammakarā* is a word of very frequent occurrence in the Jātakas. *Tr.*

3. See f.-n. 5, p. 95. *Tr.*

4. M. 3, 119: Nār. 3, 9—11 etc. Cf. Weber, I. St. 10, 125; Delbrück l. c. 567 f.

5. West and Bühler, 3rd. ed., 601, 651 f.

6. Cf. the decision in Mayne § 241.

7. B. Mullick, Essays on the Hindu Family in Bengal (Calc. 1882).

for the education, livelihood and marriage of his sons and daughters, himself takes the earnings of all the family-members and determines all expenditure. Beside him the Gṛhiṇī too carries on a no less strict government over the daughters, daughters-in-law and the maid-servants; she looks after the cooking, remains content with simple food, mostly the remains of her husband's meal which she never takes in his presence, lives a simple and frugal life and is generally bigoted and superstitious. After the Saṁskāras prescribed in the Smṛtis, particularly the investiture of the sacred thread, are performed, the sons are married at a tender age and have little power in the management of the property. Only a relic of the right of primogeniture may still be traced in the fact that posts of honour devolve on the eldest son. Servants and slaves,[1] relations on visit, often 6 to 20 in number, the Guru and Acharji *(ācārya)* complete the personnel of the joint-family of Bengal.

Joint-family outside Bengal.

Outside Bengal the principle based on the above-mentioned texts of the Mit. is observed, viz. every member of the family immediately on his birth is entitled to a share of the joint-property and therefore must be consulted in case of sale or disposition of same.[2] This principle is hardly reconcilable with the right of primogeniture and the unlimited *patria potestas*; yet they are frequently still observed particularly among noble families, inasmuch as after the death of the father the eldest son receives the family idols (as prescribed in Hār. 4, 15), represents the family at the sacrifices to the manes, marriages, depositions of evidence and similar other public duties, or, as prescribed in the Smṛtis, takes over the management of the property or even the whole in-

1. Before the abolition of slavery. *Tr.*
2. Cf. Tag. Lect. 109—113; Mayne §§ 226 f.

heritance [1]. The institution of "joint-family" is spread all over India and is found even in the customary law of the Punjab [2] which is quite free from any influence of the Smṛtis.

§ 23. *Partition.* So long as the property consisted almost exclusively of immovables the joint-property of the family certainly appeared to be the best arrangement suited to the economic condition. Traces are not wanting to prove that even whole villages formerly used the fields in common as it is found in the Punjab even to this day (§ 26). At all events, the lists of impartible properties *(avibhājya)* in the Smṛtis, often very comprehensive in themselves, indicate that there was a time when the family property was indivisible, as is the case among the Tarwaads of Malabar at the present day. Thus according to Uśanas the income out of (or claim to) sacrifices, fields, writings, prepared food, water and the wife's property should remain undivided among the relations *(sagotra)* up to the thousandth generation. Śaṅkhalikhita mentions among impartible properties a house *(na vāstuvibhāgo*, instead of which however a few commentators read *cāsti vibhāgo)*. Even according to Bṛh. 25, 93 the relations *(sapiṇḍa)*, whether their property is undivided or partitioned, have equal rights as far as the immovables are concerned, because nobody can give away, mortgage or sell the immovables alone. Elsewhere this author of course takes a more advanced view and lays down (l. c. 79-86) how things declared to be indivisible by previous authors [3] can be partitioned. Thus the clothes and ornaments should be sold and then the proceeds of it divided and the same with the bonds

Traces of a time when the family property was absolutely indivisible.

Advanced views of Bṛh.

1. Steele, Castes 178 f., 228 f., 417-419. Cf. also Tupper 2, 188 etc.

2. Tupper 2, 70 f., 137 f. etc. Cf. Kohler ZVR 7, 195-201.

3. Cf. M. 9, 219 ; Vi. 18, 44 ; Gaut. 28, 46 f.

of debt—the debt is realised and the sum is then divided; prepared food is exchanged for unprepared food; the water of a well or a tank should be used according to need; male and female slaves should be divided or work alternately in the houses of the coparceners; fields and embankments are to be divided *pro rata parte* (into shares agreed upon), the pasture ground and the common roads are to be used in the same manner. Only the presents of the father-in-law to his daughters-in-law are not included in the partition even in the opinion of Bṛh.

The father undertakes the partition.

If a partition took place, as the will is not known in Indian law, the only influence the father could exercise on the determination of the shares was to undertake the partition himself. The partition by the father is even a Vedic custom and the passage TS 3, 1, 9, 4, which declares that Manu divided his property among his sons, is even specially referred to in the Smṛtis (Baudh. 2, 3, 2; Āp. 2, 14, 11). Originally on the strength of his paternal authority, he could determine the portions just as he liked, but later he was subjected to various restrictions, see below. Whether and on what occasion the father can be compelled by the sons to undertake the partition is doubtful. Thus according to Hār. 4, 2 the partition can be made against the will of the father if he is aged, insane or sickly. But this passage cannot be found either in the Ms. of Hār.'s Dharmasūtra nor in the numerous quotations and moreover it cannot be well-harmonised with 4, 3 where it is laid down that in such a case the management of the property should be taken over by the eldest son. In other works, such as in the Mit. on Y. 2, 114, in the Dāyabhāga 41 etc. the same passage is ascribed to Śaṅkha or Śaṅkhalikhita but very often with the insertion of the negative particle *na*, so that the meaning is quite the opposite and the division of property against the

Could the father be compelled to do that?

Partition with father's consent.

will of the father is thereby altogether forbidden ; and as another passage of this author likewise denies the sons the power of partition during the father's life-time, this reading is probably the right one.[1] Also according to Gaut. 15, 19, sons who have extorted from the father a partition of the family property against his will, should not be invited to a Śrāddha. For this reason Gaut. 28, 2 allows a partition by the sons during the life-time of the father only with the consent of the latter. Also Baudh. 2, 3, 8, Nār. 3, 3, Bṛh. 25, 1 etc. mention this partition with the father's consent.

Partition deferred till the death of mother.

It is also disputed whether the partition should be deferred till the death of the mother if the sons wish to divide after the death of the father. According to M. 9, 104, Y. 2, 117 the sons should divide "after the death of the father and the mother" or "the parents", because, as M. says, they have no authority over the property so long as the two parents are alive. Śaṅkha-likhita expresses this still more distinctly with the words "so long as they have the father they are not independent, and the same so long as the mother is alive" ; yet this quotation appears only in the works of Bengali authors whose reading of the above-mentioned text about the partition against the will of the father is different from that of other authors. Also according to Nār. 1, 36 f. the sons can never be independent even if they are of age so long as their parents are alive and after the death of the father his authority devolves on the mother and only after her death, on the eldest son ; yet the same author also lays down in 13, 3 in agreement with Gaut. 28, 2 and Bṛh. 25, 1 that the partition can take place even in the life-time of the mother if she is too old to give birth to any more children and in 31, 28—31

1. Cf. Tag. Lect. 98 f.

speaks of the guardianship of the relations and the sons over the widow, cf. §20. There was thus in any case a view according to which after the death of the testator the management of the property at first devolved on his widow; perhaps the main purpose of this rule was to provide for such cases where the sons were not yet grown up and the daughters were not yet married what is often mentioned as the necessary precondition for a partition among the brothers[1]. Most authors however are of opinion, expressly or tacitly, that the death of the father is the only precondition for partition among brothers or collaterals[2]. The social death of the father is often considered to be equivalent to his natural death, viz. if he retires into the forest according to the laws of the Smṛti or joins a spiritual order or is excommunicated out of the caste[3].

The real motive of this rule.

Partition immediately after father's death natural or social.

The manner in which the partition is to be made is determined chiefly with reference to the age of those who are going to divide, at least according to the oldest authors and also the TS 2, 5, 2, 7. The most ancient rules are certainly those which allow a special extra share of the family property to each of the sons according to the hierarchy of age, particularly however to the eldest son, and in the case of polygamy also according to the order in which their mothers were married to their father. Thus according to Gaut. 28, 5-8 the eldest son should receive 1/20 as a preferential share *(uddhāra)* over and above a pair (of kine and similar domestic animals), a cart along with a yoke of oxen having incisors both above and below and a bull; the middlemost son receives the one-eyed, old, hornless and tailless domestic animals if there

Preferential shares of particular sons.

1. Nār. 13, 3 ; Hār. 4, 7.
2. Gaut. 28, 1 ; Hār. 4, 4 : Baudh. 1, 11, 11 ; Vi. 17, 23 ; Vas. 17, 41. 81 etc.
3. Hār. 4, 5 ; Nār. 13, 3 : Cf. Dāyabh. 34 (Colebrooke 1, 32 f.); Nār. 13, 25 etc.

are more than one such animals; to the youngest belong the sheep, corn, iron utensils, a house, a wagon with team as well as one of each of the (remaining) animals; the residue is divided equally.

The law of partition reveals a society of agriculturists as well as of industrials.

While the lists of the items of property mentioned here and elsewhere indicate the almost exclusive pursuit of agriculture, the purely arithmetical calculation of shares in other rules of partition, such as Gaut. 28, 9 f., M. 9, 112 ff. etc., are applicable also to property earned through commerce and industry. Analogous proportional numbers are used to indicate the shares of inferior, illegitimate and adoptive sons and not only the Smṛtis but also the Mah. 13, 47, 4 ff. prescribes a system of partition in the ratio 4: 3: 2: 1 specially for the sons of a Brahman by different wives of the four castes, and Vi. 18, 1-40 develops this system casuistically for all possible analogous cases. Yet not only unequal marriages were disapproved already at an early period (§ 18) but also the theory of the right of primogeniture and in general that of unequal division of property met with determined opposition already at a very early period and it was recognised only as a local custom (Āp. 2, 14, 6 ff.) beside the theory of equal shares mentioned by all the authors and it is later reckoned among the obsolete customs.

Unequal division condemned.

Patria potestas and partition.

In a partition taken up by the father the *patria potestas* too of course came into consideration which finds significant expression in the rule of Har. (4, 5) that the father is to become a pious hermit or a beggar after the division of his property or retain the greater part of the property or even take back something from the shares of his sons as necessity may arise or even concede still more to the sons. On the other hand, according to Hār. 4,4, after the death of the father a partition should be made only in equal shares. Even later authors such as Y. 2,114, Nār. 13,15, Bṛh. 25,4 recognise the absolute power of the father to determine the portions of the sons as he chooses. Yet a restriction was imposed on the will of the father by means of the distinction made between the inherited family property and one's own acquisition (cf. § 22); the father might have a free right of disposal only over the latter while the father and the sons had equal right on the inherited property, so that the sons could claim an equal share with the father in a partition (Vi. 17, 1 f.; Y. 2, 114, 121; Bṛh. 25, 2-4). It is doubtful, whether the rule that the father may reserve a double share for himself (Y. 2, 123; Nār. 13,12; Bṛh. 25, 5) is also to be applied only to the father's own acquisitions.

Restriction imposed on the father.

That the father reserved for himself a greater portion was all the more justified inasmuch as under certain circumstances he had to provide for his wife and the son born after the partition(*vibhaktaja*) though of course there is the rule that the partition should take place only when the parents are sufficiently advanced in age (Nār. 13, 3); there was however difference of opinion as to whether the Vibhaktaja might claim only the property of his father or was also to be provided for by his brothers (Gaut. 28, 29; M. 9, 216; Nār. 13,44; Vi. 17, 3; Y. 2, 122 etc.). In a partition the shares of the grandsons and the great-grandsons shall be adjusted *per stirpes* (according to fathers) (Vi. 17,23; Y. 2, 120, Cf. § 22).

The son born after partition.

Shares of grandsons and great-grandsons.

The wives and daughters were without doubt originally entitled only to maintenance and it is disputed even if they can retain their ornaments and the presents received from their relations when partition takes place (Āp. 2,14,9, cf. M. 9,200; Vi. 17,22). According to Vi. 15,31 the brothers have to provide for the marriage of their sisters in a manner befitting their position and according Vi. 18, 34 f. they must also give them an adequate share of the property and to the mother they shall give a son's portion. The latter rule is given also by

The wives and the daughters at the partition.

Y. 2, 123 and in 2,115 he affirms that even when the father undertakes the partition each of his wives should have a share equal to that of a son excepting when they have previously received presents by way of Strīdhana ; according to 2,124 a daughter should receive 1/4 of a son's portion to meet the expenses of her marriage. Nār. 13, 12 f., 26 f. speaks of a partition only among the brothers : they should give the full share of a son to the mother and a smaller share to the unmarried sister, they should provide for the wife and the daughter of a brother who has no son—the latter however only till her marriage. M. 9, 118, Bṛh. 25, 64 and Kāty. 24, 3[1] again speak of the fourth-part share of the daughter, but those commentators are probably right who take this term solely to mean a sum sufficient to cover the expenses of the marriage and the wife's share too, which is equal to that of a son, is explained to be nothing more than a life annuity in conformity with the rules about the dependence of the sex, cf. § 24.

Members suffering from physical or spiritual maladies were excluded from inheritance.

According to Gaut. 28, 43, Baudh. 2, 3, 37 ff. etc., those who are incapable of work or trade on account of physical, spiritual or moral defects are excluded from the inheritance such as, for example, those who are blind, dumb, deaf, lame, impotent, castrated, half-witted or deranged in mind or those who are suffering from an incurable disease, lepers, and those who quarrel with their father or have cheated their brothers or in general have committed a heinous crime which is punished with excommunicationu out of the caste, etc. Such family-members who are refused inheritance can claim only maintenance for themselves and this claim too is refused in the case of the excommunicated person (*patita*) ; however, the Patita may regain his position in the caste by performing the prescribed penances and thus the ample grounds for excommunication probably, on the

1. Bandyopadhyaya, Kātyāyanamatasaṅgraha, verse no. 754. *Tr.*

whole, served only to bring profit to the Brahmans by means of the penances prescribed by them.[1]

Authentication of a partition.

Only later authors like Nār. 13, 40, Bṛh. 8, 5 refer to the authentication of a partition by a document (*vibhāgapattra*). A disputed partition may also be ascertained by circumstantial evidence, such as if the relations perform the domestic sacrifices and their businesses separately, if each of them has his own household or if they possess movable and immovable properties and slaves separately, or give evidence for one another and go security for one another, which is allowed only to those relations who have divided their properties, etc.

Local variations are the cause of differences of opinion in the Smṛtis.

In the epoch of commentators very important local differences cropped up, specially between Bengal and the other provinces[2]. This may be taken to be an indication of the fact that also the differences in the Sṛmtis regarding the law of partition are for the most part or almost wholly based on the differences of *deśadharma*. The customary law too shows various phases which often perfectly agree with the Smṛtis. Thus in the customary law of the Punjab the father's absolute authority to dispose of the immovable property is curbed by the right of the sons and other agnate relations but not his authority over the movable property and that again only with reference to the immovable property which has been inherited in contradistinction to his own acquisitions[3]. In most cases only the sons or the nearest heirs, in Sialkot however all the descendants of the same great-grandfather, have the right of protest if the father sells the property. The father cannot be compelled to undertake the partition during his life-time, but it is equivalent to his death if he enters a religious order and partly also if he changes his religion and loses his

Partition in Punjab customary law.

1. Cf. Tag. Lect. 271–282.
2. l. c. 107–143.
3. Tupper 2, 163–171, 206. Cf. Kohler ZVR 7, 195–201.

caste. The head of the family may divide the family property according to his will, all the same whether further children may be expected or not, only, if the division is unequal, it need not be acknowledged any longer after his death when every member of the family entitled to inheritance may demand a partition. The women receive no share unless on failure of male descendants, see § 24.

The Piṇḍa decides the heir.

§ 24. *Law of heirship.* In the joint-family every fully authorised member is entitled to the privileges of a member of the family simply on account of his birth and the two expressions *dāyāda* "coparcener, heir" and *sapiṇḍa* "one who takes part in the funeral oblation, agnate," are therefore often used one for another. The latter term indicates a more primitive character of the Indian law of inheritance—its close connection with the sacrifices to the manes. "He who inherits the property, offers also the *piṇḍa*" says Vi. 15, 40, and *vice versa*, he who offers the *piṇḍa*, i. e. performs, with the consent of his relations, the funeral ceremonies for a deceased person, is frequently regarded to be the heir to the deceased according to popular conceptions. The juridical significance of this rule should not however be over-emphasieed. It is an exaggeration to consider the law of inheritance to be merely spiritual law in which the performance of the usual funeral sacrifice is rewarded with the claim of inheritance[1]. Of course in most cases the two coincide, yet however Piṇḍas are given, for instance, also to the three female ascendants and the three Mātāmahas, i. e. the father of the mother and his two male ascendants, although the offerer of the Piṇḍa does not inherit the property of these relations. [2]

But this rule is not universal.

1. Goldstücker, On the deficiencies in the present administration of Hindu Law 19 ff.
2. Cf. Tag. Lect. 168—176 ; Caland, Altind. Ahnencult 163,

First claim of the son.

The sons have the first claim on the legacy *(riktha)* of the father, primarily the sons born within the wedlock and then the secondary sons according to those authors who permit Niyoga, adoption and other forms of substitution. About the partition among the brothers and the share of a son born within the wedlock after the partition has taken place, see §§ 23 and 21. Among the Śūdras the father can give the full share of a son even to an illegitimate son, but after the death of the father the brothers have to give him only half a share ; if he is the only son and if there is no grandson of the testator by a daughter, then he receives the whole property (M. 9, 179 ; Y. 2, 133 f.). An explanation of this rule will be found in the despised position of the Śūdras for which reason only the lowest form of marriage was prescribed for them and their marriage was considered to be no higher than illicit connections (Baudh. 1, 20, 14—16 etc.).

Special laws about Śūdras.

After the sons come the sons of the sons and after them their sons ; the three descendants and the three ascendants along with the testator form the close body of Sapiṇḍa relatives (Baudh. 1,11,9 ; M. 9,137,186 f. etc.) which illustrates the connection of the funeral ceremony with the law of inheritance. Yet however the word Sapiṇḍa also often signifies all the agnates (such as in Vas. 17,81 ; Āp. 2,14,2) and the same is the case more or less also with the other expressions by which distant relations and members of the family entitled to inheritance are designated, such as Sakulya, Sagotra, Gotraja, Bandhu, Bāndhava, Jñāti etc. (M. 9,187 ; Baudh. 1,11, 12 ; Gaut. 28, 21 ; Vi. 17, 10 f. ; Y. 2, 135 ; Nār. 13, 51 ; Bṛh. 25,59,62 etc.). Near relations exclude the more distant ones (M. 9,187 ; Āp. 2,14,2). For that reason not infrequently, the father or the two parents or the brothers are mentioned at the top of the agnates (M. 9, 185 ; Vi. 17, 6 ff.; Y. 2, 135 ; Bṛh. 25, 67, 63 etc.).

Various terms employed to designate near or distant relatives.

According to Gaut. 28,27 the eldest brother is to be regarded as the heir to those brothers who are not reunited.[1]

Female members generally excluded from inheritance by the ancient authors.

The assignment of shares to the female members of the family—particularly to the widow of the testator—was a disputed question in the inheritance of a man who has died without male issue. According to Baudh. 2, 3 ,46 (and even according to Nirukta 3, 4) the women are incapable of inheriting and this is proved by a Vedic passage (TS 6, 5, 8, 2) which however refers only to the Soma sacrifice. Also Āp. 2,14, 2-4 does not at all mention the widow and mentions the daughter only subsidiarily after the Sapiṇḍas. Gaut. 28, 21 adds to the above-mentioned heirs also the widow wherewith according to Haradatta is only meant that the heirs should look after the women or should eventually make over to them a portion of the fields sufficient for their maintenance[2]. According to Gaut. 28, 22 there is another possibility of women's inheritance if the widow raises a son by Niyoga (§ 20). Vas. 17, 55-66 has only this alternative in mind. Also Hār. 4, 9 allows only the maintenance to the widow. Śaṅkhalikhita on the other hand refers to the parents or the eldest wife for inheritance directly after the brothers. Vi. 17, 4 ff. and Y. 2, 135 f. even mention the widow and then the daughters—perhaps a relic of the privilege of the daughter, see § 21—as the nearest successors when male descendants are lacking.

Chances of widow's inheritance.

The Bandhu.

It is perhaps no mere accident that just these two authors insert also the Bandhu before or after the distant family members. The expression Bandhu is of course uncertain and may signify any relation in general.[3] Yet

1. If they die without leaving male issue. *Tr.*

2. Cf. Tag. Lect. 193, 286.

3. Aparārka or Y. I, 108 expressly says that Bāndhavas are the relations of the mother's side (बान्धवाः मातृपक्ष्याः); very probably the word Bandhu too is primarily of the same meaning. *Tr.*

primarily the brother of the mother is understood by it and according to an oft-quoted text,[1] there are in particular nine Bandhus : the sons of the sister of the father, the sons of the sister of the mother, the sons of the brother of the mother, then the sons of the grandfather's sister, grandmother's sister and of the grand-father's brother and finally the sons of the maternal grand-father's sister, the maternal grandmother's sister and the sons of the maternal grandmother's brothers.

The share of cognates in the inheritance.

The share of the cognates in the inheritance is, of course, to say the least, a secondary principle like the apportioning of the women. According to M. 9, 217 (cf. Bṛh. 25, 63), when male descendants are lacking, the mother and even the grand-mother of the paternal side is entitled to inheritance ; but it is directly in contradiction to the above mentioned rules of succession and is perhaps a later interpolation[2]. According to Nār. 13, 28 f., 51 f., the widow can claim only maintenance and even that only if she lives a chaste life ; on the other hand, the daughter may inherit and Nār. also mentions the Bāndhavas as heirs. The sister too is often mentioned as a coparcener along with the brothers, yet it is not meant that she should get a full share, see § 23. In the fragmentary Smṛtis the widow's right of inheritance is often recognised, yet however it is subjected to certain conditions. Thus according to Vṛddha M. (ed. Herberich) 92 the sonless widow is said to receive the whole property of her husband if she leads a chaste and strictly religious life. Bṛh. 25, 46-71 gives a series of very exhaustive though of course also highly contradictory rules about the right of inheritance of the widow, mother and daughter. The widow is the surviving half of her husband and should therefore inherit his whole property, yet however only

The sister as a coparcener.

Widow's right of inheritance recognised in the later Smṛtis if she remains chaste.

1. Mit. on Y. 2, 136 (Colebrooke 2, 6, 1).
2. Bühler SBE 25, LXX.

under the condition that she performs his Śrāddha and other pious and charitable acts, or she should inherit only the movable property and even that only if her husband were no longer living in a joint-family with his agnates or on the whole she should receive only a maintenance.

Kāty. on the inheritance of widows.

According to Kāty. 24, 55 ff.[1] the chaste widow should inherit the property of her husband, male descendants failing, yet she cannot give away, mortgage or sell her share of the family property and must live with the agnates of her husband and the latter shall receive the property after her death. If she proves to be stubborn and wilful the agnates need give her only a small pittance. These striking differences of treatment are perhaps, for the most part, more apparent than real. The widow has to be looked after in quite a different manner if there is Niyoga. Even if she is declared to be the heiress to her husband, she could not freely dispose of his property, but remained completely under the control of his nearest agnates under whose protection she lived, cf. § 23.

The law of reversion to the king.

If there is no relation to inherit, the property reverts to the king (Gaut. 28, 42 etc.). Thus if a merchant on a sojourn from outside dies in his kingdom, even in such a case, the king shall seize his property ; if any direct heir (*dāyāda*) or relation (*bandhu*, *jñāti*) does not turn up within ten years to claim the property, then the king retains it (Nār. 3, 16-18). Perhaps Indian princes made a still more extensive use of this law of reversion than is permitted in the Smṛtis. Thus in the Śakuntalā 138 f. (ed. Pischel) it is considered self-evident that the property of a rich merchant shipwrecked in the sea, amounting to several millions, should go to the king if the merchant has no son. King Kumārapāla after his return voluntarily resigns his claim on the property of those who

1 Bandyopadhyaya, Kātyāyanamatasaṅgraha, verses nos. 708 ff. *Tr.*

died without any son to succeed them (Bühler, Hemacandra 30).

The property of a Brahman exempted from this law.

According to the Smṛtis the property of a Brahman should not on the whole be subjected to this law of reversion but should go to the spiritual teacher or pupil or to the fellow-student of the deceased or to the community of Brahmans, particularly to the learned Brahmans, cf. § 25. The verse (Baudh. 1,11, 16; Vas. 17, 86) quoted as proof of this, according to which the property of Brahmans is worse than poison, is frequently found also in the inscriptions. The privilege here allowed to the Brahmans reminds one of the special favour shown to the Brahmans when a treasure is discovered which otherwise reverts to the king (M. 8, 30 ff. etc.). Perhaps the uncertainty of the Smṛti rules about the right of inheritance of distant relations is to be attributed to this law of reversion to the king, and in part certainly also to the fact that partitions were rare in ancient times, for, in undivided families, if male descendants were lacking, the relations living with the owner on the joint property were to inherit and as the result of the catholicity of Indian law with regard to the law of sonship, such cases were not all too frequent in which no son of one kind or another could be found.

The uncertainty of the law of inheritance.

Complete system of successive heirs developed only by the mediaeval jurists.

Only the mediaeval jurists drew up a complete system of successive heirs; yet however there are very wide differences of opinion among them and here too, as in partition (§ 23), a very marked difference between the Bengali system and the other systems is in evidence, particularly in connection with the position and rights of women. One at least of these systems is partially given here; the table of the male agnates *(gotraja)* according to the Mit. is as follows [1]:

---

1. West and Bühler, 3rd. ed., 123.

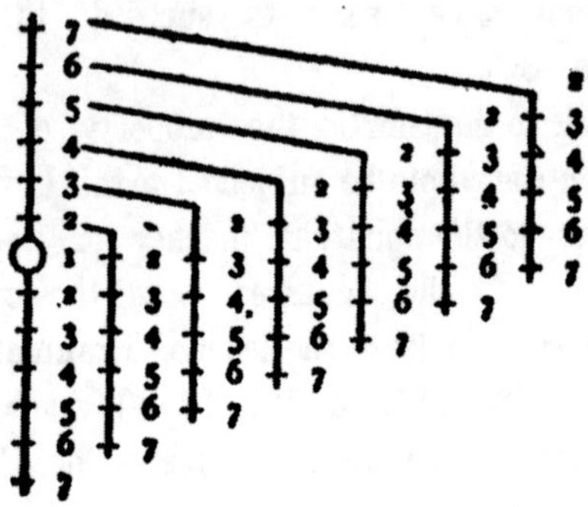

The system of heirs in the Punjab customary law.

The customary law of the Punjab has various points of agreement with the Smṛtis in this respect although it recognises no connection between the law of inheritance and the funeral sacrifice [1]. The succession of heirs is arranged strictly agnatically according to generations and with unrestricted right of representation. The family property never goes out of the *got.* If there is no male issue then the widow inherits the property, but she cannot sell the family-property because after her death it reverts to the agnates of her husband and she is on the whole more or less controlled by them in her dispositions of the property. The daughter may claim only maintenance until her marriage though a tendency to allow a share of the inheritance to the daughter is quite perceptible, but elsewhere, on the contrary, even the widow is given only a sustenance [2].

§25. *Peculiar forms of heirship.*

Stridhana.

(1) The female property (*strīdhana*) i. e. the peculium of the female members of the family and their special privilege of inheriting the same,[3] is mentioned already in the older Dharmasūtras, sometimes in substance

1. Tupper 2, 142.
2. l. c. 2, 101, 142, 258 etc. Cf. Kohler ZVR 7, 201–217.
3. Cf. Tag. Lect. 226–270.

and sometimes in name, particularly in Gaut. 28, 24 ff.; yet it is only Vi. 17, 18 who gives an enumeration of the different items of the Strīdhana. He mentions as such the presents which a woman has received from her parents, sons, brothers or relations, and what has been presented to her at the time of and after her marriage, as well as the Śulka and the compensation (*ādhivedanika*) received from her husband in case he subordinates her to another wife. By Śulka is to be understood the nuptial fee given by the husband to the wife before or at the time of the marriage (§16)—a custom also found among other peoples which was developed out of the primitive usage of the purchase of bride[1].

Items thereof described by Vi.

If the owner of the Strīdhana has children, it should be transmitted to the daughters; we have therefore here a line of heirs exclusively composed of females as in the case of the famous "Gerade" of the German law; yet it may well be assumed that on failure of daughters the sons were to inherit the Strīdhana. If a woman dies childless, enquiries are to be made as to whether she was married according to one of the four higher or lower forms of marriage (§ 16); in the former case her Strīdhana goes to the husband, in the latter, it reverts to the father. The husband should accordingly suffer a loss of property if he is not married according to one of the orthodox forms, for in such cases his marriage (cf. Nār. 12, 29) is not considered to be so firmly established as in the case of the higher forms of marriage; it should also be remembered in this connection that the Āsura marriage is the most usual of all the lower forms and that the Śulka coming from this form of marriage originally went to the father to whom it should also revert through heirship. Y. 2, 142-144 (cf. 117) agrees mainly with

Strīdhana inherited by the daughters.

Inheritance of the Strīdhana of a childless woman.

1. Cf. Kohler ZVR 3, 431; Schrader, Sprachvergl. u. Urgesch. 552 f.

Vi. and also M. 9, 131, 194, 196f., Nār. 3 1, 8 f. etc., lay down similar laws and the Mah. 13, 45, 12 (=M. 9, 131) too expresses the same views. That the daughters should inherit the ornaments and the dowry of the mother or in general her Strīdhana, is mentioned also by Baudh. 2, 3, 43, Vas. 17, 46, Gaut. 28, 24; but Gaut. (cf. Bṛh. 25, 86; M. 9, 131) says it with the interesting note that it should primarily go to the unmarried daughters who are naturally in need of maintenance and only secondarily to poor married daughters.

Unmarried daughters have the first claim.

At the time of the division of property the ornaments of the women should not be taken for partition but should be reserved for them (Āp. 2, 14, 9; Vi. 17, 22; M. 9, 200). Likewise also the Śulka, according to the oft-quoted passage Gaut. 28, 24 f., which is of course ambiguous in meaning, should firstly be transmitted to the mother and only after her death to the brothers. The view that the Strīdhana should be divided among the sons and the daughters is probably of later origin; thus according to M. 9, 192, 195, Nār. 13, 9, Bṛh. 25, 87 etc., Kāty. 24, 94-97[1] the Strīdhana consisting of the presents from the relatives is to be returned to them and the residue should go primarily to the (unmarried) daughters and on failure of such daughters to the sons and the married daughters; if the woman has no children, and if she is married according to one of the lower forms, her parents get the Strīdhana, yet however the immovables should always descend on the brothers.

Later views on the inheritance of Strīdhana.

Immovables included in Strīdhana.

The consideration of males in the line of heirs and the differentiation of the various kinds of Strīdhana including the immovables at the time of succession indicates an epoch in which the Strīdhana was developed far beyond mere ornaments and articles of use. Such a development is again revealed particularly by the highly complicated rules about

1. Bandyopadhyaya, 770—772. *Tr.*

women's right of dispositisn over their Strīdhana in Kāty. 24, 80-92.[1] She is said to be quite free to spend the presents received from her loving relations (*saudāyika*) or give them away or sell them even if they consist of immovables. Neither her husband nor her blood-relations have any right on her Strīdhana, and if they use it forcibly they should have to restore it with interest and pay a penalty for it; yet it is also remarked that she may lend her Strīdhana voluntarily to her husband—may be to help him in the pursuit of his trade. The sons would have to deliver to her the Strīdhana after her husband's death which was even only promised to her by him; but it is compulsory only if she remains with his family and not with her father.

Woman's absolute right over her Strīdhana recognised by later jurists.

Generally the greatest possible Strīdhana should be given to women, yet however not exceeding 2000 paṇas and generally no immovables should be given to her. The earning of a woman by her own labour and presents received from outsiders are not included in the Strīdhana, she can dispose of them only with the consent of her husband. Such rules were necessary at a time when the Strīdhana had assumed very large proportions; as the wife conducted the household affairs and as the daily incomes and expenses passed through her hands (M. 9, 11), she did not lack opportunities for encroachments which might sap the whole family property (Nār. 12, 92). It must have also appeared equally dangerous to let the immovables actually in her possession go down to the daughters, and thus outside the Gotra, after her death.

Amount of the Strīdhana. Immovables generally not given to her.

The frequently diverging statements in the Smṛtis about the Strīdhana and its inheritance have been a rich field of activity to the critical acumen and hair-splitting disquisitions of Indian commentators and the English

Divergent views and their result.

1. Bandyopadhyaya, 757 ff. *Tr.*

judges have found in the still more conflicting teachings of the latter a congenial field to apply their art of exposition. Thus, for instance, an almost endless discussion accumulated on the truly highly sophistical deduction of the Mit. that by Strīdhana, in conformity with the etimological meaning of the word, every favourite property of the woman is to be understood and therefore every such property should be transmitted according to the particular system of heirship which has been followed in the Smṛtis in connection with the Strīdhana i. e. the peculium of the woman.

Law of inheritance among reunited coparceners.

(2) Several divided coparceners (*vibhakta dāyāda*) may again unite their inheritance afresh. They are then called Saṁsṛṣṭin or Saṁsṛṣṭa and are heirs to one another on failare of male issue, at the exclusion of the other relations (Gaut. 28, 28 ; M. 9, 212 ; Vi. 17, 17 ; Y. 2, 138 ; Bṛh. 25, 76). But there is also the opinion that such a reunion could take place only so far as the movable properties are concerned because all the Sapiṇḍa relations have equal claim upon the immovables (Hār. 4, 22 ; Prajāpati). The well-known obscurities of the passage Y. 2, 139, which has been so much commented upon[1], are probably due to a corrupt reading of the Mit. ; if with Apar. it is read *nānyodaryadhanaṁ haret* and *sodaryo nānyamātṛkaḥ*, then we have the simple meaning that step-brothers can never be heir to one another, not even if they are "reunited"[2]. The Smṛtis leave uncertain the position of other heirs specially of the widow of a Saṁsṛṣṭin who has died without leaving behind any male issue and for this reason this question has been vigorously discussed by later jurists and is one of the

Uncertainty about the heirs of the widow of a Saṁsṛṣṭin.

1. Cf. Goldstücker, On the deficiencies 7 f.; Roth in Mayr, D. ind. Erbrecht 134 ; Mayne § 502 etc.

2, Tag. Lect. 194 f., 286

chief points of dispute between the Mit. and the Dāyabh. At the present day "reunion" appears to be very rare[1].

Inheritance on the strength of spiritual relationship.

(3) The *spiritual relationship* which in ordinary inheritance comes into consideration only when real relations are absolutely wanting (§ 24) may justify a direct right of inheritance among the members of a religious sect or order. Thus accordingly to Vi. 17, 15 f. the property of a hermit in the forest (*vānaprastha*) descends after his death on his teacher and eventually on his disciples. Y. 2, 137 extends this system of inheritance also to the property of an ascetic (*yati*) and a life-long Brahmacārin and mentions as their heirs the spiritual initiator, a virtuous disciple, a member of the same religious brotherhood or one who lives in the same holy place (so according to Apar.). Of course the practical importance of this rule is not high for when going to enter the state of monkhood a man, as a rule, gave up all his worldly possessions which were divided among his relations (§ 24). Even to this day this spiritual right of succession is met with not infrequently and the best known is perhaps the case of the Gosāvī sect[2]. Among the Gosāvīs the Guru often even in his life-time nominates one of his disciples to be his heir and successor, but a disciple's disciple, a teacher, a fellow student and other spiritual relations may also succeed him.

---

1. Mayne l. c.; Tag. Lect. 224.
2. West and Bühler, 3rd. ed., 550—567.

III. LAW OF PROPERTY AND CONTRACT

§ 26. *Possession, ownership and prescription.* Ownership and possession are fully distinguished in Indian law. Possession is expressed by the derivatives of *bhuj* "to enjoy, use, possess" and the pronoun *svam* "self" and its derivatives such as Svāmin "owner," Svatva, Svāmya, Svāmitva "right of ownership" as well as substantives such as Dhana, Dravya, Riktha etc. in the sense of "possession, property, inheritance," serve to express ownership. The essence and origin of ownership have been the subject of philosophical disquisitions even in very ancient times[1].

Clear distinction between possession and ownership.

Thus according to Gaut. 10, 39 the sources of the right of ownership are inheritance, purchase, partition, seizure (of unclaimed property) and finding, over and above which the Brahmans have the acceptance of presents, the Kṣatriyas the booty of war or conquest and the Vaiśyas and Śūdras the wages for labour. In this connection the seizure of an unclaimed property is of particular importance in establishing ownership. For this reason a person who makes a piece of fallow land arable by felling the trees on it becomes the owner of the soil (M.

Various ways of gaining ownership.

1. Applying the strict canons of law to the Smṛtis Dr. Breloer has arrived at the conclusion (Kauṭalīya Studien, I. Das Grundeigentum in Indien, pp, 36—37) that like the Greeks the Indians too never made any distinction between possession and ownership ('rechtliche Herrschaft' as opposed to 'tatsächliche Herrschaft'). As far as the older Smṛtis are concerned Dr. Breloer is perfectly right, but he seems to have taken no notice of the statement in the Smṛtisaṅgraha quoted below. The author of the Smṛtisaṅgraha (and his followers) was fully conscious that there is something indefinable in ownership which cannot be proved by circumstantial evidence but by the science of law (Śāstras). *Tr.*

9, 44). Similarly the hunted deer belongs to him who hits it first ; he who hits it later has shot his arrow in vain. A person earns a certain right even merely by cultivating a field which is lying fallow for the time being. In Indian inscriptions the expression is often met with that a village or a piece of land is presented *bhūmicchidranyāyena*. It is clearly meant by this that the donee is endowed with all the rights of him who makes a fallow land arable for the first time and this is exactly the view of the law-books[1]. According to the latter somewhat similar rights upon a piece of land may be gained if it has remained fallow for 5 or 3 years or at least for 1 year *(aṭavī, khila, ardhakhila)*. True, the legitimate owner may reclaim it from the cultivator, but the latter may keep his profit and must be indemnified by the owner for his labours (Nār. 11, 23-27).

Partial ownership by bringing under plough a piece of land lying fallow for some time.

According to other authors only the following three are the legitimate means of livelihood common to all the castes: inheritance, presents and the dowry of a wife. This classification of the means of livelihood is crossed by another, probably of later origin, according to which there are (1) seven white means of livelihood, namely, religious learning, bravery, mortification of the flesh, (the dowry of a) bride, teaching, sacrifice and inheritance ; (2) seven spotted means of livelihood, namely, lending money, agriculture, trade, the nuptial fee (for a girl), crafts, service and wages (for a service rendered) ; (3) seven black means of livelihood, namely bribe, gambling, bearing message, (causing) pain, forgery, robbery and fraud (Nār. 1,44-49. Cf. Vi. 58). The profits gained by the employment of property, specially in sacrifices and other religious deeds, depend to a large

Various means of livelihood.

1. Bühler EI 1, 74.

extent, on the manner in which this property has been earned.

Possession cannot prove ownership.

How little mere possession may give rise to the right of ownership is expressed in an oft-quoted text of the Smṛtisaṁgraha : "If anybody holds something in his hands, he does not thereby become the owner of it ; does it not happen, for instance, in the case of stolen goods, that the property of one is found in the hand of another ?" "Therefore", continues the text, "the right of ownership is to be ascertained not through mere natural observation but only by means of science *(śāstra)* for otherwise it cannot be said reasonably that the property of one has been taken away by another. The legitimate means of livelihood, namely presents, booty, trade and service according to the order of the castes, have been separately enumerated in the science." This conception that the true right of ownership may be recognised and established only with the help of science had taken root even at an early period in Indian Jurisprudence and philosophy but also a reaction set in already at an early period from the side of those who emphasised that even the means of livelihood enumerated in the Smṛtis are taken solely from the observation of daily life and after all, the legal rules of the Smṛtis like the laws of grammar, merely serve to exhibit and strengthen what is practised at all times and that therefore the right of ownership does not depend upon the science or the sacred laws *(śāstra)* but upon the experience of the world.[1] While the religio-scientific character of ownership was defended particularly by Jīmūtavāhana, Raghunandana and other representatives

It can be established only with the help of the Śāstras.

Two opposite camps representing religious and secular nature of ownership.

---

1. The arguments of this opposite camp are worth quoting. Mitramiśra says that although the Śāstras recommend certain modes of acquiring property it does not follow that ownership cannot be valid without observing those directions, just as a man does not enjoy his meal the less even though he disregards the rules about keeping one's face turned to a certain direction at the time of eating. *Tr.*

of Bengal the theory that "ownership is temporal"—*svatvam laukikam*—is represented already in the Mitākṣarā, then in the Smṛticandrikā, in the Vīramitrodaya, Vyavahāramayūkha, Sarasvatīvilāsa and other works of the south and the west. The last named South Indian work goes perhaps farthest in this direction, inasmuch as it asserts that ownership is originated only by worldly acts while the Mitākṣarā emphasises only the worldly effects of ownership.[1]

Law of prescription.

Usucaption which takes place before the eyes of the owner and with his permission is to be distinguished from the seizure of an unclaimed property which has been mentioned above as one of the means of livelihood. The general law is that the legitimate owner forfeits his rights on a property if it is occupied by another, and he, though present, does not raise any claim within ten years (Gaut. 12, 37 ; M. 8, 147 ; Vas. 16, 17 etc); the period of ten years appears also to be the usual period of prescription (Nār. 13, 41). Yet this principle was clearly regarded to be dangerous and the attempt to hinder its effect by ordaining as many exceptions as possible is unmistakable. Thus as prescription presupposes a possibility of the claim of the legitimate owner, it is not allowed when the legitimate owner is imbecile in spirit or a minor, i. e. less than sixteen years of age (Gaut. l. c. etc.). In like manner the rights of a man who is not present are to be preserved, for which reason, e. g. a divinity student who performs an observance abroad which occupies him for 36 years or a travelling merchant may reclaim his property when he returns home ; his right of ownership is lost only after 50 years of adverse possession if strangers occupy his

Numerous exceptions.

1. Mit. (Bomb. 1882) 189; Vīram. (ed. G. Sarkar) 1, 12; May. (ed. Mandlik) 32; Sarasvatīvilāsa § § 401ff.

property and it will never cease to apply where friends and relatives are concerned (Quot. from Nār. 4, 7—10) Accordingly it is emphasised in the law of inheritance that an heir coming from abroad may claim from his family members the share which is his due even though he may be a descendant of the testator who had gone away in the third, fifth or even in the seventh generation (Bṛh. 25, 22—26).

Uninterrupted possession essential for prescription.

Moreover, it is essential that the possession should continue :without any interruption; usucaption takes place only if it can be proved by means of documents and witnesses that the house or field in question was not *chinnabhoga*, i. e. its possession was not interrupted (Bṛh, 9, 15 ; Nār. 13, 48). Certain categories of proprietors enjoy this benefit of law that their property cannot in general be lost through prescription ; this advantage is enjoyed by princes and their officers, women, Śrotriyas and ascetics besides minors and halfwitted persons, already mentioned above (Gaut. 12, 38 ; Y. 2, 25 ; Bṛh. 9, 21 etc.). Prescription of course does not apply to a property which has been lent, deposited or mortgaged (Vas. 16, 18 ; Nār. 1, 81, etc.) and female slaves (M. 8, 149 etc.) are not lost through adverse possession ; this law is perhaps meant for the concubines who are said to remain with their master even at a partition of property (Gaut. 28, 47).

Exemptions from the law of prescription.

Law of prescription inapplicable to immovable properties

It is of particular importance in this respect whether the possession extends over immovables or over movable property. According to Gaut. 12, 39 besides the female slaves, animals and real estates too are not liable to prescription. This rule reminds us of one of the texts about the law of inheritance which asserts the indivisibility of the immovables (§ 23). The immovables, originally the only valuable possession, should under no circumstances be lost to the family. Later authors however stances be lost to the family. Later authors however often speak of the prescription of immovable property, only according to Y. 2, 24 its possession should extend over twenty years, that is, double as long a period as in the case of movable properties. Later Smṛtis generally advocate longer periods for usucaption and prescription ; thus Bṛh. 9, 7 speaks in general of 30 years Kāty. 8, 6[1] even of 60 years.

Or very long periods of occupation are demanded.

Prescription and the law of acquisition.

Moreover, the law of the right of acquisition or possession *(āgama)* was gradually developed. If the possessor can prove that the disputed property was earned through purchase, present or in any other legitimate way, then he must be left in the safe enjoyment of the same (Vi. 5, 185) ; on the other hand, one who cannot prove himself to be the legitimate owner by means of documentary evidence or otherwise, would be regarded as a thief and punished accordingly, however long he might have had the property in his possession (Nār. 1, 85—87). Yet however according to the later authors there is a kind of legitimate usucaption without any title of ownership.

Thus already in the case of the son of the first possessor the possession is regarded as more than mere right of acquisition if already between the first possessor and a pretender no dispute had arisen which was not afterwards satisfactorily settled. The possession (Bhukti) however becomes quite indisputable and independent of any right of acquisition when as *tripuruṣāgatā* it has lasted three generations. Thus we have expressions as *pauruṣī*, *dvipauruṣī*, *tripauruṣī bhukti*, "possession for one, two or three generations," in which each generation is reckoned by 36 years. The "possession for three generations" particularly should be considered as possession from time immemorial ; the Mit. and other commentaries explain

The opposite views of later jurists about prescription and usucaption.

1. Bandyopadhyaya, 242. *Tr.*

26

this term by a period exceeding 100 years (Vi. 5, 186 f.; Y. 2, 27-29; Nār. 1, 88-91; Bṛh. 9, 23-29; Kāty. 8, 1-8).[1] The following rules involve an encouragement of pious gifts, viz. even a possession of three generations cannot prevail against a grant (*śāsana*), and that a complex of immovables occurring in such a grant should wholly belong to him who actually possesses even only a part of it (Bṛh. 9, 30 18).

Encouragement of pious gifts.

The tendency to prevent an occupation and prescription of the family property by a stranger is connected with the original indivisibility of the same (§ 23) and may be observed even to-day in the customary law of the South.[2] For this reason the family property is lost only after 100 years of adverse possession and even then only if the possession is uninterrupted ("Nywedbhogy"=Niravadhibhoga?); if possession is interrupted ("Suwedhbhogy"=Sāvadhibhoga?) the occupier has to hand over the property occupied by him to the legitimate owner, though however he receives compensation[3]. He who buys mortgaged immovable property from the mortgagee may, after 60 years, consider it as his own free property, excepting where the original proprietor has repeatedly raised his claim and thereby has prevented its being lost to himself[4]. Even the expression Khil has been preserved in the modern dialects to signify fallow land (=Khila). In the third year after bringing it under plough it is called Kṣet=Kṣetra[5]. The rights of the absent heir is carefully preserved particularly in the Punjab, yet after returning home the heir has to make good the expenses of his relatives[6]. For the Śāsanas see § 35.

Law of prescription in modern India.

1. Bandyopadhyaya, 239 ff. *Tr.*
2. West and Bühler (3rd. ed.) 692.
3. Steele, castes 282 f.
4. l. c. 253.
5. Grierson, Bihār Peasant Life § 797.
6. Tupper 3, 145ff.

§ 27. *Common fields and boundary disputes.* It is more important for the historian to arrive at a solution of the question whether communal or private property was the chief form of ownership than to decide whether the origin of property was secular or religious. The joint property of distant family relations was doubtless very much in vogue (§ 22); but the traces of a common property of the whole village community are much less clear and the data in the Smṛtis are much less definite on this point. The village of course forms the political unit —the smallest unit in the scheme which the Smṛtis (Vi. 3, 7ff. etc.) prescribe for the management of an Indian principality. At the head of the village stands the Grāmādhipa or Grāmaṇī, Grāmakūṭa, Grāmapati or Paṭṭakila of the inscriptions—the modern Pātil, the Gāmabhojaka of the Jātakas. It is a hereditary office though however the officers are appointed by the king; the village headman exercises the authority of a criminal police, imposes taxes on the farmers or exempts them from taxes and hands over the collected taxes to his superior after taking away his own share.

Joint ownership or individual ownership.

The village organisation.

The inhabitants of a village also jointly bear the responsibility of the theft of cattle which is suspected to have been committed by one of the inhabitants of the village if the foot-marks of the stolen cattle may be followed up into their village and cannot be followed further from there (Nār. 14, 23). The village has definite boundaries on every side which mark it off from the neighbouring villages; see below. In a wide circle round the village extends the pastureland; its breadth should be 100 'bows', i. e. 600 feet, or more according as it is a large village or a "city" (M. 8, 237; Y. 2, 167). On the pasture land, which on that account is reckoned among the indivisible properties (M. 9, 219; Vi. 18, 44), graze and wander the cattle of the inhabitants of the

Joint responsibilities and properties of the villagers.

village under the surveillance of the cowherds who have to prevent the cows' doing mischief to the adjoining fields (M. 8, 240 etc.).

On the other hand the fields, mostly furnished with hedges, appear always to have belonged to individual proprietors (Kṣetrin, Kṣetrika, Kṣetrasvāmin), who therefore may demand compensation for injury done to their property (M. 8, 241 etc.).[1] The principle of ownership of the field also serves as the theme of comparisons and it is specially indicated when, for instance, it is said that if a seed is carried off by wind or water into another field and there generates into a tree and bears fruits, then it becomes the property only of the owner of this field (M. 9, 54; Nār. 12, 56). The fruits of such trees as grow on the boundary line between two fields should belong to the owners of both the fields (Nār. 11, 13). The tenant of a field who pays to the owner half the crops as rent, is called Ardhika, Ardhasīrin (Vi. 57, 16 etc.); an idle tenant will be punished and must hand over the rented field to some other person for cultivation (Y. 2, 158).[2] Moreover, the organisations mentioned by Bṛh. 14, 21—26 for jointly cultivating the soil have evidently nothing to do with the original joint possession of the fields because he recommends great caution in the selection of partners and describes these agricultural associations in connection with the rules of trading companies.

The fields were generally individual property.

Tenants tilling the fields for half the crop.

1. Dr. Breloer however says that all this does not prove individual ownership ('rechtliche Herrschaft' as opposed to 'tatsächliche Herrscheft') for even a simple possessor of the field would have enjoyed this protection of law (Kauṭalīya Studien, I. Das Grundeigentum in Indien, pp. 39 ff.). *Tr.*

2. Meyer (Rechtsschriften p. 124) has translated this passage of Y. in quite a different manner and makes it yield a meaning which in his opinion proves Y.'s dependence on Kauṭ. who lays down that fields should be taken away from idle owners. But Meyer's translation is based on a highly improbable interpretation of the word *phālāhata*. *Tr.*

Rather two anonymous texts quoted in the Mit. 191 f. (1, 1, 31 f. Colebrooke) may refer to a joint ownership and to the village community's right of cancellation. One of these texts declares the sale of immovables to be generally inadmissible and even says that it is possible to mortgage it only with the permission (of those in authority); according to the other text alienation of the ownership of a piece of land is subject to six conditions, namely the consent of the village community (*svagrāma*), of the relations, neighbours (*sāmanta*) and of the heirs and the gift of gold and water (symbol of a gift). The commentators of course interpret this text in all possible manners; as for example, they find in it the assistance of the village community etc., in merely authenticating the act; yet however the passage may be a relic of a time or region in which the community actually possessed the right of prohibiting the alienation of property.

The anonymous texts revealing a former state of joint ownership.

That in general the villages were indeed secluded from outside but inside every village private property was in evidence[1], is best proved by the rules of the Smṛtis about boundary disputes which must have been one of the most common grounds of litigation. Here we have the boundary (*sīmā, maryādā*) between two countries and villages as well as the boundary between to houses and fields.

Individual ownership and boundary disputes.

The boundary line is either visible (prakāśa) or secret (aprakāśa). By visible boundary generally the boundary marks (*setu*) are meant, which according to M.8, 245 are best visible in summer when the sun has scorched all grass and plants; the proper meaning of *setu* is "dike, ridge of earth" as the dikes are specially mentioned as boundary marks and even to-day, e. g. in Behar, they serve to indicate the boundaries of a field [2].

Visible boundary.

1. See f.-n. 1 p. 204. *Tr.*
2. Grierson, Bihār Peasant Life § 833.

Natural boundary

Natural boundaries too belong to the category of visible boundaries, particularly hills and rivers which serve to divide two adjacent countries or adjacent villages. Tall trees, as for instance holy fig-trees, palms, bamboos, banyan trees are likewise pointed out and further shrubs and briers, heaps of stones, natural or artificial elevations, ant-hills, lakes, ponds, wells, cisterns, canals, streets, depressions, ditches, sanctuaries, temples etc. serve the same purpose.

Invisible boundary.

Secret boundary marks are stones, bones, charcoal, potsherd, sand, ash, dried cow-dung and other objects not easily destroyed by earth which are filled in pots and buried in the ground on the boundary line for which reason such a boundary is called boundary of buried things (*naidhānī sīmā*). The secret marks should be shown particularly to the children and the latter, when they grow up to be men should show them again to their children, and thus the knowledge of the boundary is propagated from generation to generation (Bṛh. 19, 6 f.).

Punishment for violating the boundary.

Severe corporeal punishments and fines (Vi. 5, 172; M. 9, 291; Y. 2, 155) are prescribed for shifting a boundary as well as for encroaching on an adjoining field, as for instance, if a man violates the boundary when driving the plough and goes boyond it.

Legal procedure of settling a boundary.

In the laws about the settlement of boundary disputes principally the case of dispute between two neighbouring villages has been taken into consideration. In these cases boundary marks have to be searched and evidences are to be taken, and the evidence of ancient and respectable inhabitants who are settled (*maula*) there for a long time is regarded as decisive, although particularly at that time they may live in another place; next, the evidence of the neighbours is taken or generally of those who often have to stop in the neighbourhood of the disputed boundaries, be it for ploughing or as cowherds, fowlers, snake-catchers, hunters,

The witnesses.

fishermen, root-diggers and forest rangers of every sort. According to the commentators these people are in a position to know best the boundaries of the villages which may often lie on wastes or wildernesses on account of their unstable and changing mode of life.

In order still more to enhance the solemnity of the event the witnesses or the neighbours selected as arbitrators are to put on red robes and red garlands, sprinkle earth over their heads and in this pageantry visit the boundary and fix it; otherwise a single person who enjoys universal confidence is appointed for this purpose (M. 8, 256; Y. 2, 152; Nār. 11, 10). Such an act has the character of an ordeal ;it is therefore watched whether he who fixes the boundary is visited by any mishap within a short time in which case his decision is regarded as false (Kāty. 18, 19).[1] Attempts are made to secure dependable depositions by threats of high fines for giving false evidence. If the border people are bribed and intentionally give false evidence, distant neighbours should be heard (Kāty. 18, 10).[2] As a last resort, the king should settle the boundary ; according to M. 8, 255 the king should be appealed to as a rule in all the boundary disputes and the names of the witnesses should be entered in a document; the boundary document *sīmāpattra* is also mentioned elsewhere.

Solemn character of the proceedings.

The king interferes as that last resort.

We have a whole series of successive appeals in the case of disputes over a house or a field, namely, (1) decision of the boundary dispute by the neighbours ; if they are not unanimous, (2) by means of documents ; (3) by the elders or other representatives of the village or the city or it should be decided by (4) un-

Successive appeals for boundary disputes.

1. Bandyopadhyaya, 582. *Tr.*
2. Ibid. 572. *Tr.*

interrupted possession for ten years (Śaṅkhalikhita). Also differences over gardens, plantations, wells, temples, tanks, inns, palaces, conduits for rain water and other immovables are mentioned—all of which reveals a highly developed individual property.[1] The rules connected with the changes of a river-bed and the boundary between two neighbouring villages or fields along this river-bed remind us of the frequency of great floods in India: the gain or loss arising from it should be taken quietly as a disposition of God just as a man cannot resist a royal command; yet however if a piece of tilled ground is swept away by the floods and deposited somewhere else it should be left in the possession of the original proprietor till the harvest time (Bṛh. 19, 16—21).

Law about flooded fields.

There are special laws about the dikes (*setu*) and wells on account of their importance, which along with a series of other rules with regard to policing are generally subjoined to the chapter on boundary disputes. If anybody constructs a dike on the land of his neighbour the latter should not obstruct him if thereby only a little land is lost and the gain in water more than makes up for the loss in ground. On the other hand he who repairs an old and dilapidated dike without asking the permission of the owner of the field, will not be allowed to use it; that can be allowed only after the death of the owner and his heirs and after obtaining royal permission (Nār. 11, 17—22; Y. 2, 156). The proprietors of two adjacent houses must be careful to have due consideration for each other; thus it is forbidden to obstruct or injure a veranda, window, drainage pipe or a shop etc. or to construct a privy, a fire-place, a receptacle for leavings or to dig a pit or to open a window or to drive a drainage pipe in the immediate vicinity of the neighbouring houses (Kāty. 18, 20 f.; [2] Bṛh.

Laws of dikes and wells.

Neighbours must have due consideration for each other.

1. See f.-n. 1 p. 204. *Tr.*

2. Bandyopadhyaya, 583—584. *Tr.*

19, 24—26). A distance of at least three feet or two Aratnis must be observed (Vas. 16, 12 ; Kāty. 18, 22[1]). Also public roads, bathing places, gardens etc. cannot be misused, defiled or obstructed for similar purposes (Nār. 11,15 f. ; Bṛh. 19, 27 f.; Kāty. 19, 23—26[2]).

The joint ownership of the fields is often seen to-day specially in the Punjab. There the villages are divided into three classes according to the constitution of the land-tenure system, which in the official jargon are called Zamīndārī, Pattidārī and Bhayācāra villages. In the Zamīndārī system properties are absolutely held in common, inasmuch as the whole of the proceeds of the pieces of land is put in a common coffer and is divided among the family-heads after the expenses have been deducted from it. In the Pattidārī system the soil, held in common, is divided into lots (pattī), as is found in private property, but they can however be redistributed periodically. In the Bhayācāra (*bhrātrācāra*) system every family tills its own ground as its free property. Sometimes these three systems are regarded as historical steps from absolute common possession of the soil to pure private property [3]. On the other hand Baden-Powell is of opinion that some of the Bhayācāra villages came into existence through the decline of former village communities with joint ownership of the fields, but it is improbable that all of them came into existence in this way. The state of things described in M. is in his opinion preserved in the land tenure system of the N. W. Provinces : the land is divided into small principalities, pure private property of individual families in the villages, great land-owners, nobles etc. through the villages being bestowed upon them as fiefs and the inheritance of these

Joint ownership of fields in the Punjab.

Zamīndārī, Pattīdārī and Bhayācāra villages of the Punjab.

Land-tenure system of N. W. Provinces corresponds to the state of things described by Manu.

1. Ibid. 585. *Tr.*
2. Ibid. 589—92. *Tr.*
3. Tupper 2,2 ; Mayne § 197 etc.

fiefs in their families so that they frequently become common property till it is divided again.[1]

Pasture grounds are common property where fields are owned by individuals.

In the Punjab on the other hand joint settlements of particular tribes appear to be the usual cause of joint ownership of fields[2] ; perhaps these tribes are meant by the agricultural organisations mentioned in Bṛh. As recommended by the Smṛtis, common pasture grounds are often found even where the fields are private properties. Inscriptions often refer to fields which bear particular names or are designated by the names of their proprietors, so that here too purely private property is in evidence as prescribed in the Smṛtis. The boundaries of villages in the four cardinal points are carefully described in the donative grants, on account of which a village described in that manner is called *caturāghāṭaviśuddha* "fixed by four boundaries". Rivers, mountains, trees, hillocks, tanks etc. are utilised in marking the boundary if simply the names of the adjacent villages are not given. Also the boundaries of fields are fully described; thus in a Śāsana of 1091 A. D. the boundaries of a granted field is described in this manner : the names of the fields lying to the east and the south of it and the names of the owners of these fields are mentioned and the boundaries of a certain village are given as its western and northern boundaries.[3] About the fixing of the boundaries see § 34. In Behar even to this day there is a proverb about the necessity of keeping the boundary ridges in order, in which the farmer who does not look after the boundary ridges of his fields is compared with an ape fallen from a bough.[4]

Boundaries described in the donative grants.

1. Baden-Powell, A Manual of the Land Revenue Systems and Land Tenures of British India (Calc. 1882) 395 f.

2. l. c. 393—399.

3. E.I. 1, 317 f.

4. Grierson l. c. § 834.

§ 28. *Interests.* The movable property is differentiated from the real estate or the immovables (Sthāvara), literally "fixed and motionless property" which may consist of pieces of land, plantations, fields, woods, houses etc., including however also rents out of a piece of land and income from a donation (*nibandha, vṛtti*); very probably cattle was the most primitive form of movable property, particularly animals giving milk (*dohya*) and beasts of burden and animals used for riding (*vāhya, vāhana*). The standpoint of the Vedas that the cows are the proper medium of trade is still in evidence particularly in many Prāyaścittas and in the compensation for murder and then also in marriage (*ārṣa*, § 16). Yet metal money is predominant, particularly the already very old Kārṣāpaṇa,[1] as in the laws of punishments most of which are fines (M. 8, 131—138 etc.). The formulas of oaths and ordeals are regulated according to the value of the disputed object estimated in gold (Vi. 9,4), and thus we find here a pure gold currency. The Greek disignations Dīnāra=dynários and Dramma=draxmy are mentioned only in later works and also the Suvarṇa, which occurs at quite an early date, is later equated with the Dīnāra in value. Besides the money and the domestic animals, male and female slaves, who are comprehended in the term "two-footed," ornaments, corns, fruits, metals, and other raw products, weapons and dresses are the principal items of movable property.

Distinction between movable and immovable preperty.

Household animals were the earliest movable propertv.

A gold currency.

Other movable properties.

In contrast to assets (*dhana*) there is the liability (*ṛṇa*), and the development of the conception of the latter is the same as that of *debitum* and our [German] *Schuld* (from *skulan*). The general significance "obligation" is still retained even in the Smṛtis, and particularly in the

1. Cunningham, Coins of ancient India (Lond. 1891) 1—3,42-54.

Conception of liability and assets.

theory of the three-fold debt consisting of sacrifices, raising of a son and the recitation of the Veda, which has to be paid to the gods, ancestors and the Ṛṣis respectively. On the other hand the word *ṛṇa* is already known in the Veda in the sense of an obligation of payment and in Indian arithmetic too the conception of "minus" is expressed by *ṛṇa* ("plus" by *dhana* or *sva*).

High antiquity of the law of debt.

"Recovery of debts" is the first of the eighteen titles of law ; in most of the laws regarding procedure, complaints of debts are referred to in the first line and even the whole procedure of witnesses forms only a part of the law of debts in M. and Nār. The high antiquity of the law of debt is suggested also by its vigorous emphasis on religious motives ; unpaid debts pursue the debtor even into his future birth, so that he is reborn as a slave in the house of his creditor in order to pay off the debt by his labour and the religious merit of his sacrifices and penances is transferred entirely to his creditor (Nār. 1,7-9). On the other hand, similarly from a religious standpoint, the trade of a money-lender and particularly of the usurer (*vārdhuṣin*) is regarded as immoral. Even in the extremity of distress a Brahman should not practise usury (Nār. 1,111) ; the usurer is placed on the same footing as the thief (Y. 1,132) and in a future existence he is reborn as an epileptic (Vi. 45, 26). Also taking interest apart from all other considerations, even without exceeding the allowed rates, is a means of livelihood of doubtful quality (Nār. 1,46) and according to Bṛh. 11,2 interest is called Kusīda because it is extorted from a hard pressed man by a centemptible (Kutsita) person. This means of livelihood is however permitted to the Vaiśya and in Āpaddharma, the law in the time of distress, we find along with the above-mentioned

Usury condemned.

Even simple interest is deprecated.

prohibition also the laxer view that in such times even Brahmans may live by lending money at interest (M. 10, 116 f.; Y. 3, 42).

Rates of interest and the periods of accumulation.

As usury cannot be altogether stopped, it had to be limited as far as possible, and this the Smṛtis attempt to do particularly by rules about the limit of the permissible rate of interest and the length of the period for the accumulation of interest. It is a general opinion that where gold has been lent the interests in arrear cannot exceed the amount of the principal and that the interest stops as soon as this maximum is reached. Opinions are divergent regarding the maximum in the loan of other things which may be the result of the differences in local usages emphasised by Nār. 1, 105 f. The interest is paid in kind. According to the particularly detailed rules of Bṛh. 11, 13—16 the accumulated interest in the case of clothes and base metals may make the debt treble, in the case of corns, fruits, beasts of burden and wool quadruple, in the case of vegetables quintuple, in the case of seeds and sugar-cane sextuple, in the case of salt, oil, intoxicating drinks, sugar and honey the interest may make the debt octuple, while in the case of grass, wood, brick, thread, stuffs from which spirituous liquor can be extracted, leaves, bones, leather, weopon, flowers, fruits either (according to one reading) the interest may increase unimitedly, or (according to another reading) no interest should be charged.

Period of accumulation varies according to the material which is lent.

High rates of interest.

This extraordinary amount of interest is possible on account of the fact that the rate of interest is very high and according to a rule which M. 8, 140 ascribes to Vas. and which is actually found in Vas. 2, 51, the interest should be 1¼ per cent. per month, that is 15 per cent. per annum; but if the debtor belongs to the lower castes and in the case of insufficient security, it may rise to 5 per cent. per month, that is 60 per cent. per annum, what according to M. 8, 152 is the maximum. Debtors of higher castes should be favoured and the rates of interest decrease according as the debtor belongs to a high caste so that the Brahman has to pay only 2 per cent. per month in the case of loan without security.[1] If there is a particular risk, still higher rates may be charged; thus merchants who wish to travel through a wilderness should pay 10 per cent. and those who would make a voyage should pay 20 per cent. (Y. 2, 38) because in such loans even the principal is endangered (Mit.); generally any interest voluntarily promised should be paid by every man (Vi. 6, 3 etc.).

Higher castes favoured.

Higher rates for special risks.

The law-books seek to effect a limitation of usury also by forbidding certain particularly oppressive forms of interest and by declaring certain debts to be free from interest. Thus M. 8, 153 forbids taking interest beyond one year and also such as is unapproved i. e., according to the oldest commentaries, all short period interests, interest on interests, periodical or monthly payable interests, and usurious interests fixed on special agreement as well as body interests, i. e. those which would have to be worked off by physical labour of a man or an animal (*kāyika*, according to another explanation daily payable interest). Of course this passage and other similar passages are in open discord with the rules of other law-books; M. himself in 8, 155 permits compound interest in the veiled form that in the renewed agreement the interests in arrear should be added to the principal and the same process is observed to this day. M. also allows the working off of a debt (8, 177). *Inter alia*, the following are mentioned on which no interest can be charged[2]: reward, gambling debts, improper promises (e. g. made to

Particular Kinds of interest forbidden.

Compound interest in a veiled form allowed.

1. It is significant that Kauṭilya ignores the caste privileges in the law of debt. *Tr.*

2. Cf. my Ind. Schuldrecht, Sitzungsberichte d. b. AK. d. W 1877. 295 f.

a courtesan), deposits, the price for a purchased ware, friendly loans, loans particularly mentioned to be free of interest (*uddhāra*, which is explained as *niṣphalam ṛṇam*), and articles lent for use (*yācitaka*), as well as the property of a woman (Strīdhana) used by the male relations with her permission, liabilities for securities, fines and the articles mostly of little value such as wood, grass, thread etc. mentioned in Bṛh. 11, 16 referred to above, the reading of which however is certainly faulty. Yet under certain circumstances e. g. if the debtor refuses to the take back the property or generally after the lapse of a short period, interests could be charged on some articles of these categories and indeed at the rate of 5 p. c. per month, which is another proof of the universality of this rate of interest.[1] A loan is free of interest also when the creditor refuses to accept the due interest and particularly if the debtor deposits the interests with a trustworthy person (Y. 2,44).

Debts which are free of interest.

Usual rate is 5 p. c.

The expressions Kusīda and Kusīdin are found already in the TS and in the Nirukta and the designation of percentage by numerical adjectives, occurring in M. 8,142, was already known to Pāṇini 5,1,47 and he also uses the expression Vṛddhi "interest" and on the other hand also speaks of articles lent for use (*yācita*, *yācitaka*) which are free of interest (4,4,21). Accordingly, no importance evidently should be attached to the statement of Megasthenes fragment 27 B, where it is said that the Indians are unacquainted with the conception of interest (oute daneizousi oute isasi daneizeshai[2]). The Nasik inscriptions offer us ancient epigraphical documents for interests and the limit of the rate of interest from the first century A. D. downwards[3].

Laws of interest known in the Vedic period and to Pāṇini.

Mistake of Megasthenes.

Epigraphical evidence.

1. Hopkins perhaps goes a little too far when he says "no stipulation beyond five per cent. *per mensem* is legal" (CHI p. 287). *Tr.*

2. The Indians neither put money out at usury nor do they know how to borrow (Mc Crindle). *Tr.*

3. Arch. Surv. W. I. 4, 101 ff.

Thus there are mentioned interests to the amount of 100 for 2000 and 75 for 1000 Kāhāpaṇas (Kārṣāpaṇas) i. e., as these are very probably monthly interests, 60 p. c. and 90 p. c. respectively ; the first rate agrees with the rate of interest laid down in the Smṛtis.

High rates of interest at the present day.

Even at the present day the rate of interest is still very high, particularly in the country. Thus in Bengal the farmers have to pay 50 p. c. for advances in corn at the time of sowing to the Mahājan (Mahājana) "village banker" corresponding to the Kusīdin or Vārdhuṣin of the Smṛtis ; as laid down in the Smṛtis, the interest is paid in kind and the Mahājan has the right of a mortgage bottomry on the corn reaped. 2 p. c. per month is allowed for advance in money[1]. In Behar where the ancient expression Mūl for "principal" (Mūla), Khaduka for "debtor" (Khādaka), Udhār (Uddhāra) for loans on which no interest can be charged are still in evidence, there is a whole series of different expressions which vary from province to province to designate the interest for seed-corn to be paid in kind after harvest and for every grade of the rate of interest, which here too often amounts to 50 p. c.[2] According to Steele in Bombay, 1/2—1 p. c. per month were charged for loans on security from well-to-do farmers, but it is also seen in Puna and Southern Mahārāṣṭra that a farmer at the end of the year has to return 1 1/4 times as much or even double the amount of the grain lent to him. There is a particular word (*dāmupat*) in Mahrathi to designate the principal doubled by interests ; when this doubling takes place, the interest as a rule, as laid down in the Smṛtis, ceases to accumulate, though triplication (*tripat*) is allowed in the case of the loan of grains. Small traders have to pay sometimes even 6 1/4 per cent. per week and the rate

Duplication or triplication of the principal.

1. Phear, The Aryan Village (Lond. 1880) 62—64. Cf. also Kohler ZVR 9,352 (according to Hunter).

2. Grierson §§ 1475-81.

of interest also depends generally on the circumstances and the caste of the debtor. The money-lenders are often Brahmans. There are also loans on which no interest çan be charged [1]. Dubois says that 20 p. c. is the minimum, 100 p. c. the maximum and 50 p. c. the usual rate of interest in Mysore [2].

Liability rests with all the members of the family but chiefly on the chief of the family.

§ 29. *Debts, pledges and sureties.* The liability for debts according to the earlier developed principles of the family law and joint property (§ 23), extends over all the members of the family if the debt is incurred for the benefit of the whole family *(kuṭumbārthe)*, particularly however the responsibility lies on the chief of the house-hold *(kuṭumbin)* and passes over to his heirs, and here too as in the law of inheritance, taking admission into a religious order or disappearance is regarded as equivalent to the death of the testator (Vi. 6, 27-39 etc.). How far the debts of the testator are transmitted to the descendants is a matter of dispute, for e.g. according to Vi. l. c. and Nār. 1, 4 only the sons and grandsons are liable and according to Bṛh. 11,49 the grandsons have to pay only the principal without interests, while on the other hand, according to Nār. 1, 6 the great-grandsons too are liable for the debts of the great-grandfather. The same difference of opinion may be seen also in the commentaries. Thus the Mit. on Y. 2, 50 advocates the view of Bṛh. that the liability for the debts does not extend to the great-grandsons and that even the grandsons are responsible only for the principal shorn of interests. On the other hand, according to Asahāya on Nār. l.c. the great-grandsons too are liable for the debts and he illustrates this by an alleged case dealt with in a court of Pāṭaliputra in which the son and the grandson of the debtor quickly

Dispute over the transmission of debts.

1. Steele, Castes 266 ff., 247.
2. Dubois, People of India 496.

28

died one after another and the great-grandson tried in vain to escape the liability of payment.

The religious motive in the law of debt.

The narrower circle of Sapiṇḍa relations stretches up to the great-grandson and so here too, as in the law of inheritance, the religious motive connected with the funeral sacrifice plays a prominent part. Therefore, even the absence of assets does not free the sons from the liability for the debts of the father. On the other hand immoral promises of payment such as gambling debts and tavern scores of the father are not binding on the sons and as little binding are the debts of a father who was rendered unfit for legal business on account of some bodily or spiritual defect (Bṛh. 11,51 ; Kāty. 10,53 f.[1] etc.). The head of the family is in general not liable for those debts which the sons, the wife or other members of the family have contracted for purposes other than those of the household. Only in the case of those professions in which the man can support himself only with the help of the wife, e. g. in the case of washermen, shepherds, actors and sailors, the debts of the wife are said to be always binding on the husband (Vi. 6,37 etc.). After the death of the husband the wife is responsible for those debts of his which she contracted together with him or which she has expressly recognised and she is also liable for her husband's debts if she inherits his property or receives from him a command of payment at the time of his death ; in the absence of assets or sons the liability may fall also on him with whom the widow lives, inasmuch as he is to some extent the heir (Nār. 1,16,22).

Sons liable for the debts of father even in the absence of assets, but sometimes not.

Wife's liability for husband's debts.

Similar forms at the beginning and at the end.

At the payment of a debt as well as at the time of giving back a deposit (§ 30) the same forms are to be observed as when launching on them (Vi. 6, 1). Therefore if it was contracted orally or with written documents

1. Bandyopadhyaya, 437 ff. *Tr.*

before witnesses, the same witnesses must be present also when it is paid back (Vi. 6,24 ; Y. 2,94). If a written contract had been made, as was usually the case at least in later times, the creditor must give it back or tear it or give the debtor an acquittance ; part payments too must every time be noted down on the back of the bond of debt, or if it is not at hand, a special acquittance must be given for them (Vi. 6,25 f. ; Y. 2,93). If the creditor refuses to give acquittance for a sum which has been paid he will forfeit the rest of his dues, and moreover the amount which has been paid to him but for which he has given no acquittance begins to accumulate interests for the debtor as it had till then done for the creditor (Nār. 1,115). Accumulation of interest stops if the creditor does not accept the offered payment (out of greed, in order to get further interests, according to the commentators) ; yet according to Y. 2,44 this happens only when the debtor deposits the money with a disinterested party. Among several concurring demands, according to Kāty.[1], the oldest one is to be satisfied first ; exception however should be made in favour of the demands of a Brahman or a king which shall be satisfied before all others. The Brahmans appear to be favoured also in another way ; after the death of a creditor of this caste the debtor shall pay back the debt not only to his descendants or near or more distant relations, but shall pay it to other Brahmans on failure of such relations and if Brahmans too cannot be found, it should be thrown into water (Nār. 1, 112 f.). About the recovery of debts see § 53.

Aquittance must be given for part payments.

Otherwise the rest of the debt is forfeited.

Interest stops if creditor refuses to take money.

Earlier debts paid first.

Brahmans favoured.

Nār. 1, 117 says that the guarantee (to the creditor) may be of two kinds : a surety and a pledge. Pledge of property and personal security appear to have been equally developed, yet however the law of pledges is dealt with more fully and plays the chief

Sureties and pledges.

1. Bandyopadhyaya, 434. *Tr.*

part even at the present day. The pledge is called Ādhi "deposit" or Bandha, Bandhaka "binding, bond". Hypothecation is not mentioned in Ancient Indian Literature,[1] there is only pledge of property, all the same whether it consists of immovable or movable properties. Of the various kinds of pledges those which may be enjoyed (*bhogya*) and those that are to be preserved uninjured (*gopya*) (Nār. 1, 125 etc.) are most important. Pledged immovable properties which may be used, such as for instance, a house, a field, a fruit garden, appear as a rule actually to have been used; the income made out of it was the interest. Also male and female slaves, oxen, cows and other house-hold animals are mentioned as usable pledges.

Various kinds of pledges.

The pledgee is responsible for the injury, loss and depreciation of a pledge excepting when vis major is the cause thereof and he forfeits the interests in the case of illegal handling of the pledged property which was to be preserved uninjured and is punishable if he maltreats a pledged slave; on the other hand the debtor has to replace a pledged property which has become valueless without there being any fault on the part of the creditor, and if he does not prefer it he has to pay off the debt.

Pledgee responsible for the depreciation of the pledge.

Different grades of the right of mortgage are naturally excluded, because a pledge is valid only when it is actually in the possession of the creditor.[2] For that reason only the first mortgage is valid in the case of repeated mortgages of the same property with different creditors and if it is mortgaged with various creditors at the same time the priority of the possessor or superior right is the determinative factor or the pledge is divided among the creditors. The debtor could any time demand the restoration of the mortgaged property on payment of the debt and the accumulated

Several mortagages of the same property.

1. P. N. Sen (Hindu Jurisprudence, p. 186) has shown that hypothecation was known at least in Bengal. *Tr.*

2. But see f.-n. 1. *Tr.*

interests, which according to the rule mentioned above could not exceed the amount of the principal, for in principle "pledges cannot be prescribed." This principle is particularly applicable in the case of usable pledges which are accordingly to be given back to the debtor as soon as the redoubling of the debt takes place as the result of the accumulation of interests and the whole amount which is thus due is realised through usufruct. According to another and perhaps a later view even in the case of usable pledges either the forfeiture of the same or the cessation of usufruct after the expiry of a fixed period may be stipulated. Stipulations for forfeiture were of common practice, e. g. after a term of 2, 5 or 10 years, in the case of pledges to be preserved uninjured; even without such stipulations they would be forfeited as soon as the interests in arrear have reached the amount of the principal or after 20 years; yet in favour of the debtor a respite of 10 or 14 days is arranged or a court warrant is given for the sale of the pledged property and partly also the refunding of the excess arising out of this sale is arranged for. The creditor too may get satisfaction by reverting to enjoying the pledged property from merely holding it in custody. Gold and precious stones, garments and stuffs are particularly mentioned as properties of pledge which are merely to be held in custody, but also slaves, horses, copper utensils of cooking etc. could be pledged in this way. Such pledges could be kept in custody also by a pledge-keeper *(adhipāla)* instead of the creditor himself[1].

Pledges cannot be prescribed. Usable pledges automatically clear away the debts.

Unused pledges were forfeited.

Respite for the debtor.

Unusable pledges changed into usable ones.

Sureties, called Pratibhū "representative" or Lagnaka "bail" can be held responsible not only for the payment of a debt *(dāna)*, but also for appearance (*darśana* or *upasthāna*), for delivering the debtor's assets *(ṛṇidravyārpaṇa)*, for delivering a pledge

Seven kinds of sureties.

1. For the original documents about the above see my ind. Schuldrecht l. c. 298—307.

(*gṛhītabandhopasthāna*) and for reliability (*viśvāsa* or *pratyaya*), i. e. for the good conduct of the debtor or for his capacity to pay. In a law-suit (*vāde*), either for the complainant or for the accused, a surety may stand for the performance of an ordeal (*divya*, *śapatha*), for assurance (*abhaya*), i. e. protection against a sudden injury, or for a written document (*lekhye kṛte*). The first five kinds of sureties may eventually be held responsible for the payment of the debt, in which however the creditor has to proceed with utmost mildness and must allow respite.

Regarding the inheritance of the obligations of suretyship a historical development of the same seems to lie before us from its absolute uninheritability to its inheritability by the son, in whose case it is restricted only to the principal.[1] According to some authors even the son is responsible only in the case of the suretyship for payment and the suretyship for delivering the pledge. The choice of a surety should never fall on such persons who on account of their position and qualifications or on account of their special connections with the debtor or the creditor cannot qualify themselves for going bail. For this reason, e. g. dependants, royal officers, ascetics, unpropertied or unknown persons, friends or enemies are excluded. Near relations too cannot stand surety for one another if they live on a joint property. If there are more than one sureties it depends on the nature of the previous agreements whether they should jointly pay off the whole debt or each of them should pay off the part of the debt guaranteed by him. The regress of the surety

Inherited suretyship.

Inadmissible sureties.

Several sureties for one debt.

1. This statement is apparently based on M. 158-162. Meyer (Rechtsschriften, pp. 303-4) says however that it is wrong to hold suretyship to have been uninheritable originally, for already Kauṭ. speaks of inheritable suretyship. But even apart from the fact that Kauṭ.'s date is still uncertain it is very likely that the kernel of M. is very old (Ind. Hist. Quarterly, 1927, pp. 808ff.). *Tr.*

against the debtor generally amounts to the double of what he has paid under compulsion but in the case of natural products, under certain circumstances, it is said to rise even to the eight fold.

Law of debt at the present day.

Mutual suretyship of family members is still found in the South according to Steele, but the creditor in such cases holds the head of the family specially responsible for the debt[1]; now however by English legislation the responsibility of the heir for the debts of the testator has been restricted to the amount of the wealth inherited by him. About modern bonds of debt see § 35. Among pledges different kinds of usable pledges are seen even at the present day for which the ancient designation Bhogyādhi is still in vogue in Kanara. The pledgee has still to compensate for the pledged property if it is lost and still as in old days this obligation is escaped if the loss is due to fire, floods or another *force majeure.* Precious stones, cotton and silk stuffs, metal vessels, money in a sealed bag and similar things are handed to the creditor only to be kept by him in custody and not to be used.[2] In Behar the pledge is generally called Bandhik=Bandha of the Smṛtis; in the pledge of immovable properties distinction is made between the usufruct of a piece of land for a certain period by which the principal and the interests are annihilaied, the usufruct which serves to satisfy only the interests and the pledge which becomes the property of the creditor if the debtor cannot pay off the principal within a certain period [3]. In the Punjab too the usable pledge is the most common form of pledges[4]. According to Steele many of the rules about suretyship are still observed in the South.[5] Thus there are four kinds of suretyship:

Different kinds of usable and unusable pledges.

Various kinds of suretyship.

1. Steele, Castes 265 f.
2. l. c. 247—257.
3. Grienson § 1481 f.
4. Tupper 3, 218 ff.
5. l. c. 274—276.

for payment, for appearance, for loyal behaviour and mutual suretyship. Responsibilities of suretyship go down to the sons in the first case and under certain circumstances also in the next two kinds of suretyship. The surety is mostly responsible only for the principal. Ascetics agents, women and near relations cannot stand security.

§ 30. *Deposit and treasure trove.* The development of the law of deposits is expressive of the universal insecurity of person and property. Bṛh. 12, 2 speaks of fear of king, robbers etc. and the purpose of cheating one's co-heirs as motives for a deposit. A deposit (*nikṣepa, upanidhi, nyāsa*) may either be open or closed; the closing is usually performed by sealing up the deposit or keeping it in a casket or a bag. Also a deposit received from a third person (*anvādhi, anvāhita*), a deposit handed over in the absence of the house-holder to his family or servants (*nyāsa*), a thing lent for use in a festival etc. (*yācita, yācitaka*), that which is given to a merchant for business purposes or to an artizan for him to work upon, mutual deposits (*pratinyāsa*) and other kinds of deposits are mentioned (Nār. 2, 14 f.; Bṛh. 12, 15; Kāty. 11, 1[1].)

Different kinds of deposits.

The depositary is punished if he misappropriates the deposited property or uses it in any other way than is expressly allowed and he is also to make good the deposited property if it is lost through his own fault. In the investigation of the question of debt particular importance is attached to the point whether the depositary kept the deposit apart from his own valuable articles and thus failed to bestow upon it equal care and in general whether he did not pay necessary attention to it; he is not guilty if the deposit is lost through fire, flood, theft or through (confiscation by) the king or generelly through a vis major (*daiva*) or if he has timely warned the depositor of the threatening

Responsibilities of the depositary.

1. Bandyopadhyaya, 472. *Tr.*

danger. The most sensible act is never to accept a deposit ; yet however high religious merit may be gained by faithfully keeping a deposit, while on the other hand, its misappropriation is as great a sin as the murder of a near relative (Bṛh. 12, 6—8).

It is best not to accept a deposit.

The law-books display a great deal of imagination in laying down means of preventing the embezzlement of the deposit by the depositary which probably took place very frequently: one should choose only a reliable and well-to-do man as depositary; witnesses may be called who must be present at that time as well as at the time of giving back the deposit; also the seal etc. must be intact when the deposit is given back; where witnesses are lacking the judge should test the honesty of the depositary by having another article deposited with him through the secret police and watching whether he gives it back or not; in a difficult case an ordeal may be resorted to, particularly in the case of secret deposits (M. 8, 179—184; Nār. 2,4 ; Bṛh. 12, 14). Embezzlement of, or falsely claiming, a deposit is severely punished.

Precautions to prevent misappropriation.

The same motives which urge a man to deposit his valuables with a reliable person cause him also to bury his treasure in the earth. If such a treasure *(nidhi)* is found anywhere it becomes the property of the king because he is the lord of the earth with all that is found in it[1] ; or the finder may keep 1/6 (Gaut. 10, 43, 45 ; Vas. 3, 13 ; M. 8, 39 ; Nār. 7, 6). A Brahman, particularly a learned and dutiful Brahman, may keep the whole of a treasure trove found by him (Gaut. 10,44 etc.). This seems to have been the original theory ; usually however the king is less

King seizes the treasure trove.

1. Jayaswal (Hindu Polity, Part II, p. 174 ff.) however has shown that Hindu jurists and law-givers never considered the king to be lord of the earth. *Tr.*

thought of[1]. If a member of any caste other than that of the Brahman finds a treasure, he must inform the king and after delivering the sixth part—the usual share of the king also in taxation—he may keep the rest for himself; whoever fails to send information must deliver the whole treasure trove and may be punished also otherwise; if the king himself finds the treasure, he may retain half of it for himself; the other half he must give away to Brahmans (M. 8,35-39; Y. 2,34 f.; Vi. 3,56 ff.).

Brahman's share in the treasure trove.

Caste privileges in the law of treasure troves.

Vi. 3,59 ff. casuistically develops the result of the caste distinction in the finder. A Kṣatriya must always give away 1/4 of the treasure trove to the king and 1/4 to the Brahmans; a Vaiśya 1/4 to the king and 1/2 to the Brahmans; a Śūdra 5/12 to the king and 5/12 to the Brahmans. The procedure about lost properties which have been found and delivered to the king is connected with these rules; the king can claim a share also of these finds, he can even completely take possession of it after the expiry of a certain period (M. 8,30 ff. etc.). On the other hand he must restore the property uninjured to the legitimate owner which was stolen and was then seized by his police (M. 8,40; Y. 2,36.).

Lost properties deposited with the king.

Instances of deposit in Sanskrit literature.

In the poetical literature the Mṛcch. offers us a well-known instance of a deposit, the depositing of ornament (*alaṁkāranyāsa*); the ornament is then stolen and the depositary holds himself bound to make amends for it. In the Rājatar. 8,123 ff. a king famous for his accurate judgments uses a stratagem of the kind of tricks recommended in the Smṛtis in order to arrive at a clue in a case of embezzlement of a large sum which the owner had deposited with a merchant; the convincing proof of the faithlessness of the depositary (*nyāsadhārin*)

1. Kauṭ. however allows the king to seize the whole of a treasure trove specially if it is large. *Tr.*

is gained when he produces quite new coins as belonging to the remaining part of the deposit which could be possible only if the deposited sum had been constantly in use.

Various kinds of deposits still known.

The difference between the open, closed or sealed deposits is still expressed by special terms in Bihari which however do not agree with the Smṛtis [1]. The customary law of Bombay recognises depositary's obligation to compensate for illegal use or loss of a deposited property and other principles of ancient law [2]. According to an example occurring in Rājatar. 7, 499, the treasure trove may also be wholly the property of the king, yet however according to EI 1, 400, 27 he can transfer his claim upon the treasure trove to the donee as a special privilege when making presents of villages. Also according to the customary law of Bombay the treasures which are found on unclaimed land should revert to the government; in other cases too the share of the government is 1/6 or 1/4 as laid down in the Smṛtis; in the days of the Mahrattas the Brahmans and other higher class people were allowed to take complete possession of a treasure trove[3].

King sometimes seizes the whole treasure trove.

Strīdhana developed out of the law of presents.

§ 37. *Presents and charitable gifts.* Presents (*dāna*) play an important role not only in worldly life, as for instance it has been the primary cause of the development of the theory of the personal property of women (§ 25), but it is still more important for religion (*dharma*), for the right of accepting presents is the most important privilege of the Brahmans. In worldly connections the presents fall under the title of law *dattasyā 'napakarma* or *dattāpradānikam* "resumption of gifts" or "retraction

1. Grierson, § 1480.
2. Steele, 242—246.
3. l. c. 283—285.

or promises" (M. 8, 212—214; Nār. 4, 1—12) or, as Bṛh. 15, 1 says, the law of valid or invalid gifts—of what may or may not be given. The rules about presents and gifts of a religious nature (*dharmārtham*) are described at a much greater length in the Smṛtis and the Purāṇas —e. g. they fill a big volume of Hemādri. Even in the Vedic literature the sacrificial fee (*dakṣiṇā*) and generally all presents to Brahmans play an important part. The more valuable the present, the greater is the reward in heaven. The 10 or 16 great gifts (*mahādāna*) are particularly emphasised: according to the Bhaviṣyapurāṇa the 10 gifts consist of gold, horses, sesamum, elephants, female slaves, carriages, land, houses, girls and a brown cow; the *tulāpuruṣa*, i. e. gold or valuables of the weight of a man, tops the list of the 16 gifts.[1]

Religious gifts dealt with more exhaustively.

The 10 or 16 great gifts.

Besides gold land was very much coveted by the Brahmans. Already Vi. 3, 81 f. advises the king to present land to the Brahmans and to have a deed of gift prepared on a piece of cotton cloth or copper plates for the attestation of the gift and for the purpose of informing the future rulers of the gift; it should contain the name and the family tree of the donor, a description of the gift and a reference to the meritoriousness of the gift and the sin of every encroachment on the same. Later Smṛtis have very detailed rules for the preparation of these deeds (§ 35). Besides land particularly fields, houses or whole villages, by which only the right of taking the taxes out of it is meant, pensions (*nibandha*) too are bestowed, for instance the fixed monthly or annual payments of guilds of merchants for the maintenance of a temple. The king should also do his utmost to provide everything for the corporations of learned men, to procure them maintenance and erect a building for them in his capital (Y. 2, 185—191, cf.

Gift of land and rules for drawing up a copper-plate grant.

Other gifts besides land.

1. Hemādri 1,19.

Bṛh. 17, 2 ff.). Also real monasteries (*maṭha*) are mentioned which should be bestoweed upon Brahmans and ascetics.

Public works (*pūrta*) too are not considered to be less meritorious, such as the establishment of shelters for the poor and for travellers (*dharmaśālā*), sinking wells and constructing cisterns and water stations (*prapā*), digging tanks and laying public gardens etc. The Purāṇas deal with this subject very exhaustively[1] from which it is also clear that it was not always a gift but mere resignation of proprietory right (*utsarga*), as for instance even the liberation of a bull (Vi. 86 etc.) at the Śrāddha ceremony falls under this head. To these pious acts further belongs the establishment of images of gods and temples and the repair of the same if they are dilapidated or damaged. Important immunities and privileges are connected with the gifts. Thus exemption from taxes is warranted to the donee (cf. §35), and a man who has promised a present to a Brahman may be sued for it as for a debt (Kāty. 14, 4)[2] etc. Intentional alteration and forging of a royal grant shall be punished with the first amercement and death respectively (Y. 2, 295; M. 9, 232); if a man does not fulfil his promise of constructing a house for the assembly or a water station or a temple or of digging a tank and laying a garden, or of constructing roads and of similar pious works of public utility, his property shall be confiscated and he will be banished from the city (Bṛh. 17, 11—13).

Public works encouraged.

Banishment for unfulfilled promises of public works.

On the other hand care should be taken that gifts are not bestowed on undeserving persons; those gifts which are made with a pious intention but are spent otherwise are therefore invalid as well as if there are fraud, bribery, fear, enmity and other illegal and ignoble motives at the root (M. 8, 212; Nār. 4, 9—12; Bṛh. 15, 8—11 etc.). It is a

Invalid gifts.

1. Cf. Mandlik 333—344.
2. Bandyopadhyaya, 513. *Tr.*

A family man cannot give away his whole property.

significant fact that it is held to be necessary to put a curb on the pious zeal by declaring the gift of the whole property invalid, at least when there is male issue (Nār. 4,4 etc.) ; all that remains after the costs of maintaining and clothing the family have been defrayed may be given and if anybody gives still more then "what formerly tasted like honey should be changed into poison" (Bṛh. 15, 3). Gift once bestowed cannot be lost through usurpation by an outsider ; for this reason the property of a learned Brahman is reckoned among things that cannot become the property of another through prescription (M. 8, 149 etc.).

Gifts cannot be prescribed.

An historical instance of a Tulāpuruṣa is given by the minister Caṇḍeśvara of Mithilā who in the year 1314 A. D. gave to an assembly of Brahmans his own weight of gold [1]. Mandlik, the well-known author of "Hindu Law", gave away his own weight of silver in 1875 or 76 in Wāi near Sattārā (Bühler). The inscriptions afford us the richest documents of gifts and presents of every kind. Already king Aśoka boasts of the construction of mango parks and other plantations, wells, serais and water stations on the roads [2]. The foundation of a monastery for ascetics (*tāpasamaṭha*) is for instance mentioned in an inscription of 1114 [3] ; erection of temples and establishment of images of gods are often accompanied by special endowments for the maintenance of the same and for the observation of the cult—all of which are managed by special committees (*goṣṭhījana*) ; particularly however villages, fields and pieces of land of every sort are given to Brahmans. Also houses, gardens, shops tanks and canals etc. appear in the documents of gifts.

Historical and modern instances of Tulāpuruṣa.

Epigraphical data about donations and gifts.

Endowments and committees on them.

1. Cf. WZKM 4,72.
2. EI 2, 270–274.
3. EI 1,36

Donations payable at fixed intervals or daily[1] correspond to the Nibandha of the Smṛtis. See § 35 for the formula of grants.

A very old specimen of all possible kinds of presents is found in the cave inscriptions of Uṣabhadāta in Nāsik[2] of about the first century A. D. who relates there *inter alia* that every year he has fed 100000 Brahmans, given 100000 cows and 16 villages to Brahmans, given wives to 8 Brahmans, built a staircase at a holy bathing place on the river Banas and rectangular serais and gardens, dug tanks and sunk wells for drinking water, built ferries, inns, water stations, cisterns and a cave for monks and assigned a field to the monks living in that cave for their maintenance, and that he has invested money in guilds of merchants on interest etc.

Uṣabhadāta's munifiscence.

Various gifts for religious and charitable purposes are seen even to this day ; in Behar[3] they are called Saṁkalp=Saṁkalpa "the introductory part of the ritual of gift which proclaims the intentions of the donor," the given land is everywhere called Devotar, Devasthān "the land belonging to a god" (the latter term is found even in the inscriptions). The management of these Devotars, according to the statement in the document of the gift, is either retained in the family of the donor or it may devolve on the chief of the temple priests or of the community after whose death it goes down to his successors. Interesting statements about the magnitude of the Devotar in Rajputana at the beginning of this [nineteenth] century may be found in Tod's Rājasthān ; thus at that time a great part of the state of Mewar (Udaipur) belonged to the mendicant orders. In the monasteries the board of directors is either

Religious gifts of the present day.

Magnitude of donations in Rajputana.

1. Cf. ZDMG 44, 355 ff. EI 1, 288.
2. Arch. Surv. W. I. 4, 99ff.
3. Grierson § 1209.

elective or it is fixed by its predecessor or it is either appointed by the government or by the donor and his family. The freedom from taxation is observed even to this day in the case of lands given away for religious purposes before 1765 [1].

The duty and the wages of the cow-herd.

§ 32. *Wages, hire and compensation.* Among the rules about the wages for service those which deal with field labour are the oldest. Cowherds are usually paid in kind, inasmuch as they receive a part of the milk; according to others they receive also a certain percentage of the animals entrusted to them, e. g. a calf for every 100 cows; they are however also punishable for wickedly deserting the herd and for illegal milking. With the break of day they have to drive the cattle to the meadow and bring them back to the stall at dusk undiminished and uninjured.

Cowherd is to make good the damage to cattle.

The cowherd will have to compensate for any injury that may occur to the cattle during that time excepting when he can prove that he had not slackened necessary attention for the cattle, for instance if he had defended his herd as best as he could against the attack of wolves or cried for help in the case of an attack by robbers. For damages to fields done by the herd he suffers punishments varying according to the amount of the damage and his own guilt but the duty of compensation in this case falls upon his employer; yet however there are cases in which both of them are allowed immunity from punishment, e. g. if the field is without fence or if the cowherd was ill or if any accident had befallen him, if the cow had calfed very recently or if the cow was unusually obstinate (Gaut. 12, 18—26; Y. 2, 159—165; Vi. 5, 137—150; M. 8, 229—244; Nār. 6, 10—17; 11, 28—41 etc.). There is a difference of opinion

Owner compensates for the damage to fields.

1. H. Cowell, Tagore Law Lectures (Calc. 1870) 65—69.

in this case as to whether over and above the obligation to compensate for the injury done by his cattle the owner has to pay the fine imposed on him, in which case the cowherd comes off with a sound flogging. The generally recognised principle seems to have been that the owner alone was responsible if there was no cowherd with the cattle.

Shall the owner also pay fine ?

The punishment of flogging, according to Āp. 2, 28, 2 f. is generally to be applied to a cowherd or a field labourer *(kīnāśa)* who does not perform his duty. The wages of the field labourer or the ploughman (*kṛṣīvala*) shall consist, like those of the cowherd, if no other agreement is made, of a portion of the profit (cf. Āp. 2, 28, 1). Thus according to Bṛh. 16, 11—13 he should receive 1/5 of the produce if he gets besides it also free living and quarters and 1/3 if he gets nothing else. Nār. 6, 3 and Y. 2, 194 speak only of 1/10; on the other hand the Ardhika or Ardhasīrin (M. 4, 253; Vi. 57, 16; Y. 1, 166) performed his service, as his name suggests, for half the proceeds of the crops.

Wages of the field labourer and the ploughman.

Later authors give a classification of various wages for labour. The warrior stands first, after him comes the field labourer, load carriers and domestic servants occupy the lowest place (Nār. 5, 22—24 ; Bṛh. 16, 10 f.). In all these kinds of service, even in the case of the servant of a merchant, a share of the profit may also be stipulated for instead of the wages ; in shorter periods of work very probably a fixed sum was stipulated for as a rule (Bṛh. 16, 9). idle employees who do not perform or finish their duty shall receive no wages, or shall return double the amount received as wages or shall also pay a fine ; yet however illness is recognised as a legitimate cause of hindrance to work. On the other hand the employer who without any ground refuses to pay the stipulated wages may be compelled to do it and a fine is imposed upon him ; he

Hierarchy of wage-earners

Punishment for neglecting duty

may pay for the special performances of his employees as he wishes. The employees must look after the implements of their master and must compensate for any damage done to those implements or to any property of the master, excepting what is caused by *force majeure.*

Transporter responsible for damage to cargo.

Similar rules are applied also to transport agreements. Thus the transporters are responsible and punishable for the damage to the cargo caused by their own negligence ; in the case of unintentional negligence of the duties of agreement, they must pay a compensation the amount of which depends upon the particular circumstances. On the other hand however the the owner of the cargo has to pay compensation if he withdraws from the agreement without mutual consent and it is for him to take care of a servant who may fall ill on the road ; in the case of an interruption of the transport for which the transporter is not guilty, e. g. on account of the attack of robbers, he must pay the transporter for the portion of the journey already accomplished (Vi. 5, 153—159 : M. 8, 215—217 ; Nār. 6, 4—9 ; Y. 2, 193—198 ; Kāty. 15, 16—18 etc.[1]).

Responsibilities of the owner of the cargo.

The pupil a servant to the Guru.

The position of the pupil (*śiṣya*) with his teacher and of the apprentice (*antevāsin*) with his master is also considered in the light of the relation between master and servant (Nār. 5, 3, 8—21). The rules for the conduct of a Brahmacārin who spends the period of his learning, up to the completion of his study of the Veda, with a Guru and during this period who has to show also outwardly every kind of respect to the teacher and even to his family, are usually given in religious law, and that in the most exhaustive manner ; they constitute one of the chief factors of Āśramadharma [2]. The apprentice too must continue with his master

1. Bandyopadhyaya. 539-40. *Tr.*
2. Cf. e. g. Āp. 1, 2—12.

till the expiry of his period of learning and shall render him services; the master shall treat him as his son and must not employ him in works of a different nature. At the end of the period of learning the pupil must remunerate his teacher and the apprentice his master in adequate manner. Even in the case of prostitutes (*veśyā*) a stipulation for service is made subject to principles given above (Nār. 6, 18 f.). A relation of piety exists between the sacrificial priest (Ṛtvij), particularly the hereditary family priest (Pūrvajuṣṭa), and the laity (Yājya) who employ and pay them. Dissolution of this relation without mutual consent is punishable (Vi. 5, 113 f. etc.).

Duties of both.

The priest cannot be discharged without mutual consent.

Besides the already mentioned instances of engaging load carriers and beasts of burden or draughts animals or wagons also the rent for a house, a cistern or a shop etc. is included in the category of hire. He who does not give back at the fixed time these rented properties or hired elephants, camels and other beasts of burden, has to pay for it adequately (Kāty. 15, 19 f.[1]). Any injury to a property of the owner must be made good to the owner by the hirer excepting in the case of *force majeure* (Nār. 6, 22). If anybody has built a house on a piece of land not his own he can take away the building materials used for it when evacuating the place only if he has paid the rent of the piece of land to the owner; otherwise he must leave behind the building materials as compensation (Nār. 6, 20 f.).

Rents and hires.

Owner compensated by hirer.

The obligation to pay compensation for every kind of injury is recognised in the fullest extent and the evidence for it may be found in what has been said above. Thus the owners must be compensated also for killed household animals, felled trees, torn or injured plants, expenses of treatment must be paid for wounded men or household animals, destroyed or injured walls,

Law of compensation.

1. Ibid. 542-543. *Tr.*

dikes, houses must be reconstructed and defiled roads shall be wiped clean (Vi. 5, 51, 59, 75 f., 106—109 etc.). We find included herein also the compensation which a metal-worker working in iron, copper, lead, tin, silver or gold, has to pay to the owner of these metals who gives these to him to prepare utensils from, for the loss in smelting when it exceeds the usual amount of loss in smelting as known from experience as well as the compensation of a weaver for the yarn woven by him, rendered heavier or more valuable in the process (Nār. 9, 12—15 ; Y. 2, 178 ; M. 8, 397). In the case of a washerman it is assumed that the linen loses 1/8 of its original value at the first washing, 1/4 at the second etc. and therefore the washerman has to make good to his customers every loss which exceeds this amount (Nār 9, 8f.). It is therefore in his own interest to wash the linen as carefully as possible on a board of soft wood (M. 8, 396).

Compensation for loss in smelting metals.

Compensation from washermen.

In dealing with the obligation to pay compensation everywhere a great emphasis is laid on the point whether or not there was any bad motive or criminal negligence of duty. Thus M 8, 290 ff. gives ten instances in connection with transport in which the transporter shall remain unpunished, as for example if he called on the man going before him to make room, if a wheel, the axletree or the yoke is broken etc. ; in other cases the transporter or the inmates of the wagon would be punished. The owner of a horse, dog or ape is not responsible for the damage caused by these animals excepting when he has spurred them on to do it ; sailors are responsible for every damage to the cargo which they have caused by their own negligence, but are not responsible in the case of *force majeure* (Nār. 15, 32 ; M. 8, 408 f.). About compensation for murder see §44.

Compensation demanded only when criminal motive is in evidence.

Already the Mahābhāṣya refers to the punishment

inflicted by kings for damages to corn caused by cows[1]. The field labourer working for half the profit (*addhika=ardhika*) is mentioned already in an ancient Pallava inscription [2]. Even now there are in Behari special expressions for the share of milk and corn given as wages to the cowherd and the farm labourer [3]. In the Deccan the cowherd gets the young calf by way of remuneration, such as if he tends a pregnant cow then after two years he receives the calf for it. Hired labourers who leave their work unfinished receive no wages and transporters who delay their cargo may have their remuneration cut down. The building materials of a house which somebody has built on a piece of land not his own and in which he dwells on rent may be taken away by him when evacuating the house. In the case of damage of every kind to property distinction is carefully made between guilt and accident[4]. The washermen (*dhobi=dhāvaka*) still receive all linens for washing and in the villages are paid for this by a share of the crop and there are many proverbs about their mishandling the clothes entrusted to them [5].

Ancient laws in modern customary law.

§ 33. *Law of commerce and companies.* In the law of trade which is wholly a later development the purchase upon trial strikes us first of all. The buyer may and should personally examine the wares closely and show them to others before the purchase is regarded as completed. What the test would be depends on the nature of the ware to be sold ; it may be sold by tale e. g. betelnuts, or by weight such as gold or sandal wood, by measure such as grains, according to work such as

Testing before purchase.

1. Weber, I. St. 13, 466.
2. EI 1, 9.
3. Grierson §1205.
4. Steele 192 f., 258—262, 280 f.
5. Grierson §393.

draughts animals, according to beauty such as female slaves, according to splendour or lustre such as a precious stones (Nār. 8, 3). The seller will be punished if he uses false weights, artificially covers any actual defects, mixes with oil, salt, corns etc. substances of less value, gives a a false brilliance to precious stones, iron etc. or generally if he meretritiously attempts to raise the price of his wares or hands over quite a different article than was shown at first (M. 8, 203; Y. 2, 244—248; Nār. 8, 7; Bṛh. 18, 4 etc.).

Punishment for foul play.

Period of testing.

The data are conflicting as to the period of examination, which may partly be the result of local differences; principally however it depends on the value of the article and its durability and the difficulty of testing it. Thus according to Nār. 9, 5 f. the period of testing shall be one day in the case of iron and garments, 3 days in the case of milch cows, 5 days in the case of beasts of burden, 7 days in the case of precious stones, pearls and corals, 10 days in the case of corns, a fortnight in the case of slaves and a whole month in the case of female slaves. Even a consummated sale may be annulled, according to Nār. 9, 3, on payment of some penalty which should amount to 1/30 of the price on the second day and 1/15 of the price on the third day. After 3 days every sale is final and definitive. An earnest money (*satyaṁkāra*) which may have been paid by the buyer is forfeited if he fails to realise the purchase; on the other hand, a seller who refuses to sell an article after having promised to do so shall pay back to the buyer double the amount of the earnest money (Vyāsa; Y. 2, 61). If the buyer refuses or makes delay in taking delivery of the article the risk of damage or loss that may happen through fire, theft etc., is of the buyer and the article may be sold to another person; on the other hand the seller is to bear the risk if he refuses

Annulling a sale.

The earnest money.

Delay in taking or giving delivery.

to deliver the article even after receiving the price (Gaut. 12, 42 ; Vi. 5, 127—129 ; Y. 2, 254 etc.)[1]. If during the period of non-delivery the merchandise which has been sold loses in value, e.g. if the milk yield of a cow diminishes, or if there is a fall of price, or if in the case of export wares the chances of profit are greater—for all this the seller shall have to bear the consequences (Nār. 8, 4—10 etc.).

Mit. on the cancelling of a purchase.

After consulting the various pertinent texts the Mit. (on Y. 2, 258) has developed the theory that in the case of a ware already tested the purchaser is entitled to cancel the purchase within three days if the price is extraordinarily high and the seller may cancel the sale within three days if the price is extraordinarily low ; in the case of wares which have not yet been tested the purchaser is entitled to annul the purchase during the period of testing on the discovery of some defect; in the absence of any such ground however, even during the fixed period and in all cases after the expiration of that period, a penalty of $^1/_6$ of the price should have to be paid when annulling a sale or purchase.

A ware should be bought only from the proper owner.

The purchaser should try to protect himself not only from illusive representations and other treacherous manipulations of the seller but he should also be on his guard that he buys only from the real owner. The "sale without ownership" (*asvāmivikraya*), which already forms one of the 18 titles of law in M., is invalid and the legitimate owner may reclaim the sold property any time from the temporary proprietor. As it appears, regular markets used to be held. One should purchase only in the markets and even that before witnesses, during usual market time from honest vendors and at reasonable prices ; otherwise the purchaser will be punished if he is not able to

Conditions of a legal purchase.

1. In Stenzler's translation of Y. 2. 255 "seller" wrongly stands for "purchaser" (*kretur*).

identify the vendor who will have to give him back the purchase price paid by him, while the purchased property is restored to the proper owner. Even when the seller cannot be found, but if the purchase has at least taken place in an open market, the purchaser receives no punishment, yet he must however give the article back to the owner. The seller however is punished in any case, whether he is a relative of the owner or not and all the same if it is an embezzled pledge or a deposit or if it is something found or stolen (Vi. 5, 164—166; M. 8, 197—202; Y. 2, 168—170; Nār. 7, 1—5 etc.). Even the owner must have his right to the disputed property corroborated by witnesses or other well-known means of proving. If he cannot show the proof he shall pay as penalty twice the amount of the value of the property falsely claimed by him. Even when he has proved his claim he shall pay to the purchaser half the price when the latter gives the property back to him if he had bought it *bona fide* in a bazaar *(vaṇigvīthī)* before royal officers (Bṛh. 13, 4—9).

Unauthorised seller punished.

Owner must prove his claim.

The control and interference of the king is a very remarkable feature in every part of the law of trade. The king shall fix the market price[1] every five or fourteen days or when he thinks fit in view of the rapidity of the fluctuation of price, so that the profit of the traders in indigenous wares may be 5 per cent. and of those in foreign wares 10 per cent.; he should take for himself 1/20 of the value of the merchandise and under certain circumstances even 1/10 of the same after making due consideration of the market price and the costs of the journey, the maintenance of the servants and the escorts of the transports; he shall collect duties and ferriage at the customs houses (*śulka-sthāna)* and the ferries (*tara*) and impose heavy fines

Royal interference.

Profit of the traders assured.

Customs houses.

1. Cf. the royal valuer in Jātaka I, 124 ff.; II, 31. See also the parallel rules in Kauṭ. II, 16, 21, 22. *Tr.*

on merchants who try to evade the customs houses; he should examine the measures and weights and have them verified twice a year—falsification of measures, weights and coins is severely punished; he should try to stop the formation of cliques among the merchants which aim at bringing about artificial rises and falls in the prices (M. 8, 398—405; Y. 2, 249—253, 261—263; Vi. 3, 29—31; 5, 130 f. etc.).

Cliques of merchants.

The king should also watch over the gambling houses and draw his share of the profits from them (Y. 2, 200; Nār. 17, 8). These and similar probably highly lucrative sources of income for the royal treasury will be dealt with in the State Antiquities[1]; I wish to point out here that the king himself appears as an industry captain, inasmuch as not only the whole or at least half of the profits of the mines belong to him (Vi. 3, 55; M. 8, 39), but even factories are run by him (M. 7, 62) and the production and the sale e. g. of saffron in Kashmir, precious stones in the south, horses in the west, fine stuffs and wool in the east and elephants always belong to the royal monopolies (Medh. on M. 8, 399).

King's share in the gambling house.

King an industry captain.

Also companies, guilds and corporations of all sorts shall enjoy the special protection of the king. The law of partnership has however been developed only in the later Smṛtis, apparently in connection with the religious brotherhoods and associations which are already mentioned in the older works. Thus Vi. 5, 167 speaks of the punishment for the embezzlement of articles belonging to a religious corporation *(gaṇa)*. M. 8, 206—211, in agreement with the Śrautasūtras, sets forth the division of the sacrificial fee *(dakṣiṇā)* in the ratio of 48 : 24 : 16 : 8 among the four classes of sacrificial priests and declares this scheme to be generally

Guilds and corporations.

1. See f.-n. 5, p. 95. *Tr.*

Law of trade guilds fully described in later works.

applicable; in 8, 218 ff. he briefly describes the punishments for transgressing the rules of a corporation. On the other hand in Nār., Y., Bṛh. and other later works the laws of trading associations are exhaustively discussed and from these discussions, which are based on foundations much more real than the theory of the four Varṇas, a very interesting side-light into the development of the castes may be obtained. Everywhere warning is given against combination with incapable, sick or inactive persons; one should combine only with noble, clever, active, enterprising, honourable and experienced men. The division of the profit in a trading company should take place according to the capitals laid out and the expenses and actual losses too are to be divided in the same manner. He however who injures the company through negligence or arbitrary actions will have to pay compensation. On the other hand he who has saved the property of the company from a danger by dint of his own activity, e. g. by repulsing an attack of robbers, shall receive 1/20 of the property thus saved as extra remuneration. Companies for the cultivation of the soil must be particularly careful in selecting a proper piece of land and powerful beasts; the partner who is guilty of the loss of cattle or the produce in corn must make it good to the other partners. If an apprentice, a comrade, an expert and the master work together in a craft, the profit will be divided in the ratio of 1: 2: 3: 4, that is, exactly in the proportions laid down by M. for sacrificial priests as mentioned above. Freebooters and robbers too shall divide their booty in the same manner. Among masons, tank-diggers and tanners the leader or the master shall have a double share and the leader among musicians gets 1½ shares (Nār. 3, 2-7; Bṛh. 14 1—32; Kāty. 13, 1—6[1] etc.).

Profits and losses divided according to capital.

Remuneration for special services.

Larger share for experts in the corporations of craftsmen.

1. Bandyopadhyaya, 504 ff. *Tr.*

According to Steele the custom of testing an article before purchasing it is very much in vogue even to this day in the south and to some extent also similar periods of testing are found as laid down in the Smṛtis, e. g. a week in the case of precious stones and gold and silver wares. Delay in giving or taking delivery is similarly punished. If anybody sells a thing which is not his own the purchaser must restitute it to the legitimate owner if the seller cannot be found in the bazaar or if the price paid for it was extraordinarily moderate. Trading corporations in which profit, loss and expenses are divided in proportion to the capitals laid out or according to special arrangements, are often met with, e. g. among traders in cloth, grains and butter and among bankers and brokers [1].

Law of trade at the present day.

§ 34. *Forms of transactions.* In many cases not only the contents of agreements were enough for their validity but also certain particular forms of concluding agreements had to be observed. Ceremonious and symbolical actions and certa verba (word of assurance) are generally connected with most of the legal transactions, particularly if in any way they have a religious character. About the ceremonies at the marriage and the adoption see §§ 16, 21. Such ceremonies (*saṁskāras*) take place in all important epochs of life and are exhaustively described in the Gṛhyasūtras. Gifts of every kind are ratified by an offering of water. For this reason an offering of water is made also when handing over the bride to the bridegroom and surrendering the rights over a piece of land (§ 27). Numerous and detailed data about the ceremony of the consecration of temples, tanks, wells, serais and other pious bequests useful to the public are contained in the Purāṇas[2].

Importance of the form.

Gifts always accompanied by offering of water.

The settlement of a disputed boundary is a ceremonious

1. Steele, Castes 276—281.
2. Mandlik, 322—344.

Ceremonies of settling boundaries.

act in which the person or persons enjoying the confidence of both the disputing parties are called upon to do it; they have to put on garlands of red flowers after fasting previously and wear a red mantle and strew earth on the head; the boundary then fixed by them shall be regarded as definitive if the party entrusted with the charge does not fall into any misfortune within a short time (§ 27). If a royal servant finds an unclaimed property in a forest or elsewhere, the find should be proclaimed by beat of drum which generally accompanies all royal proclamations, so that the owner may announce himself (Medh. on M 8, 30). If anybody has borrowed money of a Brahman and if the Brahman and all his legitimate heirs are dead, he will have to throw the money into water (Nār. 1, 113) as also the king throws into water the money of a fine which he imposes unjustly (M. 9, 244; Y. 2, 307).

Unclaimed property.

Confirming and manumitting a slave.

Among other ways of confirming slavery one is this: a free man gives himself up to anybody with the words *tavāham* "I am yours." At the manumission of a slave his master pours out a pot of water with unshelled grains and flowers on the head of the slave and during the process thrice declares him to be a free man; the pot is then dashed to the ground so that it is broken (Nār. 5, 27, 34, 43 f.). Against a stubborn debtor the creditor may use the methods of compulsion known as Prāya, Prāyopaveśana and Ācarita which signify that he sits and fasts before the house of his debtor as long as his demand is not satisfied; if the creditor dies in this way the debtor is considered to be his murderer (M. 8, 49 etc.).[1] Promises and assertions on oath, the binding power of which is enhanced

Ways of realising a debt.

1. In the Sanskrit literature we find not infrequently that a king is beseiged by fasting Brahmans and from Rājatar. 6, 14 we know that the king had a special officer whose duty it was to look after these Brahmans on hunger strike. *Tr.*

by the ordeal of the sacred libation, are resorted to in many cases and play an important role specially in the deposition of witnesses at the court. Witnesses should preferably be called to be present at transactions of every kind, such as loans, deposits, purchase and sale, particularly of immovables, pledges and also on the occasion of pious bequests, documentary authentication, repudiation of a married wife, etc. The witnesses also may be invited secretly so that from some place of concealment they may overhear a verbal agreement, for which they may afterwards also give a written document (Nār. 1, 150).

Witnesses should be called at every transaction.

The offering of water at the time of bestowing gifts is also frequently mentioned in the inscriptions. The custom of sitting on Dharna is no less known or less widely in vogue and it has continued even to the present day (§ 53). Even now boundary disputes are settled in this way: the disputing parties at first come to agreement over an arbitrator who after bathing in a holy stream puts on (red) basil plants or other sacred flowers round his neck, prays before an image of god and besmears his forehead with (red) sandal wood. He now walks across the disputed land and the line followed by him would be the future boundary. Yet however his decision is regarded as false if in a short time after it he or his family falls into a misfortune.[1]

The old customs still observed.

§ 35. *The documents.*[2] Perhaps traditions would have been far richer in forms and symbolic usages if written documents had not been in use already in very early times. In the older Dharmasūtras writing is generally not yet mentioned,[3] for which, as Bühler

Documents known from very early times.

1. Steele. Castes 288.

2. Most detailed information on this point may now be had from the highly interesting newly published work "Lekhapaddhati" (Gaek. Oriental Series).

3. Meyer (Rechtsschriften, p. 304). following the commentators,

suggests, perhaps the religious character of these works is responsible which allowed them to omit things profane, belonging more properly to the Arthaśāstra,[1] such as the documents. On the other hand already Vas.,[2] Vi. and M. frequently refer to written bonds and documents and the later Smṛtis contain a mass of detailed informations about them.

Different kinds of private documents.

According to these sources primarily a distinction is to be made between royal and private documents (*rājakīyam* and *laukikaṁ* or *jānapadaṁ lekhyam*). The private documents are divided into documents of partition, gift, purchase, pledge, combination, slavery, boundary, truce, cession and debt (*pattra* or *lekhya* for *vibhāga*, *dāna*, *kārya*, *ādhi*, *saṁvit*, *dāsa*, *sīmā*, *saṁdhi*, *anvādhi*, *ṛṇa*) : a receipt (*viśuddhi-pattra*) may be given even for a penance which has been performed.

The form of a bond of debt.

In the bonds of debt, which were most commonly used, the date (*kāla*) and further the reigning king (*rājan*), the land (*sthāna*), the locality (*nivasana*), the creditor (*dāyaka*), the debtor (*grāhaka*) as well as their fathers, the caste of the debtor (*jāti*), his race (*gotra*), the branch of the Veda he studies (*śākhā*), the thing that is lent (*dravya*), the pledge (*ādhi*), the value of both (*saṅkhyā*) and the rate of interest (*vṛddhi*), should be mentioned and it should contain the signature of the debtor (*grāhakahasta*) and finally that of two knowing witnesses (*viditārthau sākṣiṇau*).[3] The debtor is to give his signature at the end of the document and write "I, the son of such and such, am agreed to the above";

---

translates the word *anibaddhaḥ* in Gaut. 13, 4 by "not bound down by written documents." But this translation is too far-fetched. *Tr.*

1. For interrelation between Dharmaśāstra and Arthaśāstra see Jolly, ZDMG 1913 and Kalidas Nag, Theories diplomatiques de l'Inde Ancienne pp. 114 ff. *Tr.*

2. Bühler, Ind. Studies 3, 6 f. (1895).

3. ZDMG 44, 369 f.

then the witnesses should write down their names and those of their fathers with the words "I, such and such am a witness to this"; at the end the writer should state "I, N. N., the son of N. N., have written the above at the order of both the parties" (Y. 2. 84—88).

A debtor or a witness who does not know how to write may appoint some one else to write for him. A deed of debt which is throughout written by the debtor is however valid even without the signature of witnesses, but it is not valid if the writer has to write it under compulsion or if fraud, bribe or enmity plays any part in it or if it contains the signature of a witness who has been bribed or whose character may be questioned in any way. Generally if a question is raised every document has to undergo a close examination in which the contents and the form of the document as well as the capacity of doing legal business and the character of the writer of the document and the witnesses and the general circumstances are put to test. The art of forging hand-writings has been particularly warned against, for which comparison of hand-writings and a very close examination of the documents are necessary. In the case of an old document it is difficult to prove its authenticity, particularly if all or a part of the persons who gave their signature in it are no longer alive; for this reason it is rocommended that the document should be shown and read to the debtor on every opportunity and that he should be reminded of it repeatedly, for otherwise after 30 years the document will become invalid even though the witnesses are still alive. If a document is lost, e. g. through fire, or if it is injured, another document is to be given for it (Vi. :7, 6—13; M. 8, 168; Y. 2, 89—92; Nār. 1, 135—146; Bṛh. 8, 20—31.)

Bond written by debtor valid even without witnesses,

Testing a document.

Forgery warned against.

Document becomes invalid in thirty years if debtor is not repeatedly reminded of it.

Of public or royal documents [1] the following kinds

1. l. c. 350—359.

Various kinds of royal documents.

are mentioned: Śāsana (documents of gift), documents about lands etc. presented to a functionary or an officer and other people as sign of royal favour *(prasādalikhita)*, the document of a verdict which is given to the victorious party after the decision of a suit *(jayapattra* or *paścāt-kāra)*, the edicts which are meant for vassals, governors and other subordinates *(ājñāpattra)* and courteous summons or proclamations which are issued for the priest, the spiritual initiator and other venerable persons *(prajñāpanapattra)*. Moreover private documents "attested by the king" (*rājasākṣita*) are mentioned; they are to be drawn up at the royal court by a royal scribe and to be signed by the judge (Vi. 7, 3). Documents of pious gifts (*śāsana*) have been described by far most exhaustively in the law-books. Copper-plates (*tāmrapaṭṭa*) or cotton cloth (*paṭa*) are to be used as writing materials. The royal seal (*mudrā*) must not be omitted; it should represent an animal, e. g. a boar or the mythical bird Garuḍa.

Private documents attested by the King.

Writing material.

Royal seal.

Contents of a royal grant.

As regards contents, the Śāsana, like the private documents, but more exhaustive, shall give information on these points or they should be explicitly mentioned: (1) the place of drawing up the document, (2) the donor and his forefathers, (3) the village etc. which is given away and the province in which it is situated, (4) the assembled witnesses, (5) the pious intention of the donor, (6) the exact position and the boundaries of the gift, (7) the receiver of the gift, (8) the period over which the donation will continue, (9) the inheritance of the same; (10) that it cannot be taken away, (11) its freedom from taxes and other privileges, (12) future rulers shall be informed of the gift by this document and (13) it should contain the corresponding passages of law and (14) the signature of the king and (15) of the person who draws up the document and (16) the date too should be mentioned in it. The forging of such a Śāsana, as also of every document, is mentioned as a crime which is punished by death.

Bühler has proved that the borrowing of the North Semitic alphabets, the source of the Brāhmī script of India, is to be dated at about 800 B. C.[1] It is therefore not at all surprising that already in the Jātakas bonds of debt (*iṇapaṇṇāni*), royal proclamations and instructive speeches engraved on golden tablets are mentioned [2]. The famous edicts of Aśoka are proclamations of this kind and may be compared with the Prajñāpanapattra and Ājñāpattra of the Smṛtis. By far most frequently however the Śāsanas are found among the inscriptions which are generally engraved on copper plates and composed exactly according to the above-mentioned formulas of the Smṛtis. Even the seals found on them are in comformity with the rules inasmuch as e. g. the seals of the Calukyas exhibit the boar and those of the Guptas the Garuḍa[3]. For an ancient epigraphical specimen of the document of verdict in a suit, which was found in Java, see § 18. The Sandhipattras and Dānapattras too may be verified epigraphically; forgeries, particularly of documents of pious gifts, were also in evidence already at a very early period, as e. g. king Harṣa in an edict of 631—32 refers to a forged grant (*kūṭaśāsanam*) which a Brahman had used as a title of possession[4].

Epigraphical comforation of the Smṛti rules.

Steele gives specimens of modern bonds of debt which are remininscent of the Smṛtis in a high degree. Thus it is said in it: N. N. acknowledges to have received from N. N. such and such amount of Rupees at X per cent. interest to be paid back on such and such date; then follow the date, the signature or a sign,

Modern bonds of debt.

1. Bühler l. c. 80. (This theory will of course now have to be reconsidered in the light of the discovery of Sumerian seals in Sind. *Tr.*)

2. Jātakas 4, 256, 7; 2, 371, 381; Bühler l. c. 10 f.

3. ZDMG l. c.

4. l. c. 360.

then the signatures of the witnesses. Bonds of debt wholly written by the debtor are also valid, but the authenticity of the same must be ascertained by comparing the hand-writings and usually every document has to be subjected to a close examination [1].

---

1. Steele, Castes 272—274.

IV. CRIME, PENANCE AND PUNISHMENT

§ 36. *Religious transgressions.* The expressions for the general concept of "crime, 'trangression" are very numerous, but are mostly of a religious nature ; by way of example I mention here agha, āgas, enas, pāpa, pāpman "evil, sin", aśubha, kalmaṣa, paṅka, mala "filth, sin", adharma "injustice", kilbiṣa, doṣa, duṣṭa "omission, transgression", unmārga "going astray", hiṁsā, aparādha, apakāra "infraction, transgression," atikrama, dharmavyatikrama, apacāra, duṣkṛta, vikarman, vikṛta "transgression, evil-doing", patanīya, saṁkarikaraṇa, jātibhraṁsakara, pātaka as well as the derived words atipātaka, mahāpātaka, anupātaka, upapātaka signifying "crimes which cause the loss of caste." The last group of expressions is specially important because they exhibit the close connection between the criminal law and the caste system. Impenitent sinners and those whose sins are generally unatonable, not only go to hell and later undergo low births, but they are also excommunicated out of the caste.

Various terms signifying religious transgressions.

The systematic lists of sins in the Smṛtis are arranged according as re-acceptance into the caste may be secured easily, with difficulty or not at all, on the performance of certain penances ; of these lists that of Vi. 33-42 is the most exhaustive and may be given here: (1) Sins punished by death (*atipātaka*), namely sexual intercourse with mother, daughter or daughter-in-law ; (2) great sins (*mahāpātaka*), namely murder of a Brahman, indulging in spirituous liquors (*surā*), theft of gold belonging to a Brahman, sexual intercourse with the wife of the teacher (*guru*), association with those who have committed any of these crimes ; (3) sins which are equal to great sins (*anupātaka*), and indeed equal to the murder of a Brahman:

Lists of sins.

Sins equal to a Mahāpātaka.

the murder of a Kṣatriya or a Vaiśya actually engaged in a sacrifice, of a woman in her courses or of a woman who has not bathed after temporary uncleanness or of a pregnant woman or of an embryo of unknown sex or of one who begs for protection; sins equal to the drinking of spirituous liquors are: giving false witness and murder of a friend; sins equal to theft of gold are: usurpation of land belonging to a Brahman and the embezzlement of an entrusted property; sins equal to the sexual intercourse with the wife of a teacher are: intercourse with the wife of father's brother, of a maternal grandfather of a father-in-law, of a king, and other incests; (4) lesser crimes (*upapātaka*): are hypocritical bragging, denunciation before the king, false accusations against a teacher, to revile or forget the Veda, abandoning parents, son, wife or the sacred fire intentionally, indulging in forbidden food and drink, usurpation of property belonging to others, adultery, sacrifice for low people, improper occupation, receiving unlawful presents, killing a Kṣatriya, Vaiśya, Śūdra or a cow, selling forbidden articles, marriage of the younger brother before that of the elder, every kind of abetting to these transgressions, the mode of life of an outcast (*vrātya*), teaching and studying the Veda for a reward, work in the mines, manufacturing big machines, injuring trees or plants, earning livelihood by means of the wife, magic, violent actions, neglect of sacrifices, Vedic studies and other religious duties, reading bad books, atheism, the profession of a dancer or a singer, intercourse with women who take spirituous drinks; (5) crimes which entail excommunication out of the caste, namely injuring a Brahman, smelling of disgusting things and spirituous liquors, dishonesty, sexual intercourse with beasts or men; (6) crimes which degrade the perpetrator to a mixed caste, namely injuring household or wild animals; (7) crimes which render the perpetrator unfit to accept

Lesser crimes.

presents, namely accepting presents or alms from contemptible persons, trade, money lending, mendacity and serving a Śūdra ; (8) crimes which entail defilement: killing birds, amphibious animals, aquatic animals, worms or insects and to partake of substances which came in contact with spirituous liquors (or are like them) ; (9) miscellaneous crimes namely all that has not been specially mentioned.

Vi.'s list of sins not exhaustive.

Even this last expression shows that Vi.'s enumeration does not claim to be exhaustive and in fact still many more crimes may be collected from the parallel passages of other ancient authors, as for instance, sea voyage, medical practice, murder of husband, regicide and other important cases of murder, intentionally abandoning nearest relations, various cases of theft, etc. Further sins of commission and omission are seen particularly in the rules about penances (Vi. 50 ff. etc.), in the teachings about retaliation *(karmavipāka)* in which particularly the various forms of theft are discussed with lively symbolism (he who steals flesh is reborn as a vulture Vi. 44, 21 etc.), in the Snātakadharma (Vi. 71 etc.) and in the enumerations of those Brahmans who should not be invited to a Śrāddha (Vi. 82, etc.).

Uncertainty about meaning.

Many crimes in these lists appear to be disconcerting and almost phantastic and about some of the expressions used therein even the commentators are of divided opinion. Thus the crime of earning livelihood by means of the wife (M. 11, 64 etc.) is interpreted not only by the prostitution of the wife but also by the appropriation of her earnings or her own property or by the sale of the wife.

Antiquity of these categories.

On the whole there is no part of the Brahmanical codes of law whose roots reach so far into antiquity and which with all its peculiarities has maintained itself tenaciously up to the present day as the theory of crimes and the penances for those sins. The Sūryābhyudita and the Brahmahan, Bhrūṇahan, Parivitta, Didhiṣūpati, Agredidhiṣū and other categories of sinners may be traced back even to the Vedic Saṁhitās (Kāṭh. 31, 5; AV 6, 112, 3 etc.)[1]. The Taitt. Brāhm. 3, 2, 8, 11 ff. contains an enumeration of sinners which agrees almost literally with Āp. 2, 12, 22. Konow in his translation of the Sāmavidhānabrāhmaṇa has pointed out many parallel passages out of the Smṛtis to the rules of atonement contained in it. Over and above those parallel passages I compare Sāmav. 1, 5, 6—9 (disrespectful conversation with Brahmans and relatives) with M. 11, 205, Y. 3, 292; 1, 5, 12 (smell of impure things) with Vi. 55, 8; 1, 8,2 (sale of animals with two rows of incisors) with Vi. 45, 23, and 1, 8, 5 (forcibly carrying away a girl) with the Rākṣasa marriage of the Smṛtis. The deadly sins and the minor sins of the Smṛtis are mentioned also in the Mah. 12, 165, 34 ff. as well as in inscriptions e. g. EI 1, 366, 39 *(gohatyābrahmahatyādi mahāpātakam)*. The Buddhist lists of sins exhibit many points of agreement with the Smṛtis[2].

Parallel passages in Sāmavidhāna Brahmaṇa

Even now in Bombay among many castes the following are considered to be the chief sins: murder of Brahmans, women and children, incest, indulging in spirituous liquors and forbidden foods, omission of the funeral ceremonies on the death of a relative and also every intercourse with people of low caste and Muhammedans. Also the killing of a cow is considered to be a particularly grave act of murder and stealing gold is considered to be the most heinous act of theft[3]. Similarly in Nepal the 5 chief crimes *(pañc khāt)* are taken from the 5 deadly sins of the law-books, namely Brahmahatyā, Strīhatyā, Bālahatyā, Gohatyā and

Categories of sins at the present day.

1. Cf. Weber I. Str. 2, 210f.
2. Kern, Der Buddhismus 2, 100—138.
3. Steele, Castes 147—152.

Agamyāgamana[1]. Also according to Alberuni the following were regarded as deadly sins in the mediaeval age: murder of a Brahman or a cow, drinking wine and incest, particularly with one's own mother and the wife of the teacher[2]. How the religious fanaticism of the Hindus always flares up in the case of a transgression of the law of diets, particularly in the case of eating beef, is well-known from Indian history; even now the society for the protection of cows espouse the cause of the cows against Muhammadans as well as Europeans.

§ 37. *The penances.* As old as the lists of sins is the theory of penances *(prāyaścitta)* the determination and prescription of which was one of the most essential means of maintaining the influence of the Brahmans and frequently was also a lucrative source of income for them. It is not improbable that the principle of spiritual punishment goes back even to the Indo-Germanic epoch, because frequent use of prayers, presents of every kind to the priests and the use of cow's urine on the occasion of penances are often met with also in the Vendidād. In India the Sāmavidhānabrāhmaṇa, as already mentioned, seems to contain the oldest detailed exposition of the penances. On account of its connection with the Sāmaveda it mentions particularly many Sāmans the chanting of which is said to produce the effect of a penance; in 1, 3 however it also mentions the three penances *(kṛcchra)*. The Kṛcchra in the narrow sense consists of taking unspiced food during the first three days only in the morning, during the next three days only in the evening, for further three days eating only that food which may be obtained without asking for it and fasting during the last three days. The Atikṛcchra is an intensified form of this

Penances probably of Indo-germanic origin.

The three Kṛcchras.

1. Hodgson, Ess. 2, 215.
2. Alberuni. 2, 162.

penance in which one may eat only as much at each meal as the mouth can hold at a time ; the Kṛcchrātikṛcchra however is to be regarded as the most difficult of penances in which one has to live only on water.

Of the Smṛtis Gaut. 26 has taken the three Kṛcchras verbatim from the Sāmav. and they are found also in other works, particularly the Kṛcchra in the narrow sense, which however is generally called Prājāpatya, i. e. the penance discovered by Prajāpati. Other Kṛcchras are : the hot penance in which during three periods of three days each one has to live on hot water, hot milk and hot clarified butter respectively and to fast completely for the last three days, the cold penance in which the same fluids are to be taken in cold state, the penance of leaves, the water penance, the penance of roots, the quarter penance etc. (Vi. 46, 10-23 etc.). The lunar penance of the Smṛtis (also Mah. 12, 165, 69) should be specially mentioned with its varities Yati, Śiśu, and Sāmānyacāndrāyaṇa—so called, because the quantity of food taken is increased or decreased according as the moon waxes or wanes (Vi. 47 etc.). The Parāka penance consists of a complete fast for twelve days (Y. 3, 321 etc.). In the Sāṁtapana penance which, in an intensified form is called Mahāsāṁtapana, one may take cow's urine, cowdung, milk, sour milk, butter and a broth of Kuśa grass in one day and must fast on the second day (Y. 3, 315 f. etc.).

Various other penances.

"The five things of the cow" (pañcagavya) mentioned in this penance appear also in other penances, and thus almost everything what comes from this holy beast, even when in itself it is extremely impure, may be used as an instrument of purification and expiation. In the Govrata (Vi. 50, 24 etc.), the penance for killing a cow, the sinner should accompany the cows to the meadow and serve them in every way, inhale the dust raised by their hoofs,

The cow cultus and penances.

bring them into safety in case of inclement weather and danger even at the risk of his own life and live on nothing but the Pañcagavya. Even if one scratches the back of a cow and lets himself be wetted by the drops of water falling from the horns of a cow, one may derive thereby an expiating effect (Vi. 23, 59 f.).

Penances through prayers.

The prayers play even a more important role than the cultus of the cow in the penances. Among them the Sāmans are the most important and their power of effecting penances is already referred to in the Sāmav. The most important prayers have particular names (Vi. 56 etc.). The more a man repeats them the greater is the effect attained by him; thus according to Baudh. 4, 5, 31, he who murmurs the Gāyatrī 1008 times at sunrise may get absolution from all sins excepting the murder of a Brahman. Frequently the recitation of prayers is accompanied by other observances, thus for instance, in the Anaśnatpārāyaṇa we have the recitation of the whole Veda along with fasts and other self-mortifications (Baudh. 3, 9).

Penance by presents to Brahmans.

Another mode of atonement with which the authors of the Smṛtis are naturally in full sympathy consists of presents given to Brahmans. Baudh. 3, 10, 14 mentions as fitting substances of present gold, cows, dresses, land, sesamum, clarified butter and food stuff; Gaut. 19, 16 mentions moreover the horse; in the case of particular sins however many more presents are mentioned which have to be given for their expiation. Thus in connection with the penance for killing beasts it is laid down that for killing a snake an iron spade should be given, for a boar a pot of clarified butter, for a partridge one Droṇa of sesamum, for a parrot a two-year-old calf, for a peacock and other birds or for an ape a cow, for a horse a garment, for an elephant 5 black bulls, for an ass a one-year-old calf, for a camel one Kṛṣṇala of gold, for a beast of prey a milch-cow and for stealing gold belonging to a Brahman one's own weight of gold should have to be given, etc. (Vi. 50, 25 ff. etc.). That the presents are intended for Brahmans, and primarily for the Ācārya who has prescribed the penance, is indeed expressly mentioned only in a few passages (Vi. 50, 31, 33; M. 11, 131 etc.) but it is implied in the connection in which it is mentioned. In Baudh. 1, 19, 6 of course the expiatory presents for killing a swan and other animals are set on an equal footing with the indemnity that is to be paid for killing a Śūdra,—the source of the very important penance, often amounting to 1000 cows, which is to be performed in expiation of homicide, is at all events to be sought in blood-money (§ 44). Yet presents and gifts of every kind form an important feature of the religious law even from its very beginning, cf. § 30. Other means of expiation are visiting holy places, of which Vi. 85 alone enumerates 51 in all parts of India, a mendicant life in which one lives only on alms, baths mostly with the clothes on, sacrifice, sleeping on the ground, sitting in the sun, shaving of the hair, living in the forest, humble apologies and obseisance, etc. The penances for secret crimes (rahasyaprāyaścitta) form a particular category; according to Mit. on Y. 3, 301, a sinner who is well-acquainted with the Dharmaśātras should impose on himself these penances which mostly consist of prayers; an ignorant man on the other hand should approach one who knows these things and enquire about the proper penance under the pretext that somebody else has committed the crime.

Hardly any mention of Brahmans in this connection.

Other means of expiation.

Secret penance.

The graver the sins the more difficult are the penances; for this reason a deadly sin may be expiated for only by suicide. According to Mah. 12, 165, 46 ff. the murderer of a learned Brahman (*bhrūṇahan*) shall plunge into the turmoil of a battle in order to obtain

Deadly sins expiated for only by suicide.

absolution from sin through death at the hand of the enemy, or shall throw himself into fire. He who takes intoxicating drink will be pure if he drinks hot water till he is scalded to death. He who has defiled the conjugal bed of his teacher shall embrace the iron image of a woman glowing with heat till he dies of it or cut off his organ and the testicles and holding these limbs in his hands he should walk till he falls dead on the ground or he should sacrifice his life in defending a Brahman from the danger of life. Yet, for instance, the drinking of spirituous liquor may be expiated for through fasting, chastity and sleeping on the ground. The above-mentioned and similar other modes of suicide for the expiation of deadly sins are met with in most of the Smṛtis, yet later on the penances leading to death have been reckoned among the customs no longer in vogue in this age.

Elaboration of the theory of penances.

The later Smṛtis seem to have attempted to fill up the gaps in the theory of penances and elaborate it casuistically. Thus now besides the killing of a cow the case of more or less serious injury to the same is also taken into consideration. If children, sick persons or women have committed sins they should have to perform only half the same penance. The consulting Brahmans shall give their opinion about the Prāyaścitta for the particular case in writing (Bṛh., Kāty. etc.). Equivalents in money may be always substituted for the penances.

Penances in mediaeval and modern times.

Already Alberuni 2, 172f. mentions the vows of fasts —Kṛcchra, Parāka, Cāndrāyaṇa etc. Even at the present day the principles of the Dharmaśāstra are in force for the penances which are still always prescribed by the Brahmans learned in law (*dharmādhikārin*) who give their opinions in writing. Fines or presents are most common ; they are either directly exacted or, as is most usual, the man who performs the penance has to give a feast to all the members of his caste with prescribed entertainments. The Pañcagavya and the cultus of the cow in general also play an important role in the religious expiatory ceremonies, e. g. as recorded by Dubois, who also speaks of a rite comparable with the Govrata of the Smṛtis in which one has to accompany the cow to the meadow and receive the urine in vessels actually brought for that purpose [1]. For graver crimes going on pilgrimage is regarded as the proper penance [2]. Also the Rahasyaprāyaścittas, decided either by the sinner himself or by the head of the family, are still in evidence, at least in Kashmir [3].

§ 38. *Excommunication out of the caste.* Nobody can escape the performance of the prescribed penances if he does not wish to run the risk of being excommunicated out of the caste. The ceremonies of excommunication (*tyāga*), the outward sign of which is to overturn or break the water vessels and the victim of which becomes fallen (*patita*) and thereby forfeits all his rights, are according to M. 11, 183-188 and the parallel passages and commentaries somewhat as follows. If anybody has committed a great sin (*mahāpātaka*) and is therefore accused by his Guru, his relations or the king, he is, if he confesses his crime, ordered to approach an Ācārya who prescribes him the proper penance. If he does not comply with this and refuses to perform the penance inflicted on him, the ceremony of overturning water-pots takes place. His relations and his spiritual initiator hold a meeting on an inauspicious day, in which, just as if he were dead, they perform for him all the funeral ceremonies beginning with the offering of water. Upon this a slave or a servant

Ceremonies of excommunication.

1. Dubois 29.
2. Steele 150.
3. Bühler, Kashmir Report 22.

or a kinsman of low lineage brings a broken pot from a heap of sweepings or an impure dish, fills it with water out of the water-pot of a female slave and upsets it with his left foot ; on this the relations of the person who is going to be excommunicated touch it after loosening their hair ; the female slave or even the relations themselves may upset the pot. In this act the name of the person who is going to be excommunicated is proclaimed and it is said that the offering is meant for him and that he is going to be deprived of water for all time to come (*anudakaṁ kar omi*).

When leaving the place the relations, in token of their contempt for the excommunicated person, turn their left side to him and then go home after taking a bath. Henceforth it is forbidden to speak to the excommunicated person, to sit by him, or in any way to come into intercourse with him ; he who speaks to him has to perform penance and he who continues to be in intercourse with him for a year shall himself be an outcast. The Patita is excluded from all religious ceremonies and businesses of his caste, he is even disinherited (cf. § 24) and if he is the eldest son he loses his right of primogeniture as well as the privileges connected with it. After his death he goes to hell (Gaut. 21,6) ; moreover no funeral sacrifice is performed for him but instead of the offering to the dead a female slave upsets a pot of water on the day of his death with the words "drink this" (Vi. 22,57). Excommunicated women are treated in the same way ; yet however she should be allowed sustenance and a place of abode should be assigned to her in the neighbourhood of the family house (Y. 3, 297 etc., cf. § 19).

After-effects of the ceremonies.

Outcast woman is allowed sustenance and lodging.

Re-acceptance of the excommunicated person into his caste may take place on the resolution of his caste people in case he has performed the prescribed penances. The cere-

Re-acceptance into the caste.

monies which take place are just the antithesis of the ceremonies of excommunication. A new pot of clay or gold is brought, it is filled with water out of a sacred tank or river and then it is overturned or poured upon him while his relations too bathe in the same water. Mantras from the Veda, presents to Brahmans and the same festivities which take place at the consecration of a new-born child accompany this sacred ceremony. Yet before the excommunicated person is taken into society another test shall take place: he offers grass to the cows as fodder; now only if the cows eat this grass he is again considered to be fit for mixing in society (Y. 3, 300, M. 11, 197). After his re-acceptance into the caste he can no longer be kept down in any way; everybody must have intercourse with him in every respect (Y. 3, 296). Vas. 15, 18 contains a remarkable statement: people should walk before those who re-admit a person into society gamboling and laughing and walk before those who excommunicate a person weeping and sorrowing.

Excommunication and its effects at the present day.

Even to this day the excommunication out of the caste is effected by the ceremony of Ghaṭasphoṭa[1], and even to this day it is everywhere feared although the effects thereof falling into the sphere of civil law have been abrogated by an act of English law in 1850, and the re-admission of the culprit into society, excepting in the case of the gravest crime, may take place if he submits to the judgment given on him and pays a fine. So long as the period of excommunication continues the excommunicated person cannot eat together with any one of the members of his caste, cannot get the services of the spiritual advisor, the washerman and the barber of the village and with his whole family is excluded from connubium with his caste.[2] Dubois 28 f. lucidly describes the humiliating

1. West and Bühler, 3rd. ed., 58.
2. IG 6, 199 f.

proceedings to which the excommunicated person has to submit himself in order to obtain his re-admission into the caste. In the mediaeval age the Hindus who were able to run away from the slavery of Mohammedans had to fast in their house, lie for a long time in a mixture of cowdung, cow's urine and milk and to use it as food before they could again be taken into their caste.[1]

The two systems of punishment developed independently.

§ 39. *Relation between spiritual and worldly punishments.* Is the secular criminal law in India later than the law of spiritual punishment and has the former been evolved out of the latter? Burnell [2] has answered both these questions in the positive, but certainly Weber, Barth and Konow are more correct who are of opinion that on the whole the two systems of punishment had developed independently of each other. Even though the theory of religious expiation had been codified as an important feature of the Dharma at an earlier period than the theory of punishment yet however the power of punishment has always been an essential attribute of royalty. Nothing stood in the way to prevent the welding together of spiritual and worldly punishments and the punished criminal moreover performed also the penances prescribed in the Dharmasūtras in order to gain re-admission into his caste [3].

Burnell however was right in saying that in all the Smṛtis an elaborate admixture of spiritual and worldly punishments is in evidence. Thus according to M. 9, 240 criminals of every class may escape the branding by the order of the king and pay only a fine if they perform the prescribed penance. On the other hand, it is said that "the criminals who have received their punishments from the king are purged of guilt and go to heaven

1. Alberuni 2,162 f.
2. Sāmav, XIV ff.
3. Cf. Bühler in "Festgruss an R. v. Roth" 47 note.

Admixture of spiritual and temporal punishments.

like holy men" (M. 8,318 ; Vas. 19, 45 ; Nār. App. 48) ; for this reason the thief who goes to the king with a club, confesses his crime and asks the king to strike him down to the ground is purified all the same whether the king acts according to this or grants him forgiveness ; though of course the sin of the thief in the latter case is transferred to the king (M. 8, 314 ff. etc.). According to Nār. 14, 11 in the case of the Sāhasas of the first and the second grades the criminal may again be received into his caste ; but he who has committed the Sāhasa of the highest grade shall for ever be excommunicated from his caste. Gaut. 23,14 f. and Mah. 12, 165, 64f. mention among Prāyaścittas a penance for adultery in which the woman is torn to pieces by a dog and the man is roasted on a bed of glowing iron. Usually (M. 8, 371f. etc.) this punishment is referred to in the criminal law. Also the branding of the great sinners (*mahāpātakin*), e. g. the murderer of a Brahman with the brand of a headless man, is always met with among the punishments inflicted by the king (Baudh. 1,18,18 ; Vi. 5, 3-7 etc.) ; according to M. 9, 236 however it takes place only subsidiarily in the place of a penance. Originally the Mahāpātakin, as even the name shows, certainly belonged only to the spiritual law. The blood-money (§44) on the other hand, has gone over to spiritual law from secular law.

Points of agreement and distinction between the two systems.

There are many more instances of exchange and analogies between these two systems of punishment. Thus in both of these systems the caste-distinction and the privileges of the Brahman have been fully recognised which stand out prominently particularly in the punishments and penances for murder, maiming, adultery, theft, injuries and other grave crimes.[1] In civil law too the

1. Kanṭ. however almost wholly ignores such caste distinctions in criminal law. *Tr.*

gradation of penances, which is seen e. g. in Sāmav. 1,6,8, for withholding the interests on a loan, according as the creditor is a Brahman or not, may be compared with the various rates of interest according to the caste of the debtor and the privileges of the Brahman as found in the law about the recovery of debts. Further in the penances as well as in the punishments the existence or absence of criminal intention is taken into consideration. Y. 3, 226 even expresses the view that penances are proper for sins committed unintentionally and punishments are appropriate for sins committed intentionally (*kāmataḥ*), and it corresponds to the religious belief that for the existence of a sin which has to be expiated for only the actual facts of the case and not the evil design come into consideration.

Penances for unintentional and punishments for intentional crimes.

Penances also for intentional crimes.

Yet often Prāyaścittas are prescribed for the expiation of intentionally committed crimes. Thus according to M. 11, 46 prayers are to be resorted to in the case of unintentional crimes and Prāyaścittas in the case of intentionally committed crimes. The general rule is that the penances for unintentional crimes are doubled when there is evil intention in evidence (Mit. on Y. 3,226). According to Viśvāmitra the intentional killing of a cow is to be expiated for by 4 Kṛcchras and unintentional killing by 2 Kṛcchras. Raghunandana (228 Calc. ed.) explains it in this way: it is not to be regarded as intentional killing of a cow if anybody mistakes it to be a bos gavaeus and strikes it dead or if the arrow meant for another object accidentally hurts a cow. The commentators such as Nandapaṇḍita mention all the penances referred to in the Smṛtis whether connected with intentional or unintentional crimes. Accordingly the conceptions of dolus (evil design) and culpa (crime) are as much in evidence in the religious law as in the secular law, cf. § 32.

Penances aggravated when evil intention is in evidence.

Crimes in self-defence remain unpunished in both systems.

The same is the case also with the conception of permissible self-defence. For killing an assailant *(ātatāyin)*, even if he is learned in the Veda, neither punishments nor penances are prescribed ; the fury of the assailant in such a case meets the fury of the defender (M. 8, 350 f. etc.). Yet however the killing of a Brahman in self-defence is one of the customs now obsolete *(kalivarjya)*. The participation in a crime is judged likewise from the same point of view both in the religious law and in the secular law. Thus he who eats or serves, cooks and sells the flesh of a killed animal commits as great a sin as he who himself has killed it or has cut it into pieces (Vi. 51, 74 etc.). The Mit. on Y. 3, 227, in the theory of penances, quotes a text, said to be of M., according to which among a troop of men carrying weapons not only he who gives the mortal blow should be considered to be the murderer but his companions too are as guilty as he himself. Similarly Āp. 2, 29, 1 speaks of the rewards of heaven and the tortures of hell which are shared by the instigator (*prayojayitṛ*), helper (*mantṛ*) and the perpetrator *(kartṛ)* of an evil deed.

Abetment condemned in both the systems.

Repetition of a crime severely punished in both the systems

Also the repetition of a crime has been taken into consideration in the same way both in punishments and in penances. Thus according to Āp. 2, 27, 11 ff. in the case of repeated adultery the penance for the adulterer is more and more intensified. Similarly M. 9, 277 in criminal law affirms that the cut-purse when caught for the first time shall have two fingers cut off, the second time a hand and a foot and the third time will lose his life and Vi. 3, 93 declares that the king should not let a twice repeated crime go unpunished. In theft the penances as well as punishments are graded according to the value of the stolen property. Thus also for penances in general it is said, e. g. Y. 3, 294, that in cases of crimes not specially provided for in law the penance is to be fixed on consideration of Deśa, Bala, Vayaḥ, Śakti and Pāpa just as according to Y. 1,367 the king should determine the punishment after consideration of Aparādha, Deśa, Kāla and Bala.

Consideration of particular circumstances in both systems.

In this thorough parallelism of the two systems it is quite natural that they should have very many particular sins and crimes in common with one another. As already mentioned, in such cases it is to be assumed that penances and punishments were both prescribed at the same time and this is sometimes even expressly mentioned. Thus according to Baudh. 1, 19, 4 he who kills a bull shall finally, that is after paying the fine, also perform the penance Cāndrāyaṇa. According to Nār. 12, 77, in the case of grave sexual crimes *(agamyāgamana)*, the king should decree a punishment ; at the same time however the sin should have to be destroyed by Prāyaścitta. There being no fine line of demarcation between penances and punishments both may be applied indiscriminately. In the mediaeval age according to Alberuni 2, 162 f. in punishing an act of murder the penances and punishments were arranged in this way : in the case of the murder of people of lower castes by a Brahman, only penance consisting of fasts, prayers and alms-giving was ordained ; in the case of acts of murder among people of lower castes, penance as well as punishment, and in the case of murderous deed and other grave crimes among Brahmans and Kṣtriyas, only punishments consisting of confiscation and banishment were prescribed. Probably the line of demarcation between the church and the state was never fixed with any certainty and it is also to be remembered that princes with religious zeal themselves used to enforce the performance of the penances prescribed in the Dharmaśāstras, cf. § 47.

Penance as well as punishment prescribed for a crime.

§ 40. *Secular crimes and transgressions.* The secular crimes and transgressions, i. e. those that are punished by the king, are also dealt with along with the corresponding punishments in the Dharmaśāstras in the chapter on the duties of kings without any trace of systematic arrangement. In M. the criminal law, divided into real and verbal injuries, theft, violence and sexual crimes, constitutes the contents of 11.—15. of its 18 titles of law. In Nār. the laws about punishments, dealt with in 14.—16. titles of law, consist of violence or grave crimes (*sāhasa*), real and verbal injuries, and these 3 titles are subdivided into 15 sections; moreover in Nār. the 12. and the 18. titles contain things connected with criminal law—their titles being "duties of man and wife" and "miscellany"—as well as an appendix which like M. 9 deals with theft and robbery and the destruction of evil-doers (*kaṇṭakaśodhana*). Also a quotation from Nārada (Quot. 1, 11f.) enumerates the 10 chief crimes (*daśāparādha*) as follows: violation of a royal command, murder of a woman, mixing of castes, adultery, theft, pregnancy as the result of criminal intercourse, verbal injury, gross abuse, real injury and abortion of the embryo. But only Bṛh. 2, 5-10 expressly makes distinction between civil and criminal cases (*dhanodbhavāni* and *hiṁsodbhavāni*); according to Bṛh. the latter consist of real and verbal injuries, violence and adultery and each of these four crimes is again divided into three grades.

The ten chief crimes.

Bṛh. makes distinction between civil and criminal cases.

According to Kāty. the king should himself investigate and give judgment over the 10 chief crimes (*daśāparādha*) as well as the *chalāni* and the *padāni nṛpateḥ* even though nobody complains to him about them. The following 50 are the *chalāni nṛpasaṁnidhau* according to Pitāmaha 1, 8-18: (1) obstructing the road; (2) raising hand in a threatening manner; (3) leaping over a fence; (4) breaking a cistern or (5) a temple; (6) filling up a ditch; (7) betraying the weakness of a king (to his enemies); (8) unlawful entrance into the harem, (9) sleeping chamber, (10) treasury and (11) kitchen of the king and (12) prying in when (the king) is at his meal; (13-16) uncovering the body or making water, blowing nose or passing wind in the presence of the king; (17, 18) to sit before the king with folded legs or to take the foremost seat; (19-22) to enter the audience hall in a dress more gorgeous than that of the king, to enter alone, to enter not through the door or to enter at an improper time; (23-25) to lie on the couch of the king, to sit on his seat or to put on his shoes; (26) to go near the king when he is taking rest on a couch; (27) to serve his enemies; (28) to occupy an unoffered seat; (29, 30) to use gold in garments or in ornaments (?); (31) to accept and enjoy alms without being invited; (32) to presume to speak without being asked; (33) to insult the king; (34) to wear only one cloth; (35) to anoint oneself; (36) to untie hair; (37) to hide the face; (38) to paint the body; (39) to wear a garland; (40) to shake the dress; (41) to cover the head; (42) to spy into the weak points (of the king); (43) to touch him (?); (44) to shave the hair; (45-47) to point to the nose, the ears and the eyes; (48) to pick the teeth; (49, 50) to cleanse the ear or the nose. These prohibitions mostly contain rules of etiquette for deportment at the presence of the king.

Fifty crimes in which state directly intervenes

More serious are the 22 *padāni nṛpateḥ* in which likewise the king should directly interfere, namely (1) killing (an animal); (2) destruction of corn; (3) arson; (4) defloration of a maiden; (5) misappropriation of a deposit or treasure; (6) breaking a dike or (7) a hedge of thorn; (8) to let the cattle graze on other people's field; (9) to cut down the trees of a forest; (10) poisoning;

The more important group of 22 Padāni.

(11) intrigue against the king; (12) to break the royal seal; (13) to cross king's plans; (14) liberating a prisoner; (15—18) embezzlement of a tax, fine, present or a sold property; (19) to render the sound of the drum inaudible; (20, 21) embezzlement of unclaimed property confiscated by the king; (22) to hinder the mutilation of a criminal ordered by the king (Pitām. 1, 19—23).

Epigraphical corroboration of the above.

The destruction of evildoers, literlly "removal of thorns" *(kaṇṭakaśodhana)* appears also in the inscriptions as one of the chief duties of an able ruler, as for instance, in the inscriptions of the 12. and 13. centuries, EI 1, 198, 210, 334. The inscriptions are also familiar with the Daśāparādha or Daśāpacāra (IA 15, 306) and how popular this conception of ten great sins was may be understood from the fact that there was an officer who was actually called 'Daśāparādhika' (IA 14, 167; 15, 306).

§ 41. *Crimes with regard to property.* Many points indicate that crimes against property were investigated at a very early period and that very energetically. Thus in ṚV 6, 45, 1 there is perhaps already a reference to an act of stealing cattle and to a class of spies corresponding to the modern Khojis [1]. At all events such spies, experienced in tracking the marks of feet or hoofs, were known to the authors of the Smṛtis.

The espionage system.

When cattle and other properties are lost they are to trace the track up to its starting point; the inhabitants, the headmen or the proprietors of the village or meadow concerned have to make the required compensation excepting when they can prove that the track goes further out of that place (Nār. 14, 22 ff., App. 16—18; Y. 2, 271 f.). If the thieves cannot be caught the king is personally

1. ZAL 182 f. Cf. Elliot, Memoirs (Lond. 1869), 276 ff.

liable to make good the loss (Vi. 3,67 etc.); the king however may charge the loss from his officers and the guards of thieves (cauragrāha, cauroddhatṛ, the cauroddharaṇikas of the inscriptions) in whose jurisdiction the robbery took place (Nār., Y. l. c.). The tragic figure of the penitent thief who with flying hair—the sign of his submission—goes to the king with a club on his shoulder and confesses to him his crime and asks him to strike him dead (Gaut. 12, 4?-45 etc.) certainly belongs to the most ancient part of the penal law; this appears to be personal dispensation of justice thinkable only in the case of petty chiefs of small tribes.

King is to make good the stolen property.

King dispensing justice with his own hands.

Another noticeable point is that in the rules about evidence (Nār. I, 1, 42; Bṛh. 2, 13) and punishment theft appears to be the typical crime. "Like a thief" (*cauravat*) is to be punished, for instance, he who binds freely roaming cattle or sets free cattle that are bound fast (M. 8, 342), he who drives the cattle to other people's fields (Y. 2, 162), he who uses other peoples' property without obtaining permission for it (Nār. Quot. 7,10), he who misappropriates a treasure trove (Nār. 7, 7), he who kills a man through carelessness (M. 8, 296), etc. For this reason various sorts of crimes have been put in the category of theft. Cheats of every kind, particularly falsifiers of wares, measures, weights or coins, soothsayers, people living on bribe or extortion, quacks, jugglers, treacherous arbitrators, false witnesses—they are considered as "word thieves" (Nār. 1,228)—unjust judges, gamblers etc. are "open thieves" or robbers (*prakāśataskara*, M. 9, 256 ff.; Nār. App. 1—3; Bṛh. 22, 2—4). Opinions are however divided as to whether gambling is permissible or is it to be condemned as it appears already from Bṛh. 26. Thus M. 9, 221—228, Gaut. 12, 41, Baudh. 2, 2, 16 etc. also strongly emphasise the sinful character of gambling, while

Theft is the typical crime.

Various crimes included in the category of theft.

Difference of opinion about gambling.

on the other hand Āp. 2, 25, 12 ff. regards gambling to be a lawful amusement of the higher castes and Nār. 17 and Y. 2, 199 ff. raise only the demand that the king should receive his share and that there should be no foul play. Even in the Vedas gambling is frequently mentioned (ṚV 10, 34 ; 1, 41, 9 ; AV 7, 50 etc.), and in the Mah. the gambling scene is the central theme of the whole plot[1]. Thieves proper, burglars, highwayamen, cut-purses etc. are considered to be "secret thieves" (*aprakāśataskara*) (Bṛh. 22, 5 etc.). According to Bṛh. 22, 2 varieties of thieves are thousand-fold.

Secret thieves.

The detection of theft and cheating and keeping watch over the thieves is one of the most important duties of princes according to the Smṛtis. Thieves are to be looked for specially in the gambling houses (Y. 2, 203 ; Bṛh. 26, 2) and also in public houses and houses of evil reputation, shops, forests, festive gatherings etc. the king, through spies and agents provocateurs (*cāra*), should keep watch over them and cause them to practise their profession in order to bring them into his power (M. 9, 261—269). Even a mere suspicion, e. g. if anybody expends very large sums of money or is in intercourse with criminals, or if he drinks or gambles or goes about in disguise or under false names, makes enquiries about houses of other people, sells articles that have been lost, lives in a house of doubtful reputation or is known as a criminal by nature or if he behaves in an unusual manner at the court etc., is sufficient to get a man under arrest[2] and he must prove his innocence by means of human or superhuman witnesses to escape being punished as a thief (Y. 2, 266—269 ; Nār. App. 8—12 ; Bṛh. 22, 6). The possession of a stolen property (*loptra, hoḍha*) or a foot-mark (Y. 2, 266 ; Nār. App. 6) is regarded as sure proof of guilt.

Haunts of thieves.

Spies and agents provocateurs.

Arrest on suspicion.

Accused has to prove his innocence.

1. Cf. Hopkins R. C. 122 f.
2. Cf. Kauṭ. IV, 6. *Tr*.

The punishments for theft are very heavy. In all cases of serious crimes the accused is sentenced to death: he is impaled, hanged or drowned and often his hands are hacked off and other tortures are inflicted for the purpose of aggravating the punishment. The same punishments are ordained also in the case of burglary, frequently repeated instances of picking pockets, robbery, stealing cows, horses or elephants or more than 10 Kumbhas of grains, more than 100 Palas of precious metals, particularly valuable jewels or stuffs etc. (Y. 2, 273; M. 8, 320 f.; 9,276 f., 280; Bṛh. 22, 17—19 etc.). Forging of royal grants and even of private documents is punished by death (Vi. 5, 9 f.; M. 9, 232); the king should have a dishoṇest goldsmith cut to pieces, i. e., according to the commentaries, those who use false weights, touch-stones, alloys and practise other kinds of fraud (M. 9, 292). In determining the magnitude of the punishment according to the value of the stolen property often three grades are distinguished. Thus Y. 2, 275 speaks about the theft of small, middling or large properties and similarly speak Nār. 14, 13; 15, 6; App. 29 and Bṛh. 22, 24. Enumerations of objects of about equal value are generally given along with data about the punishments for misappropriating the same, which, besides the already mentioned cases of capital punishment, consist of the hacking off of a hand or a foot and other kinds of mutilation and fines in most cases amounting to many times the value of the stolen property. No distinction is made between robbery and theft as regards punishment and moreover taking part in these crimes, abetting of every kind or refusing to render help is regarded as equally criminal (Nār. 14, 12, 19 f.; Y. 2,276 etc.).

Capital punishment for theft.

Capital punishment for other crimes.

Various punishments for theft according to the value of the stolen property.

The caste of the thief and the person whose property has been stolen likewise come into consideration in determining the punishment.[1] Thus the Brahman

Caste distinction in criminal law.

1. See p. 264, f.-n. *Tr.*

remains unpunished if he takes away the property of his Śūdra slave (M. 8, 417) or if, when on journey, he takes two stalks of sugarcane and two eatable roots out of a field (M. 8, 341; Nār. 18, 39). On the other hand stealing gold which belongs to a Brahman is punished by death. However, on the other hand the responsibility and culpability for an act of theft is heavier as the thief is of higher position and intelligence (M. 8, 337 f.; Gaut. 12, 15-17; Nār. App. 51 f.). For cheating mostly fines are prescribed varying according to the amount of the damage done (Bṛh. 22, 13 f. etc.).

Penal laws of mediaeval and modern times.

Impaling as the punishment for theft is found also in literature, as in Mah. 1, 63, 92. The gradation of the punishment according to the value of the stolen property and the three grades of culpability was known also to Alberuni 162; he says that in the case of the theft of particularly valuable properties culprits of the Brahman caste are blinded and a hand and a foot are hacked off by way of punishment, Kṣatriyas are mutilated without being blinded and the culprits of lower castes are punished by death. According to Hodgson death sentence is still given in Nepal for stealing properties of great value or in the case of repeated theft; in less serious cases only mutilation and heavy fines are inflicted. According to Dubois[1] mutilation was in vogue also in Mysore; the owner received only a portion of the stolen property recovered from the thief while the king and his officers got the lion's share. Even to this day in Bombay the chief of a locality has to pay compensation for what has been stolen within his jurisdiction[2].

The capital offences.

§ 42. *Other crimes.* Besides theft and robbery murder, manslaughter, arson, high treason, real and

1. People of India 499.
2. Bühler on Āp. 2,26,8.

verbal injuries, rape, adultery and other sexual crimes are included among the chief offences. Often the capital offences, in so far as they are connected with violence, are called by the consummate title "act of violence" (*sāhasa*) which is the secular counterpart of the mortal sins (*mahāpātaka*) of the spiritual law. Thus according to Nār. 14, 2—6 there are four kinds of Sāhasa, namely man-slaughter, robbery, rape and real or personal injuries; he however distinguishes two lower grades of it consisting only of injury to property. The punishments for Sāhasa are regulated according to the gravity of the crime but caste distinctions exercise a definite influence on them; the Brahmans particularly enjoy the privilege that they cannot be condemned to corporeal punishments or death sentence[1] (Vi. 5, 2 f. etc.).

Advance from blood-money to legal punishments.

Death sentence is by no means universal in the case of murder and manslaughter, rather the composition system was originally prevalent (§ 44), according to which the cows given as recompense fell to the lot of the family of the deceased. Later on in the place of this blood-money punishments, partly secular and partly spiritual in character came in vogue which were determined by the Brahmans who of course did not forget themselves in the performance of their duty if the punishments concerned were of a religious character; cf. § 37. Of the secular punishments, according to Baudh. 1, 18 f. etc., the death sentence as well as confiscation of property is ordained only when the person killed is a Brahman and the assassin a man of a low caste; if the culprit is a Brahman he shall be branded and banished; if the person killed belong to a non-Brahman caste he shall pay the proper compensation in coin or kind. According to Y. 2, 279

Death sentence given only when a low caste man kills a Brahman.

1. Kauṭ. (IV, 11) however under certain circumstances allows the Brahman the dubious privilege of being drowned instead of being burnt alive. *Tr.*

a female poisoner or a female incendiary and also the woman who murders her husband or her child shall be cruelly executed. According to Y. 2, 273, Bṛh. 22, 27 f. etc. all murderers in general, open as well as secret, shall be punished by death and the confiscation of property. The death sentence is ordained also particularly for the murder of women and children (M. 9, 232 etc.).

Punishment for high treason.

High treason (*nṛpadroha*) is punished very sternly. He who forges a royal edict or bribes the ministers of the king or serves his enemies or is in an understanding with them or being a man of low origin strives for royal position, or opposes the royal commands will be sentenced to death (M. 9, 232, 275; Vi. 5, 14). If a man raises his hand against the king, even though he is wicked, he shall be impaled and burnt to death because his sin is worse than killing 100 Brahmans (Nār. 15, 31). He who expresses inimical views about the king (e. g. if he praises his enemies, Mit.) or vilifies him or betrays his plan shall have his tongue cut off and will be banished; if a person mounts the animal on which the king rides or sits on his throne, he shall pay the highest amercement (Y. 302 f.). High treason as well as the violation of any of the very numerous rules of etiquette about deportment at royal court belongs to those crimes which the king himself can investigate on his own initiative and pass sentence even though he has not been informed about it by any complainant (§40). In such cases the performance of a divine ordeal too may be imposed on the suspected criminal (§52). Crimes against public order are likewise subjected to heavy punishments, e. g. the breaking of a dike is punished by death (Vi. 5, 15; Y. 2, 278; M. 9, 279).

In verbal and real injuries (*vāk* and *daṇḍapāruṣya*) particular attention is paid to the castes of the insulter and the insulted; the sentence is fixed according to Varṇa and Jāti (Y. 2, 206). Thus a Kṣatriya will be fined 100 paṇas if he abuses a Brahman and 200 paṇas if he actually assaults him; a Vaiśya shall pay 1½ times as much as the Kṣatriya; on the other hand a Brahman who insults a Kṣatriya pays only 50, for insulting a Vaiśya only 25, and for insulting a Śūdra nothing at all (Gaut. 12, 8-13 etc.).

Punishments for real and and verbal injuries.

Injuries done by a Śūdra to a man of a higher caste is punished with particular severity; thus if a Śūdra reviles a virtuous Aryan his tongue shall be cut off; if he reviles the name or the caste (of a twice-born) a piece of red-hot iron ten fingers in length shall be forced into his mouth or if he dares to learn Vedic texts by heart his body wtll be cut in twain (Āp. 2,27, 14; M. 8, 172; Gaut. 12, 6 etc.). In general the insulter or the assailant of low caste loses the particular limb with which he insults or assails a member of a higher caste (Vi. 5, 19 etc.); thus if he sits on the same seat with a high caste man his backside shall be brandmarked; if he spits on him his lips shall be cut off. In such cases the assailed person may also take the law into his own hands by whipping the assailant on the spot, for by extorting a fine from such unholy persons the king himself will only be defiled (Nār. 15, 11-14). In injuring an equal only a fine, small or big, has to be paid according as only the skin has been scratched or if blood too has flowed or if a bone has been broken or if both the eyes have been knocked out, etc. (Vi. 5, 66-72 etc.); the fines for insulting an equal is still more insignificant. When two persons have insulted each other he who began is the criminal (Nār. 15, 9). In the case of injury to property as a rule a fine has to be paid (Nār. 14, 4 f.). About paying compensation see § 32.

Cruel laws for a Śūdra.

Lex talionis.

Nominal punishments when both are of the same class.

Also on the occasion of adultery *(strīsaṁgrahaṇa)* the distinction of castes is of the greatest importance, and more-

Punishment for adultery varies according as the woman was guarded or not.

over it makes all the difference if the adulteress was properly guarded *(guptā)* or not, because if necessary surveillance was lacking the sentence will be mild and particular importance is attached also to the question if violence was applied. Thus for adultery with the wife of an Aryan the Śūdra shall have his organ cut off and his property confiscated and if the woman was under guard he shall also be executed (Gaut. 12, 2 f. etc.). On the other hand

Caste privileges in adultery

a Brahman for a similar crime has to pay only a fine of 500 paṇas if the woman was willing, and 1000 paṇas in the case of forcible violation (M. 8, 378 etc.); for a Kṣatriya and a Vaiśya there are proportionally higher punishments aggravated by incarceration, shaving of hair and the pouring of urine on the head (M. 8, 375 ff. etc.). A similar gradation is found in the sentences for

Grades of sexual crimes

the defloration of a maiden; the fines are lowest in the case of forced sexual intercourse with courtesans and female slaves, and they are higher in the case of unnatural sexual intercourse with a cow (Y. 2, 288—291 etc.). Moreover, secret conversation at a bathing place, in a wood or in any improper place in general at any improper time and particularly sending flowers, ornaments and other presents, touching, pranks and jokes etc., are considered to be adulterous actions (Nār. 12, 62—68 etc.). A particularly grave crime which is punished by castration is the criminal intercourse with the wife

Punishment for incest.

of the spiritual initiator and incest with mother, sister and other female relations and sexual intercourse with a queen, a nun *(parivrājikā)*, a nurse, a pious woman, a Brāhmaṇī etc. is also considered to be no less heinous a crime (Nār. 12, 73—75 etc.) but this crime rather belongs to the sphere of religious law. Intercourse with a woman of the lowest caste is also heavily punished (Y. 2, 289, 294 etc.) and the abortion of the foetus is punished in the same manner (Y. 2, 277). :Public punishments are imposed on adulteresses but in most cases only if their crime is exceptionally flagrant; they are then sentenced to a cruel death (M. 8,371; Vi. 5,18 etc.); ordinarily merely the insulted husband or the insulted family inflicted the proper punishment on the adulteress (cf. § 19).

Criminal laws of mediaeval and modern times.

At the time of Dubois[1] in Mysore almost only high treason was punished by death, otherwise only fines were imposed which sometimes amounted to the confiscation of the whole property. In Nepal the death sentence is or was given for murdereing the father, elder brother, teacher, wife, a child or a cow and according to another source for every kind of murder without any distinction of person, as well as for high treason, incest, adultery or sexual intercourse of a man of low caste with a high caste woman—particularly a Brahman woman—poisoning and arson. Yet however the Brahman is not executed but only banished after the confiscation of his property and various insults; as for instance his hair is shaved and his sacred thread is torn away[2]; for Alberuni's statements on this point see §§ 36,39. In the Mṛcch. 154 the judge following M. (perhaps M. 9,241) advises the king not to have the Brahman Cārudatta, who was convicted of murder, executed for the crime but only to banish him but without confiscating his property.

§ 43. *The punishments.* The utility and necessity of punishment (*daṇḍa*) has been vehemently and often extravagantly emphasised. The word Daṇḍa, really meaning "stick," is said to be derived from the root *dam* "to restrain" (Gaut. 11, 28), and to bind down peoples by means of punishments appears to be the

1. People of India 499.

2. Hodgson, On the Administration of Justice in Nepal, AR 20,1,94—134 and Ess. 2,235.

principal duty of a good ruler, who for that reason is called Daṇḍadhara "the holder of Daṇḍa," i.e. the power of punishment, and is called an incarnation of Yama, the judge of the dead souls. If the king ceases to punish the subjects who swerve from the path of duty, the whole world will be destroyed, Brahmans will leave their brother Brahmans, Kṣatriyas their brother Kṣatriyas, the Vaiśyas will not do their work, the Śūdras will rule the world and the strong will roast the weak on the spit like fish. The punishment is identical with Dharma ; it is the dark, red-eyed god, the son of the creator of the world under whose mighty rule the world feels itself secure. Punishment protects mankind and keeps watch when mankind sleep. The whole world is held in order by means of punishment, for a faultless man is very rare ; even the gods and demigods are driven to perform their duty by the fear of punishment (M. 7, 14-30 ; Vi. 3,95 ; Y 1,353-356 ; Nār. I, 1,1 etc.).[1]

Importance of Daṇḍa for the state.

M. 8, 129 divides the punishments into 4 categories: admonition, reproof, fine and corporeal punishment. Nār. App. 53 ff. makes distinction only between corporeal punishments and fines ; the former extends from imprisonment to execution and the latter from one *kākaṇī* to the confiscation of the whole property. According to M. 8, 124 f. (=Nār. App. 36 f.) there are 10 places on which the punishment may be applied in the case of the three lower castes—the Brahman suffers no corporeal punishment ; the ten places are the organ, the belly, the tongue, the hands, the feet, the eyes, the nose, the ears, the property and the body, i.e. life. Usually the fines are divided into three grades : Pūrva or Prathamasāhasa estimated at 250 (or 270) paṇas, the

Four kinds of sentences.

Limbs on which corporeal punishments are applied.

1. Cf. the beautiful ode to Daṇḍa in Mah. 12, 63, 28-29. It appears that Daṇḍa should be translated by 'internal administration' and not merely by 'punishment' which was its original meaning. *Tr.*

Madhyamasāhasa at 500 (or 540) paṇas, Uttamasāhasa at 1000 (or 1080) paṇas (Vi, 4,14 etc.). Bṛh. 27,4-12 distinguishes between four kinds of punishments just like M., but he attaches particular importance to imprisonment and banishment ; in cases of grave crimes he recommends an accumulation of different kinds of punishments and mentions 14 instead of the 10 traditional places for the infliction of corporeal punishments in which besides the above-mentioned limbs also neck one half of the feet, the thumb and index, the forehead, the lips, the hindpart and the hips are named.

Three grades of fines.

Bṛh. mentions 14 limbs.

In point of fact the fines are mentioned most frequently in the Smṛtis in connection with the rules of punishment, either graded in the manner already referred to or otherwise in fixed amounts, or without any mention of amounts, or in relatively fixed amounts, i. e. fixed according to the value of the disputed property. Perpetrators of grave crimes suffer confiscation of their whole property, yet in such cases the weapons of a warrior, the instruments of a musician and the implements necessary for earning livelihood cannot be laid hold on (Nār. 18, 10 f.). In the case of mutilation and execution, as in other ancient systems of punishment, the principle of retaliation (Talion) as well as symbolical punishments come into play. The offender or the robber shall lose that limb with which he assaults or injures anybody. The slanderous tongue shall be torn out, the adulterous limb shall be cut off, the hand raised for a blow or the foot raised for kicking shall be cut off, red-hot iron shall be pushed into the mouth of the slanderous Śūdra or boiling oil shall be poured into his mouth and ears, and for a stolen property many times the same has to be paid by way of fine. The lips which spit on a man out of hatred and the thievish finger of a pickpocket shall be cut off. The adulterer shall be roasted

Fines are most frequent and graded variously.

Implements necessary for livelihood cannot be confiscated.

Lex talionis.

on a red-hot bed of iron and he who pierces a dike shall be drowned. Moreover, the brandmarking of the murderer of a Brahman with the figure of a headless man, of the drinker with the flag of a tavern and of the incestuous person with the mark of feminine pudendum are also symbolical.

Detracting punishments.

Detracting punishments such as riding on an ass, shaving of the hair, sprinkling urine on the head, hanging a garland of dices round the neck of a dishonest gambler, etc. and many Prāyaścittas are no less symbolical in character.

Various forms of execution.

Gruesome forms of execution are impaling, roasting, burning, cutting into pieces, trampling down by elephants, tearing to pieces by dogs, drowning etc. The flogging punishments are mentioned mainly for women, childeren and persons of low castes. Forced labour too appears as a public punishment as in working off a debt. In the ancient works punishment by imprisonment is rather rarely

Imprisonment rare.

mentioned. According to M. 9, 288 prison-houses should be built on public roads so that everybody can see the suffering and disfigured criminals, who, as the commentaries elucidate it, with their bodies emaciated with hunger and thurst, disordered hair and beard, often fettered in

Prisoners exposed to public gaze.

chains and mutilated—their hands or other limbs being amputated—produce a horrible impression on the onlookers. Banishment is mostly, but never in the case of Brahmans, accompanied by the confiscation of property, and there are also other combinations of punishments.

System of punishment from other sources till modern times.

Even Megasthenes (fragment 27) speaks about the Talion through amputation of that limb of the culprit who maimed the same limb of another person and the classical authors too know that hands were cut off and the hair was shaved by way of punishment (cf. LIA 3, 344). Hiuen-Thsang[1] says that in India the usually inflicted punishments are life-long imprisonment, specially in the case of rebels, mutilation of nose,

1. Mém. 1, 83 f.

ears, hands, feet, banishment and ransom, and the money equivalent frequently paid to escape punishment. Alberuni 2, 162 speaks *inter alia* of the combination of the confiscation of property with banishment and with various kinds of mutilation. Of the death sentences impaling, which is mentioned also in the Mah., Rājatar. and in the literature of fables, was in vogue for instance in Golconda even in the 17. century, [1] in Kolhapur until the period of British rule[2], and the trampling down by elephants mentiened also in Mṛccha. 146 and the Jātakas (Fausböll) 1, 199 ff., was universally practised in the Mahratta states[3]. Moreover under Mahratta rule, specially in Central India, the following are said to have been the customary punishments: fines, flogging, imprisonment, putting in stocks, forfeiture and sale of the whole property, amputation of hands, fingers or nose and other corporeal punishments; the hands of a forger of base coins were crushed with one blow of the hammer which is apparently a symbolical punishment.[4] Fines were particularly in vogue in Rajputana according to Tod[5], in Mysore according to Dubois [6] and in Kolhapur according to the Gazetteer; among the Prāyaścittas fines still play the chief role, cf. § 37. In Nepal, besides the very frequent fines, sometimes amounting to the confiscation of the whole property, banishment and detracting punishments such as the shaving of the hair (§ 42) as well as the horrible mutilations and death-sentences of the Smṛtis are still in vogue. Imprisonment is of temporary nature inasmuch as the prisons are emptied from time to time and the prisoners are

Alberuni.

Impaling and trampling under feet by elephants.

Various punishments in Mahratta period.

Smṛtis followed in Nepal.

---

1. Fryer in Wheeler, Hist. 4, 487.
2. BG 24, 267.
3. l. c.
4. Grant, C. P. Gazetteer 70 f.; Malcolm A Memoir of Central India, 2nd. ed., I, 558.
5. Annals of Rajasthan 1, 142 f.
6. People of India 499 f.

handed over to the executioner for corporeal or capital punishments[1]. Detracting punishments such as Prāyascittas ordained by the caste people, take place in India even to this day not seldom. Thus among the Bedars of Bijapur a wife excommunicated from the caste must have her hair shaved with a razor and touch a piece of red-hot coal with her tongue before she may again be accepted into her caste[2].

The institution of blood-money betrays a primitive society.

§ 44. *The blood-money.* However. closely the penal laws of the Smṛtis may agree with the principle of state justice, yet traces of a state of things have been preserved when the atonement for murder and slaughter was still regarded as a private affair and when the blood-money used to be paid[3]. Roth has referred to the Vedic expressions *śatadāya* and *vairadeya* and has proved that in the Vedic age a blood-money of 100 cows was paid to the relations of a murdered person. Baudh. 1,19,1 prescribes fines of 1000, 100 and 10 cows and a bull to be paid to the king for the murder of a Kṣatriya, :a Vaiśya and a Śūdra respectively. Generally the same indemnity has to be paid for the murder of a woman as for the murder of a Śūdra as well as for an ox or a cow (excepting milchcows, draughts animals) and also for a swan, a peacock and other birds and animals. As Bühler ingeniously suggests, probably the king did not keep these fines for himself, but gave them to the family of the murdered person. The blood-money of 100 cows reminds us of the 100 cows which have to be given as price for an adoptive son or as the price for a bride.

Various amounts of blood-money.

In Baudh. the above mentioned indemnities form a

1. Hodgson AR 20, 1, 94–134.
2. BG 23, 93 f. Cf. Kohler ZVR 10, 174–177.
3. Roth, : Wergeld im Veda ZDMG 41, 672–676 ; Bühler, Das Wergeld in Indien and L. von Schröder, Indogermanisches Wergeld in Festgruss an R. von Roth 44–52 ; Leist, Altar. jus gentium 294–307 ; ZDMG 44, 339 f.

part of the "duties of the king", but in Āp. 1, 24,1 ff. they top the list of Prāyaścittas and the bull is given *prāyaścittārthaḥ* (another reading *prāyaścittārtham*) and in any case it was received by the Ācarya or the Dharmādhikārin who determined the indemnity while the cows as composition, probably even according to Āp., go to the family of the murdered person ; Gaut.'s treatment of this question is more enigmatical (Gaut. 22,14—18). According to Y. 3,266 f., and M. 9, 128—131 the cows too are presented to a Brahman as Prāyaścitta, i.e. the blood-money has been completely changed into a spiritual atonement. Vas. and Vi. seem no longer to be acquainted with the blood-money even in this form and prescribe other Prāyaścittas in their place.

The bull goes to the Ācarya while the relations get the cows.

Blood-money later changed into a spiritual atonement.

Even in the modern period the blood-money as *mund-kati* (*muṇḍakāṭī* "severing of the head"), consisting of pieces of land or villages, was in vogue in Rajputana. Sir A. Lyall speaks of a case of robbery in very recent times of a half wild frontier tribe in Rajputana, which ended in this way that the tribe consented to pay "the usual blood-money" for a Brahman shot down in the fight. In another part of Rajputana regular meetings are held in which prices of the murdered men, children, old men, young or old women, cows etc. are fixed according to certain principles and the compensations to be paid are regulated accordingly[1]. Also in Central India the price of blood was known[2] yet the relations had to give their consent to such a composition.[3] In Kolhapur in the Mahratta period the murderer was occasionally compelled to indemnify the family of the murdered person ; the land given as composition was called Khunkat.[4]

Blood-money in modern times.

1. Tod, Annals of Rajasthan 1, 161—164,209, App. XVIII : Lyall, As. Studies 159 ; Bhüler l. c.
2. Malcolm 1, 557 f., 576 f.
3. Grant, C. P. Gazetteer 70 f.
4. BG 24, 267.

V. JUDICIAL PROCEDURE

§ 45. *The king as judge.* The administration of justice,[1] the punishment of the criminal, appears to be one of the chief duties of a good king. If the punishable person remains unpunished the king shall fast one day and he shall fast three days if an innocent person is punished (Vas. 19, 40-43). In order to pass the right judgment he should learn the right law for each caste from authoritative persons and in doubtful cases take the advice of learned Brahmans (Gaut. 11, 22-26). Every day the king shall repair to the hall of justice in the company of learned Brahmans and experienced councillors and courtiers and there sitting or standing shall examine the cases of the complainants (M. 8, 1 f.; Y. 1,359 etc.). This patriarchal method of administering justice can go so far that the king even with his own hands may strike down a confessing thief with an iron club (Gaut. 12, 43-45 etc.). The king is also advised not to begin a law-suit himself (M. 8, 43) because the fines are a lucrative source of income to the king. He must throw into water the money of those fines which were unlawfully imposed or he shall give to the Brahmans thirty times that amount (M. 9, 244; Y. 2, 307). The king superintended also the performance of the Prāyaścittas of the religious law (§ 47).

King's penance for wrong judgment.

Must consult learned persons.

King not to begin a law-suit led by the greed for fines.

The council of the king is responsible together with the king himself for the injustice which the king commits by passing a wrong judgment. Of the sin thus originated a quarter falls on the person wrongly condemned or released, a quarter on a false witness, a quarter on all the

Divided responsibility for a wrong judgment.

1. Cf. Colebrooke, On Hindu Courts of Justice (Ess. 1, 490—527); ZDMG 44, 342—362; Kohler, Altindisches Processrecht (Stuttgart, 1891).

assessors of the court, and a quarter on the king (Gaut. 13, 11 ; M. 8, 18 etc.). The assessors (*sabhya*, *sabhāsad*) shall speak out their opinion even unbidden (*aniyukta*) and shall not agree, out of selfish motives, with a king who is giving wrong judgment, for in that case they themselves become his accomplices in the crime and would go to hell along with him (Nār. I, 3, 2 ; Kāty. 1, 7 f.[1]). The house priest (*purohita*) of the king occupies a high place among the assessors who therefore has to expiate for a sin originating from a wrong judgment of the king by adequate fasts (Vas. 19, 40f.).

Assessors must give their free opinions fearlessly.

Composition of the court.

The later Smṛtis also mention the chief judge, the ministers, the ancients, the Brahmans and the retinue as the companions of the king. The law-court has been compared to the human body in which the king is the head, the chief judge is the mouth, the assessors are the arms, etc. More accurately, the functions of the limbs or parts (*aṅga*) of a law court, which are ten in number, are thus defined : the chief judge passes the judgment, the king inflicts the punishment, the assessors or judges investigate the merits of the case, the law-book furnishes the decree, gold and fire are used when ordeals are resorted to, the water is to refresh, the accountant calculates the value of the disputed property, the scribe records the proceedings and the court servants have to summon the accused, the assessors and the witnesses and hold both the parties in custody if they have given no surety (Bṛh. 1, 4—10). Vyāsa mentions also "the keeper of the disputed property" (*sādhyapāla*), a Śūdra who as a kind of beadle or executor of the verdict has to look after the execution of the judgment, and the Sabhāstāra who should hold discourses about morals (*dharmavākya*) for the edification of those who are present. In Mah. 4, 1, 24 however the Sabhāstāra appears only

Various functions of the different members.

Religious discourses at court.

1. Bandyopadhyaya, 26-27. *Tr.*

as a courtier (*sabhya*, Nīl.) who is particularly interested in gambling; moreover mention is made also of the recitals from Purāṇas, Dharma and Arthaśāstras in the court (Bṛh. 1, 23). Also some respectable merchants (*vaṇij*, *naigama*, Kāty. 1, 12[1]; Mah. 16, 7, 8) should be invited to the court in order to win over the people (*lokarañjanārtham* Mit. on Y. 2, 2).

Respectable citizens called to court to please the people.

The court shall sit in an edifice situated in the middle of the fortress *(durga)* of the king; the court hall shall be situated in the east and should be decorated with statues, pictures, idols, jewels, garlands and furnished with a throne (Bṛh. 1, 19). The forenoon is considered to be the proper time for holding the court, more accurately the time from the second to the fourth eighths of the day (Kāty. 1, 19[2]). In passing judgments the king shall follow the Dharmaśāstra and the opinion of his chief judge (Nār. 1, 1,:35).

Place and time of the court.

Already Megasthenes, fragment 28, points out that in the time of peace Indian princes leave their palace, if not for sacrifice or chase, only for the purpose of giving verdicts and continue at it the whole day even when four servants massage them with wooden cylinders. In the inscriptions too the examination of law-suits appears as one of the most important virtues of the administrator, thus IA 9, 170 speaks about a Nepalese king and the Rājatar. mentions many instances of Soloman like verdicts of Kashmirian princes (6, 14 ff., 42 ff., 8, 123—156). In Nepal too even now the state council (*bhāradar sabhā*) which is presided over by the king, functions partly as the highest court of appeal in law-suits and sometimes it inflicts heavy punishments as a court of the first instance[3]. The same was the case in Central India in the Mahratta period when law-

Megasthenes on Indian law-court.

Indian law-court from other sources.

Law-cour in Nepal and Mahratta.

1. Bandyopadhyaya, 22-23. *Tr.*
2. Ibid. 40. *Tr.*
3. Hodgson, Ess. 2, 213—215.

suits over an amount of money exceeding 100 rupees went directly to the Raja, in other cases his court was the highest court of appeal. The king gave judgment mostly according to the advice of a Śāstrin [1]. Already in his inscriptions Aśoka prides on having established a kind of religious department (dhaṁmamahāmāta) for the superintendence of the pious conduct of his subjects [2].

§ 46. *Other courts in the state.* Even the oldest Smṛtis permit the king's being represented by a learned Brahman who is to investigate and decide the law-suits for him (Gaut. 13, 26; Vi. 3, 73; Vas. 16,2 etc.). Details about the position and the function of the chief judge (*prāḍvivāka, adhikṛta, adhyakṣa, dharmādhyakṣa, sabhāpati*), who assists the king when he is present and represents him when he is absent, may be derived from the later sources. The name Prāḍvivāka is derived in this way: he questions (*pṛcchati*) the parties and then gives his verdict (*vivecayati*). As an expert surgeon removes the thorn or morbid matter out of a wound, even so the Prāḍvivāka should remove the thorn of injustice out of a law-suit by means of investigations and enquiries. In caste he should be Brahman or at least belong to one of the higher castes, the Śūdras are absolutely excluded from the post of a judge. His knowledge should comprehend not only the 18 titles of law along with their sub-divisions but also extend to logic and other sciences and to Śruti as well as to Smṛti. He should also be determined, firm, patient, virtuous, impartial, pious, kind-hearted and of a good family. As insignia of his position he carries the seal (mudrā) of the king, which is particularly necessary for the summons of the parties; the court conducted by him is therefore called *mudrita* "furnished with the

Court of the chief judge.

Caste and qualifications of the chief judge.

Court of the royal seal.

1. Grant, C. P. Gazetteer 70 f.; Malcolm, Central India 1, 557.
2. Bühler ZDMG 48, 53.

royal :seal" (Bṛh. 1, 3, 12, 24 ; Nār. 1, 3, 16 ; Quot. 1 1 etc.).

The assessors of the chief judge.

The assessors of the chief judge must be like himself respectable, pious, learned, truth-loving, impartial, incorruptible men of any one of the three higher castes (Vi. 3, 74 etc.). They are subordinated to the chief judge as well as to the king ; yet the Sabhyas too under certain circumstances have formed independent colleges of judges in which decisions were arrived at by a majority in votes or by unanimity. Thus according to Nār. I, 3, 17 the thorn of injustice may be removed only when the whole college of judges *(sabhyo janaḥ sarvaḥ)* are unanimous about the decision.

The college of judges.

The three courts of appeal.

Appeals too are preferred by the Sabhyas to the chief judge and by the latter to the king (Bṛh. 1, 30 f.), or by the village court to the city court and by the latter to the king (Pitām.). The commentators too distinguish between these three courts of appeal ; on the other hand, Y. 2, 30, Nār. I, 1, 7 etc. are acquainted with only the two courts of the king's judge and of the king himself,—a state of things quite in conformity with the simpler circumstances of an older period.

Courts are ambulant or stationary.

The law-courts may again be of two kinds : standing (*pratiṣṭhita*) courts which sit in a city or in a village and ambulant (*apratiṣṭhita*) courts which have no fixed seat (Bṛh. 1, 2 f.) ; they can however signify mere private arbitration courts. The headman of the village (grāmaṇī, grāmādhipa, grāmapati), whose post was hereditary, acts as the village judge. According to Vyāsa the competence of the lower courts is restricted merely to administering reproofs, for the infliction of punishments involving confiscation of property and corporeal punishments is a privilege reserved for the king. According to Bṛh. 1, 6, generally the king alone shall dictate the punishments. Yet the pursuit of the culprit in the villages which was

Competence of the lower courts.

a principal duty of the village headman (Vi. 3,11, etc.) contained in any case in itself a great measure of the power of punishment. The unjust judge shall pay a fine of double the amount of the disputed sum (Y. 2, 4, 305 ; Nār. I, 1, 66) ; they can however be punished still more severely, particularly by the confiscation of property and banishment (Vi. 5, 180 ; M. 9, 231, 234 ; Bṛh. 22, 10 etc.).

Punishment of the unjust judge.

The appointment of intelligent persons in the place of the king for the examination of the law-suits is recommended also in the Mah. 12, 69, 27. The ninth act of the Mṛcch., called the law-suit (Vyavahāra), describes the judicial proceedings held by one of the chief judges (Adhikaraṇika) of the king in his capital. The constitution of the court is here essentially the same as in the royal courts of the Smṛtis (§45), even the terminology is in agreement with the Smṛtis. The college of judges (adhikaraṇika, niyukta, adhikṛta, draṣṭṛ) assemble in the court hall (adhikaraṇa-maṇḍapa, adhikaraṇa, likewise Vi. 7, 3) which seems to have formed a part of the royal palace. Also the expression *rājakaraṇam* [1] in the first monologue of Cārudatta seems to refer to the court assembly and the following are mentioned as members of it (144, 12 ed. Stenzler) : the minister (*mantrin*) absorbed in deep meditation, the messengers (*dūta*) hurrying here and there, the spies (*cāra*, mentioned in the Smṛtis particularly in connection with the tracking of thieves and rebels) like voracious crocodiles, the talkative herons i.e. the informers (corresponding to the *stobhaka* and *sūcaka* of the Smṛtis), the scribes (*kāyastha*) a brood of snakes ; also the elephants and horses necessary to

Description of the law-court and procedure in the Mṛcchakaṭikā.

Functionaries of the court.

1. This is according to the Calcutta editions and the commentary and it is perhaps better than the *rājabhavanam* of Stenzler, because *karaṇa* is often used in the Smṛtis in the sense of "law-court" and the connection shows that a court is meant here.

trample down the criminals are mentioned (cf. §43). The functions of the chief judge are confined (as according to §45) to directing the investigation in which the assessors help him, and the passing of judgment, while the punishment is fixed by the king (Pālaka). Among the assessors the chief of the guild and the scribe (*śreṣṭhikāyasthādibhiḥ parivṛto 'dhikaraṇikaḥ*) are specially mentioned, who approximately correspond to the merchants (*naigama*) and the clerk (*lekhaka*) of the Smṛtis. The Śodhanaka "purifier" appears as the servant who sweeps the court hall and keeps the seats in readiness and then ushers in the judges, the parties and the witnesses like the Rājapuruṣa of the Smṛtis. The Rājapuruṣas also appears in the drama besides as police officers who seize the condemned criminal.

Chiefs of guilds called to court.

Of the fables I mention here only the Pañc. 1,21 (similarly Kathās 4 and 19 ; 5, Kathā 1 and others), where the disputing parties come to the royal court (*rājakula*) and are heard by the judges (*dharmādhikāriṇaḥ, sabhyaḥ*). The police too are mentioned in the fables. In Nepal the highest criminal court, which however in important cases is the court of first instance, has 251 officers excluding the judge, who for the most part are police officers or beadles. The chief justice (*ditha*) presides over this body and the other three courts (*nyāyasabhā*) of the capital, each of which possesses two other judges besides him. The state council (*bhāradar sabhā*) is the highest court. In the provinces there are four other courts, yet the jurisdiction mostly lies in the hands of the Governors. and the village headmen.[1] In India itself in the Mahratta period the executive and the judicial departments were mostly unseparated and were entrusted to the village headman (*pāṭil*) in the villages who was helped by his secretary

Court procedure in the fables.

Law-courts in Nepal.

Law-courts in the Mahratta period.

1. Hodgson AR 20, 1, 94 ff. Ess. 2,212—216.

mostly a Brahman; above the Pāṭil stood the governor (*kamāvisdār* or *māmlatdār*), above them the prince. The land-owners too could give judgment excepting in cases of capital offences. There were also judges proper (*nyāyādhīśa*) but their jurisdiction was very narrow[1]. Already in the Jātakas (I, 199 ff.) the village headman makes a considerable income out of the fines he imposes (*daṇḍavali*).

§ 47. *The private courts and the penances.* When the government is weak and powerless and the government officials tyrannise over the people, it cannot but happen that the people, specially in the provinces, should by preference obey the *ad hoc* or permanent arbitration courts at least in civil cases.

According to Vi. 3,12 ff., the village headman, if he cannot get the better of the criminals in his village, should apply to the chief of the district and the governor, and it may be thus assumed that this took place quite frequently. The oppression of the people by the Kāyasthas, the rivals of the Brahmans, is referred to, for instance, in Y. 1,335 and Rājatar. 4, 351 f., 621 ff., 5,439 etc. The particular jurisdiction of corporations of every kind is recognised in the fullest measure even in the Smṛtis, cf. § 1. The right of making laws for their corporations and composing disputes has been given tc farmers, craftsmen, cowherds, money-lenders, members of a sect, robbers, actors, artisans etc. It is particularly recommended to the king to recognise and support the arrangements of and punishments inflicted by the chiefs of a family, of a guild or of a corporation; only when a dispute breaks out between the chiefs and their subordinates the king shall interfere; cases of grave crimes (*sāhasa*) are however exclusively reserved for the king. For forest-dwellers the court shall

Criminals often defied authority.

Tyranny of Kāyasthas.

Guilds and corporations made their own laws.

King interferes only in the case of insubordination and grave crimes.

---

1. BG 10, 305ff; 24, 266—268; Malcolm, Central India 1, 557 ff. 563, 567; Grant, C. P. Gazetteer 70 f.; Dubois 499 ff.

be held in the forest, for warriors in the camp and for merchants in the caravan (Gaut. 11, 20—22 ; Bṛh. 1, 25—28 ; 17, 17—20 etc.). Successive appeals are also preferred by the clans or families (*kula*) to the guilds or corporations (*śreṇī*), e. g. of horse-dealers, betel-sellers, weavers, shoemakers (Mit. on Y. 2, 30) and by these to the local committees or courts (*gaṇa, pūga*) ; then appeal may be made to king's judge and also to the king in person (Bṛh. 1, 29—32). The whole title of law named "violation of agreements" (M. 8, 218—221 ; Nār. 10 ; Bṛh. 17), which has been often misunderstood, intends only to place the rights of corporations, particularly of religious ones, under a very great measure of state protection.

Lower corporations prefer appeal to higher ones.

Hereditary or elected chiefs (mahattama, mukhya) represented the official organs of the corporations and they were thus entrusted with the whole jurisdiction and they are said to have been assisted by committees of three or five persons (Bṛh. 17, 9 f.) ; mentions are made also of arbitrators about the election of whom both the parties had to be unanimous (*ubhayasaṁmata*) particularly on the occasion of the frequent boundary disputes (Bṛh. 19, 11). Also the penances of the spiritual law are dictated by such permanent or specially elected judges. In later works on Prāyaścitta the Pariṣad, composed of three to ten learned Brahmans, eventually only of one Brahman, which is to affirm what is right in doubtful cases (Gaut. 28, 48 ff. etc.) is called the proper court for fixing due penances in every case.

Hereditary or elected chairman of corporations.

Arbitrators had to be chosen unanimously.

The chief source about the proceedings to be observed on the occasion of the imposition of a penance is Āp. 2, 10, 12—16 along with the commentary. If a grown-up man has committed a sin, his spiritual advisor (*śāstṛ*) shall dictate to him a penance according to the rules of the Dharmaśāstra. If he does not perform the penance the Śāstṛ shall take him

The proper proceedings in a penance.

to the king and the latter shall refer him to his Purohita learned in law with the order to prescribe for him a proper penance. If he proves refractory even against the Purohita he shall be brought round to the resolution of performing the penance by means of confinement, starvation and other modes of compulsion, yet however without corporeal punishment or enslavement if he is a Brahman. Naturally this intervention of the king does not exclude the intervention on the part of the chiefs of the caste, who could impose the punishment of excommunication from the caste (*tyāga*) on the sinner who is unwilling to perform the penance (§ 38).

Criminal compelled to perform penance.

The Mahattaras or Mahattamas of villages are often mentioned also in the inscriptions. An example of an elected arbitrator from a drama is found in the judge Asajjātimiśra in the farce Dhūrtasamāgama who as the disinterested party *(madhystha)*, keeps for himself the Hetaera Anaṅgasenā, for according to Y. 2, 44 the disputed property may be deposited with a Madhyastha. Another treacherous arbitrator appears in the Pañcat. 3, Kathā 4. The caste chiefs and the village headmen exercise a great influence even to this day[1]. Besides it the *pañc*, *pañcāyat* "committee of five", so called because it is composed of at least 5 members, is a popular institution and has been recently reinstated in the Deccan by the Deccan Ryot Act and it has been put under the superintendence of a special judge[2]. The committee of the five was composed in Rajputana of the headmen and secretaries of any two villages which the complainant and the accused were free to mention; the Hakim gave his seal to the verdict[3]. In the Mahratta states too each of the parties was permitted

Epigraphical and literary evidence.

The Pañcāyat system.

1. Cf. Steele, Castes 79-156; BG 23, 241, 244 etc.; see above § 46.
2. Bühler (communication by letter).
3. Tod, Rajasthan 2, 171 f.

to elect an equal number of members in the *pañc*, which was then presided over by a government official, and there were also permanent *pañcs* of the most respectable people [1], in conformity with the ancient saying that that is no Sabhā in which ancients (*vṛddhāḥ*) are wanting (Nār. I, 3, 18; Mah. 5, 35, 58). In Nepal too the *pañcāyats* appointed by the parties or by the Government on their desire, decide half of all the law-suits [2]. In Kolhapur a refusal to submit to the verdict of a *pañcāyat* was regarded as a proof guilt [3].

Dharmādhikārins carrying on the traditions of the Pariṣads.

The traditions of the religious courts of the Pariṣads are still carried on by the hereditary Dharmādhikārins and other people learned in the law who have to prescribe penances. Even in 1875 there were 5 hereditary Dharmādhikārins in Kashmir who decided the Prāyaścittas and the Rājā saw that they were actually performed.[4] In Nepal too everybody who has sinned through forbidden intercourse with other castes or otherwise against the order of the castes, has to consult the Dharmādhikārins and perform the penances imposed by them[5]. The Mahratta princes, themselves endowed with great religious zeal used to dictate penances for religious transgressions[6]. At the present day in India the caste assembly sit in judgment over such transgressions and commands the guilty person in the old formula: *ācāryaṁ labhasva, prāyaścittaṁ samācara* to consult a spiritual advisor and to do penance[7].

---

1. Malcolm 1, 558, 570; BG 16, 304 ff.; 24, 266.
2. Hodgson AR l. c.
3. BG 24, 267.
4. Bühler, Kāśmīr Report 21 f.
5. Hodgson, Ess. 2, 214.
6. Telang, Gleanings from Marāṭha Chronicles in Transactions of 9. Congr. 1, 255, 257.
7. Bühler ZDMG 48, 53. Cf. Elliot, Memoirs 1, 281.

§ 48. *The court expenses appeal and wager.* Not only the numerous and considerable fines (*daṇḍa*) were a lucrative source of income to the kings and their judges but fees too were imposed on the defeated party to meet the expenses of the court. Thus according to Vi. 6, 20 and Y. 2, 42, fees to the amount of 10 and 5 per cent. of the disputed sum had to be payed by the debtor and the creditor respectively. The fines which a complainant or an accused or one who performs an ordeal has to pay if convicted of treachery, is equal or twice the disputed sum (Y. 2, 11; M. 8, 59; Nār. Quot. 6, 86). According to another view indeed only the debtor has to pay a fine, which is doubled if he denies the debt and is then convicted (Nār. 1, 133; M. 8, 139 etc.). Also the Brahman who prescribes the penance for a murder receives a bull as his fee (§ 44). According to other texts, which Raghunandana 226 quotes, the Brahmans who prescribe a penance shall receive from him who performs it, a milch-cow, a bull or at least some trifle. Whether the king's judge received any fixed salary *(vṛtti, nibandha)* over and above the court fees, has not been expressly mentioned; yet however, analogy with the executive officers, who also exercised judicial functions suggests it (M. 7, 118 f.). The court fees are higher in the case of an appeal. He who thinks that the verdict given against him is unjust, may demand a renewal of the law-suit, but must bind himself to pay twice the fine decreed by the first verdict in the case of a defeat; if he is victorious in the second suit this poena dupli (double fine) is inflicted on his opponent and at the same time on the unjust judges (Y. 2, 4, 305 f.; Nār. I, 1, 65 f., cf. Bṛh. 6, 5 f.).

Respective fees from winning and defeated parties.

Fee to Brahman prescribing penance.

Remuneration of the judge.

Fine is doubled in case of defeat in an appeal.

The wagers on law-suits too were a source of income for the judges; at least according to Mit., Apar. and Vīram. on Y. 2, 18 the staked sum is to be paid to the king or to the judge, while of course according to the Burmese law,

Wagers on law-suits a lucrative source of income to the court.

derived from Indian law, only 10 per cent. go to the judges and the advocates, the rest on the other hand goes to the victorious party [1]. According to Nār. I, 1, 4 and the commentary thereon the wager (*paṇa*) is to be stipulated in writing. It shall take place only when the plaint and answer are already filed and the procedure of witnesses has already begun. Either only one party lays wager by promising, in the heat of the dispute, to pay a certain sum in the case of defeat, or both the parties lay wager in which the stakes however may be quite different; the amount of the wager is also independent of the amount of the disputed sum, e.g., very small stakes are allowed in the case of valuable properties of dispute.

Rules of wager.

In the Mahratta period in Central India both the parties had to pay court-fees each amounting to one-fourth of the disputed sum [2]. In Nepal in law-suits about debt even to this day the parties have to pay 5 or 10 per cent. of the disputed sum. If the debtor denies, the case is decided by an ordeal. The complainant and the accused each takes a rupee in his hand and strikes the earth with clenched fists, thus asserting the truth of his statements. The court receives the two rupees; in like manner 5 other rupees are given as sign that the parties submit themselves to an ordeal for the decision. The court officers receive this money; after the decision of the ordeal four other fees have to be paid which are received by the government [3]. The Dharmādhikārins who prescribe the penances mostly enjoy a hereditary Vṛtti (*vattan*) [4].

Court fees in Mahārastra and Nepal.

§ 49. *Civil and criminal procedure.* Law-suits (*vyavahāra*) are divided into civil and criminal cases

1. Richardson, Dhammathat 73.
2 Grant, C. P. Gazetteer 70f.; BG 16, 87 ff.
3. Hodgson, Ess. 2, 220—223.
4. Bühler ZDMG 48, 53f.

(*dhana* and *hiṁsāsamudbhava*) which are treated in different manners in important cases. Thus in the cases of adultery, theft, real and verbal injuries, violence and other grave crimes everybody may bear witness (Gaut. 13, 9; Nār. 1, 189 etc.), while otherwise the qualifications of the witnesses shall be subjected to a close scrutiny. A similar exception in favour of the grave criminal cases is made on the occasion of ordeals, which otherwise would be resorted to by the accused only if the other party is ready to accept the punishment in case of defeat (§ 52). In criminal cases the answer of the accused has to be given immediately while otherwise pretty long periods are allowed him (Gaut. 13, 28—30; Y. 2, 12; Nār. I, 1,44 f.). On the other hand, he can bring a counter suit e.g. for the compensation of an insult with another insult (Y. 2, 9). The accused may be represented at the court by another person but it is not allowed in criminal cases (Kāty. 2, 11—13).[1] In the case of the 10 principal crimes and 72 other crimes the king may interfere, even though there is none to complain (§ 40), while ordinarily the procedure of accusation is followed [2]. The cases in which anybody may be convicted merely on suspicion even though there is no witness to prove it, are all criminal cases; thus he who is seen with a firebrand will be known as an incendiary; he who is seen with a weapon, as a murderer; he who is seen with the wife of another, as the adulterer; he who is seen with an axe in his hand will be known as the destroyer of forests (Nār. 1, 172—176). The lower competence of caste-assemblies corporations, families, arbitrators and similar others had probably nothing to do with important criminal cases.

Special laws for criminal cases.

No proxy allowed.

Arrest on suspicion in criminal cases.

In general however the proceedings of civil and criminal cases, as described in the later Smṛtis, are the same.

1. Bandyopadhyaya, 57-58. *Tr.*
2. Cf. Kohler, Altind. Processrecht (Stuttg. 1891) 15.

Acceptance of the plaint and the summoning of the accused.

The judge asks the complainant modestly entering the court "What is your complaint, what wrong have you suffered? From whom, how, when and why? Have no fear, speak out." The plaint which now follows is subjected to a preliminary examination by the judge. If for instance the complainant is halfwitted, drunken, a woman or a minor or in general incapable of doing legal business, the plaint may be summarily dismissed. Also a law-suit between father and son, man and wife, master and servant, teacher and pupil is not allowed. If the plaint is accepted the judge shall summon the accused by a sealed warrant (*mudrā*) or by a court messenger *(puruṣa)* (Kāty. 2, 1—3[1]; Y. 2, 32; Nār. Quot. 1, 6 f. etc.).

Accused may be arrested even before the suit is filed.

Until the legal summons (Nār. I, 1, 47) has been issued or even before filing a suit (Vīram.), the plaintiff may place the accused under arrest by preventing him from leaving his house or undertaking a journey or a religious ceremony by means of an appeal to the king for that purpose (Mit.); the transgression of such a prohibition entails legal punishments excepting under special circumstances, e. g. when somebody is arrested in a dangerous or miserable condition, and moreover anybody who is just about to marry or to offer a sacrifice or to give alms, a cowherd who tends his cattle, a warrior in battle and other persons engaged in pressing business, cannot be arrested (Nār. I, 1, 48—54 etc.). In similar cases legal summonses too are not to be issued and moreover noble ladies, idiots and other persons incapable of legal procedure, cannot be summoned; excepting these, whoever fails to obey is punished with fines varying according to the gravity of the situation and he also loses his suit. The complainant has to bear the cost of the court messenger so long as he is

Persons who cannot be arrested at all.

Punishment for disregarding the summons.

1. Bandyopadhyaya, 45-47 *Tr.*

engaged in searching out the accused (Kāty. 2, 7, 14 f., 25;[1] Nār. I, 2, 32, etc.).

Only when both the parties or at least their representatives are present at the spot the procedure proper may begin, which according to the later authors, for the first time in Y., is divided into four parts, plaint, answer, trial and verdict. The written plaint or declaration (*bhāṣā*, *pratijñā*, *pakṣa*, *pūrvapakṣa*, *vāda*) is called the kernel (*sāra*) of the procedure and for this reason it is composed with particular care. The judge has the deposition of the complainant at first noted down on a writing board probably of black wood[2] then the fair copy is made on a sheet; or the plaint is written down on the floor and the whole procedure recorded in this way. The plaint may also be afterwards modified and improved so long as the answer is not tendered. The plaint which is obscure and self-contradictory and which is absurd, contrary to good custom or which contains any other defects shall be disallowed by the judge. The complainant shall come first to prove his case and his witnesses shall be heard at first; for this reason dispute about priority may easily arise between the two parties[3] which is then decided not only according to priority of time but also according to the contents of plaints of both the sides or according to the castes of the parties. Both the parties must give sufficient security, otherwise the court servant takes them into custody and the object of dispute too may be taken care of by a Sādhyapāla (Nār. I, 2, 7—20; Quot. 2, 1—20; Bṛh. 3, 4—14; Y. 2, 10).

Procedure begins when both the parties are present.

Recording the plaint.

Defects of a plaint.

The complainant has to prove his case at first

The answer (*uttara*, *pratipakṣa*, *vāda*), likewise in writing, has to follow immediately only in important or urgent cases; otherwise longer or shorter respites are

1. Bandyopadhyaya, 50, 59-60, 69. *Tr.*
2. Burnell, Palaeogr. 87.
3. That is, when there is doubt as to who is the plaintiff and who the defendent. *Tr.*

The answer and the respite for it.

allowed according to the nature of the cases; they sometimes extend over a whole year and sometimes even any period is allowed that may be asked for (see above). The answer in writing shall exactly correspond to the contents and the line of thoughts of the plaint and it must be clear, precise and not confused or evasive. There are four kinds of answers : denial (*mithyā*), a confession (*sampratipatti*), protest or a special plea (*kāraṇa*, *pratyavaskandana*) and reference to a previous verdict in a similar case (*prāṅnyāya*). The denial is fourfold: "It is not true, I do not know it, I was not present there, I was not yet born at that time." It is an instance of protest when the accused says: "I of course received 100, but I have returned the amount to you" (Nār. I, 2, 2—6 ; Quot. 3, 1—7 ; Bṛh. 4, 8 f. ; Hār. 1, 20—25 etc.). Silence or refusal to answer is considered to be equivalent to confession. At first it is tried to extort such a confession showing the inducement that half the punishment shall be excused if the accused confesses his guilt (Nār. I, 2, 32 f. ; Quot. 3, 10 etc.).

Various kinds of answers.

Who is to prove his case?

Before the third part of the procedure, the trial, can begin the judge has to decide on which party the burden of adducing proofs shall fall. In general, in the case of denial the plaintiff, and in the case of protest or reference to a previous verdict, the accused has to begin the act of proving (*kṛiyā*) ; in the case of a confession generally no trial takes place (Hār. 1, 29 etc.). In doubtful cases an amicalble settlement is recommended to the parties which may also be ordered by a royal mandate (*rājājñā*), but it will have to be performed at the proper time if the payment of a fine, amounting to double this disputed sum, has to be avoided (Bṛh. 5, 10-13).

Amicable settlement recomend-ed.

Court procedure in the Mṛcch.

In the Mṛcch. the plaintiff (*kāryārthin*) is ordered by the judge to present his plaint, which the court scribe records on the floor (likewise in the Dhūrtasamāgama);

Cārudatta, accused of murder, is courteously summoned to the court, and in the procedure it is attempted to extort from him an admission of guilt even under the threat of flogging. Alberuni 2, 158 mentions the plaint in writing, furnished with data about the proofs. Also in the Mahratta period plaints and answers in writing were often in use[1]. Dubois 497 speaks of a legal usage analogous to the Āsedha, in which the plaintiff goes to his opponent with the words "I arrest you in the name of such and such", mentioning thereby the name of the prince or the governor; the man spoken to in this manner can do nothing until he has tendered his answer for it. In Nepal in the case of civil cases the judge asks the plaintiff about his complaint, and on his paying for it gives him a court servant with him to fetch the accused. In criminal cases it is attempted to extort from the accused an admission of guilt by flogging him; in civil cases it is tried to effect an amicable settlement, and it is done mostly with success[2]. Also the court scene in Pañc. 1 Kathā 21 ends with an amicable settlement.

Legal usages in mediaeval and modern times.

§ 50. *Procedure of witnesses.* The trial (*kriyā*) is mainly based on the deposition of witnesses, particularly according to the older sources. The knowledge of the witness is based on what he has seen (sākṣin), or what he was present at (deśya, anubhāvin) and what he has understood (jñātṛ), and he is primarily an eye-witness or an ear-witness; yet indirect witnesses (uttarasākṣin) too are known who are somehow instructed by a direct witness or who somehow manage to get wind of the statements made by the direct witness (Nār. 1, 147f., 150 etc.). The indirect witness is one of the "appointed" (kṛta) or solemnity witnesses who were called in by the parties for the authentication of

Varieties of witnesses.

Appointed witnesses.

1. BG:16, 304 ff.; 27, 266.
2. Hodgson, Ess. 2, 220-224.

purchase and sale, deposit and other legal transactions. Moreover, the witness of a document, the secret witness, who is stationed behind a wall to overhear a negotiation without the other party knowing it, one who was accidentally present and the reminded (smārita) witness who is repeatedly reminded of what took place in his presence so that he may not fall a prey to his forgetfulness—all of them are "appointed" witnesses. The judge and the king are regarded as unappointed witnesses (akṛta) for what was discussed before them, the village community are unappointed witnesses for what took place in the village, particularly in the case of boundary disputes and family members, acquaintances, and employees are unappointed witnesses for what was known to them on account of their relations with the parties (Nār. 1, 149—152 ; Bṛh. 7, 1—17 ; Kāty. 6, 5-10[1]).

Un-appointed witnesses.

The minimum number of witnesses is usually set at three. Bṛh. 7, 16 ff. speaks of 9, 7, 5, 4, 3 or 2 witnesses, but he however makes distinctions among them. Thus only 2 witnesses are said to be sufficient if they are learned Brahmans or secret witnesses or witnesses by whom documents are attested while on the other hand in the case of voluntary, reminded, family or indirect witnesses always 3 to 5 witnesses are necessary. In general, no notice shall be taken of a single witness, yet the deposition of a messenger, accountant, accidental witness, king and the chief judge may be valid even if he is the only witness. Others allow a single witness if he is acknowledged by both the parties ; a single witness shall also be heard when it is about a deposit or an article borrowed for use (yācita) or if he is the manufacturer of the disputed property or if the witness for some other reason particularly deserves to be trusted, and specially in criminal cases the competence of the witnesses must not be examined too strictly (Vi. 8,

Minimum number of witnesses varies according to their special qualities.

Sometimes even a single witness is heard.

Everybody can bear witness in a criminal case.

1. Bandyopadhyaya, 249-254. Tr.

5 f., 9; Gaut. 13, 9; Y. 2, 72; Kāty. 6, 16 f.[1] etc.). If the depositions of witnesses are contradictory, the statement made by the majority of the witnesses shall be taken and if the witnesses are equally divided the decision depends on the respectability or the extraordinary memory of some witnesses (Vi. 8, 39; Nār. 1, 229; Bṛh. 7, 35 etc.).

Decision by majority.

Generally as a rule only respectable, honoured, pious and reliable persons, of the same caste as the accused if possible, shall be allowed to give evidence. Inadmissible witnesses (asākṣin) are friends or enemies, relations or servants of anyone of the parties concerned and people interested in the issue of the case, men of bad reputation or of bad conduct or of despised position, such as a bad character, a gambler, or one who was formerly guilty of perjury or a notorious criminal and traitor, one who is excommunicated from his caste, actors or singers, snake-catchers, slaves, as well as persons who are incapable of carrying on a law-suit or who have no experience of the world, such as women, children, half-witted persons, ascetics, those who are learned in the Vedas or are studying the Vedas (Gaut. 13, 1-4; M. 8, 61-72; Nār. 1, 177-187 etc.; Mah. 5, 35, 44). He who gives a deposition without being ordered or asked is regarded as unreliable, but also omission or refusal to give the deposition or non-appearance inspite of a summons is punished (Gaut. 13, 5 f.; Nār. 1, 161; Bṛh. 7, 31 etc.). The rejection of unreliable witnesses is primarily the concern of the opposite party but this protest has to be raised at the proper time and the judge shall examine it along with the reply of the other party (Bṛh. 7, 24—26). Yet it is naturally one of the chief duties of the judge to estimate the reliability of a witness, in which signs of the consciousness of guilt such as bodily disquietude, cold sweat, pallor, incoherent

The desirable witness.

Inadmissible witnesses.

The unreliable witness may be rejected on the protest of the opposite party.

Outward signs of an unreliable witness.

1. Bandyopadhyaya, 256-257. *Tr.*

speech etc. are to be particularly taken into consideration (Vi. 8, 18 ; Nār. 1, 193—196, 230—234 etc.).

Witnesses take oath.

Even the oldest Smṛtis contain long lectures with which the judges shall exhort the witnesses in order to prevent them from giving false depositions. Often the witnesses take oath with prescribed formulas varying according to the status of the witness (Vi. 8, 19—23 etc. ; differently Gaut. 13, 12). For the enhancement of the solemnity of the occasion the hearing of the witnesses may take place before a glowing fire and near (a jug of) water, in the presence of the king, Brahmans, gods i. e. images of gods (Āp. 2, 29, 7 ; Gaut. 13, 13). The witness shall also put off his shoes and turban, take gold, cowdung or holy grass in his right hand and stretch it out (Bṛh. 7, 23). A mishap, particularly illness, burning by fire or the death of a relation, happening to the witness within seven days of giving evidence is regarded as a sign of perjury. In the case of giving evidence in a boundary dispute, this period is extended to 6 weeks (Kāty. 18, 19[1])

Solemn ceremonies at the time of giving evidence

Punishment for perjury and concocting false witness.

False witnesses are punished with fines and banishment. Bribed witnesses have to pay particularly heavy fines and bribing or seducing to give false evidence is likewise punished with heavy fines and with the confiscation of property and banishment and leads to the loss of the suit. The last punishment is also inflicted on him who tries to influence the witnesses of the opposite party in his favour (M. 8, 120—123 ; Y. 2, 81, Kāty. 6, 26[2] ; Nār. 1, 165). Over and above the temporal punishments there are the most terrible hell tortures and low rebirths and the perjured person by his false evidence throws into hell long lines of predecessors and relations—their number depends on the value of the disputed property ; this belief

1. Bandyopadhyaya, 582. *Tr.*
2. Ibid. 289, 296. *Tr.*

is met with not only in the oldest Smṛtis and Mah. 5, 35, 32-34, but it appears also in the Vendidād and therefore seems to go back to the Indo-Aryan period. The hierarchy of *paśvanṛta*, *gavānṛta*, *puruṣānṛta*, *bhūmyanṛta* exactly correspond to the *pasu-mazo*, *staoro-mazo*, *vīro-mazo*, *daṅhu-mazo* of the fourth Fargard, and also the *mithro aiwidrukhto* may be compared with the *mitradruh* of the Smṛtis, in so far as the sin of the latter may be placed on the same footing as that of a false witness [1]. The Smṛtis mention only a single case of permissible perjury, namely when the life of a man, particularly of a Brahman, is at stake; yet the sin committed through such an untruthful act, has to be expiated for by a sacrifice (Vi. 8, 15,—17; Gaut. 13, 24; Bṛh. 7, 34 etc.).

The belief about the hell tortures of the perjured person is of Indo-Aryan antiquity.

Perjury pardonable when a man's life is at stake.

Already Megasthenes (fragment 27) speaks of mutilation as punishment for false evidence and corporeal punishments may be actually inflicted in the case of the false evidence of a low caste man according to Mit. on Y. 2, 81. According to Alberuni 2, 158 at least four witnesses had to be taken and only an exceptionally reliable man might be an only witness. According to Steele 285ff. minors, men rendered infirm by old age, a deaf man, one diseased in mind, an unusually quarrelsome person, one who is avaricious, one who is addicted to drink or opium, or one who is related with or friendly or inimical to a party, women and slaves were regarded as inadmissible witnesses; yet in the case of murder and other serious criminal cases everybody who was accidentally present should be heard. The minimum number of witnesses was two, yet in particular cases and when the witness had good qualification a single witness was also permissible. False witnesses were punished with fines or detracting punishments excepting when a human life was saved or any pious gift was made thereby. According to Dubois 497 witnesses always had to take oath,

Law of witnesses in mediaeval and modern times.

1. Cf. Spiegel ZDMG 30, 366 ff.

usually with the hand laid on the head of an image of a god, yet perjuries were very frequent. In Nepal the false witness forfeits his property and even suffers corporeal or capital punishment[1].

§ 51. *Other methods of proving.* Already Āp. 2,29,6 speaks of the divine ordeal (daiva) along with the proof by inference (liṅga). Later authors give a complete system of the methods of proving, namely (a) human or worldly proof (mānuṣī or laukikī kriyā), consisting of proof by means of documents and witnesses and circumstantial evidence or documents, witnesses and possession or merely by documents and witnesses; (b) divine intervention (daivikī kriyā) consisting of oaths and ordeals (Nār. I, 1, 3; 1, 69, 235-239, 247 ff.; Bṛh. 5, 18; 9, 32; Y. 2, 22 etc.). According to Bṛh. 9, 32, of worldly proofs witnesses are superior to inference and documents etc. are superior to witnesses; a possession for three generations however overrules everything. As a rule, the proof by ordeal shall be resorted to only in default of worldly proof (Y. 2, 22 etc.).

Worldly proofs and ordeals.

In selecting the method of proving the nature of the case and the competence of the court shall be taken into consideration. Thus in the case of a breach of promise, resumption of a gift, recission of a purchase or a sale, dispute about property, gambling and wagers, only the proof by means of witnesses is resorted to. On the other hand, in the case of disputes about setting and using a gate or a road or a canal, possession alone is the decisive factor. The arbitration courts of the castes, corporations, etc. shall allow only documents as means of proof. In serious criminal cases or when crimes which were committed in secret or a long time ago have to be investigated or when the case concerned is about the denial of a deposit or the genuineness of a document or the validity of the deposition of a witness,

The method of proving varies according to the merits of the case and the court.

1. Hodgson, Ess. 2,226.

etc.—in all these cases only oaths or ordeals are admissible. In the case of suits about debts documents, witnesses, circumstantial evidence or ordeals are allowed; no ordeals are allowed in law-suits about immovable properties (Kāty. 9, 1ff.[1]; Nār. 1, 241 f.; Bṛh. 13, 2f.; 17 etc.). Of course, these rules are not to be taken literally; they are to be regarded as advices for the judges.

Ordeals not allowed in law-suits about immovable property.

About the proof by means of witnesses see § 50, about documents § 35, about possession § 26. Pañc. 1, 86 contains this list: documents, witnesses and ordeals. Authenticity of the documents shall be very carefully examined. The proving of the authenticity may be greatly facilitated if the holder of the document shows it from time to time and reads it to the other party. Also documents written under compulsion or with treacherous motives or those which are not drawn up by persons who are legally capable of doing it, are regarded as unauthentic (Nār. 1, 135-146; Vi. 7, 7-13; Bṛh. 8, 20-26 etc.).

Defects of a document.

The circumstantial evidence or argumentation (yukti, liṅga, tarka, anumāna, upadhā) is based on a careful consideration and co-ordination of all remarkable and suspicious circumstances. The appearance is the first consideration (§ 49), such as if a man suspected of murder is found with a bloody sword or a man suspected of theft is found with the stolen property. Yet the judges have to be on their guard in this respect against treachery, as for instance, anybody may artificially produce a wound on his body and denounce his enemy as the perpetrator of the crime (Nār. 1, 176). The consciousness of guilt may also be manifest from the conduct of the parties at court, as in the case of false witnesses (Y. 2, 13-15.; Pañc. 1, 35 f.). Thieves can be convicted not only on the strength of the possession of the stolen property, but they can also be convicted if it is found that they are. making extra-ordi-

Proof by inference.

1. Bandyopadhyaya, 178-181, 235. *Tr.*

narily large expenses, mixing in bad company and they may be discovered for their thievish propensity or their crime may be laid bare by a sharp cross-examination etc. (Nār. App. 8-12). Also the words which the parties let slip when in a passion shall be carefully recorded (Nār. I, 2, 18).

Appearance is often misleading.

Of course appearance may be misleading, just as there is no fire in the glowworm although it lights up like fire. Liars may produce the impression that they are speaking the truth and truthful men may be suspected of falsehood. Documents may be forged and ordeals may be eluded; for this reason the judges cannot believe in appearances and must strain all their acumen (*yukti*) to come to the bottom of the affair (Nār. I, 1, 30, 40, 68-73; 1, 238 f.). How even a holy man may be suspected to be a thief is exemplified in the story of the pious Māṇḍavya (Nār. I, 1,42) which is related in the Mah. Flying robbers concealed themselves and their booty in his hut. The police found the booty and took the holy man to the king who impaled him as a robber, but later, as he was still alive, set him free and asked for forgiveness. In the Mṛcch. a suspicious utterance, which the plaintiff (*saṁsthānaka*) lets slip, is at once recorded on the floor. The unjust sentence against Cārudatta is the result of a whole line of points of suspicion dexterously pieced together, among which the possession of the ornaments, apparently the stolen ones, plays the chief part.

Story of Māṇḍavya.

The ordeal.

The divine judgment (*divya*, *daivikī kriyā*, *samayakriyā*, *daiva*) is based on the belief in the direct intervention of the deity in order to expose the guilt or to vindicate the innocence and to expiate for the violation of law which has occurred. In simpler cases the oaths (*śapatha*) come to be first applied which signify variously formulated solemn spells, varying according to circumstances and the caste of the swearer, and the customs of the land etc., and they bring down misfortune and degradation on the man

Oath in less important cases.

who takes oath or on the person who is dearest to him, in case his deposition proves to be false. The Smṛtis mention that already in former ages such oaths were taken by gods and Ṛṣis and they trace the name of the ordeal (*divya*) back to them (Nār. 1,243 f.; M. 8, 110 ; Pitām. 2,1). An oath formula actually occurs already in the ṚV 7,104,15 which exactly agrees with the oath of Vas. handed down by Medh. on M. 8,110. Numerous oath formulas are found in Mah. 13,93,115-135, in which there is also the legend of the Ṛṣis accusing each other of the misappropriation of lotus stalks, also referred to by M. and Nār. The man who is taking oath may touch the head or the feet of a Brahman or his wife or his son or the feet of an image of a god, or may take in his hands the blades of Durvā grass or sesamum or silver or gold or earth out of a furrow made by the plough, according as the value of the disputed property is great or small, or he may stretch his hand into fire or water ; the ordeal of the sacred libation too is mentioned in this list (Vi. 9,4—10 ; Bṛh. 10,6 f.; M. 8, 114; Mah. 3,10,32; Raghun. etc.). All these oaths and ordeals are however regarded as valid only if the person who has taken the oath is not visited by any misfortune or affliction (ārti) within a short time, such as an illness, burning by fire, loss of property, death of a son etc. (M. 8, 115 and comm.). The period of watching for the possible misfortune of the swearer should, in this case, according to Mit. on Y. 2,113, be 1,3,5 or more days according as the complaint is more or less serious, cf. § 50. Neither can an oath be taken thoughtlessly or without the command of the judge ; on the other hand, perjury for the sake of a cow, a marriage, a Brahman, or a woman and in similar other cases is considered to be excusable (M. 8, 111 f. etc. ; Vi. 5, 118 ; cf. the oath of the witness, § 50). Alberuni 2, 158 f. also speaks of

Oath formula in ṚV.

Swearing on those who are near and dear to heart.

Oath is valid only if the swearer is not soon visited by misfortune.

Perjury excused under certain circumstances.

Oaths in mediaeval and modern times.

"many oaths", varying according to the value of the disputed property and enumerates as such the oath before 5 learned Brahmans and six kinds of ordeals. Even now oaths are taken by touching the Harivaṁśa, Ganges water, or an ammonite (śālagrāma), an idol, the feet of a Brahman, the head of the son, the tail of a cow etc.; there is also a period of waiting to watch whether any misfortune befalls the person who has taken oath.[1]

The terms Sapatha and Divya are interchangeable.

Discrimination between oath and ordeal.

In an ordeal the other party must accept punishment in case of reverse.

One-sided ordeal.

§ 52. *Ordeals.* Between oaths and ordeals[2] there is only a difference of degree but there is no difference of quality; for this reason the term *divya* "divine judgment" may also comprehend the oath and the divine judgments too are signified by *śapatha* "oath."[3] In simpler cases only the oath is to be taken but in serious and important cases the ordeal is ordained and the value of the stolen, embezzled or otherwise disputed property is estimated in gold in order to decide whether an oath or an ordeal is to be applied and in the latter case also to decide which one (Vi. 9, 2-17 ; Nār. 1, 250 ; Bṛh. 10,7). It is a necessary condition for an ordeal that the other party should take upon itself the fine or other punishment which is eventually decreed in case of defeat. As a rule, the defendant performs the ordeal, but according to special conditions the plaintiff too may perform it. Ordeals effective for one side only, where the opposite party is not punished is case of reverse are ordained in exceptionally heinous crimes, particularly high treason, and also when

1. Grierson § 1451 ; Hodgson, Ess. 2,226 ; Steele 155 f.; BG 18, 3, 8.

2. Cf. Ali Ibrahim Khan, On the Trial by Ordeal AR 1, 389-404; Stenzler, D. ind. Gottesurteile ZDMG 9, 661-682; E. Schlagintweit, D. Gottesurteile d. Inder (Münch. 1866); Bühler, A Transl. of the Chapter on Ordeals JBeAS 35, 1, 14 ff.; Weber I. St. 13, 164 ff.; Kägi, Alter und Herkunft d. german. Gottesurteils in the Festschr. zu d. Züricher Philol. vers. (Zürich 1887); Kohler, Altind. Process-recht (Stuttg. 1891) 38-50.

3. Cf. WZKM 2, 175.

king suspects one of his own officers or if anybody wishes to remove some suspicion about himself by means of an ordeal (Vi. 9, 22; Nār. 1,257,269 f.; Quot. 6,3; Y. 2,95 f.). According to Pitām. 2,11 only the ordeal of the sacred libation, the easiest of them all, may be performed as the one-sided ordeal. Kāty. 9, 18[1] in some cases also allows substitutes in ordeals. In all divine judgments, in conformity with their religious character, special ceremonies are observed, particularly invocations and prayers by means of which the judge or the accused try to secure the co-operation of the Deity. The chief judge, by order of the king, shall conduct and superintend the whole procedure like a priest in a sacrifice. A writing is fastened on the head of the accused, on which the plaint and a prayer are written (Pitām. 2, 26—28; Nār. 2, 276, 195 etc.). The ordeals shall be performed in public, best in the court hall, or at the gate of the royal palace, or before a temple, or at a crossing (Nār. 1, 265).

Substitute in ordeal.

Solemn ceremonies at an ordeal.

From the two main forms of divine judgments, by water and by fire, mentioned in M. 8, 114 f., gradually an intermediate series of 5 ordeals was developed and at last we get 9 different ordeals, of which it is perhaps possible to say that this part of them is later than that[2]. The nine ordeals are:[3] (1) The balance (*dhaṭa, tulā*). The person performing the ordeal is twice weighed on a scale; if at the second time he appears to be lighter than before, he is considered to be innocent; if he is heavier he is guilty. It is disputed how it is to be construed if the weight remains the same or the balance is broken in two. (2) The fire (*agni*). A glowing iron ball has to be carried to a certain distance; the accused however, in

Number of ordeals grows from two to nine.

Ordeal by balance.

Ordeal by fire.

1. Bandyopadhyaya, 318—321. *Tr.*

2. Cf. Bühler SBE 25, CII. Hopkins in C.H.I., p. 283; Meyer, Rechtsschriften, p. 89.

3. Bṛh. 10, 4f., 19-33; Vi. 9-14; Nār. 1, 247-348; Y. 2. 95-113; Pitām. 2.' Kāty. 9 etc. (=Bandyop.. 300-340).

order to protect his hand from being burnt, may at first cover his hand with a layer of leaves. He will be considered not guilty if his hand is not burnt. If he lets the ball fall too early, or if it is doubtful whether he has been burnt or not, the trial is to be repeated. (3) Water (*salila*). The man who is going to be tried immerses himself into a lake or a river and he must keep himself under water until an arrow, which was shot away at the same time is brought back by a fleet runner. (4) The poison (*viṣa*). A certain quantity of poison has to be taken and for sometime it is watched whether the poison begins to act or not. (5) The sacred libation (*kośa*). An image of a deity is bathed in water and the accused is given that water to drink ; then if within a short period—three weeks at the most—any misfortune befalls him or his nearest relation, it will be taken as a proof of his guilt. (6) Grains of rice (*taṇḍula*). Consecrated grains of unhusked rice shall be chewed and then spitted out on a leaf ; if now blood is seen with them the guilt is proved therewith. (7) The hot gold-piece (*taptamāṣa*). A coin has to be fished out of a vessel full of a boiling fluid such as butter or oil ; if in doing this his hand is not injured the accused is acquitted. (8) The plough-share (*phāla*). The accused has to lick a red hot plough-share without however having his tongue scorched thereby. (9) The ordeal by lot (*dharmādharma*). Figures or pictures of justice (*dharma*) and injustice (*adharma*) are put in a vessel as lots ; now it depends on the accused's hitting on the right lot.

Ordeals by water and poison.

Ordeals by the sacred libation and rice grains.

Ordeals by the gold-piece and the plough-share.

Ordeal by lot.

Choice of the ordeal depends on various considerations.

The choice among these various ordeals depends on the circumstances and also the nature of the suit and the personal character of the accused are to be particularly taken into consideration. Thus when the value of the disputed property ranges from under one Kṛṣṇala to five Kṛṣṇalas various oaths shall be taken ; if the value is below 1/2 Suvarṇa, the ordeal of sacred libation is ordained; if the value is higher, ordeal by balance, fire, water or poison shall take place; yet however these value limits are in force only for Śūdras and they are higher in the case of the higher castes (Vi. 9, 4—17). According to another view the ordeals by fire, poison and balance shall not take place if the disputed property is not worth at least 1000 paṇas (Y. 2, 99). According to still another opinion the figures are 100 to 1000 in the case of ordeal by lot, sacred libation, rice-grains, coin, fire and poison and for members of higher castes they are proportionally higher (Bṛh. 10, 9-12).

Graded value-limits for the different castes.

The ordeals by rice-grains and plough-share should be administered to thieves, the latter specially to thieves of cows (Nār. 1, 337; Bṛh. 10, 11, 29). The ordeal by sacred libation, as the easiest of them all, is also appropriate for the removal of suspicion, particularly in the case of imagined misappropriation on the occasion of a partition, or for gaining confidence even in some proposed transaction (Pitām. 2, 9f.; Bṛh. 25, 98; Vi. 9, 16). As it is not dangerous, the ordeal by balance shall be preferably administered to Brahmans, women, children or to old, blind, lame and sick persons; on the other hand, the poison ordeal as the most dangerous one shall never be applied to such persons (Vi. 9, 23, 27; Y. 2, 98 etc.). A similar spirit of moderation is in evidence in the rule that he who suffers from a disease of the biles shall not be subjected to the poison ordeal, he who suffers from a disease of the mouth shall not be subjected to the rice ordeal, and that the blind and the asthmatic shall not be subjected to fire and water ordeals respectively. On the other hand, it would however be considered an undue favour to prescribe fire ordeal for a smith and water ordeal for a fisherman. The ordeal by sacred libation cannot be administered to an unbeliever or evil-doer or in a period of

Fields of application of the different ordeals.

Spirit of moderation.

No undue favour.

universal pestilence and scarcity (Vi. 9, 25-32; Nār. 1, 255, 334f.; Quot. 6, 6-11 etc.).

From outside literature Vatsa walking through fire, still singing, offers perhaps the oldest instance of an ordeal[1]. Sītā too remains uninjured in fire[2], and indeed according to Nār. 1, 242, *strīṇāṁ śīlābhiyogeṣu* an ordeal is to be performed. In the Chāndogyopaniṣad 6, 6 the thief takes a red-hot axe as prescribed in the Smṛtis. The reference to the ordeals *viṣa*, *salila*, *tulā* and *agni* in the Mṛcch. 156 exactly agrees with the Smṛtis. Hiouen Thsang (7. cent.) mentions the same four ordeals; but their application markedly differs from the Smṛtis, particularly in the case of water and poison ordeals[3]. Suleiman (841) mentions the two ordeals of hot iron and boiling water[4]. Alberuni (11. cent.) describes the ordeals by poison, water, sacred libation, balance, hot gold-piece and hot iron in a manner greatly in agreement with the Smṛtis. Ibrahim Khan (1788), ostensibly according to ancient sources, mentions a variety of the plough-share ordeal in which a fiery pit has to be stepped over, and a variety of the poison ordeal with poisonous snakes[5]. In the most recent times in various parts of India and in Nepal the following ordeals used to take place: hot iron, hot oil, walking over glowing coal and various forms of water and poison ordeals, rice chewing, ordeal by lot etc.[6] Ordeals are now prohibited in India.

Instances of ordeals from outside literature.

Ordeals in mediaeval and modern times.

§ 53. *Verdict, execution and self-help.* The verdict (*nirṇaya*) has to be drawn up in writing and this "deed of

1. Pañcaviṁśabr. 24, 6, 6. About the imaginary fire ordeal hymn AV 2, 12 see Bloomfield JAOS 13, 221 ff.; Grill, Hundert Lieder (2nd. ed.) 86 f.

2. Rām. 6, 116-118 (Bomb.).

3. St. Julien, Mém. 1, 84f.; Beal, Records 1, 84f.

4. Cf. Lassen IA 4, 920; Kāgi l. c. 50.

5. l. c.

6. Steele 287f.; Dubois 497f.; BG 18, 1, 468 f.; 20, 167; 24, 266 (cf. Kohler ZVR 10, 186 ff.); N. W. P. Gaz. 4, 285 f. (cf. Kohler l. c. 11, 194); Hodgson, Ess. 2, 221f.

victory" *(jayapattra)* which shall also contain the plaint, answer and the main points of the proceedings and furnished with the signatures of the king or the judges and with the royal seal, is to be handed over to the victorious party, so that reference may be made to it when necessary, e. g. on the occasion of the legal defence in the form of *prāṅnyāya*, "reference to a previous judgment." Cf. § 35. Also the seized properties are on this occasion given over to this party along with the profits arising from them (Bṛh. 6, 1—4 ; 8, 19 ; Kāty. 7, 4—7[1] ; Nār. I, 1, 43 ; Quot. 1, 15). The judgment is null and a renewal of the procedure takes place if the given evidence or the judgment proves to be false, or if the procedure was conducted at night, or outside the proper place, or in the interior of the house, or if it was caused by the enemy, or if it was decided by the application of force or treachery, or if it was decided by incompetent men or without the hearing of the witnesses and the examination of other evidences, or if it was begun by some person incapable of doing the business or by a person who is not fit for it (Vi. 8, 40 ; Y. 2, 31 f. ; Nār. I, 1, 43 ; Quot. 1, 14 ; M. 8, 117). Under certain circumstances the discovery of a new evidence may cause the renewal of procedure, although an evidence which is not produced at the right time is not considered to be valid, just as rains falling after the corn is ripe are of no use (Nār. I, 1, 62 f.). About the appeal see §48.

A deed of the verdict given to the victorious party.

Causes justifying a renewal of procedure.

The duty of enforcing the judgment appears to have been entrusted to the lower officials mentioned in § 45,—execution and mutilation apart, which were entrusted to the hated Caṇḍāla (Vi. 16, 11 etc.), and in the Mṛcch. too the Rājapuruṣa appears for the former and the Caṇḍāla for the latter ; yet however in civil cases self-help, although not permitted in the case of still disputed claims (Nār. I, 1, 46 etc.), is allowed in the largest measure in recog-

Execution of the verdict.

1. Bandyopadhyaya, 186—189. *Tr.*

Self-help in the law of debt.

Creditor takes the law in his own hands.

nised claims, for which the law of debts offers a remarkable example (M. 8, 49 f. ; Nār. 1, 122 f. ; Y. 2, 40 ; Bṛh. 11, 54—59 ; Kāty. 10, 79—92[1]). Where friendly persuasions (*dharma*, *sāntva*) are of no avail, even trickery (*chala*, *upadhi*, *vyāja*), as for instance the borrowing of something from the debtor, is of no use, the creditor may take the debtor bound hand and foot to his house and force him to fulfil his obligation under blows, threats etc., or make him work off the debt as a slave (*ṛṇadāsa*), yet however no detracting or unstipulated work should be thrust upon him. Moreover Brahmans shall be exempted from forced labour. If the debtor is not in a position to work, he may be confined, excepting when he is a Brahman or otherwise a respectable man ; yet however if he gives security he shall be let go home at night and by day at the mealtimes and in order to perform the necessary functions of life.

The "usual" method of realising debt.

Quite peculiar is the realisation of a debt by the "usual way" (*ācarita*), which is explained by "fasts" (*abhojana*) or "waiting for the death by refusing food" (*prāya*, *prāyopaveśana*), also often mentioned in the Rājatar. and also by killing, taking away and confining (*hatvā*, other readings *hṛtvā*, *ruddhvā*, *baddhvā* Bṛh. 11, 58) the sons, wife and the cattle (of the creditor himself or of the debtor) and by investing the door of the debtor. Probably all these different modes of action were actually in vogue. According to Asahāya on Nār. l. c., instead of the creditor also his son or servant may fast, or the creditor may confine his own son and threaten to kill him, etc.

The forced labour and slavery on account of debts are still in evidence, at least n modified forms ; often negotiations to that effect take place even when the

1. Bandyopadhyaya, 419 ff. *Tr.*

loan is being taken[1]. In the Mahratta period the other methods too of compelling the debtor to pay were in vogue. Thus in the south the Takāzā was the usual form, i. e. the house of the debtor was guarded or formally invested by hired servants whom the latter had to pay, or the creditor threatnened to commit suicide, until the debtor paid his debts[2]. The Dharna (*dharaṇa*), formerly in vogue everywhere in India and even now practised in Nepal, is connected with it. In a Dharna the creditor, particularly if he is a Brahman, fasts before the house of the debtor until the latter yields. The debtor has to fast likewise and give up all his business. If the Brahman dies in this manner, then he brings upon the debtor the sin of the murder of a Brahman[3]. A similar old custom of realising gambling debts has come down to this day which even according to the Mṛcch. is as follows: the creditor draws a magic circle round the debtor (*dyūtamaṇḍalaṁ kṛtvā*), which the latter cannot cross until he has paid his debt.[4]

Realisation of debt in modern times.

Note. An interesting specimen of a Sanskrit Jayapattra regarding the proprietory right over a female domestic slave *(ceṭī)* has been discovered in a village in Darbhanga and explained by Jayaswal in JBORS, 1920, pp. 246-258. This Jayapattra which dates from 1794 A.D. corresponds fully to the rules of the law-books to which it expressly refers. On the mediaeval Jayapattra discovered in the island of Java see § 13. Jolly.

---

1. BG 5, 373 f.; 16. 121f.; 17, 304 etc.; Steele 264f. Cf. Kohler ZVR 8, 125f.; 10, 163 ff.
2. Wilson, Glossary s. v. Takāzā; Steele 267 f..; BG 16. 304 ff.
3. Wilson s. v. Dharnā; Hodgson, Ess. 2, 234f.
4. Pischel in Philol. Abh. (Berl. 1888) 74.

VI. CUSTOMS AND USAGES

§ 54. *The Brahman student and the house-holder.* Of the three chief parts into which the Dharma is divided according to Y. and the later authors,—custom, law and penance, now custom (*ācāra*) only remains to be reviewed. As however important points of the laws of custom have been already described above, particularly in connection with the laws of marriage and family, and as the law of castes and classes is to be dealt with in the State Antiquities[1] and as the Śrauta and Gṛhyasūtras, particularly important for the history of customs, and the Private Antiquties[2], shall be separately dealt with in this encyclopaedia, I may therefore confine myself here only to a few remarks about the Āśramas and Saṃskāras, the "five great sacrifices", and the sacrifices to the manes and the rules about funeral ceremonies, purificarion and diet.

The four stages of life.

Along with the four castes of Brahmans, Kṣatriyas, Vaiśyas and Śūdras the Brahmanical law ordains the four stages of life (*āśrama*): students, house-holders, forest-hermits and mendicants. After he has been taken into school with the initiation ceremony (*upanayana*, § 55), the Brahman student shall dwell with his teacher (*guru*) and study the Veda under his guidance.[3]

---

1. See f.-n. 5, p. 95. *Tr.*
2. See f.-n. 1. *Tr.*
3. Women too could take a similar course of study with the accompaniment of the same ceremonies in the opinion of Hārīta: द्विविधा स्त्रियो, ब्रह्मवादिन्यस्सद्योवध्वश्च । तत्र ब्रह्मवादिनीनामुपनयनमग्नीन्धनं वेदाध्ययनं स्वगृहे च भिक्षाचर्येति । सद्योवधूनां चोपस्थिते विवाहे कथञ्चिदुपनयनमात्रं कृत्वा विवाहः कार्य्यः । See quotation in Smṛticandrikā, Saṁskārakāṇḍaḥ, p. 34. (I am indebted to my honoured teacher Prof. H. C. Chakladar for this reference). That this law was not a mere theory is proved by Bhavabhūti's unique character Ātreyī in the Uttararāmacarita. It will be remembered that Hār. is the oldest Smṛti (p. 18). *Tr.*

For each of the three or four Vedas a study of twelve years is held to be necessary, so that thus the maximum length of the period of study comes to be 48 years, while the minimum shall amount to 12 years (Āp. 1, 2, 12—16; Gaut. 2, 45—47 etc.). Yet one need not study the Vedas longer than it is necessary to master them and according to an ancient saying the sacred fire should be kindled, that is, the period of study should be completed, before gray hair appears (Baudh. 1, 3, 5). By way of an exception the student may devote himself to a spiritual life as a Naiṣṭhikabrahmacārin; in that case, if his teacher dies, he must serve the son or even the widow of the teacher or an older fellow student or eventually the sacred fire, as he formerly used to serve the teacher himself (Gaut. 3, 4—9; Vi. 28, 43—46 etc.).

Period of study.

One of the principal aims of the authors of the Smṛtis is to regulate most accurately the conduct of the students towards their teachers. Even at the first dawn of day the student has to announce himself to his teacher and respectfully clasp his feet after saying his morning prayers;[1] he cannot sit beside him, cannot first speak to him, cannot seat himself in a careless posture in his presence, cannot pronounce his name without an honorific predicate, cannot dispute with him or scoff at him, must follow him at his word, etc. He must show respect even to the wife and the son of theteacher, yet he must be reserved in his conduct towards a young wife of the teacher (Vi. 28, 14—16, 23—27, 31—33; 32, 10—15; Āp. 1 3, 9—23; 7, 25—30 etc.). To observe chastity is one of the principal duties of the Brahmacārin and moreover he cannot dance, sing, gamble and cannot anoint himself and cannot eat flesh, honey or spices, he cannot injure a living being, and cannot lie, slander or quarrel, etc. (Vi. 28, 11; M. 2, 177-197 etc.). Every day he has to go out for alms and collect faggot for

Detailed rules about the conduct of Brahmacārins.

1. Cf. Delbrück, D. indog. Verwandtschaftsnamen 559 ff.

Daily life of the Brahmacārin.

the sacred fire which is entrusted to his care; he must however hand over the food he collects by begging to his teacher and shall receive of it only what the teacher leaves for him (Vi. 28, 9 f.; M. 2, 182—187 etc.). Further he shall also regularly say the morning and the evening prayers, sacrifice to the gods, sleep on earth and rise before sunrise (Vi. 28, 2—5, 12, 53; M. 2, 176 etc.). When instructions for study are given he must listen attentively; if he is inattentive or disobedient the teacher may chastise him but not too harshly. At the end of the period of his study he shall make a present to the teacher as his resources permit and return to the house of his parents (Nār. 5, 11—15; M. 2, 245 etc.).

The final bath of the Brahmacārin.

Certain ceremonies, specially a bath of purification (*snāna*) took place at the end of the school period, after which the absolved student was called Snātaka "the bathed one." Such an absolved student has a claim to particular distinction, specially when he goes somewhere as a guest, but he has to observe special ceremonies (Gaut. 9, 1 ff.; Āp. 1, 30 etc.). Soon after his return to his paternal home the young Brahman proceeds to marry (§ 16) and therewith enters the stage of the house-holder (*gṛhastha*). The Gṛhastha life too is covered with a thick net of religious duties (Vi. 60—70 etc., cf. §§ 56—59). Even before the break of day he shall leave the bed and come out to perform the duty of evacuating

Daily duties of the householder

the bowels; very detailed rules are given about the selection of a spot for this purpose and the cleansing of the body with the left hand by means of water and earth. Then follows the cleansing of the teeth with pieces of wood of the thickness of the little finger which are freshly cut from specially recommended trees. Moreover, water is sipped and the mouth and the throat are rinsed with it, which has to be performed in sitting posture with certain parts of the hand and the fingers while the head is to be turned to the east or the north. The bath should be performed at dawn, best in the Ganges or at least in some other flowing water; the clothes too have to be washed and during the bath and afterwards prayers shall be said, holding of the breath (*prāṇāyāma*) performed and libations and sacrifices shall be offered. The Saṁdhyā of the morning shall be followed by another similar Saṁdhyā in the evening. There are only two proper meals, in the forenoon and in the evening; the wife eats after her husband what the latter leaves of his food, but the man shall not take food before he has given food to the gods, particularly the household gods and the manes, and entertained his guests. The animal sacrifice, corn sacrifice, Soma sacrifice, sacrifice to the manes and other religious performances are included in the daily duties which should take place periodically or on particular occasions, and a crowd of general rules about customs and conduct, particularly about bad omens, journeys, about giving way to one another, about the clothing and the ornaments (gold ear-rings), places to stop at, about looking before and treading on something, about keeping fire and water pure, about the cultus of the Brahmans, images of gods, cows, self-restraint and piety, etc. (Vi. 63, 1—51; 71 f. etc.).

The two Saṁdhyās.

Megasthenes' statement (fragment 41) about the 37 years which Indian philosophers spend in the company of fellow students and teachers in chastity and self-mortification, before they set up a family, reminds us of the 36 years of Vedic studies. The data in Alberuni 2, 130—135 about the student and the house-holder thoroughly agree with the Smṛtis, but probably they are mostly taken from that source. At the present day studying at the house of a Guru is no longer obligatory and takes place only in isolated places; the Naiṣṭhikabrahmacārin is still seen in various sects of the present day in which similar rules between the pupil and the teacher are in force as

Ancient laws in mediaeval and modern times.

laid down in the Smṛtis. Usually "the ceremony of being admitted by the teacher" *(upanayana)* is considered only as a form followed almost immediately by "the return from the teacher," which too has become a mere ceremony, cf. §56. From economic grounds it is not improbable that these brief ceremonies date from quite an ancient period. On the other hand, the duties of the Gṛhastha are still more or less observed, [1] such as the cleansing of the body with the left hand, the use of the tooth-pick mentioned also by Hiouen Thsang, morning and evening prayers, avoiding treading on potsherd, bones etc., wearing gold ear-rings, institutions for divine service, cf. §§ 56—59.

§ 55. *The forest-hermit and the mendicant.* At the beginning of old age when one sees his skin becoming wrinkled and the hair turn gray and sees the son of his son, the Gṛhastha should enter the stage of the forest-dweller (*vānaprastha*) (M. 6, 2 etc.). His wife shall either accompany him to the forest or remain behind with his sons. According to the Vaikh. sū., in the former case he is called Sapatnīka and as such is either Audumbara, Vairiñca, Vālakhilya or Phenapa ; without the wife he is called Apatnīka and as such belongs to one of the numerous varieties such as Kālasika, Uddaṇḍaka, Aśmakuṭṭa, Dantolūkhalika, Uñchavṛttika, Bailvāśin, Pañcāgnimadhyaśāyin, etc. Their names are based on the various kinds of self-mortification which the Vānaprasthas inflict on themselves. All of them shall clothe themselves in barks of trees or skin, let their hair and nails grow, live on fruits, plants and the roots of the forest, morning and evening offer sacrifice in the Śrāmaṇaka fire kindled on special ceremonies, generally perform the five Mahāyajñas as before, observe chastity, bathe three-times a day and

Various kinds of forest-dwellers.

Rules common to all.

1. Dubois, 147—166; Bühler ZDMG 40, 541; Hiouen Thsang, Mém. 1, 55, 71; BG 22, 60—90 etc

sleep on earth (Vi. 94; Gaut. 3, 26—36; Baudh. 2, 11, 15 etc.). As special self-mortifications they shall expose themselves in summer to the heat of the sun enhanced by four fires, in the rainy season sleep on earth, in winter wear wet clothes, roll about on earth, stand all day long on the toes or sit down and stand up alternately, stand with hands stretched upwards or with a stick raised high, shall gaze steadfastly at the sun or keep the face turned to the earth, remain under water for a long time, would not speak. fast for a whole month, etc. (M. 6, 22—32; Vi. 95: Vaikh. Dharmasū. 1, 7—11). Ṛṣi Vikhanas is said to have been the founder of the order of forest-dwellers, after whom they are also called Vaikhānasas (Baudh. 2, 11, 14); an apparently later shoot of his teachings is the Vaikhānasasūtra (§3). Perhaps this order was never universally recognised.[1] The class of the forest-dwellers belongs to the institutions obsolete in the present age (*kalivarjya*) and even Gaut. and Āp. mention the mendicant before the forest-dweller, and according to Baudh. 2, 17, 2—5, Y. 3, 56 etc., one may directly enter the state of the Bhikṣu from the stage of the Gṛhastha or the Brahmacārin.

Special self-mortifications.

Perhaps the forest-dwellers existed merely in theory.

The mendicant or the ascetic (*bhikṣu, yati, sannyāsin, parivrājaka, pravrajita*), according to the usual conception, is the fourth stage in the life of the Brahmans.[2] As the *bhikṣu* can own no property, at the time of entering this state one should perform a smaller sacrifice (*iṣṭi*) to Prajāpati in which the whole property is given away as the sacrificial fee (Vi. 96, 1 etc.). About other ceremonies on the occasion of this act see Baudh. 2, 17; without home or property (Vas. 10, 6) the monk shall roam about as a beggar, shall stay nowhere for a long time, sleep on

The stage of the mendicant.

The austerities of a mendicant.

1. See Charpentier, C.H.I. p. 151. *Tr.*
2. Cf. Kauṭ. I, 3 where the main features of the life of the Parivrājaka have been described in a masterly fashion. *Tr.*

earth, wear a loin-cloth as his only dress, shave his head bald, hold in his hand three staffs intertwined with each other and a beggar's bowl and a water-pot, eat only what is given to him voluntarily, yet never any meat or sweets. He shall enter a village only to beg, but only in the evening when the time of taking meal is past ; he can beg for alms only in seven houses, but shall not be depressed if he gets nothing, nor exult if he gets something. On the whole an unruffled temper and philosophical equanimity are the main things for the *yati* ; he shall wish neither for death nor for a long life and shall not even trouble himself to see whether somebody is hacking off his hand with an axe or is sprinkling sandal powder on him. He should meditate over the short duration of life, the impurity of the body, transitoriness of beauty, tortures of hell, infirmities of old age and diseases, separation from the beloved, co-existence with the enemies and the endless transmigrations of the soul. Thus gradually shaking off all mundane propensities, roaming about alone, speaking to none, he is finally dissolved in the universal soul. It is remarkable that the *bhikṣu* is permitted to stop his wanderings in the rainy season and to stay in one place, corresponding to the *vasso* of the Buddhists and the Jains (Gaut. 3, 11—25 ; Vas. 10 ; Baudh. 2, 17 f. ; Vi. 96 etc.) [1]. It is not allowed to leave the order of the mendicants ; those who faithlessly leave it shall be slaves of the king during their lifetime (Nār. 5, 35 ; Y. 2, 183 ; Vi. 5, 152).

Philosophical equanimity.

Parallelism with the laws of Buddhists and Jains.

To the Vānaprasthas correspond the Ulobioi of Megasthenes (fr. 41) who remain in the forests, live on leaves and fruits of wild trees and wear clothes made of barks of trees. Alberuni describes the Vānaprastha and the Bhikṣu as well as the two primary Āśramas just like the

1. Cf. Bühler on Gaut. 3, 13

Smṛtis but the picture seems to have been taken merely from literature and not from actual life. Penances like those of the Vānaprasthas are mentioned about the "fakirs" of the present day [1]. The modern "bhikṣuks" are the spiritual Brahmans as distinct from the worldly Brahmans, the Gṛhasthas[2]. Among the Sannyāsis there are ascetics of various sects, specially Śaivas. Worldly men now-a-days rarely enter religious orders ; on the other hand, the spiritual people of many sects and castes may marry as according to the Smṛtis the Vānaprasthas could have their wives with them. That it was not compulsory to go over to the spiritual life from the Gṛhastha life, is indicated in the Smṛtis in this way that they often call the Gṛhastha class the best without which the other classes could not exist (Gaut. 3, 36 : M. 5, 87—90 etc.).

Parallelism with the present age.

§ 56. *The sacraments.* Ceremonies connected with divine service in the widest sense of the term are called the sacraments, of which Gaut. 8, 14—21, quoted as the standard passage also in later works such as Nīlakaṇṭha's monograph on the Saṁskāras, the Saṁskāramayūkha, mentions 40: the ceremony of fecundation (garbhādhāna), the ceremony (at the time of the first movements of the child) the purpose of which is to secure the birth of a boy (puṁsavana), parting of the hair of the pregnant woman (sīmantonnayana, in the 6. or the 8. month), the ceremony of birth (jātakarman), the giving of the name (nāmakaraṇa, on the 10. or 12. day), the feeding with rice (annaprāśana, in the 6. month after the birth) the cutting of the hair (caula, in the 3. year of life), introduction to the teacher (upanayana), the four vows at the time of the study of the Veda, the bath (at the end of the

The forty sacraments of life

1. Cf. M. Williams, Indian Wisdom (3rd. ed.) 104—106.

2. Cf. e. g. BG 18, 1, 108 ff; M. Williams. l. c. 252f ; Wilson, Glossary 81 463.

Vedic studies, also called Samāvartana, "return"), marriage, the five great sacrifices (§ 37), the seven minor sacrifices (pākayajña), the seven offerings of the fire (haviryajña), the seven Soma-sacrifices. The fire-offerings and the Soma-sacrifices are described in the Brāhmaṇas and the Śrautasūtras, the minor sacrifices are described in the Gṛhyasūtras. According to Hār., the sacrifices are to be taken as *daiva saṁskāras* and the other ceremonies of divine service as *brāhma saṁskāras.* Only the latter are to be taken as Saṁskāras in the proper sense, but various other ceremonies are often attached to them, such as the act of Anavalobhana,[1] Garbharakṣaṇa, as protection against a miscarriage at birth, the ceremony of the first going out with a child in the 4. month after its birth in order to show it the sun (niṣkramaṇa, ādityadarśana), perforation of the ears (karṇavedha), cutting of hair as the sign of majority at the age of 16 (keśānta, godāna), etc.

Two classes of sacraments.

Saṁskāras too in the strict sense fall within the jurisdiction of the Gṛhyasūtras, for every Vedic school performs them in a particular way. The Smṛtis deal somewhat fully only with the ceremony of initiation and investiture with the sacred thread of the young Brahman[2] as it is the most important Saṁskāra (Vi. 27, 15—29 ; M. 2, 36—50, 68 etc.). For the Brahmans the 8. year is considered to be the most proper age for it. The Kṣatriyas and the Vaiśyas too have a right to be invested with the sacred thread (yajñopavīta) which is the external sign of the Ārya, who attains his spiritual rebirth through the Upanayana and along with it the right of calling himself a twice-born (dvija). Yet in their case the ceremony takes place a few years later, and moreover their sacred thread as well as the garment and the girdle,

Only Upanayana fully described in the Smṛtis.

1. Cf. Caland WZKM 8,370.

2. About the earlier history of *upanayana* see Oldenberg, D. Religion d. Veda 466—571

skin and staff, shall be of other materials than those of the Brahmans. The spiritual significance of the initiation ceremony lies therein that the right of studying the Veda and reciting the sacred prayer Sāvitrī is earned by it and for this reason the whole ceremony is also called Sāvitrī. The teacher (ācārya) who initiates the young Brahman and teaches him the Sāvitrī will therefore be regarded as his spiritual father and the Sāvitrī his spiritual mother. The young Brahman's going out for alms is an important part of the ceremony for which he first applies to his mother and other female relations. The expenses of the Saṁskāras, which in part are not inconsiderable, have to be defrayed by the parents and if they are not living by the elder brother, and the same in the case of the girl, for whom however there is only one proper Saṁskāra which is accompanied by sacred Mantras, namely the marriage[1] (*vivāha*, Nār. 13, 33, 27; Y. 2, 124; 1, 13 etc.).

Spiritual significance of Upanayana.

The ceremonies Garbhādhāna, Jātakarman, Nāmakarman, cutting of the hair, perforation of the ears and the investiture with the sacred thread are also mentioned by Alberuni 156 f., 130, though, it is true, with the additional remark, that Garbhādhāna is not performed for the feeling of shame. At the present day just this ceremony often takes place and marks the advent of puberty in the female and the beginning of the conjugal life (§ 17); the chief ceremony is often this that the lap of the young wife is filled with rice, cocoanuts and other fruits probably as the symbol of fecundity. The following ceremonies are generally practised even now among the Chitpavan Brahmans of Puna[2]: Jātakarman, Karṇavedha on the twelfth day after birth, Sūryāvalokana in the fourth month, Annaprāśana in the 6., 8., 10. or 12. month, Caula

Sacrament in mediaeval and modern times.

Ceremonies observed by Chitpavan Brahmans.

1. But see f.-n. 3, p. 320. *Tr.*
2. BG 18, 1, 108–148.

in the 1.--5. year, investiture with the sacred thread in the 7.—10. year, the return of the student *(samāvartana)* after an interval of 12 days to one month, then marriage in the Brāhma form (Brāhmavivāha), Garbhādhāna at the time of the puberty of the bride, Puṁsavana at the time of pregnancy, Anavalobhana in the 4. month of pregnancy and Sīmantonnayana in the 6.—8. month. Excepting marriage, investiture with the sacred thread (jenvī, janeo= yajñopavīta) is always regarded as the most important

Initiation ceremony.

ceremony[1]. For the Brahmans the initiation ceremony consists of this : the young Brahman takes in his hand a staff of palāśa-wood which reaches up to his hair (as in Vi. 27, 21 f. etc.)., wears an antilope skin and the sacred thread and a loin-cloth, puts on a gridle of Munj grass (as in Vi. 27, 18 etc.) and his father whispers the Gāyatrī (sāvitrī) in his ear ; in the evening follows the ceremony of begging (bhikṣāval), on which occasion his mother and other ladies give him handsome presents. At the time of the Samāvartana ceremony, which follows shortly, he finally makes the air of starting on a pilgrimage to Benares but lets himself be persuaded to return. A similar survival is to be found in Bengal on the occasion of

A survival in Bengal.

the investiture with the sacred thread, inasmuch as the young Brhman dressed as a Brahmacārin declares his resolution to enter the spiritual order and is dissuaded from this purpose only with great difficulty,[2] cf. § 54. The investiture with the sacred thread is not even now confined to the Brahmans.

§ 57. *The five great sacrifices and the Śrāddha.* The regular performance of the five great sacrifices (Mahāyajña, Vi. 59, 19—26 etc.) is one of the most important duties of the Gṛhastha. The sacrifice or the

1. Cf. Wilson, Glossary 230, 463 f.: Dubois 92—99: Bühler, Kaśmīr Report 22; Bose, The Hindoos as they are 183—186.

2. Bose l. c. 185 f.

divine service which is connected with the Veda, consists of the recitation of the Veda, the sacrifice to the gods by the offering of butter poured into the fire (homa), the sacrifice to the manes by the libation (tarpaṇa), sacrifice to the demons or all creatures (bhūta) by scattering food as offering (bali), sacrifice to men by entertaining guests, particularly Brahman ascetics. The last four sacrifices are called the Pākayajñas; the sacrifice to the Veda stands high above them and even above the Vidhiyajñas which are performed in the three sacred sacrificial fires; particularly the recital of the Gāyatrī (sāvitrī) at the time of morning and evening prayers produces as much merit as the study of the Veda, and this religious merit can never be destroyed although the reward for good deeds is transitory (Vi. 55, 12-21 etc.). Which Vedic texts should be recited and how the other Mahāyajñas are to be performed—all this depends on the Śākhā of the Veda to which the Brahman concerned belongs; these differences are minutely described in the Gṛhyasūtras, while the Smṛtis as usual give the general norm.

The five sacrifices of the householder.

The sacrifices to the dead (śrāddha) are a special development out the sacrifices proper and there is a whole literature devoted to it which extends from the Vedic Saṁhitās down to the Dharmanibandhas; of the latter the edition of Hemādri's Śrāddhakalpa in the Bib. Ind. covers 1717 pages. Already the Smṛtis discuss the Śrāddhas very exhaustively; thus Vi. in 14 chapters (73-86) deals with the ceremonies on the occasion of a Śrāddha, as well as the predecessors to be worshipped by it, the proper time, the effects of the Śrāddhas, the choice of sacrificial offerings, conduct towards the invited Brahmans, the fitness or unfitness to be invited to it, the proper spots for the performance of sacrifices to the dead and the ceremony of liberating a bull often connected with the Srāddha. "Connected by the sacrificial lump (at the

Extensive literature on Srāddha.

Śrāddha determines relation-ship.

offering to the dead)" (*sapiṇḍa*) is an usual designation of near relations, particularly agnates. Accordingly the Śrāddha which is performed at the latest one year after the death by kneading the Piṇḍas of the dead person and the predecessors, effecting thereby the inclusion of the person who is dead among the Sapiṇḍas, is called Sapiṇḍikaraṇa. At first the deceased gets monthly Śrāddhas, particularly however the Ekoddiṣṭa is performed shortly after his death when the period of mourning is past. Other kinds of the Śrāddha are the Nitya, i.e. the daily libations (see above), the Kāmya performed to attain some desired object, the Ābhyudayika or Vṛddhiśrāddha performed on the occasion of some joyous ceremony such as marriage, the Pārvaṇa performed on the days of the month called Parvan, etc.

Varieties of Srāddha.

Evolution of Śrāddha from older institutions.

Caland seems to have found the thread of Ariadne in this labyrinth[1]. Thus the Śrāddha in which three invited Brahmans, considered to be the representatives of father, grandfather and great-grandfather, are entertained, is originated from the Piṇḍapitṛyajña appearing in older sources, in which the same ceremonies take place but are directed towards the fathers supposed to be present there in spirit. The latter sacrifice seems on its side to go back to the Pitṛyajña mentioned already in the Vedic Saṁhitās in which yet no Piṇḍas were offered and the "fathers" collectively, without the restriction to the three male ascendants of the sacrificer, were invoked. That the motive of the sacrifice to the dead is merely the fear of the spirits of the dead (*preta*), is indicated, for instance, by the belief that they would return to the earth and annoy their relatives if no sacrifices are performed for them (Vi. 20, 32).

The motive of the Srāddha.

Every orthodox Brahman even now says the morning

---

1. Altind. Ahnencult 152—165,173—181 ; worship of the dead 1—47 ; cf. Oldenberg l. c. 548—562.

and evening prayers with corresponding variations according to the school of the Veda he belongs to. The main features of the morning prayer for a follower of the Rigveda are approximately the following (cf. § 55) : the bath (snāna), sipping of water (ācamana), the holding of the breath (prāṇāyāma), the many times repeated murmuring of the Gāyatrī and the recital of many other texts, proclaiming the family tree of the devout person, repeated Ācamanas, the Veda sacrifice (brahmayajña) in the narrow sense which principally consists of the recital of the initial words of various Vedic and later works, and finally the libation (tarpaṇa) which here is directed to the gods, Ṛṣis and the fathers[1]. The Homa in the morning and the evening and the other Mahāyajñas are still partly in vogue. Moreover the Śrāddha with the Piṇḍas still always plays a chief role in the cultus particularly of the Brahmans, and also among other castes[2]. The liberation of a bull on the occasion of a Śrāddha is still practised[3]. A famous Śrāddha (ekoddiṣṭa) in Bengal is said to have cost over a million rupees, and in well-to-do families not less than five to six thousand rupees are spent there at the first Śrāddha.[4] Even now Śrāddhas are preferably performed at certain holy places, particularly at Gayā in Behar,[5] as prescribed in Vi. 85, 67.

Ancient laws observed in modern times.

§ 58. *Funeral ceremony and impurity.* The funeral rites or the obsequies (antyeṣṭi), are not reckoned by Gaut. 8,14 ff. etc. among the sacraments but they

1. M. Williams, The place which the Ṛigveda occupies in the Sandhyā, 5. Or. Congr., Indog. Section 157—188.

2. Cf. BG 13,78 (Golaks) ; 85 (Sarasvats) ; 18. 1. 167 (Kanojs) ; 175 (Shenvis) ; 180 (Tailangs) : Risley. The Tribes and Castes of Bengal 1. 149 (Rahri-Brahmans) etc.

3. Dubois 298 f.; BG 22, 85f. Cf. Pañc. 1,5 (Kielhorn).

4. Bose, The Hindoos as they are 255-271.

5. M. Williams, Modern India (3rd. ed.) 97—107 ; cf. Rājatar. 6, 254 7,1008.

belong to the ceremonies in which Vedic Mantras are recited (M. 2, 16), and these Mantras are mostly taken from: Vedic funeral hymns, but neither these nor the data in the Gṛhyasūtras will be exhaustibly dealt with here[1]. The Antyeṣṭi, in contradistinction to the Śrāddha which brings happiness (maṅgala), is considered to be evil-bringing[2] (amaṅgala), and this may be the reason that the Smṛtis have so little to do with it. According to Vi. 19 and Y. 3 1-18 the procedure of the funeral ceremony is as follows. The mourning train of the relations, arranged according to age (Mit.), brings the corpse to the burning place (śmaśāna). Arriving there they burn the corpse to the accompaniment of the recital of texts appropriate for the ceremony. Then they turn round the pile of woods from left to right, that is to say, by turning their left side to it. Then follow a purificatory bath (cf. Āp. 2, 15, 10; Baudh. 1, 11, 23 etc.), inasmuch as they go into water with clothes on, and an offering of water is given for the deceased, invoking him by name; a Piṇḍa too is offered to him on kuśa grass. Then they rise out of the water and sitting on a grass plot hear a sermon about the transitoriness of human life. Then the train of mourners go back home, the children this time leading; they halt at the door once more in order to chew Nimba leaves, sip water, tread on a stone etc. and step slowly into the house only after finishing this ceremony. So long as the impurity caused by the death lasts sacrifices have to be daily performed for the deceased, inasmuch as an offering of water and a Piṇḍa are given to him, vessels with milk and water are hung by a rope for him, etc. On the fourth day after the cremation the bones are collected and thrown into the Ganges. Children under

Difference between Antyeṣṭi and Śrāddha.

The funeral ceremonies.

Ceremonies after cremation.

1. Oldenberg, D. Religion d. Veda 570—591.
2. Cf. M. Williams, Hinduism 65.

two years of age are not however cremated but buried. Later works mention many other ceremonies[1], the chief aim of which is to lend arms, legs etc., and finally the head, to the spirit of the dead (preta) by means of the Piṇḍas offered to it, so that it is transformed into a "father" (pitṛ) and is then fit to be received into the Śrāddha.

Various periods of impurity after birth and death.

The impurity on account of death [2] is parallel to the impurity caused by a birth and like the latter its term is generally 10 days. It is not improbable that the birth impurity of which the term of 10 days is probably based on a natural ground was responsible for the fixation of an equal term for death impurity too. This period undergoes important fluctuations according to the age, sex and the position of the deceased and the nearness of relationship. Thus the death of a still-born child or a child which dies soon after birth or before teething, causes no impurity. The death of a married woman makes impure only her husband and his relations, but not her own blood-relations. At the death of the father of the mother there is an impurity only of three days. For people of lower status than that of the Brahmans the period of impurity may in general extend from 11 days to a month (Vi. 22, 1—4, 26 f., 33, 42 etc.).

Austerities in the period of impurity.

So long as the impurity exists one may eat only purchased or presented foods and no flesh, sleep only alone on earth, and one cannot beg or study or have intercourse with any one for fear of defiling him (Gaut. 14, 37—39; Vas. 4, 14 f.; Vi. 19, 14—17; 22, 6 f. etc.). After the expiration of the term of impurity the ceremony of purification takes place. Women are impure not only through a death and their low origin, but also by the menses, which even according to a Vedic legend are the result of a sin which Indra drew upon himself by

1. Colebrooke. The Religious Ceremonies of the Hindus in Ess. 2, 172—195.

2. Cf. Leist, Altar. jus gentium 194—201, 262; Delbrück, D. indog. Verwandtschaftsnamen 568—572.

killing Vṛtra. Only on the fourth day the menstruating woman is pure by a bath. A bath with the clothes on is necessary after touching a menstruating woman, a woman in child-bed, a carrier of a dead-body, a Caṇḍāla, a dog etc. (Vas. 5, 4—9; Gaut. 14, 30ff. etc.).

Defilement and purification of various things.

After the treatment of the defilement of the human body usually purification of things (Dravyaśuddhi) is dealt with (Vi. 23 etc.). Spirituous liquors, drinking of which is a mortal sin (§ 36), leavings and fluids out of the human body such as sweat, tears, urine, excrements, semen, blood, etc. are held to be particularly impure. If earthen or wooden vessels are defiled by them there remains nothing to do but to throw them away; on the other hand, implements of iron, horn, ivory etc. may be purified in the fire or by scrubbing, washing etc. Defilement by a fatty substance is also very bad; defilement by leavings of food etc. are less serious; they can, as a rule, be set at right by simple washing and rinsing. Other kinds of purification are rubbing with ash, cow's hair and other things, straining (in the case of liquids), repeated burning (in the case of earthenware) sprinkling with water, milk, cow's urine or earth, besmearing with cowdung, sipping by a cow (in the case of stagnant water) etc., and in this connection the quality of the cow as a sacred animal must be remembered. Yet in many cases a rational stand-point has been taken. Wares in a shop, the hand of a workman, particles of food sticking to the teeth, hair of the beard which comes into the mouth, a shadow and dust are never impure; on the other hand, the dog is pure when catching a wild animal, a suckling calf is pure when milk flows and a woman's mouth is pure at the time of kissing, a bird is pure when it pecks the fruit; dirty and defiled roads are purified by sun and wind.

A rational view.

The ancient funeral ceremonies are still preserved

wholly or in part among the Brahmans and other castes[1], as for example the train of mourners led by the nearest relative as the "performer" (kartā) of the obsequies, the cremation of the corpse to the accompaniment of Mantras, turning round the heap of woods keeping it to the left side or from left to right, the water libation and the purificatory bath, the return of the mourning party and the halt at the door, chewing of Nim (Nimba) leaves, the offering of water and Piṇḍa and the hanging of a water-vessel on the following days up to the 10., the collection of bones, which is even now called *asthisaṁcayan*,—mostly on the 3. day—in a pot, in order to throw them later into the Ganges when possible, non-cremation of children (below 3 years of age), the belief that the deceased successively receives back his limbs through the Piṇḍas and recital of consolatory Mantras, particularly out the Garuḍapurāṇa. During the period of impurity, which as a rule extends over 10 days, it is forbidden to cook, to take sugar, milk or meat, to use ointments, sandal power or betel-leaves, to wear the turban or the shoes, to go out, to have the hair cut or to be shaved, to study the Vedas or to perform the service of the household god; moreover, one shall take only the foods sent by the relations and shall sleep on earth alone. Already Alberuni 2, 165—170 mentions some of these usages. Defilement through touching (Sparśadoṣa) a man of low caste, a menstruating woman, a dog etc. is still always expiated for by a bath. Women in child-bed shall remain one month and a menstruating woman 3 days in the "birth chamber" giving up all intercourse with men. That earthen and wooden vessels were thrown away after being used once and that metal vessels used to be rubbed

Ancient laws of the funeral ceremonies at the present day.

Law of impurity at the present day.

1. Cf. BG 13, 1, 83, 127; 18. 1, 148, 163, 167, 175, 267, 273, 280, 309 f.; 21, 98, 107: 22, 84 f. etc. Dubois 286—293: M. Williams, Modern India (3rd. Ed.) 97—99.

after every meal, is mentioned already by Hiouen Thsang [1], and even now a similar distinction is made between earthen and other vessels [2]. Also the use of cow-dung and cow's urine is very often resorted to for cleansing purposes[3]. Regarding the defilement caused by fatty substances it may be remembered what a part the cartridges besmeared with tallow had played in the insurrection of 1857.

Various kinds of spirituous liquors: forbidden only for Brahmans.

§ 59. *Rules of diet.* Eating pure food is considered to be more effective than all external means of purification. He who keeps himself pure in his nourishment is truly pure and not he who purifies himself only externally with earth or water (Vi. 22, 89). Of liquors spirituous ones (§§ 36, 58), and of solid foods meat, are strictly forbidden. 13 kinds of spirituous drinks, called *surā* or *madya*, are mentioned. Distillations of molasses, Madhūka flowers or rice-flour are called Surā; intoxicating drinks extracted out of sugar, grapes, cocoanuts etc. are Madya. Yet all these drinks are forbidden only for the Brahmans, while the Kṣatriya and the Vaiśya may enjoy them to some extent (Vi. 22, 82—84; M. 11, 91—99; Gaut. 2, 20). Meat-eating and alcoholism are in general placed on the same footing (M. 11, 96), yet the first sin is not considered to be a mortal one and the Smṛtis contain many relics of the Vedic animal sacrifice and a laxer conception of Ahiṁsā which declares certain animals to be eatable. Thus a well-known memorial verse says that an animal may be killed when entertaining an honoured guest, for a sacrifice and for the manes but never otherwise (M. 5, 41; Vas. 4, 6 etc.). Therefore, says Vas. 4, 7, the killing of animals

Relaxation of the principle of Ahiṁsā.

1. Mém. 1. 70f.
2. Dubois 108—114.
3. l. c.; BG 21, 95; Cf. § 37.

in a sacrifice is no killing in the true sense of the word; in M. 5, 48, Vi. 51, 71 of course another principle is met with in its place: "therefore, one must avoid eating meat." According to M. 5, 56 it is no sin to take meat or spirituous drinks or to cohabit, i. e. if it takes place at the time fixed by law (cf. 5, 22, 27). Sheep, goats, antilopes, buffaloes and other animals shall be sacrificed specially at the sacrifices to the dead, and, as it is believed, their flesh satisfies the "fathers" for a longer period than vegetable offerings (Vi. 80 etc.). It is often expressly permitted to sacrifice even oxen and cows and then to eat their flesh (Āp. 1, 17, 30; M. 5, 18). The flesh of the rhinoceros, iguana, hare, porcupine, wild boar and the tortoise may be eaten any time (Vi. 51, 6 etc.). Birds of prey and many other birds cannot be eaten but the partridge, francolin, quail and the peacock are excepted from this prohibition (Vi. 51, 31). Fishes are likewise forbidden but here too some exceptions have been stated (Vi. 51, 21 etc.). The eating of wild animals if not fully allowed, is however less blameworthy than to eat household animals, particularly cows, house fowls, pigs and monkeys (Vi. 51 3 etc.). Generally, to avoid animal food is regarded as a special austerity of particular merit and thus it is not given as a compulsory rule (M. 5, 53 f. etc.). For this reason it has been ordained for the austerities during the period of impurity and for the ascetics that no meat can be eaten (§§ 55, 58). Of vegetable foods, garlic, leek, onion, mushroom and plants growing on excrements should be avoided. Also presents from low persons, food which is refused, leavings of a meal and food touched by impure animals or men cannot be taken (Y. 1, 160—171, 176 etc.).

Sometimes beef-eating allowed.

Vegetarianism not a compulsory rule.

Not only what is eaten but also how, when and where the food is eaten, is of importance in this respect. Thus one cannot eat standing, lying, naked or in wet clothes, nor

Various other prohibitions about diet.

out of a broken or impure vessel, nor out of the hand ; one cannot eat in the open air, in a temple or in an empty house at midday or midnight or at dawn, nor at the time of the solar or the lunar eclipse or when any misfortune has occurred to the king, to a Brahman or to a cow ; nor can one eat during a period of indigestion or to surfeit or more than twice a day or too late or too early. Before eating, gods and Brahmans must be fed, sacrifice must be offered in the fire, etc. ; at the time of eating one must look towards the north or the south and be anointed and garlanded and after the meal the mouth and the hands must be washed (Vi. 68 etc.).

Brahmanical laws of diet in agreement with those of Buddhists.

The oldest exactly datable prohibition to eat animal food is found in the inscriptions of Aśoka who speaks in unambiguous terms against killing and sacrificing animals, but as laid down in the Smṛtis, makes an exception in favour of peacocks and antilopes [1]. In general, the rules of diet among the Buddhists are in complete agreement with Brahmanical rules, especially those for Brahmanical ascetics, inspite of the Buddhists' strict commandment of Ahiṁsā which they share with the Jains [2]. The Mah. preaches Ahiṁsā but the chief heroes go for chase and eat flesh[3]. Alberuni 2, 151 f., 155 says that it was allowed to kill sheep, goats, gazelles, hares, rhinoceroses, buffaloes, fishes, aquatic and land birds such as sparrows, francolins, doves, peacocks and other birds which are not harmful or disgusting ; on the other hand the flesh of cows, horses, mules, asses, camels, elephants, house fowls, crows, parrots, nightingales and further eggs, wine (allowed to Śūdras), onions, garlic, certain cucumbers and roots, and the *nāli* (lotus) reeds are mentioned by him as forbidden to eat. That the Brahmans could not eat

Alberuni's statement.

1. Cf. Bühler ZDMG 37, 91—94 ; 48, 49 f.
2. Kern, D. Buddhismus 1, 237 ; 2, 73—84.
3. Holtzmann, Zur Gesch. 33—36.

garlic is seen also in the medical literature from the fifth century downwards [1] and in the Rājatar. 1, 342. At the present day the Brahmans (excepting those of Kashmir) [2] avoid animal food as well as eggs and all spirituous liquors and onions and garlic [3]. Particular sects of the Jains and the Lingayats practise this abstinence still more strictly and in general this is the rule among most of the higher castes; repugnance to beef is particularly strong [4]. Yet the Rajputs eat the meat of goats, stags, hares, doves, quails, ortolans and fishes [5]. The Śivaite sects too eat and offer sacrifices with certain animals and drink spirituous liquors, while the Vaiṣṇavas are perfect abstainers [6]. It is also generally forbidden to eat together with a member of another caste, particularly that of a low caste, and to eat the food cooked by him, or to eat with women or to eat the leavings of food.

Present-day practices.

THE END

1. Cf. Festgr. an Roth 19.
2. Bühler, Kaśmīr Report 23.
3. Cf. e. g. BG 22, 61; Census of India 1891, 13, 265
4. M. Williams, Hinduism 155—157.
5. Risley, The Tribes and Castes of Bengal 2 191
6. Census of India 19. 111.

SANSKRIT INDEX

ERRATA

P 1	line 6.	*read* prohibition.
„ 22	„ 20.	*for* is *read* in.
„ 24.	„ 29.	*read* of.
„ 24.	„ 36.	*read* school.
„ 36.	„ 4.	*read* Mānavācārya.
„ 40.	„ 30.	*for* of law *read* law of.
„ 42.	„ 9.	read *nāṇaka*.
„ 56.	„ 20.	*for* Brh. *read* Bṛh.
„ 58.	„ 30.	*read* Thus.
„ 59.	„ 34.	*for* 463 *read* 71.
„ 67.	„ 14.	*read* 'work of Govindarāja.'
„ 72.	„ 14.	*read* Nandapaṇḍita.
„ 74.	„ 20.	*read* He is
„ 76.	„ 20.	*for* the and *read* and the
„ 78.	„ 5.	*for* Lakṣmīdavī *read* Lakṣmīdevī,
„ 88.	„ 17.	*read* towards
„ 103.	„ 2.	for *ekasyā* read *ekāyāḥ*.
„ 111.	„ 24.	*read* Gāndharva
„ 114.	„ 13.	*read* purchase
„ 123.	the f. n. No. 2 is translator's	
„ 124.	„ 22.	*for* spiritual *read* mental.
„ 145.	„ 18.	*read* according
„ 146.	„ 10.	*read* practices
„ 150.	„ 20.	*read* persuasions
„ 152.	„ 33.	*read* stranger
P 132.	line 21.	„ *for* spiritual *read* mental.
„ 184.	„ 23.	*read* over-emphasised.
„ 194.	„ 5.	*read* etymological.
„ 194.	„ 15.	*read* failure.
„ 195.	„ 7.	*for* accordingly *read* according.
200.	last line to be deleted.	
„ 207.	„ 26.	for *sīmāpattra* read *sīmapattra*.
„ 213.	„ 25.	*read* unlimitedly.
„ 218.	„ 13.	*for* spiritual *read* mental.
„ 221.	„ 28.	*adhipāla* read *ādhipāla*.
„ 223.	„ 34.	read Grierson.
„ 227.	„ 23.	*for* 37 read 31.
„ 228.	„ 1.	„ or „ of
„ 245.	the f. n. no. 2 is translator's.	
„ 252.	„ 6.	„ witness *read* evidence
„ 253.	„ 18.	„ retaliation *read* retribution.
„ 256.	„ 18.	*read* varieties.
„ 267.	„ 28.	„ Kṣatriyas.
„ 272.	„ 8.	„ highwaymen.
„ 276.	„ 15.	„ burnt.
„ 277.	„ 14.	„ will.
„ 283.	„ 20.	„ mentioned.
„ 293.	„ 7.	„ *daṇḍabali*.
„ 297.	„ 7.	„ paid.
„ 318.	„ 32.	„ in.